Creating a Portrait in Sculpture

featuring George Washington sculptures created by Avard T. Fairbanks

Compiled by

Eugene F. Fairbanks

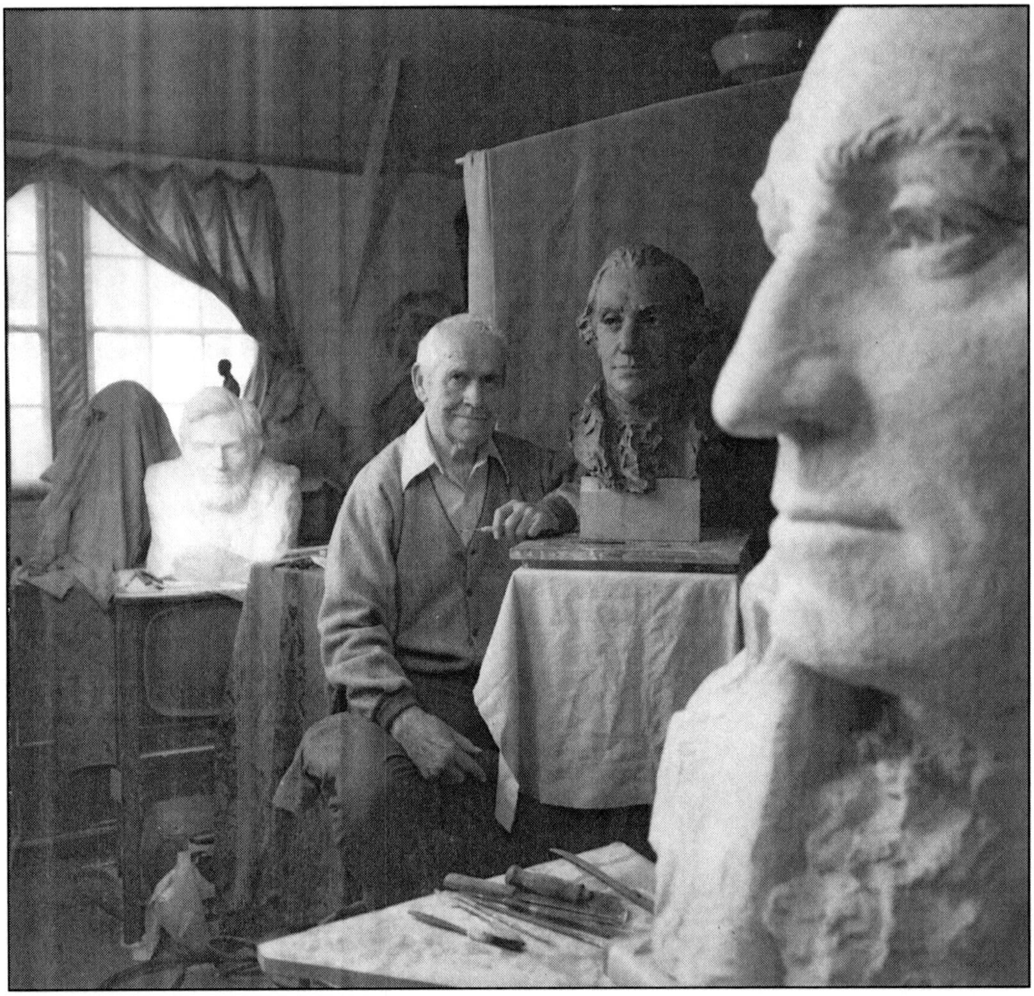

Dr. Avard T. Fairbanks in his studio in 1981, working on a George Washington portrait, with a marble bust of Abraham Lincoln in background. Photograph by Busath Photography Studio, used with permission.

Creating a Portrait in Sculpture

featuring George Washington sculptures

created by

Avard T. Fairbanks

Compiled

by

Eugene F. Fairbanks

Creating a Portrait in Sculpture
featuring George Washington sculptures created by Avard T. Fairbanks

Compiled and written by Eugene F. Fairbanks, with sections by Justin F. Fairbanks, and the lecture notes of Avard T. Fairbanks.

Fairbanks Art and Books
Eugene Fairbanks
2607 Vining Street
Bellingham, Washington 98226-4230
http://www.fairbanksartbooks.com

ISBN-13: 978-1482724639
ISBN-10: 1482724634
Printed through CreateSpace Independent Publishing Platform

Typography, book and cover design, prepress: Kathleen Weisel, Bellingham, WA
weiselcreative.com

Cover, frontice piece, and page xviii photos by Don Busath
©1981 Busath Photography Studio, used with permission.
The Busath Photography Studio, in Salt Lake City, Utah, has kindly permitted the use of a copyrighted prize-winning photograph of Avard Fairbanks in his studio while modeling a portrait of General George Washington, with a marble bust of Abraham Lincoln in background.

Dedication

This book is dedicated to the memory of Avard T. Fairbanks, sculptor; to his father, John B. Fairbanks; to his older brother, J. Leo Fairbanks; and my brothers, Avard F. Fairbanks and Elliott F. Fairbanks who assisted father in their youth; and to Justin F. Fairbanks who assisted and collaborated with him for many years.

Avard T. Fairbanks, Sculptor

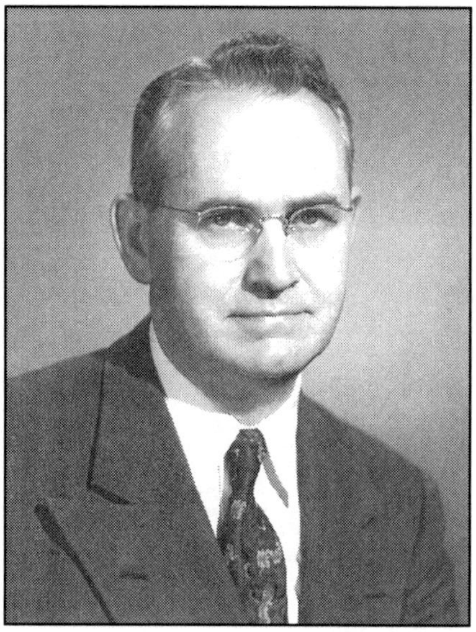

Avard Tennyson Fairbanks was born 1897 in Provo, Utah, to a family profoundly interested in art. His father and oldest brother were professional artists. He began to study sculpture at the age of twelve and in 1910-11 received scholarships at the Art Students' League in New York City where he had James Earl Fraser as an instructor. His work was exhibited at the National Academy of Design in 1911. Two years later he went to Paris to study at *Ecole des Beaux Arts* with Injalbert, at *Academie Colorossi,* and at the *Ecole de la Grande Chaumiere.* The outbreak of World War I forced him to return to the United States.

At the beginning of his professional career he created a number of large statues at the Latter-Day Saints Temple at Laie, Hawaii. While in Hawaii, he sent for his sweetheart, Maude Fox, and they were married in Honolulu. His career of teaching sculpture at the college level began in 1920 at the University of Oregon. In 1925 he earned a Bachelor of Fine Arts degree from Yale University. In 1927 he was awarded a fellowship by the Guggenheim Foundation, which enabled him to pursue further studies in Florence Italy. In 1929 he was awarded a Master of Fine Arts degree by the University of Washington. He was appointed to the Institute of Fine Arts faculty at the University of Michigan in 1930, and while teaching, earned a Master of Arts and Doctor of Philosophy degree in Anatomy there. The human proportions study in this book was a part of his doctorate thesis, titled, *Anatomic Design.*

During 18 years at Michigan while teaching sculpture he created many fine portraits, garden figures, and monuments. In 1948 he moved to the University of Utah where he was appointed Dean and asked to organize a College of Fine Arts. Many of his impressive portraits and heroic monuments were created in Utah. After being designated Emeritus Professor, he was appointed Resident Sculptor at the University of North Dakota for two years.

He has erected nearly one hundred public monuments and has created nearly another fifty significant portraits, garden figures, and bas reliefs. Many honors were awarded him during his career, including two honorary degrees. In 1982 he was honored for 75 years of professional sculpture. He died in 1987 at nearly ninety years of age. He left a legacy of creative, dynamic, and expressive fine art that is carried on by family members, students, and others. Many have benefited from his teachings and have utilized his principles.

Regarding family affairs, Maude and Avard were proud parents of eight sons and two adopted daughters. Two sons studied engineering, two became artists, and four became doctors of medicine. One daughter is a housewife and the other is a teacher of music. All retain an active interest in art.

Contents

Other Statuary of George Washington by Avard T. Fairbanks

Form is Fundamental to a Portrait

Illustrations

Proportional Measurements

Anatomy

Sculptured Anatomical Displays . . . 152

Appendix . . . 154

Preface

Since Avard Fairbanks presented many demonstration lectures to attentive audiences, it is appropriate that one should be recorded in book form, presenting students and serious amateurs an opportunity to observe, learn, and be inspired to create fine pieces of sculpture.

The tradition of Fine Art in the Fairbanks Family began with John B. Fairbanks by encouragement from his mother, Sarah Van Wagoner Fairbanks, and a fond friendship that developed between him and John Hafen, another dedicated amateur as they went sketching together in the countryside. This led to an advanced training in the Art Schools of Paris, France. He became a western Pioneer Landscape Painter and Photographer. J. Leo Fairbanks, his oldest son learned greatly from his father, and later, he also studied Art in Paris. J. Leo Fairbanks became an inspiring art teacher and was appointed as a professor of Fine Art and a Department Chairman at Oregon State University. Early in the younger brother's (Avard Fairbanks) career, J. Leo was a mentor and an important source of inspiration. The Creed, expressed by J. Leo deserves to be repeated.

Eugene F. Fairbanks

Creed

Art is for service; for making things beautiful as well as useful;
for lifting men above the sordid things that grind and depress:
to give a joyous optimism in one's work;
to realize, during one's leisure, the ideals that have been
contemplated in one's most precious moments;
to take pleasure is seeing beauty as it exists in what man has made
as well in one's immediate environment;
to see the ideal in the real;
and to realize transitory hopes in enduring tangible material.
To me, the purpose of art is to visualize ideals, to realize ideals,
and to idealize realities.

J. Leo Fairbanks

Foreword

There were multiple inspirations for this book. Nat Washington, a descendant of Lawrence Washington, George's older brother, and a senator in the Washington State Legislature from Ephrata, WA, had written an article deploring that most of George's portraits were solemn and he desired a smiling portrait of the Father of our Nation.

Having attended many demonstration lectures of my father, Avard Fairbanks, I recognized the need for a recording of his system and technique of developing a portrait. It would be beneficial to students and serious amateurs, intent on creating fine realistic and dynamic creative sculpture. Such a recording could outline and explain the multiple steps toward modeling a portrait while demonstrating the importance and significant anatomy and its manifestation at rest and in action. During the development of the portrait and in the discussion, there was a parallel presentation of idealism and expression, so that the art conveys a message and a communication from the subject to the observer.

During my teens, I often assisted in studio chores: making armatures, applying preliminary clay, assisting the plaster caster, and developing photos in the darkroom. One time, I was asked to improve illustrations by adding background colorations for my father's doctoral thesis. I was excited to be contributing to the production of a book, even though there were only a few thesis copies assembled. He later used many copies of the thesis illustrations in his sculpture classes. He mentioned that few sculptors have written books and that as a result, there were not many available for student instruction.

Years later, when I was in the Seattle City Library, I checked on sculpture books. The collection was limited to one shelf. The same situation was recognized in other large libraries.

I have often researched important information in medical libraries and there are great libraries in medical schools and fine libraries in most city hospitals. It has made me feel that there is a serious deficit in our society for persons seeking information about the techniques and procedures necessary for creating fine dynamic sculpture. Fortunately, several skilled sculptors have recently published some fine books on sculpture techniques. I hope that this and other books on sculpture that I have compiled, using information taught to me by my father, will help to fulfill a part of this need for artists and society.

Acknowledgements

The Busath Photography Studio, in Salt Lake City, Utah, has kindly permitted the use of a copyrighted prize-winning photograph of Avard Fairbanks in his studio, taken while he was modeling a portrait of General George Washington. Don Busath was honored after submitting this portrait that received a top-scoring print award in an Annual International Competition of the American Society of Professional Photography. It is also archived in the Photography Hall of Fame. It was published on several covers of photography journals as an outstanding example of portrait photography. It is now on permanent display at Abravenal Hall in Salt Lake City as part of the Honors in the Arts Exhibit. The Fairbanks Family is deeply appreciative to be permitted to use this photograph as the cover illustration of this book. A horizontal version is used in black and white on page ii. Another photograph, printed with permission, demonstrates more detail of Avard Fairbanks working on the plasteline portrait of George Washington.

The filming of the demonstration lecture by Avard Fairbanks was arranged by Al Swift at the KVOS Television Studio in Bellingham, Washington, September 1962. Permission was granted to copy images of the 16-mm black-and-white movie film that was recorded for a broadcast feature. Tape recordings were made at other times—during demonstration lectures at Bellingham High School, arranged by Robert Safston; and another lecture at Western Washington University in Bellingham. These recordings were transcribed and correlated with the television recording for the text that accompanies the illustrations.

My brother, Justin Fairbanks, was a professional sculptor, a frequent assistant to my father, and a professor of Art at Eastern Arizona State College. During a recorded discussion, he outlined many pertinent details that are important to modeling a portrait, and considerable additional information that added to portrait refinements.

The doctoral thesis by Avard Fairbanks was reviewed and illustrations were copied from original drawings, particularly about anatomy. Other information, recorded by Avard Fairbanks, was used or adapted to text where it was appropriate. Some tracings of his originals were used to accompany the text. His proportions illustrations of male and female heads were included in the section on portrait proportions. Many of the photographs of portraits in sculpture were filmed by Avard Fairbanks and then printed by him in his studio darkroom.

The knowledge of the photographic process, taught to me during my youth by my father, has been very helpful in preparing many of the illustrations used in this book.

Pre-publication preparation of this book was accomplished by Kathleen Weisel. She is an artist and a sculptor and is experienced in publishing. Her recommendations added considerably to the organization of the text and placement of illustrations.

Appreciation is also expressed to my wife, Florence, and to my family for their patience and understanding, during the years of accumulating illustrations and the composition of text.

Eugene F. Fairbanks

Portraits of George Washington Created by His Contemporaries

By the time of the revolutionary war, the artists in the colonies had acquired skill in painting by studying in Europe under master artists. George Washington became a popular subject for graphic and oil portraits after became commander in Chief of the Continental Army and even more popular after he became president.

One of the first important portraits was created by Charles Willson Peale, when Washington was in his forties. He created several more significant portraits between 1778 and 1779. Both John Trumbull and Charles W. Peale served in the Continental army. John Trumbull painted a smaller-than-life-size in 1775 at Washington's headquarters while in New York. Between his first painting in 1775 he made twelve additional paintings of Washington by 1790, but, some were copies.

There were about nineteen important portrait artists that created a likeness of George Washington during his lifetime. Among them were relatives of Charles Willson Peale that include two sons, a brother and a nephew. To some of the artists who made copies for sale it became financially rewarding. Some likenesses included miniatures and silhouettes that were popular. Many more portraits were created by other artists in the century following Washington's death, using images created by the contemporary artists.

Books have been compiled to honor the "Father of Our Country" that emphasize many of his portraits. Elizabeth Bryant Johnston authored a book entitled, *Original Portraits of Washington,* published in 1882 by James R. Osgood and Company in Boston. A later and more comprehensive documentation, *Portraits of Washington,* was recorded in a three-volume study by G.A. Eisen that included all of the artistic representations of George Washington during his lifetime and in the first century after his death. It was published by Robert Hamilton & Associates, of New York in 1932.

One of the most famous likenesses was the unfinished portrait created by Gilbert Stewart. It appears on paper currency of the one dollar bill. He could have easily finished the blank background along the border of this painting, but the unfinished effect was thought to render to it an unusual quality. He painted three portraits of Washington during 1795-96 and made many copies for sale.

While Benjamin Franklin and Thomas Jefferson were in Paris, they had an order from the State of Virginia to offer a commission to a sculptor for creating a statue of George Washington. Jean Antoine Houdon, a prominent sculptor in Paris who had already created a portrait of Benjamin Franklin, accepted the offer and accompanied Franklin and Jefferson to Virginia. While in the United States he made portraits of George Washington, Thomas Jefferson, Alexander Hamilton and other significant persons. He made a portrait of Washington that was cast in plaster, and several copies were made. One copy is presently on exhibit at Mount Vernon, VA.

Houdon was a master sculptor and the images were of very fine quality. He also made a life mask of Washington. After returning to France, using the plaster portrait, he carved a full length marble statue of Washington and portrait busts. The completed statue of George Washington was erected in the state house of Virginia, and presently remains there at Richmond. Another sculptor, Joseph Ceracchi, created busts in 1791-95 and three or four copies were carved in marble.

Kinncaid, Clark. *George Washington, The Pictorial Biography.* New York: Bonanza Books, 1958.

Events Leading to a Television Feature of a Demonstration Lecture

Early in the decade of the nineteen-sixties, Senator Nat Washington was prominent in the Washington State Legislature. He was a descendant of Lawrence, an older brother of George Washington. He was quoted in the newspapers about that time that he deplored the failure of a fine portrait of the father of the nation to be placed in our State Capitol. The remark was especially significant, since President George Washington was the illustrious person for whom our State was named. Furthermore, Nat Washington urged that a pleasant, smiling portrait be sought. All the portraits make him seem overly sincere, even stern or glum. Nat contended that "Uncle George" was a pleasant fellow with a very fine sense of humor.

Soon after reading the article, I sent a letter to Nathaniel Washington who lived in Ephrata, Washington. In it, I suggested a fine portrait bust could be created, preferably by my father, Avard Fairbanks. There was a friendly reply indicating that he intended a painted portrait.

About that time, Al Swift, then a television commentator of KVOS (Bellingham, WA) gave an informative talk to a Parent-Teachers' Association meeting regarding quality feature television programs and the benefit to educational efforts. The thought intrigued me regarding the opportunity of having my father, Avard T. Fairbanks, present a demonstration lecture on television. After the meeting, I suggested this possibility to Al Swift. He seemed interested in recording a demonstration for a television program. My father had been giving many demonstrations about how to model sculpture since he was fourteen years of age. After I showed some photos of Avard Fairbanks' sculpture, Al Swift agreed to arrange for a recording opportunity during my father's next visit to Bellingham.

During the next year, Avard Fairbanks made a careful study of George Washington's contemporary portraits and personal history. He accumulated a substantial library of Washington books and read appropriate sections of them. He then planned to come to Washington State. Arrangements were made for an afternoon that was spent filming his demonstration lecture of modeling a portrait. The subject chosen was appropriately a gently smiling portrait bust of George Washington, as a young commanding general in the Continental Army. Instead of choosing a traditional pose, a dynamic and younger energetic military officer was portrayed. Al Swift and the KVOS staff were very well pleased with the presentation. By editing the film, the usual time of two hours of modeling was condensed to a twenty-minute television feature. Still the important steps of modeling a portrait in clay were emphasized.

After the filming, Avard Fairbanks carefully packed the portrait in a large suitcase and took it to his studio in Salt Lake City, Utah, for completion. Later he received a commission, by the Salt Lake City Airport Authority, to make a colossal, three times life size bust of George Washington for the 1976 Bicentennial of the Declaration of Independence. The KVOS portrait served as the working model. During the next few months, the colossal portrait of General George Washington was modeled in clay, cast in plaster, and then cast in bronze at the Adonis Bronze Foundry.

Three casts in bronze were made. One was for Salt Lake City Airport. One was given to a son Dr. David Fairbanks, a Professor at George Washington Medical School. He donated it to that school and it was erected and dedicated at the college campus in Washington DC. The third cast was given to me, Eugene, his second son, for placement in the Washington State Capitol Building.

At that time, the Mother Joseph Foundation erected a statue of Marcus Whitman by my fa-

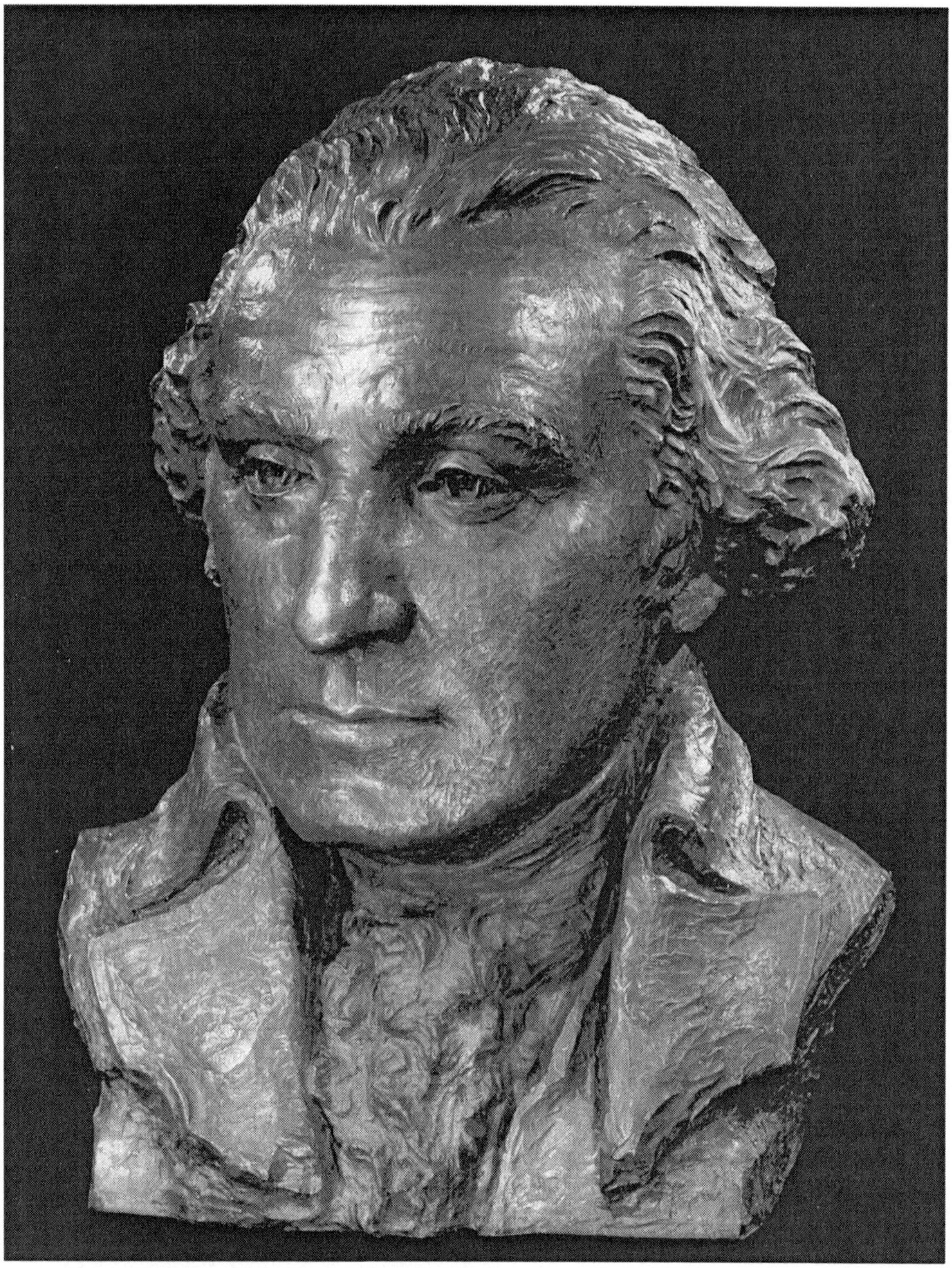

The colossal portrait of George Washington in bronze.

ther at the State Capitol. It was dedicated during the erection and dedication of a statue of Mother Joseph by another sculptor. Both bronze monuments for the State Capitol were copies of heroic statues representing the State of Washington at Statuary Hall in Washington, DC.

The Mother Joseph Foundation expressed an interest in the colossal portrait of George Washington. Since they had demonstrated a sincere attitude in fine sculpture, it was donated to the Foundation for placement in the Legislative Building at the Capitol. Dedicatory ceremonies were held in 1984. Later, the city of George in the State of Washington had an opportunity to acquire another copy. Now that city proudly displays a copy of the colossal portrait. Since that time, more than 25 additional copies of the colossal portrait have been erected in prominent locations throughout the nation.

Eugene Fairbanks, M.D.

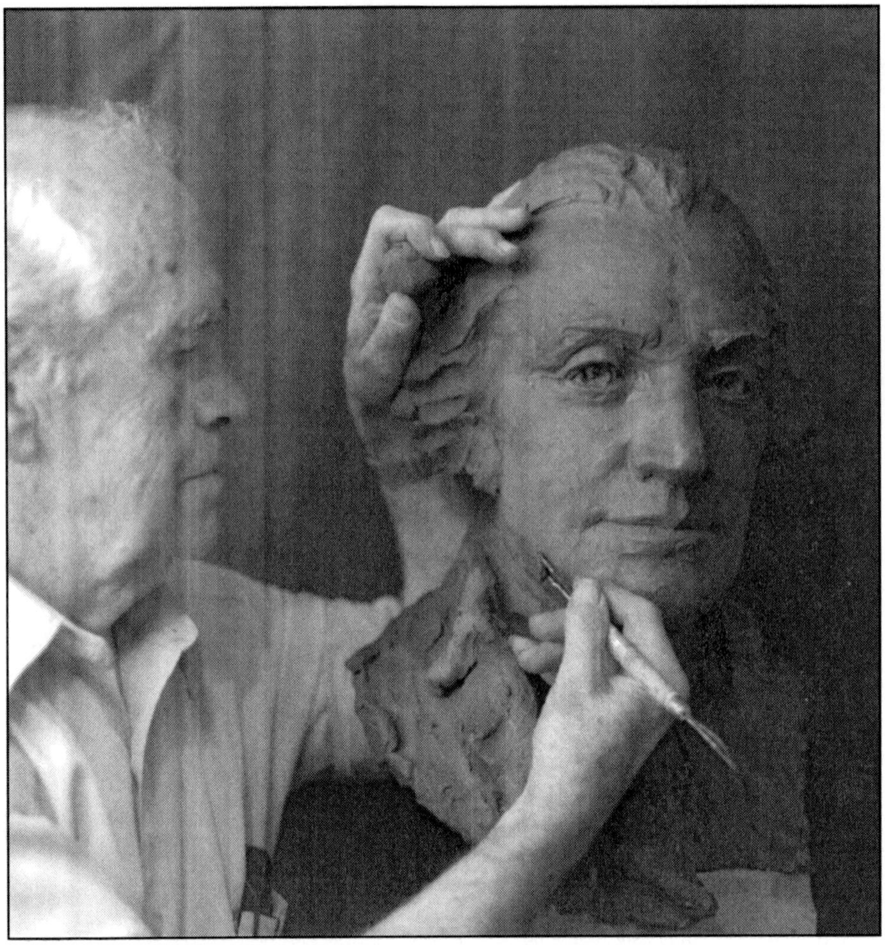

Avard Fairbanks modeling the portrait of General George Washington.
Busath Photography, ©1981.

Creation of a Portrait in Sculpture of General George Washington

Since the early days of his career, Avard Tennyson Fairbanks was a popular speaker. His first demonstration lecture was delivered to a metropolitan junior high school when he was 14 years of age. When he was appointed to be a professor, he lectured not only to his college classes but also to numerous groups interested in art, sculpture and design and he frequently included pertinent history in the discussion. These lectures usually took the form of demonstration lectures during which he modeled the figure of a person or a portrait and explained the modeling process as he worked, beginning with an armature and rolls of clay. Besides the physical form, he stressed action and animation. It seems fitting that some of his teachings and discussions were recorded, transcribed and included in a text with a series of photographs illustrating the process.

From his youth Dr. Fairbanks had an unusually astute recognition and fascination with form and anatomy. It is not surprising that he earned advanced degrees studying anatomy in the University of Michigan School of Medicine. Therefore, some of his anatomical sketches of skeletal and muscular components are included to elucidate the development of a portrait. The muscles of expression and their effect are stressed. Dynamics of the body action are also emphasized. A portrait is not complete by when only gross features have been modeled. The fine details must be included and expression needs to be added for the finished creation. During the description of modeling, human proportions are discussed in the text to facilitate instruction and comprehension.

Avard Fairbanks was endowed with a photographic memory. When planning a portrait or a statue, he thoroughly researched a subject as to features, costume and mannerisms. When creating a portrait of a living person, he studied an individual during conversations and noted characteristic gestures and expressions in order to include personality into the portrait. Therefore it was a representation of not only the features, but also a personality study for a re-creation of the individual character in a moment in time.

He often said that he recognized talent in many people, but to become a skilled artist, a person needs to study, seek instruction by a master, and pursue considerable practice. His father was an artist—a landscape painter, and his older brother, J. Leo, his mentor, was a master of landscape, portrait painting and sculpture. Both had studied in Paris art schools.

Avard, in his youth, studied under Daniel Chester French and others masters at the Art Students League in New York City and under Injalbert at the Ecole de Beaux Artes in Paris. He later studied in the Florentine Academy in Florence, Italy; and he often consulted with Dante Sodini, a leading Italian sculptor. He learned early to observe features with careful attention to details and the recognition of special individual characteristics.

This book is intended to serve as an introduction to modeling of sculpture with the hope that future artists may be encouraged not to only study and appreciate the sculpture of the masters of past ages but also to study human form an anatomy and create masterpieces of their own. The present fund of information regarding human anatomy is vast and detailed. Anthropometry, the study of human proportions, has been carefully recorded. The materials available for sculptors have never been as varied or of such high quality. As people have more leisure time and a greater awareness of quality, we may be on the brink of a great new age in the fields of artistic endeavor.

Equipment

The equipment and material that he used for this demonstration were relatively simple. Modeling tools are either smooth wooden tools with one flat tip and the other rounded, resembling a very small finger; or are fitted with wire loops, facilitating small details or smoothing surfaces. (See illustrations in Appendix.)

Armature

The wooden upright is placed into the wooden bracket for support of the modeling board or plinth. It becomes a simple armature that is portable and allows some flexibility. The armature is a supportive structure. It may be an upright of wood with a small wooden cross to support the head, and a crosspiece to support the shoulders, as shown in Figure 1, or it may be made of metal as a gas pipe screwed into a floor flange secured to the base. All worthwhile things with which we deal must have good support. We must support our institutions, our schools, our churches, our civic organizations, our governments, and all those forms of social structures which are striving to work for the advancement of society and for the benefit of mankind. Armatures may also be made of wire, of iron bars with wood and wire mesh and various other combinations. Those persons familiar with electric motors will recognize the word "armature." The term has been borrowed from art and architecture by engineers to describe the framework on which wires are applied to the rotor of an electric motor.

In architecture, an armature is defined as any means for bracing, stiffening and supporting a weak structure and as supports for slender columns. In sculpture, it is the framework supporting the clay while modeling, because clay may not support its own weight. (See illustrations in Appendix.)

Clay and *Plastilina*

Clay is man's oldest plastic material. It is the basic material for pottery, terra cotta, porcelains, and many building materials such as brick and tile. Clay has served mankind very admirably not only in ancient times but also very much in modern society. Although the use of it is old, many new and exciting developments are occurring and may yet occur, involving clay and other ceramics. However, modeling clay (often called water clay) is the most facile and plastic material of the sculptor's media. When water is added, it is easy to manipulate, since it is pliable and it retains its form. The form in clay may then be cast and the form may be converted into other materials or even fired into permanent shape as terra cotta or ceramic ware. Clay is therefore elemental for instructions and for mastery in sculpture. The disadvantage is that it must be kept moist until it is cast, and if it is allowed to dry, it may crack

Another type of modeling clay has been developed with an oil base, which does not dry. It is called *plastelina,* (often Anglicized to plasteline) and it was first compounded, according to an old Italian formulation, with sulfur, suet, and clay. The plasteline shown here has an olive gray color; however many colors and textures are available in modern formulations that are sulfur free. It is most easily handled by first rolling it into various lengths and size of rolls between the hands. These rolls will then be applied to the wooden armature according to the needs.

Some thoughts of Avard Fairbanks are included here that seem appropriate:

> "The art of sculpture is very old, but it has many aspects, which are new and exciting. There are always current or recent events and persons deserving of honor and memorialization. Whenever we produce fine works of sculpture there is considerable significance and meaning. Fine art may express the story of a people, the history of a race, the meaning of humanity, and all those aspects of a culture that we hold dear. If the ideals to which men and women strive are worthwhile, they can be, they should be, and frequently they are memorialized in sculpture.
>
> "Figures in plaster, wood, stone, or bronze

become the permanent and enduring form into which ideas and ideals are communicated to express the concepts and aspirations of mankind in its cultural activities and its growth. Monuments become the permanent record of a people and a civilization. That is why sculpture is so very important to the people that constitute the nations, and that create governments. It is also important for the sculptor's work to be anatomically and historically correct, for these governments may pass away while the sculpture lives on.

"John C. Van Dyke, in a poem in his book *What is Art* readily explains this in words he has written:

> *All passes, art alone enduring stays with us. The bust outlives the throne, the coin Tiberius.*

"The great thrones of the monarchs may be no more, but the coins, which they had struck, honoring themselves, for use in trade and in commerce, may now be treasured by museums and collectors. Nevertheless, the art of sculpture carries on the message and the legends of the civilizations. The hopes and ambitions of individuals, nations, and cultures become enduring memorabilia through the art of sculpture.

"There are many processes in the development of sculpture, and of necessity, there are many approaches to the completion of a fine work of art. The process of modeling a portrait can be more easily comprehended when one watches a series of steps. It is also important that the artist convey through his work the personality and aspirations of the character that is portrayed."

During Avard Fairbanks' Demonstration Lectures to attentive audiences, he described the process of modeling, frequently referring to features using anatomical terms. He first modeled the form of a skull that is a fundamental beginning. Soft tissues were then added. As the portrait progressed, he discussed concepts of art and history that was pertinent to the study. Details and refinement were added during the last phase. A recording of his discussion is included with photographic illustrations for better appreciation and comprehension.

In order to better present the process of modeling, a transcription of a demonstration lecture is included in the text. It reproduces the informal atmosphere of work and discussion by using the sculptors own words and expressions. There are some added explanations and discussion included, but there has been a minimum of editing.

Modeling a Portrait of General George Washington

By Avard Fairbanks

This is an opportunity to present a demonstration lecture on how a sculptor works. First of all, I shall take off my coat and then get the clay, actually plastilina, out of the case and begin modeling. Now I shall roll up my sleeves and pitch into the work. I hope you will excuse this informality. Very few lecturers assume this freedom when speaking, that is to roll up ones sleeves and appear working in a physical manner. It is much more dignified to remain in proper attire, but in this kind of work, one cannot remain that proper.

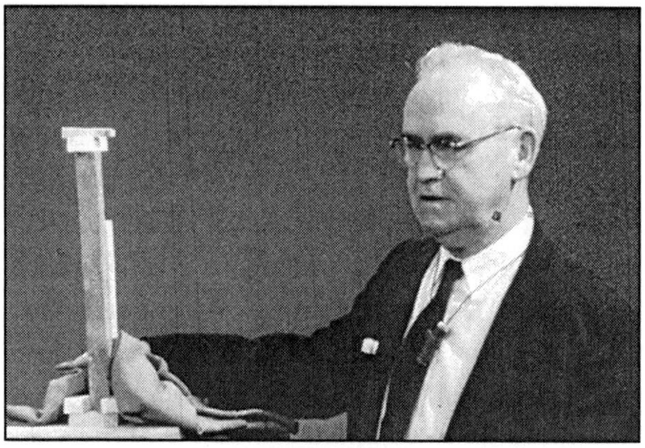

Fig. 1. Avard T. Fairbanks, with the simple armature and plasteline, prepares for a demonstration lecture creating a portrait of General George Washington.

The Modeling Begins

This material may seem to be a very crude substance. *Plastelina* as you see is a very plastic material. When I do my work in a three dimensional form of a sketch, I use this *plastelina,* but often refer to it as plasteline or simply clay. I may begin by making a few rolls and putting it on this wooden upright with a crosspiece. I will then fasten them by firm application onto this wooden armature.

A sculptor may start with some unimpressive objects, a board, a support, a stick and a pile of rolled clay. Bringing the clay together in just a mass, and working it about or just twisting and distorting it, will have no meaning in particular. Piling clay upon clay without meaning or guidance, without objective purpose is like life itself without purpose, or a civilization without a purpose, a direction, or a destiny. Just existing from day to day, without having goals or aspirations, is like clay piled upon clay. Like a civilization, if it falls down, it fails. We do not wish to have our civilization fail. We wish our nation and civilization to be strong and dynamic. Therefore there needs to be purpose and direction.

Now I will start pressing the rolls of clay onto the armature and begin by making a central structure with the first applied roll (Fig. 2). It is just the beginning of a face. It is yet only a two dimensional profile. A second roll of plasteline is applied (Fig. 3). On this central roll, I begin to form the structure, which is primary to the planned finished portrait. Subsequent rolls of plastelina are applied to create a midline form (Fig. 4, 5). It is extremely important in all sculpture to indicate the centerline or midline so that whatever we create will have two sides, which are equal, or in symmetry. Now it is necessary to make a wider form. By adding more rolls to each side gives three dimensions to the beginning form (Fig. 6). Notice that while I am modeling this, I work with two hands, not just one hand. A sculptor must be ambidextrous. Working with two hands in what he does, increases speed and facilitates designing with symmetry (Fig. 7).

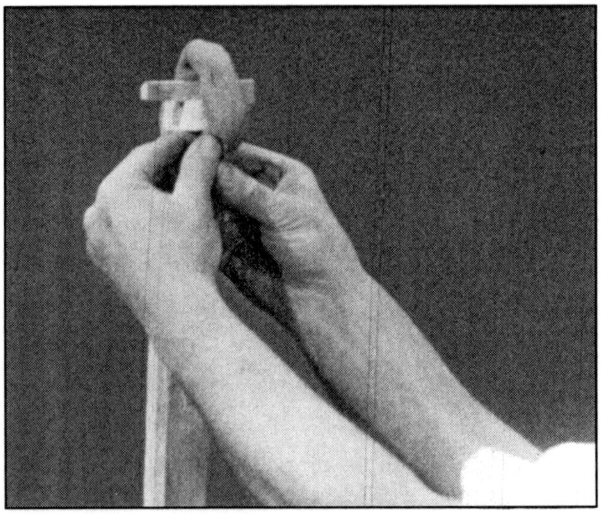

Fig. 2. The modeling begins and first roll of plasteline is applied to the armature, the beginning of a head.

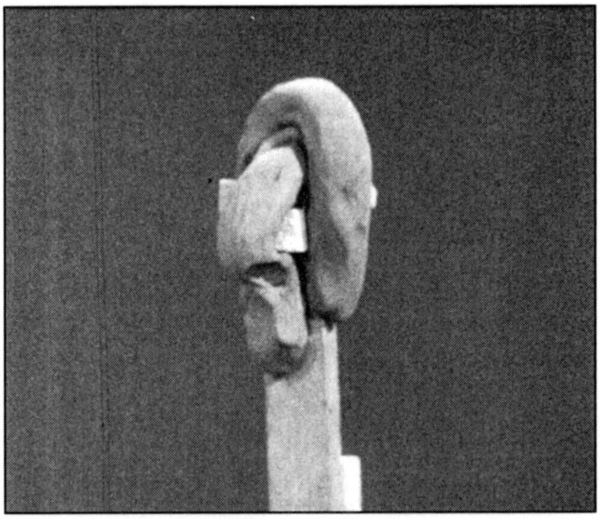

Fig. 3. Second roll of plasteline is applied to the armature for the head.

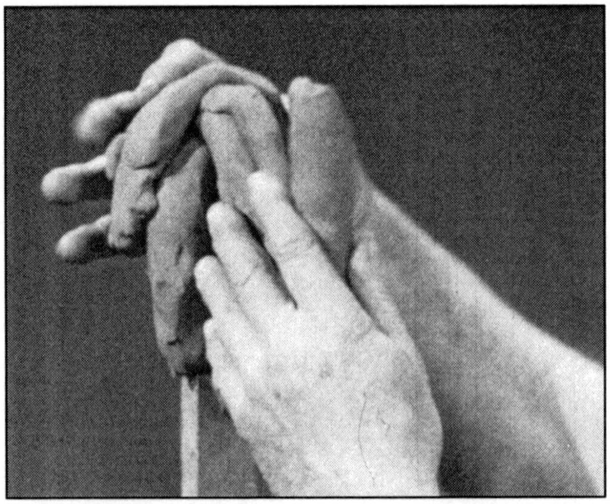

Fig. 4. More rolls of plasteline are added and the form of the head begins to develop.

Still a centerline is maintained; with the stroke of a modeling tool from the vertex downward (Fig. 8). On this centerline, Now I will place a horizontal roll so that the form of a cross is made in the development of a head (Fig. 11). This divides the form of the head into the upper one third and the lower two thirds. This horizontal roll will become the eyebrows. A centerline is again inscribed (Fig. 12).

An Arch and a Dome are Formed

The next step is to form an arch by applying horizontal rolls of clay across the central rolls (Fig. 14). The next three rolls on each side are placed above the cross roll and will become the forehead of the skull (Fig. 15). A roundness is then modeled to shape the skull, resembling a dome. With more rolls, you will see this arch forming to produce the cranium of the skull. The rounded arches of the rounded head, essentially a dome, are just the beginning of a form that is basic and fundamental to this design.

Now, as you see, I am making a skull. Roman designers discovered that an arch and a dome are the strongest structures for the least amount of material. This was found to be a principle of construction important to architecture and engineering throughout the following centuries. While I am forming the clay into a roundness in the shape of a skull, you may ask, "Why do I do this first?" Because it is the underlying structure, and we must know the structure that is beneath, before we can model the superficial tissues toward the outside surfaces.

In this work, the centerline is again considered; this line is known as the midline or midsagittal plane of the cranium. It is a technical term used in the field of anatomy.

(Note: *sagitta* in Latin is for 'arrow that, during battles, penetrated victims from anterior to posterior'.)

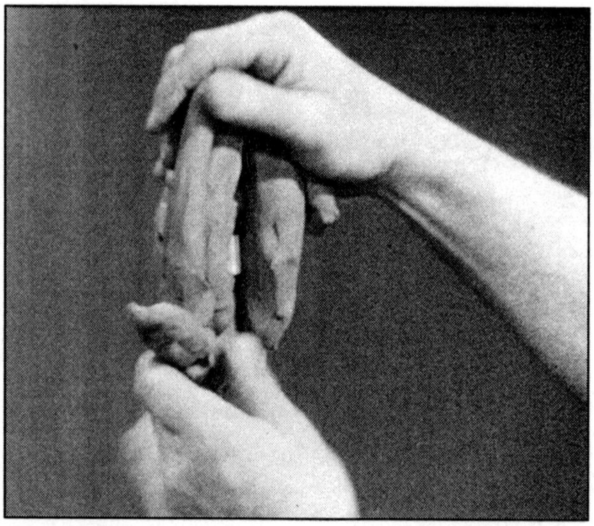

Fig. 5. Additional rolls of plasteline are applied in the midline.

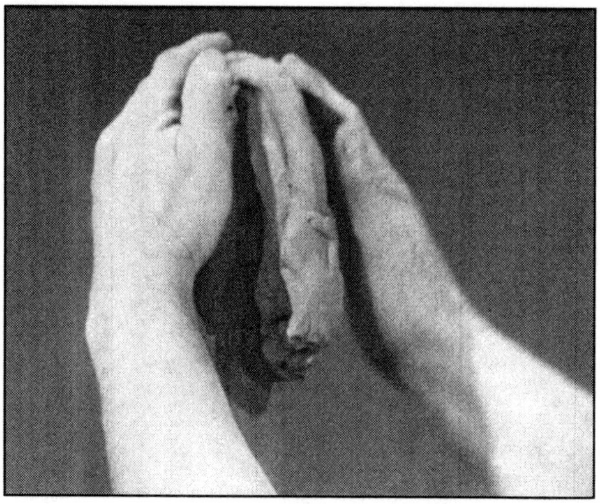

Fig. 6. A Lateral roll of plasteline is added to those in the midline.

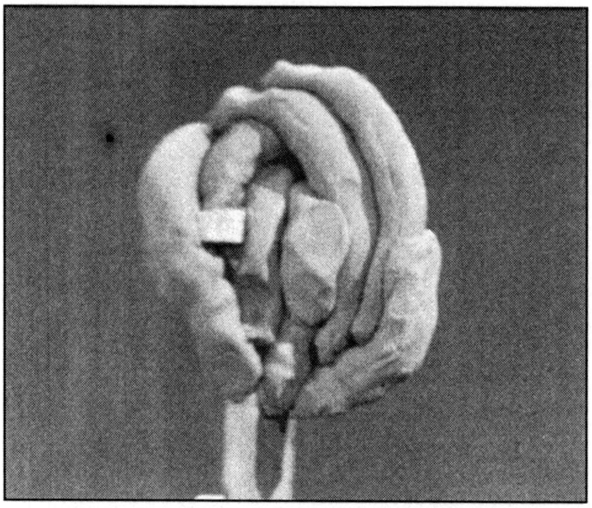

Fig. 7. An initial two dimensional form is created.

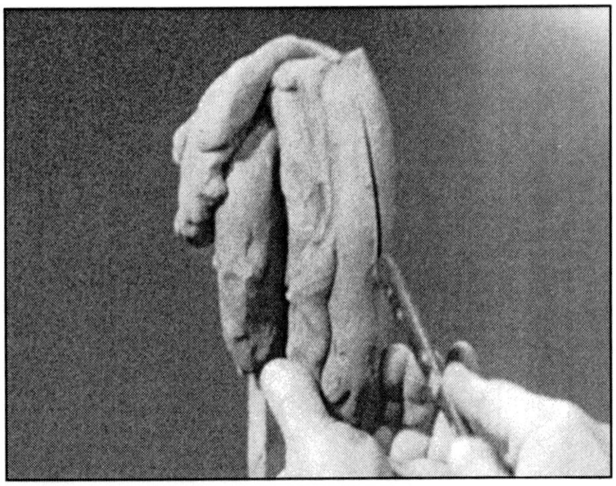

Fig. 8. A vertical mid-central line is incised in a roll with a wire tool.

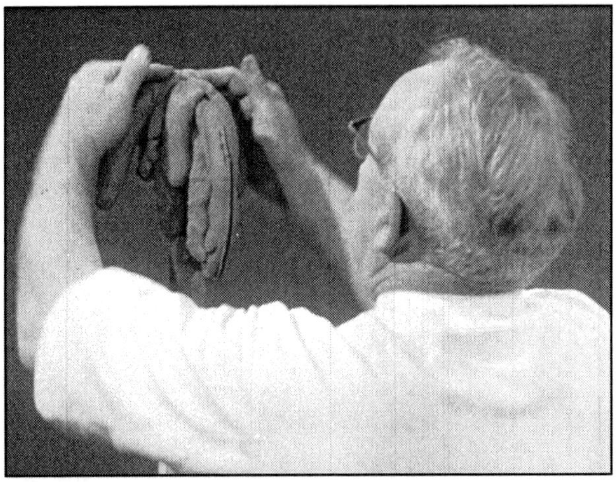

Fig. 9. More lateral rolls are added to better resemble the form of a head.

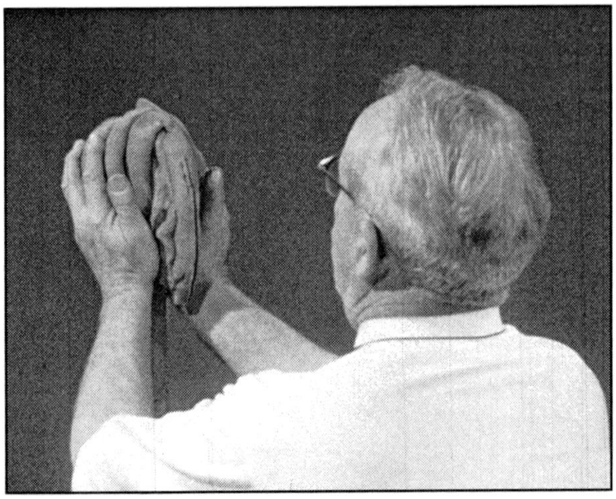

Fig. 10. Rolls are pressed together by the action of the sculptor's palms.

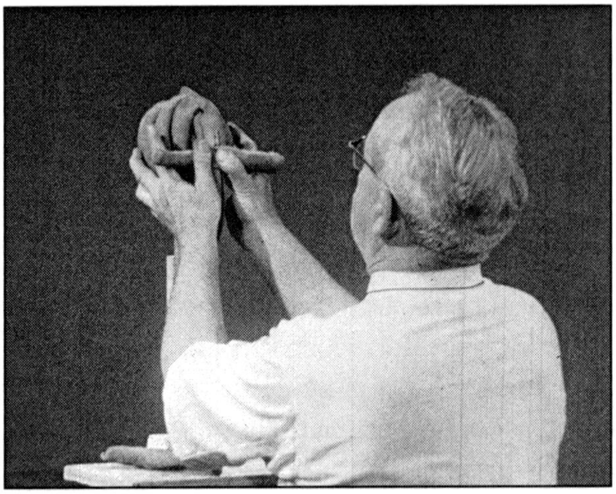

Fig. 11. A transverse roll is added indicating the beginning of a brow.

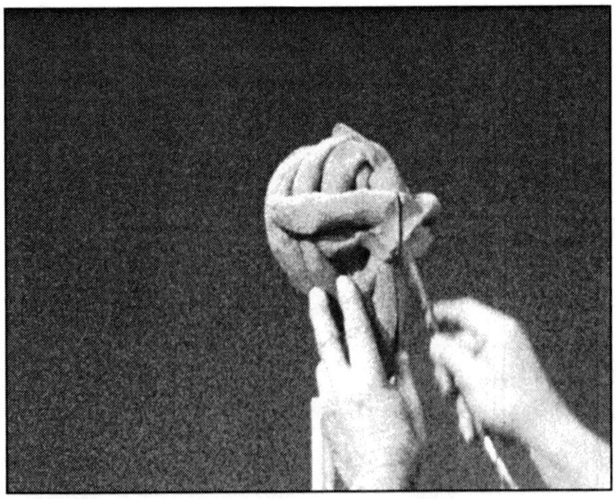

Fig. 12. A central, vertical line is again incised on the anterior roll of clay to maintain balance.

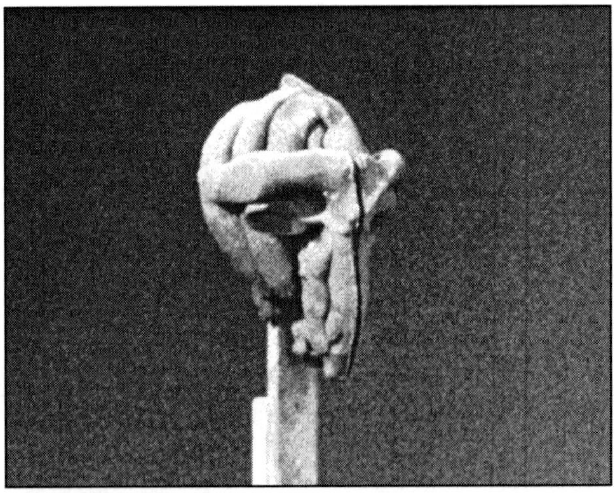

Fig. 13. A view is shown of the early stage of the developing skull.

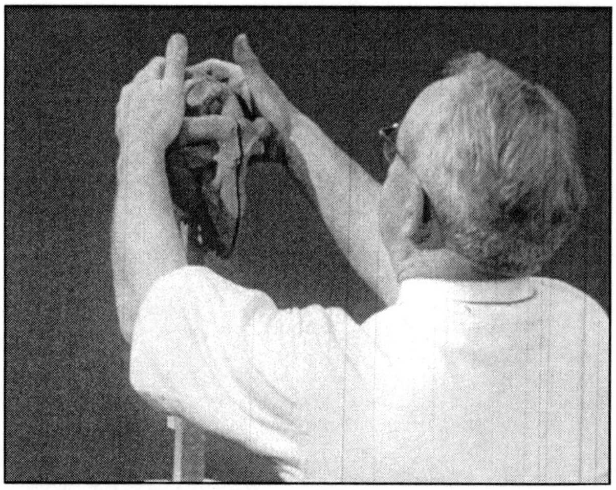

Fig. 14. Rolls are added above the brow roll to improve the dome shape of the skull.

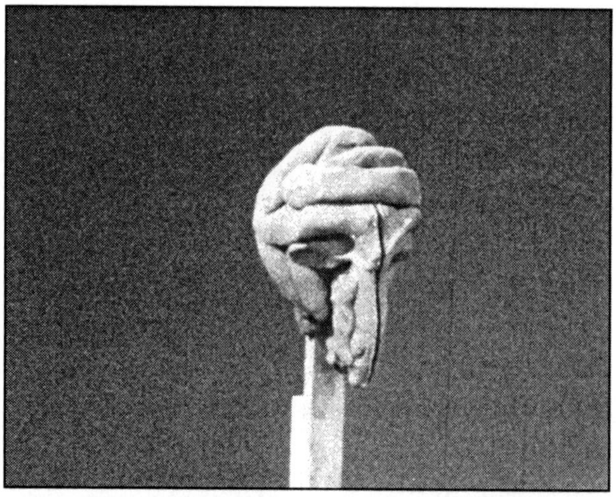

Fig. 15. A view is presented of the developing cranium.

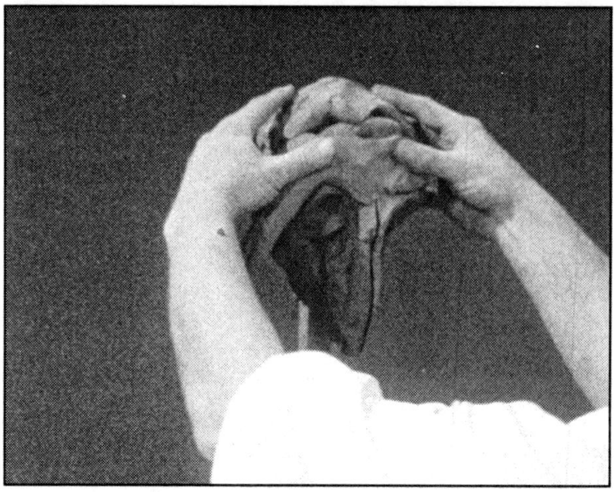

Fig. 16. A smoothing of forehead is performed using thumb strokes.

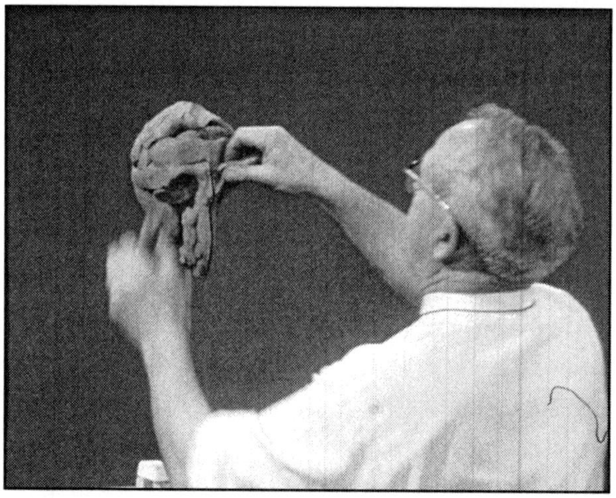

Fig. 17. A smaller roll of clay is applied to represent the supraorbital ridge.

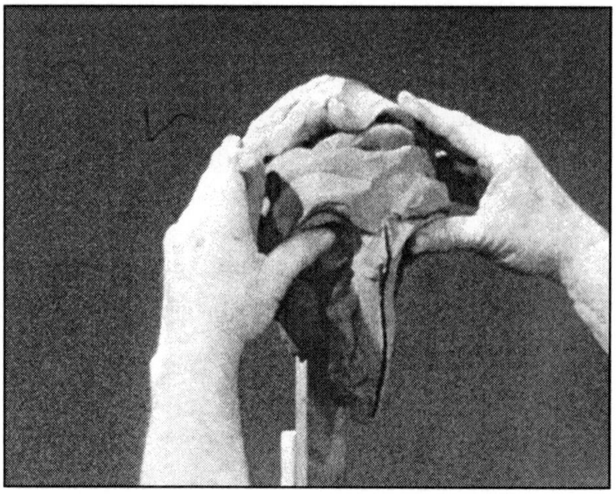

Fig. 18. Using thumb pressure, the orbits of skull begin to form.

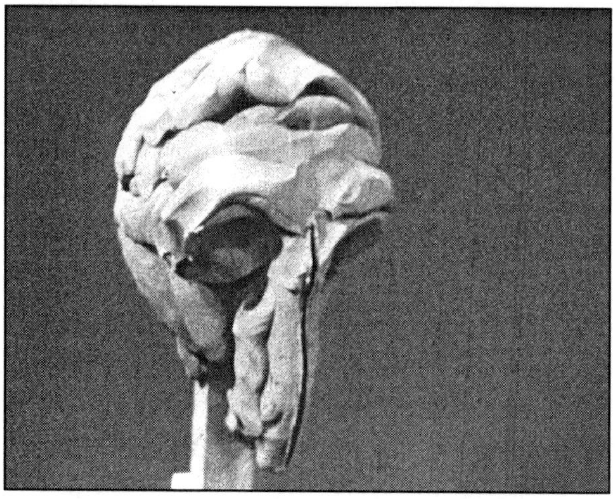

Fig. 19. A view is shown of the early progress of skull development.

Orbits for the Eyes are Modeled

In order to develop the sockets of the eyes, anatomically called orbits, additional clay is applied for the brows, (Fig. 17) and pressure is applied inward and upward with both thumbs, forming two arches (Fig. 18). These arches are called the supraorbital arches, meaning above the orbit or eye socket. Ridges above these are called the supracilliary arches, meaning the arch above the eyebrow. The applied rolls of plasteline begin to form the upper one third of the skull. These help to give a massiveness to the skull (Fig. 16). More plasteline is added and smoothed with thumb and fingers (Fig. 17-19). In the growth and development of the skull, there are certain prominent parts. These include the arches above the eyes; the maxilla, or cheek bones below the eyes; the lateral zygomatic arches that are above and lateral to the joint and attachment to the temporal bone of the jawbones, or mandibles.

The skull, as seen from above, reveals a modified oval or egg shape (Fig. 20). There is some flattening and a rounding of the forehead to gently divergent vertical planes in the temporal area with the greatest width just posterior to the ears at the parietal bossae or prominences and a rounding about the occiput or posterior area of the cranium.

There are paired eminences on the forehead of the frontal bones. Plasteline is applied to form these forehead eminences (Fig. 21). There is a gentle midline ridge in the upper forehead. There are also prominences of the brow over the frontal sinuses. These may be felt by a person on his or her own head. Using two hands not only steadies the work, but they also help to maintain symmetrical development. Temporal ridges, from the forehead back above the ears are modeled on the side of the skull by firm strokes of the thumbs (Fig. 23). The temporal ridge of the skull receives attention as I model appropriate form to the temporal area, behind the lateral aspect of the brow ridge or supracilliary arch. The temporal ridge is another arch and is situated on the lateral aspect of the cranium on two gently diverging vertical

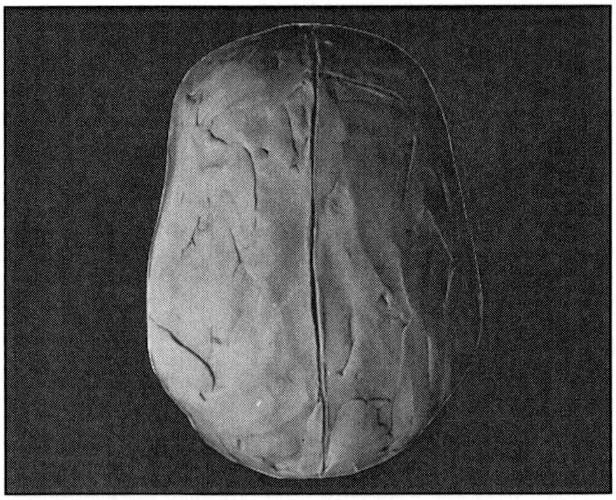

Fig. 20. The skull, when viewed from above, appears ovoid, (egg shaped) and the forehead is at the narrowest aspect.

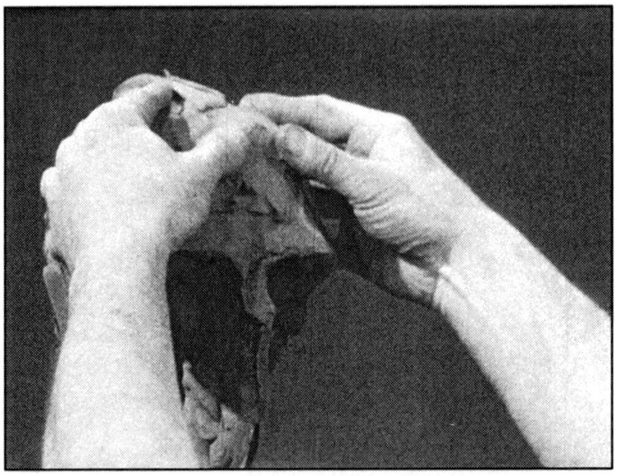

Fig. 21. Additional plasteline is added to the forehead to represent the frontal prominences.

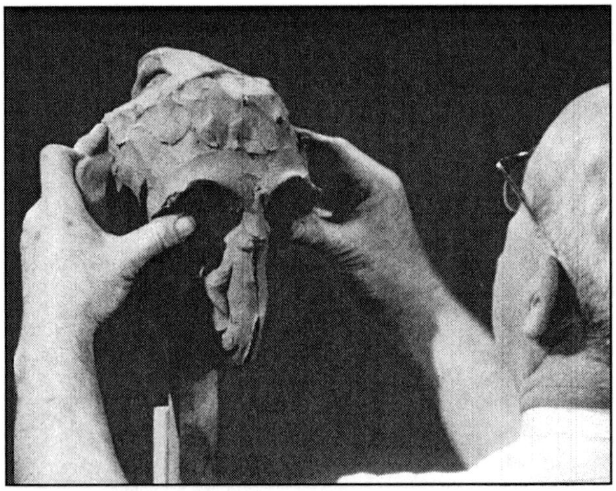

Fig. 22. The lateral borders of the orbits are improved by thumb strokes.

planes (see illustrations in Form and Anatomy sections). The temporal muscle originates along this ridge and is attached to the mandible or jaw bone. One can feel this ridge above the ear, and as one chews, the contraction of the temporal muscle may be palpated.

Rolls are placed below the eye sockets to form the cheek bones or maxilla (Fig. 25). The infraorbital ridge below the eye socket is modeled symmetrically by pressure of a sculptor's thumbs (Fig. 26). Firm pressure exerted deepens the hollow. A continuation of this bone formation sweeps around towards the ear and represents the zygomatic arch (Fig. 27). This improves the clay model's resemblance to the human skull.

The infraorbital ridge, below the eye socket is modeled symmetrically by a sculptor's thumbs. With firm pressure to deepen the hollow, This gives a roundness to the orbit. With the modeling of the maxilla and the zygoma, the form of the infraorbital arch becomes the lower border of the orbit or socket of the eye. The lateral border of the orbit is slightly lateral and posterior to the prominence of the maxilla or cheekbone. Note that the center line is still maintained.

The development of the arches of the skull is a very important consideration in modeling. The arch of the skull and the arches above and below the orbits have been modeled. A better form of the infraorbital ridge is modeled by the thumbs (Fig. 27). There is another arch of the maxilla, the arch of the roof of the mouth that is called the hard palate. There are also arches of the cheek bones The symmetry gives balance, and the arches with curved lines give rhythm to the design.

More plasteline rolls are added to the cranium. It is also modeled with the sculptor's thumbs and fingers of both hands to smooth in some areas and build up in others. The general form of the head is developed and increases when several rolls are added to indicate hair. As more plasteline rolls are also added to the back of the head as well as to the forehead, we become more aware of the massive features of the skull.

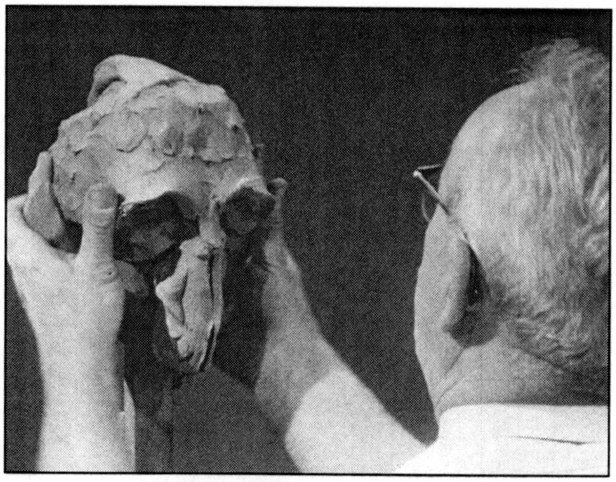

Fig. 23. More form is added to the temporal aspect of the skull.

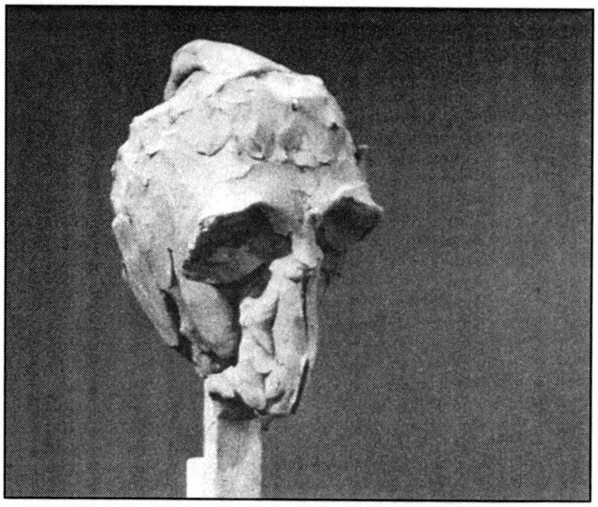

Fig. 24. A view of progress is shown that includes the supraorbital arches.

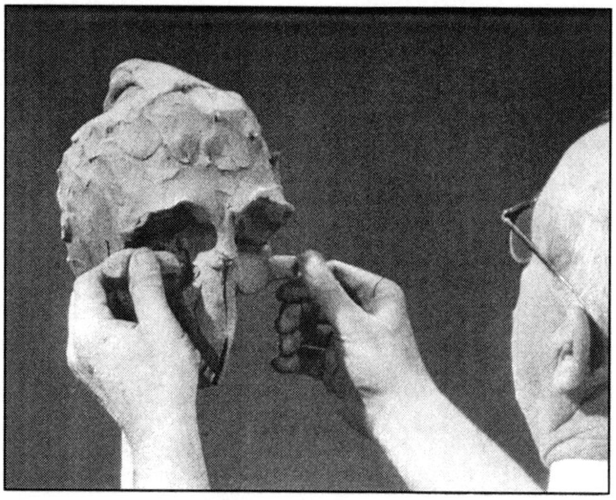

Fig. 25. More rolls of plasteline are applied to represent maxillae or cheek bones.

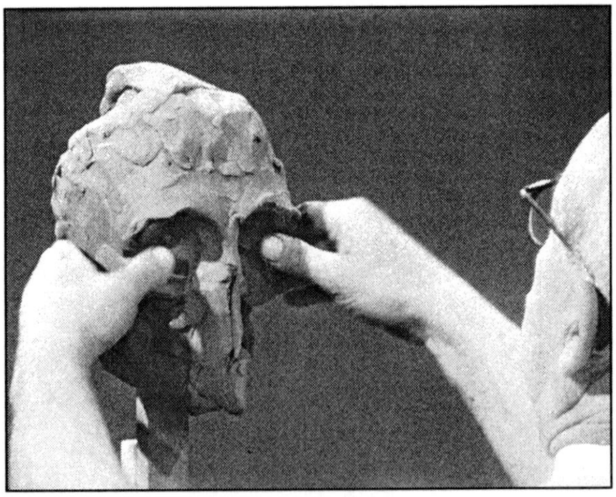

Fig.26. The temporal borders of the orbits are improved.

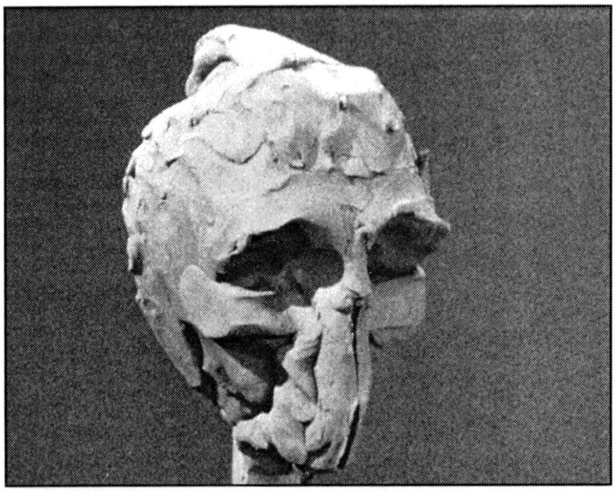

Fig. 27. The progress of skull development is presented, showing infra-orbital arches.

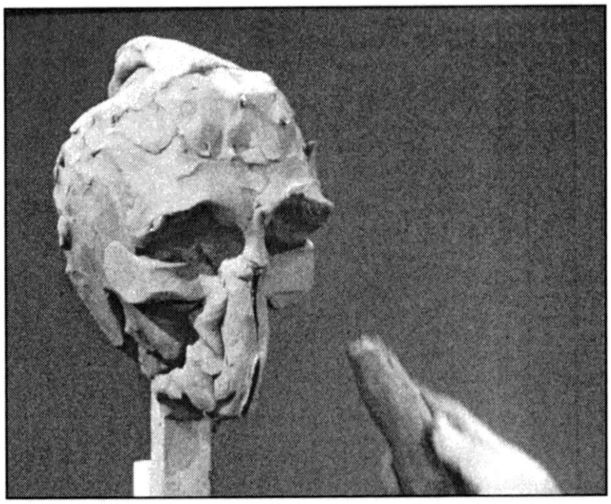

Fig. 28. A roll of Plasteline is made ready for the left mandible.

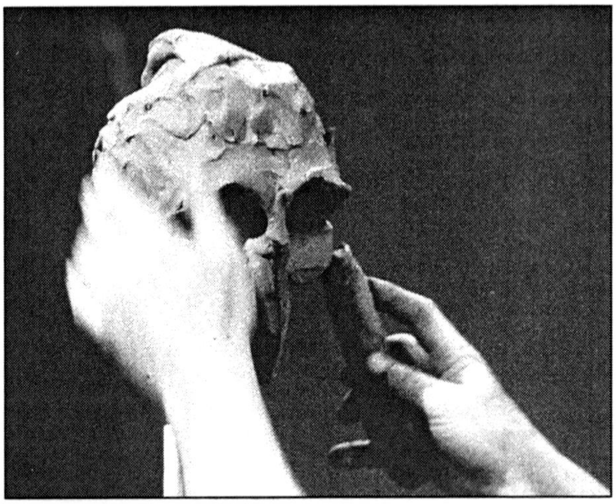

Fig. 29. The roll for left mandible is applied below the zygomatic arch.

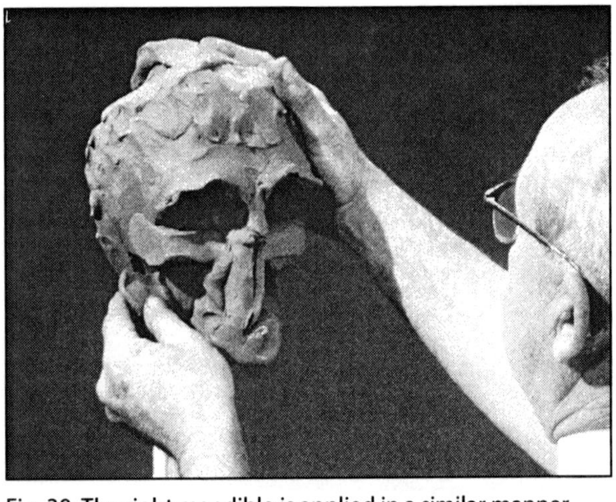

Fig. 30. The right mandible is applied in a similar manner.

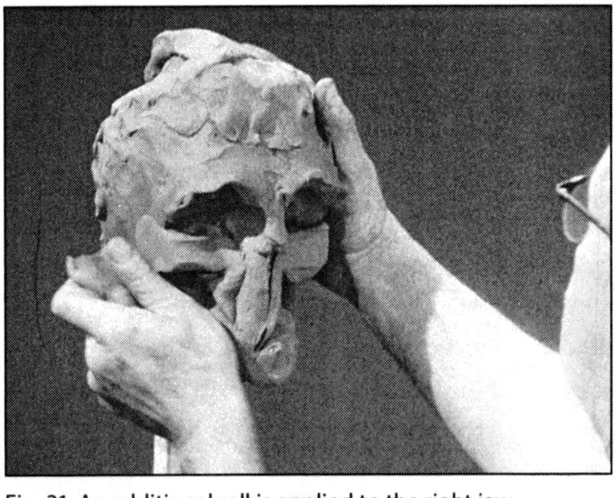

Fig. 31. An additional roll is applied to the right jaw.

The Mandible or Jaw is Modeled

There is one movable bone of the skull. This is the mandible or jaw bone. It can move side to side as well as up and down. Therefore, the next prominent feature to be added is the massive mandible. I have modeled the features of the zygomatic arch and maxilla, which join to form the cheek bone or upper jaw. After producing these, you will notice that I make the big jaw bone, or mandible as it is anatomically named. The mandible is begun with large rolls of plasteline (Fig. 28, 29). Additional modeling and pressure joins these rolls to the skull, making the mandible better formed and with a prominent chin (Fig. 30-34). This improves the shape of the skull. It is very necessary that this fundamental form of the skull be carefully modeled, because everything that we make whether it is one person or another, the subsequent modeling and fundamental form of the human head depends on the shape of the skull regardless of the person portrayed. The fundamental design of the human head and soft tissue features must conform to the skull. Now that the mandible has been added, the form more nearly resembles a skull (Fig. 35).

After doing this, we return to this center line (Fig. 36). On this center line, we begin to form the features. Again, symmetry is stressed.

The mandible, originating just under the zygoma extends down nearly vertically about two inches (5 cm). At the angle of the jaw, it extends forward at an obtuse angle of about 115 degrees and inward or medially to the chin, varying slightly with individuals. The right and left mandible approach the chin at about a 60-degree angle. This angle is apparent when another person looks up at the ceiling. The male skull has a larger mandible with a more prominent chin. It also has heavier brow ridges and cheek bones than the female skull. In childhood and youth, the male and female skulls are similar and mandibles are less prominent.

After modeling the mandible, the center line is again drawn with a modeling tool (Fig. 36). From this center line, one can begin to form the facial features. Whenever a feature is made

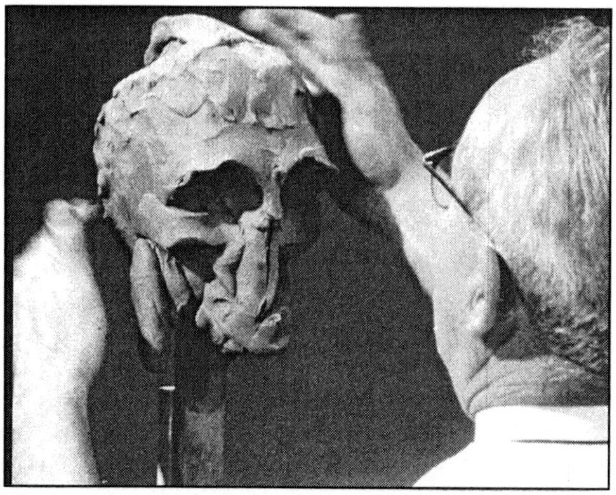

Fig. 32. The additional roll of plasteline is properly placed.

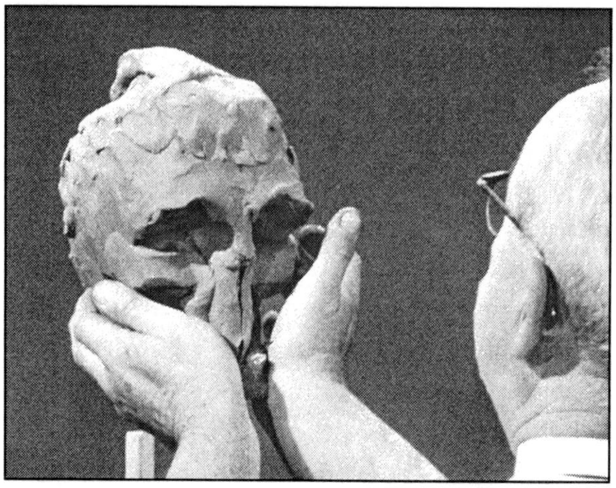

Fig. 33. Pressure is applied with the palms of both hands to form the mandible.

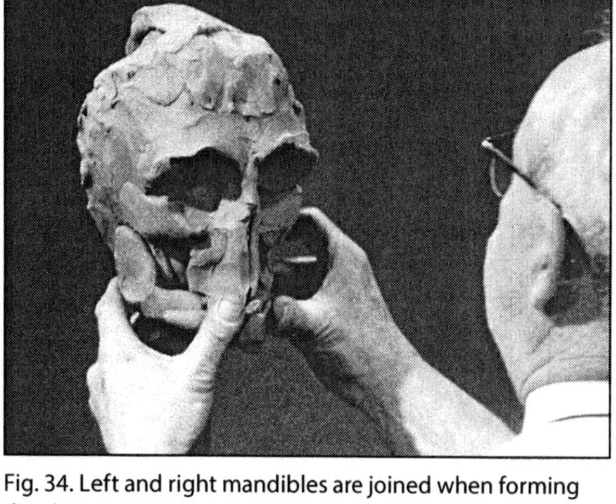

Fig. 34. Left and right mandibles are joined when forming the chin.

on one side, it must be made on the other side. This form of symmetry is fundamental in all construction, whether it be by work of art or by nature, in cells or crystals, or in plants and animals. When there is construction in architecture there usually is symmetry, for its name (architecture) refers to arches that manifest symmetry.

Head Proportions

During the modeling of the skull, careful attention to features is observed. The larger features are constructed first. Simultaneous attention must also be directed to proportions. The height of the skull, (vertex to chin) is nearly equal to the anterior-posterior dimension (depth), while breadth is approximately five eighths the height, (0.625, nearly 2/3). There are some variations in ratios of height to breadth with adult individuals. There are changes in age, and there are some variations according to ethnic backgrounds, but the proportions are similar. These facial proportions can be divided into halves and thirds. The chin to an eye, or center of orbit, equals an eye to the vertex. It also equals the chin to the sternal notch. From the hairline to the chin, the face may be divided into three nearly equal parts: 1) the hairline to brow; 2) the brow to the nose at the lip juncture; 3) and the nose to chin. (See illustrations of human proportions later in this book.)

It is essential that careful attention be given to these general contours and proportions. The fundamental form for every portrait, which a sculptor models, depends on the shape of the human skull. The overlying soft tissues generally conform to the supporting structures, which are essentially the contours of the skull.

The Nose is Added

Having modeled the fundamental form of the skull with the massive features, let us now add some of the more detailed features. The base of the nose was apparent in the early modeling of the skull. The soft part of the nose, which is supported by cartilage, may be modeled by adding a roll of plasteline.

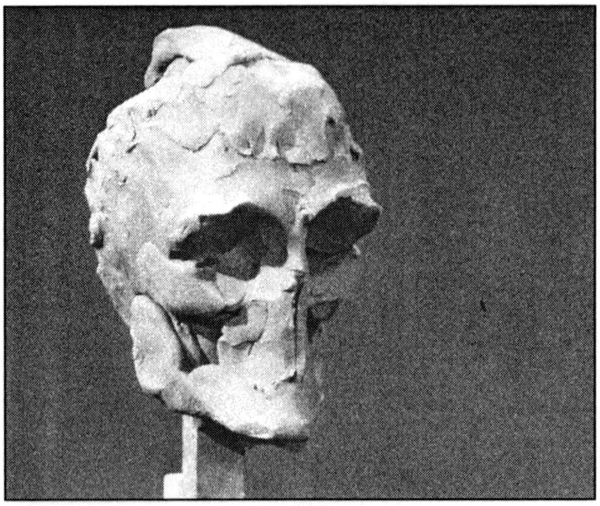

Fig. 35. A view of progress demonstrates the formed mandible with the chin.

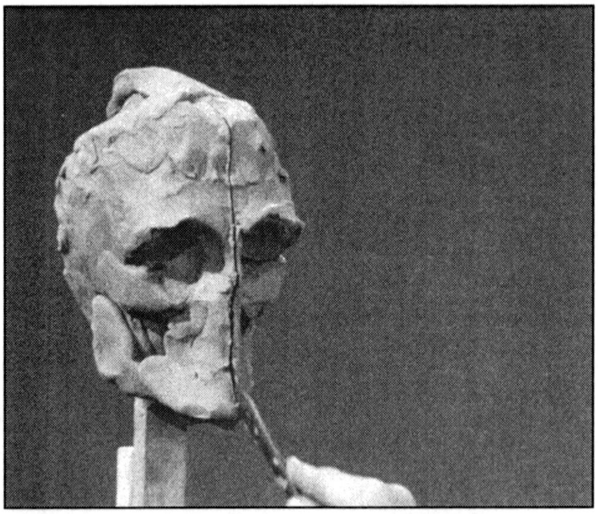

Fig. 36. A center line is again incised to demonstrate symmetry.

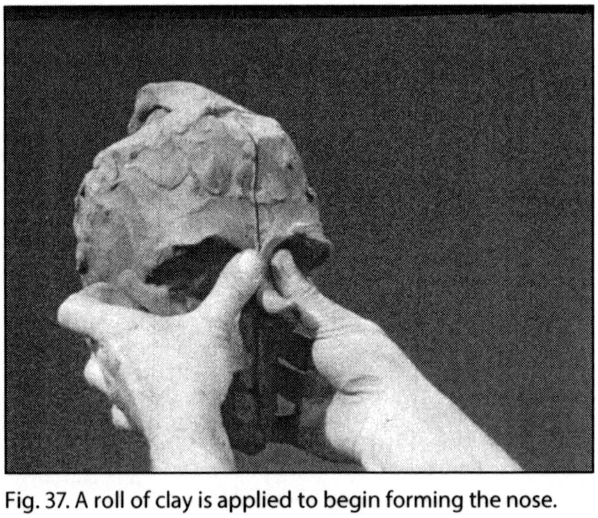

Fig. 37. A roll of clay is applied to begin forming the nose.

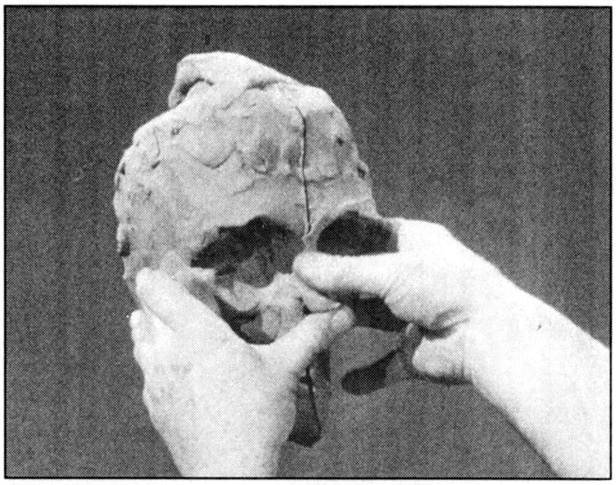

Fig. 38. The formation of the nose has begun.

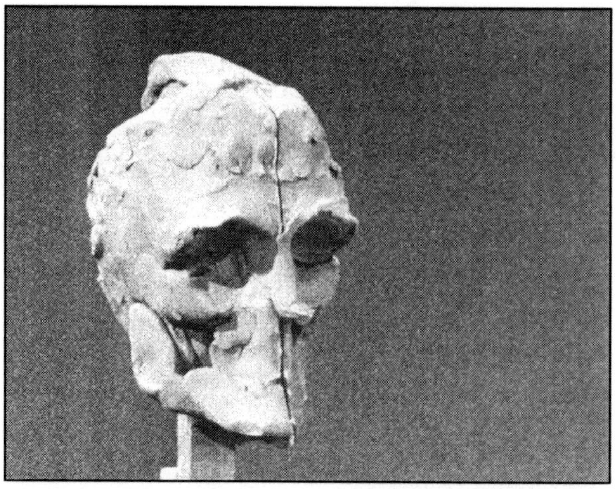

Fig. 39. A view shows the first step in the formation of the nose.

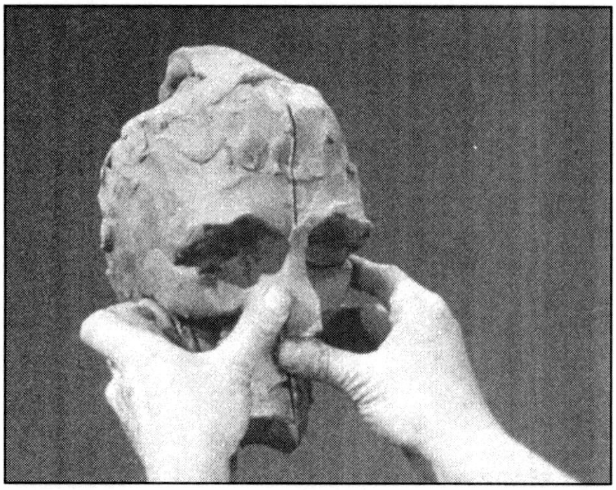

Fig. 40. Additional form of the nose is modeled by thumb and finger strokes.

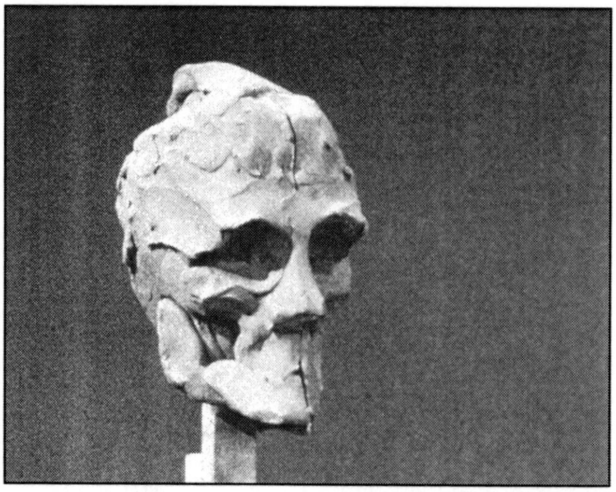

Fig. 41. A view demonstrates progress of nose development.

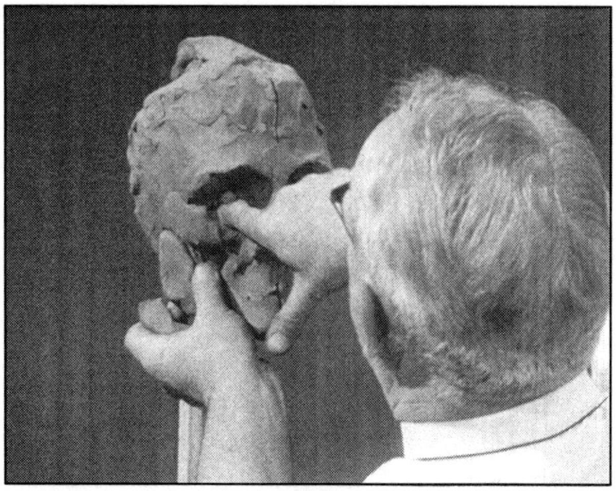

Fig. 42. The right infraorbital ridge is developed by finger strokes.

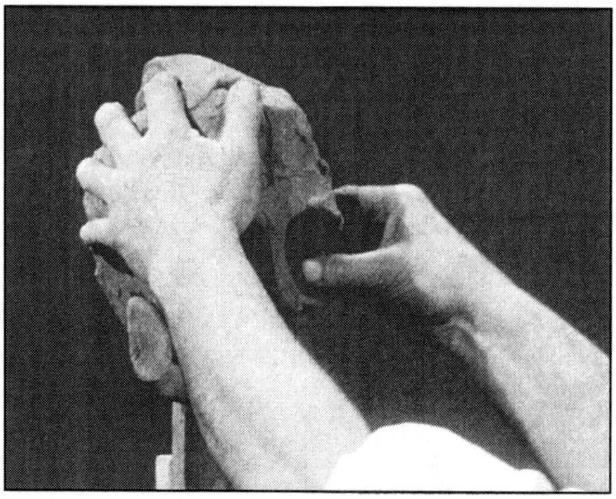

Fig. 43. The left infraorbital ridge is developed in the same manner.

The upper third of the nose is supported by bone. The middle third is supported by a midline cartilage, in the septum and lateral cartilage plates named the superior lateral cartilages. The lower third is supported by the septum and the lateral inferior cartilages that also form the nostrils. Plasteline is added to begin forming the nose (Fig. 37, 38). As more plasteline is added, a more preliminary form is given to the nose, yet more careful modeling and better form for the nose will be needed later (Fig. 40, 41). Only the basic contours are approximated. Finish details can be modeled later. The maxilla or upper jaw and mandible have been placed together, leaving voids where the cheeks will be added with plasteline.

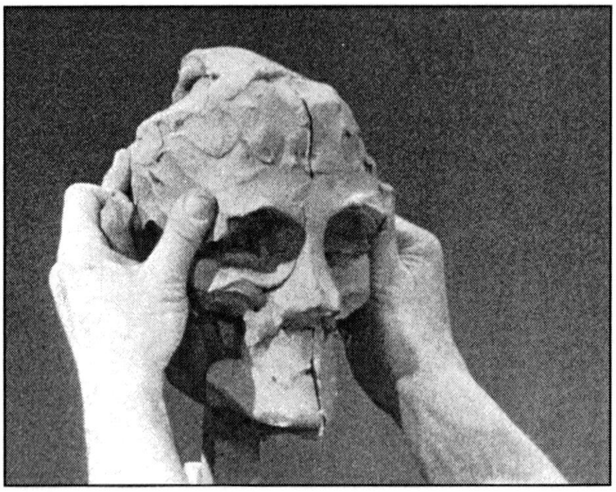

Fig. 44. The lateral ridges of the orbits ridges are improved.

Addition of Hair

The form of the orbits or eye sockets is given better outline by adding the infraorbital ridge below the eye (Fig. 42, 43). The lateral borders of the orbits are also developed (Fig. 44). These features may easily be palpated on one's own face.

More rolls of plasteline are placed on the upper part of the head to form more hair (Fig. 45). These larger features may be modeled early in the work and nearly simultaneously as the portrait develops. It helps to give the artist perspective and direction. They also begin to render a sense of personality to the work. Additional hair is added as rolls are pressed on the head sweeping down toward the shoulders (Fig. 46). Hair is modeled as locks and tresses, not in strands or individual hairs. Texture may be applied later to the locks to render that impression. In order to make hair, we must consider what period of time the person lived, the styles, and the customs of that period of history (Fig. 46, 47).

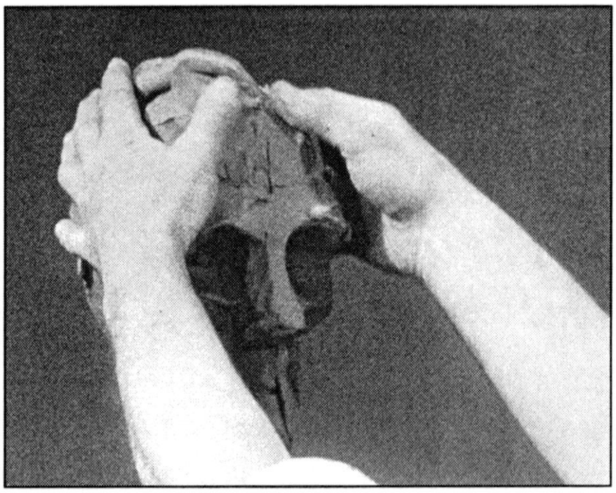

Fig. 45. Additional hair is applied above the forehead.

We must consider who the person is and what he did for humanity that makes him worthy of being given the recognition of being honored by a great monument. Naturally, my business is making great monuments, so the monuments we produce are to the men or women who are worthy of being heralded and remembered in the public monuments.

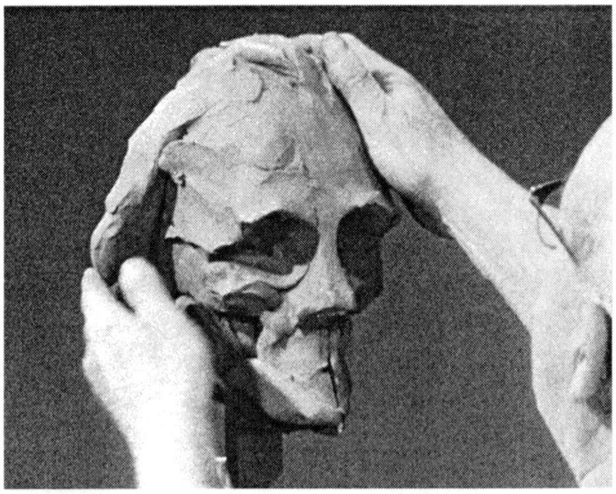

Fig. 46. A lock of hair is applied to right side of the head.

Lips Are Added

At this stage of modeling, the portrait is just a beginning and it looks rather strange. Now plasteline is pressed on and roughly shaped by applying a roll from side to side over the anterior mandible, maxilla and teeth where the lips will later be modeled (Fig. 48, 49). The lips conform to the contour of teeth. Voids in the cheeks are also partly filled in (Fig. 50). So far, only a few of the features have been added to the skull. Very few of the soft tissues have been represented. In modeling, we must go from one feature to another in order that all may progress together (Fig. 51). Now having modeled basic features, I begin making other features. The larger features are always the ones that need to be constructed first.

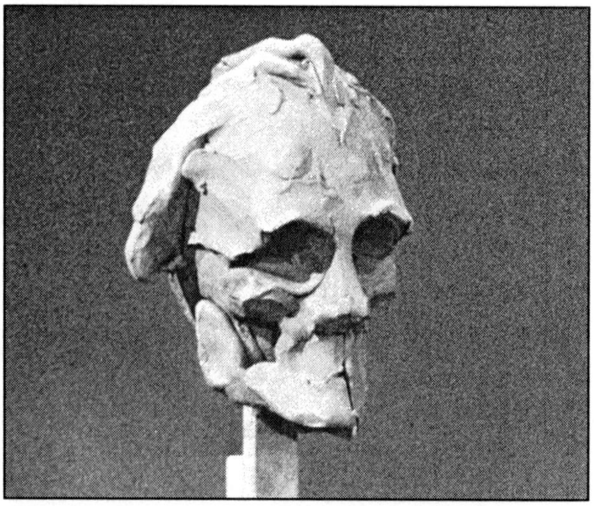

Fig. 47. A view is presented demonstrating progress.

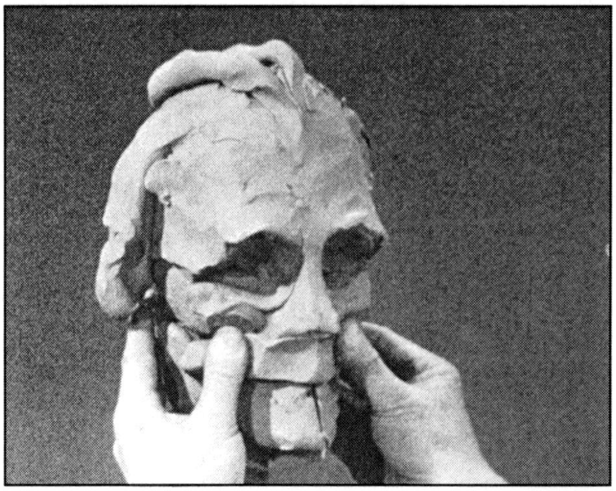

Fig. 48. A roll of plasteline is applied that represent the lips.

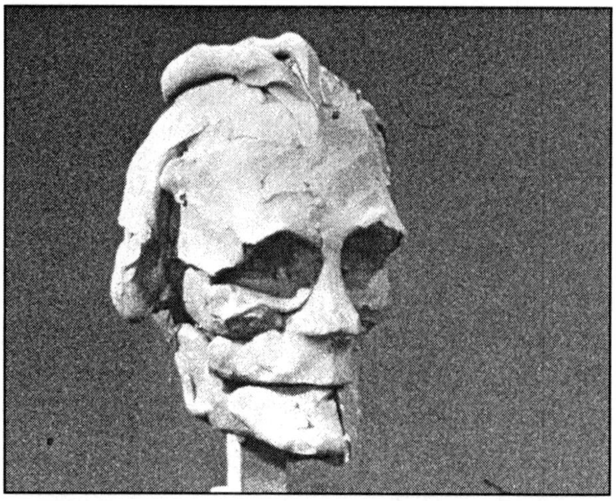

Fig. 49. A view of head demonstrates progress with initial lip form.

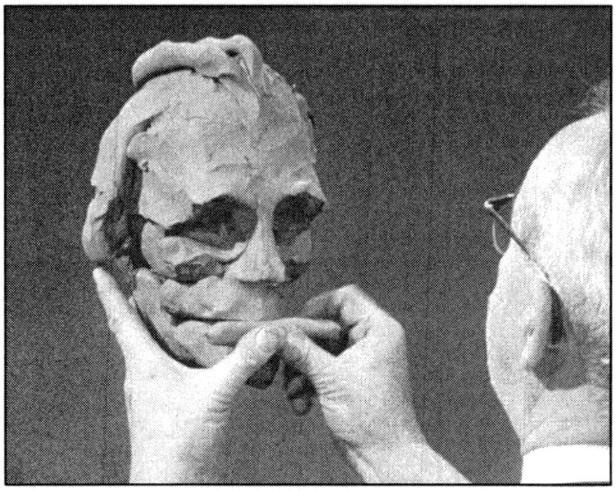

Fig. 50. An additional roll of plasteline is applied for the lips.

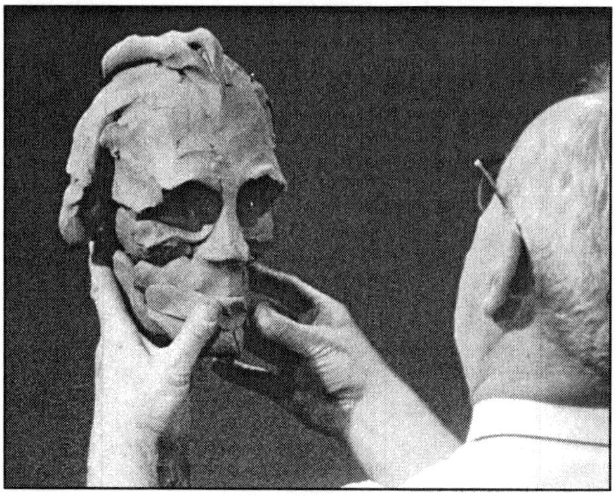

Fig. 51. The rolls are smoothed onto the face.

Muscles of the Shoulders and Neck

In order to have the modeling progress for the whole portrait, attention is now directed to the posterior aspect of the neck and shoulders. Now it is necessary to give him a backbone or vertebral column and shoulders. The form of the neck must be considered and it is appropriate to give the portrait supporting structures. It needs muscles in the neck and the shoulders. I am placing rolls of clay representing very large muscles out to the shoulders. The head is supported on the neck vertebrae, not only by ligaments but also by large muscles extending, from the occiput of the skull, down to the thorax along the vertebrae. There are the group of erector spinae muscles, which, with others, function to keep the head erect. There are also several additional layers of deep muscles in the posterior neck, which assist in balancing the head and controlling movement. Rolls of plasteline are applied to the neck and back representing the muscles located there (Fig. 52-55).

Shoulders are modeled by placing several rolls of clay to represent the very large, deep muscles of the posterior neck and the bones with the attached muscles of the shoulder girdles (Fig. 56-58). I am placing very large muscles out and onto the shoulders. These are known as the trapezius muscles. All the deeper layers are overlaid by the trapezius muscles, which originate in the base of the skull and from the spines of the vertebrae half way down the back. (See anatomical illustration.) Muscle fibers give support to the head by extending out to and along the spine of the scapula, or shoulder blade.. They insert on the point of the shoulder called the acromion process of the scapula. This bony process is also attached to the clavicle or collar bone with dense ligaments (Fig. 59). At the shoulders, on each side of the body, these two muscles each form a trapezium (a four-sided figure with no parallel lines, hence the name trapezius). Together the right and left trapezius muscles form the outline of a kite shaped figure. These muscle masses give the portrait some strength and support, and make it seem more secure.

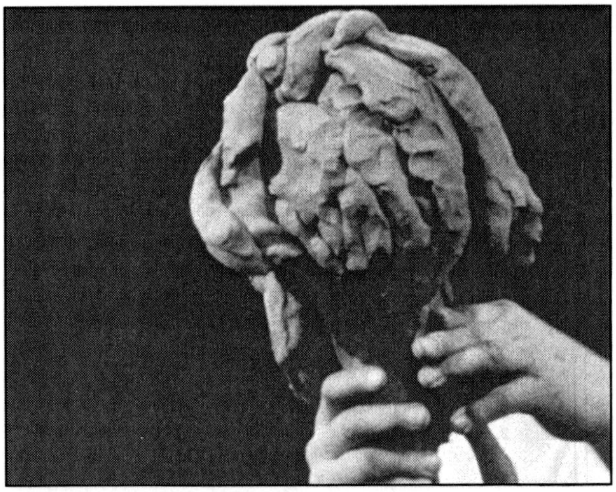

Fig. 52. A roll of plasteline is added representing deep neck muscles.

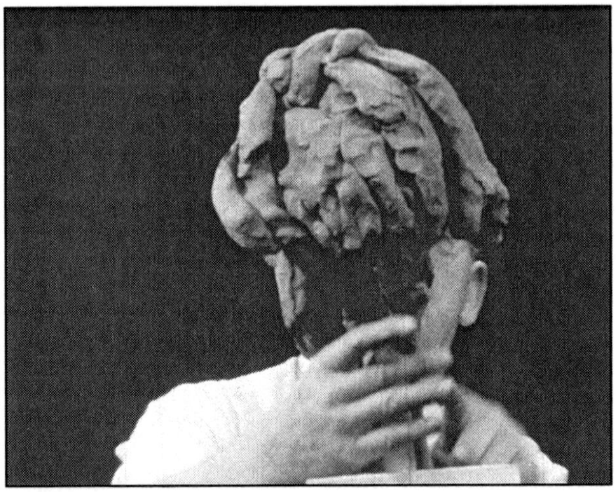

Fig. 53. An additional roll is added.

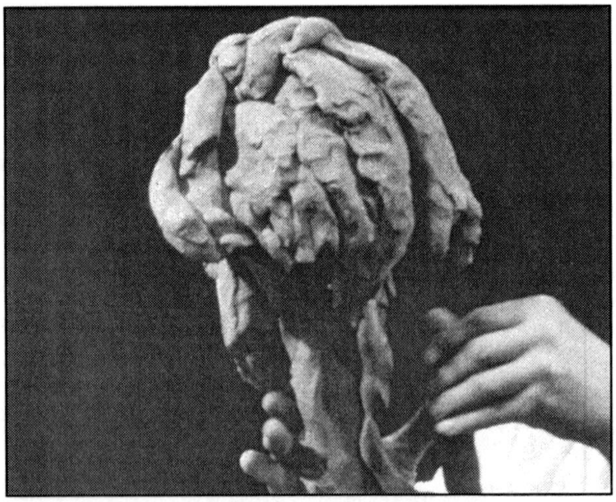

Fig. 54. Additional large rolls of plasteline are added.

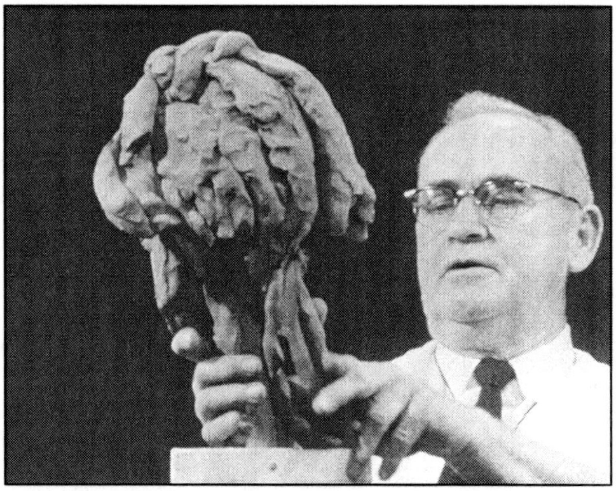

Fig. 55. The muscle mass on the right builds up with added clay.

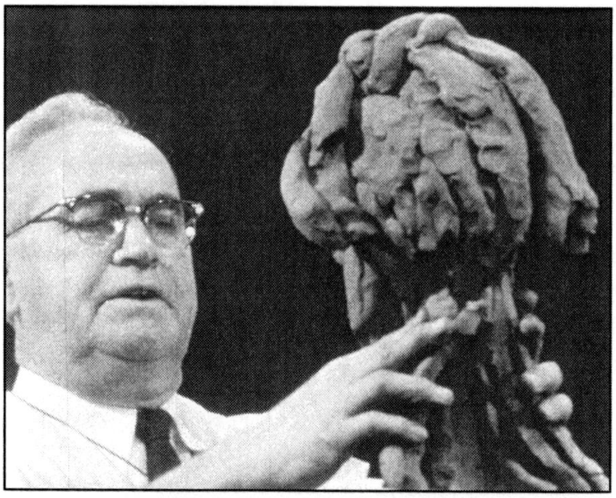

Fig. 56. Rolls are applied to the left side in the same manner.

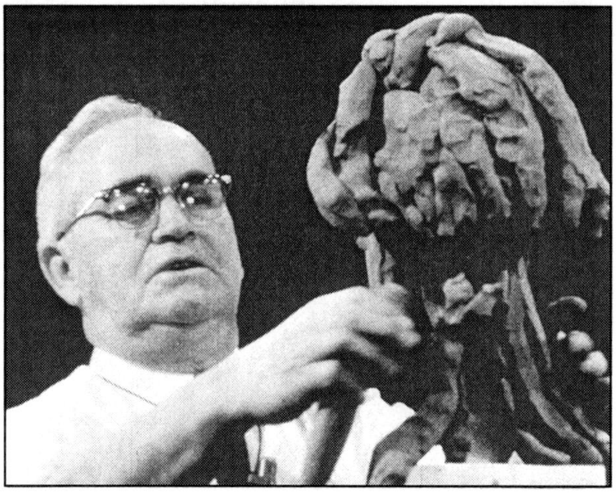

Fig. 57. Additional mass is applied to the left side.

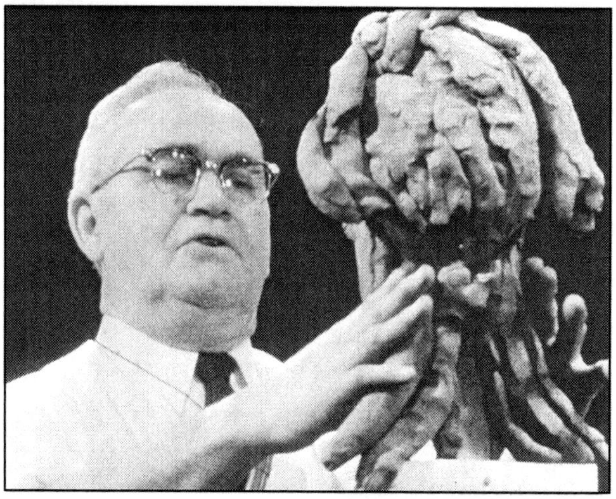

Fig. 58. The rolls representing neck muscles are pressed together by both hands.

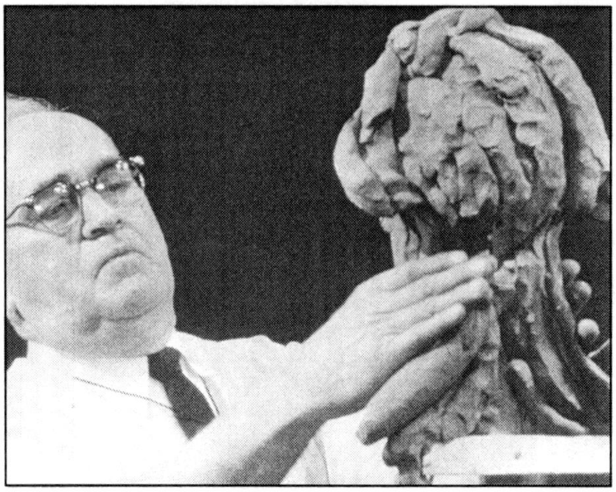

Fig. 59. The neck form representing the trapezius muscles is formed with hand pressure.

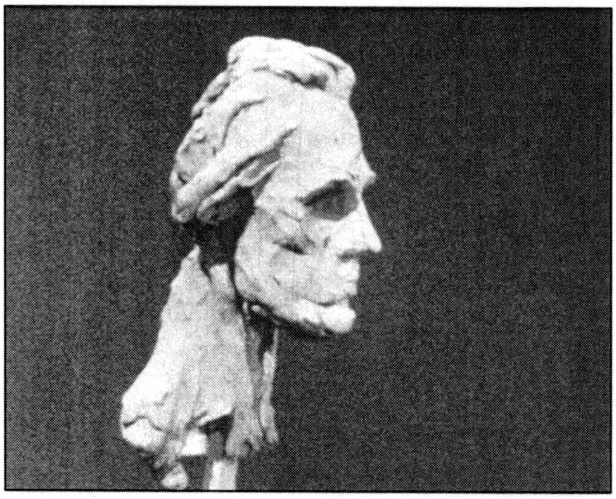

Fig. 60. A lateral view demonstrates the trapezius and the sternocleido mastoid muscles.

Anterior Neck Muscles

Deep in the anterior neck, there are three scalenius muscles on each side, that aid in the stability of the neck. They originate on the vertebrae and angle out diagonally and down attaching on the first rib, like guy wires of a telephone pole. Now I apply two large muscles, the sternocleidomastoid muscles, which extend up the side of the neck from their origins at the joint of the breast bone, or sternum and the attached collar bones or clavicles (Fig. 60).

These paired muscles angle up the neck laterally to attach to the mastoid processes of the temporal bones on each side of the skull, located just behind and below the ears (Fig. 60); hence the name sternocleidomastoid (sometimes called the sternomastoid muscles) These also give the portrait strength and support.

The sternum, or breast bone, in the center of the anterior chest, is a large flat bone (Fig. 61). The next features to model are the clavicles, commonly called the collar bones. These are not a straight bones but have a gentle "S" curve. They are attached by strong ligaments to the sternum and laterally they are attached to the acromion processes of the scapulae near the most prominent point of the shoulders. A roll of clay is applied for a clavicle (Fig. 62-64).

It is necessary to construct these features before making the upper muscles of the chest. These are the large, broad pectoralis major muscles, which originate on the sternum and medial portions of ribs and extend laterally to the arm near the shoulder, inserting on the humerus, the bone of the upper arm. Addition of these features begins to give a better base for the head of this portrait. Now that these are added, it begins to demonstrate more solidity and strength.

As a little point of interest, a short roll of plasteline is pressed into the neck between the sternocleidomastoid muscles to represent the larynx (voice box or Adam's apple) (Fig. 65, 66). This begins to give the neck a proper form. Between the chin and the larynx there is a broad thin muscle shaped like half of a cone called the myelohyoid muscle that is to be added during finishing details. As you have observed, this modeling has been constructed in accordance with anatomical knowledge and understanding.

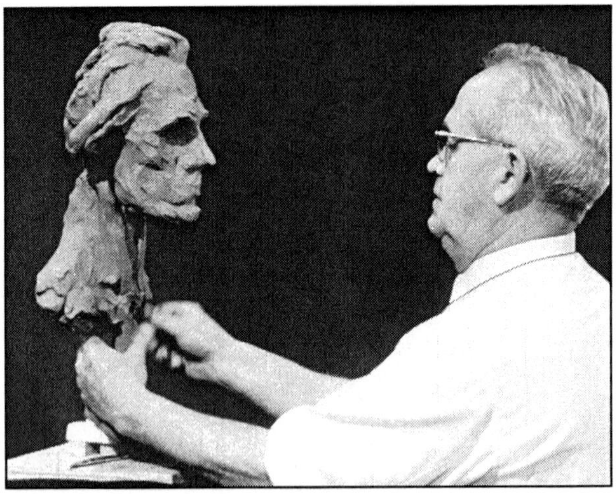

Fig. 61. Plasteline is applied representing the sternum or breast bone.

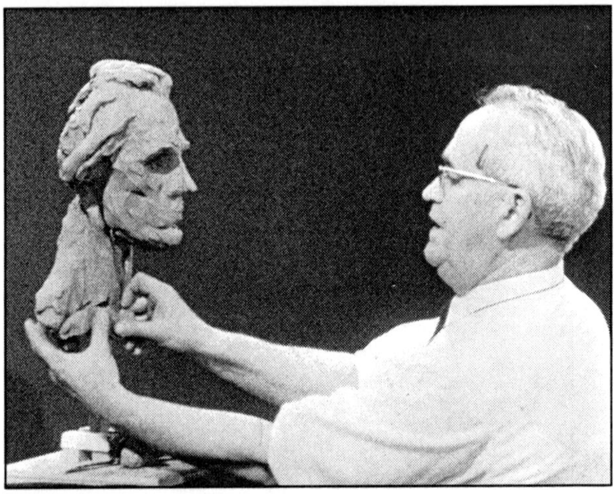

Fig. 62. A roll of plastiline is applied for the clavicle or collar bone.

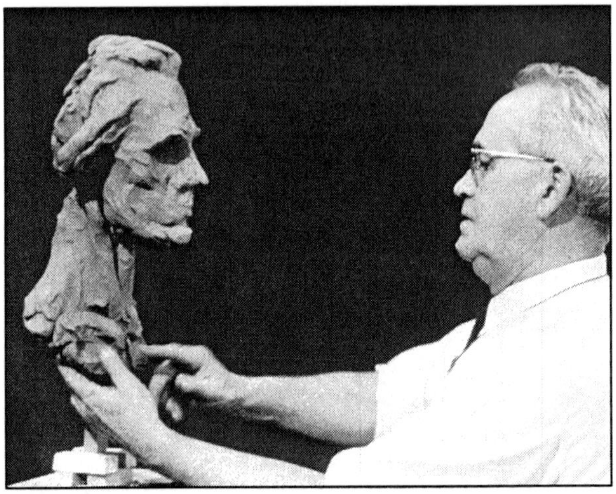

Fig. 63. The shape of the clavicle is formed with finger strokes.

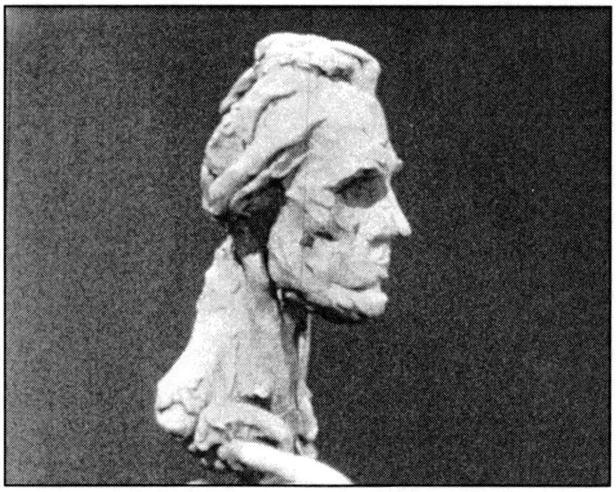

Fig. 64. A right lateral view is demonstrates progress.

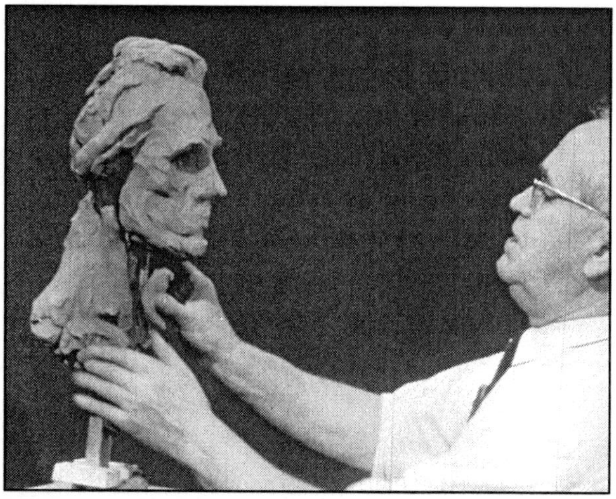

Fig. 65. A roll is applied to represent the larynx or Adam's apple.

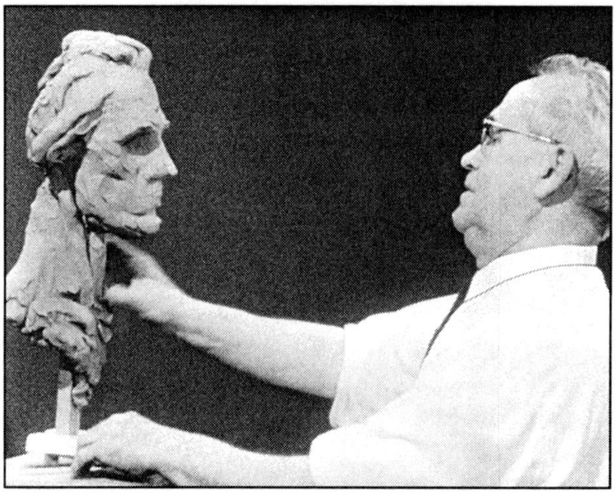

Fig. 66. The larynx is modeled into the upper anterior neck.

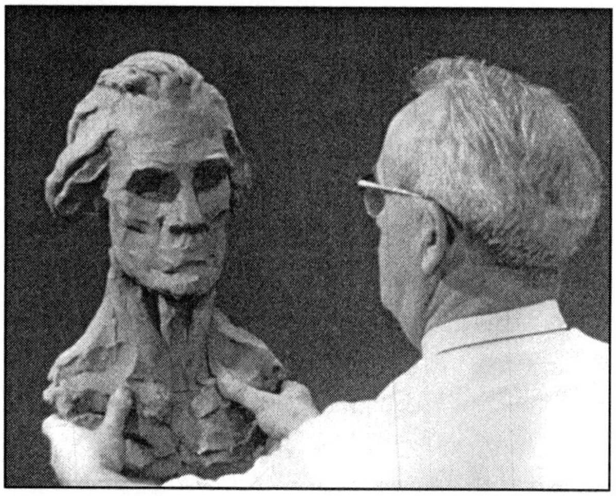

Fig. 67. A concavity above the clavicles is formed with thumb and finger strokes.

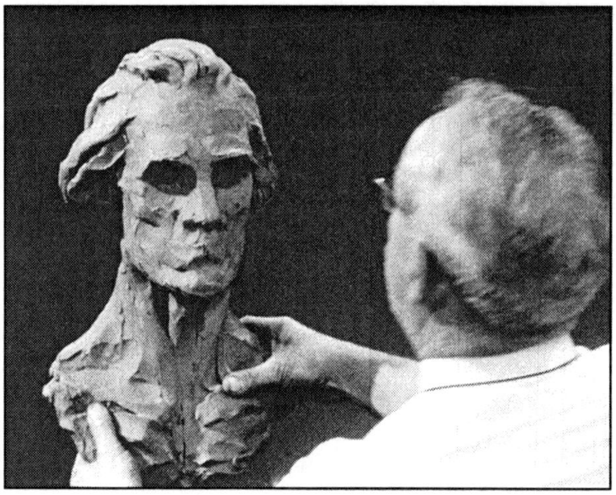

Fig. 68. Additional form is applied to each clavical or collar bone.

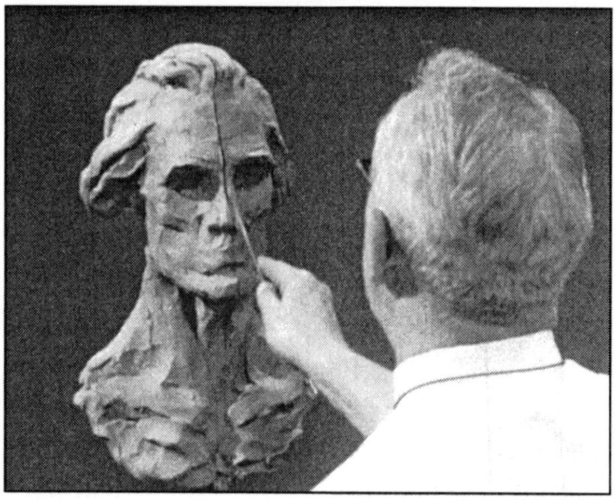

Fig. 69. A center line is again inscribed with a tool stroke.

Symmetry

Additional plasteline has been added to the cheeks and lips (Fig. 68). The form of the forehead has been refined by smoothing it with fingers Whenever as artists we form a feature on one side, we must make a similar shape on the other side which is the counterpart. That is called symmetry and in the development of this in a symmetrical manner, we must understand a fundamental law, the law of design. We must study design and the basic structures of design and appreciate their importance. One of the first principles of design is symmetry. This requires a balanced relationship of one side to another.

Again, to stress symmetry, a vertical line is drawn with a modeling tool from the midline down the nose, over the lips, the chin, and the larynx to the sternal notch. Symmetrical modeling may then be re-appraised (Fig. 69). A transverse line, drawn across the brows by a stroke of the tool, allows an evaluation of proportions (Fig. 70). The face may be divided into three parts, the hairline to brow, the brow to below the nose, and the nose to chin. Another set of three equal parts is the vertex to the corner of eye, the eye to chin and the chin to sternal notch that is between the inner borders of the collar bones.

After the lines have served to demonstrate balance, with symmetry and proportion, they may be erased (Fig. 73). The midline mark on the chin and lips is smoothed over by a stroke of the thumb as the sub-labial crease is accentuated. The vertical mark on the neck is then erased by a thumb stroke and the transverse line across the brows is also erased by thumb strokes (Fig. 73-75). Small segments may remain for later reference.

Up to this point the modeling has been definitely symmetrical and in accordance to a pattern and design. Symmetry deserves to be emphasized by repeated calls of attention. Whenever an artist makes a feature on one side, he should make a similar shape to its counterpart on the other side. Symmetry requires a balanced relationship of one side to the other. This is a formal symmetry. An informal composition

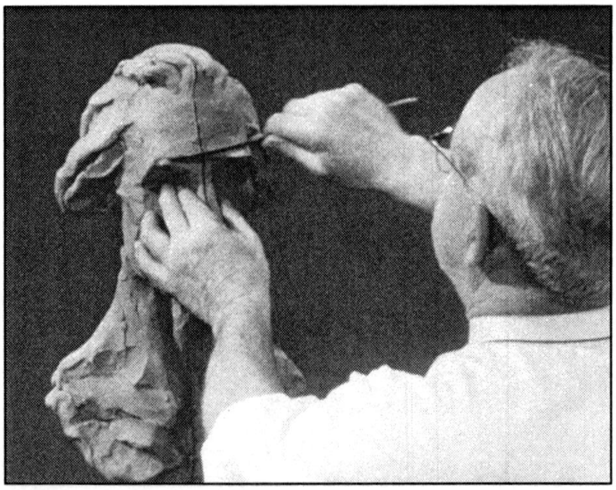

Fig. 70. A transverse line is inscribed with a tool stroke over the brows.

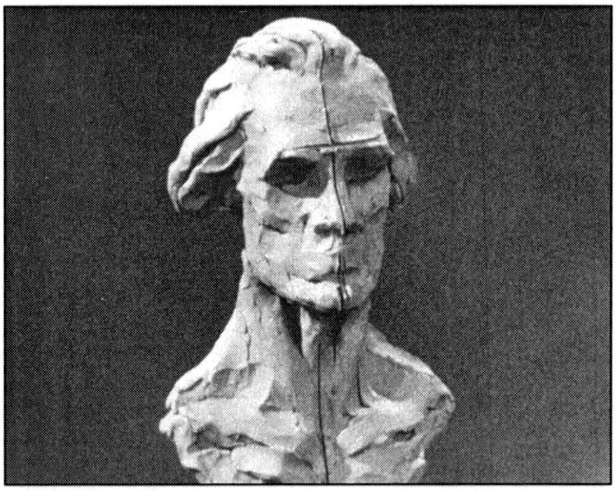

Fig. 71. The inscribed lines demonstrate symmetry and proportions.

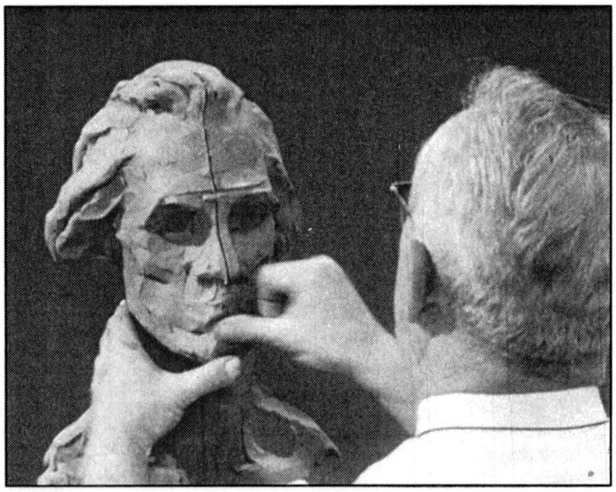

Fig. 72. The center line over the lips is erased.

will allow for action within a state of symmetry rather than being static. We must first understand static forms in order to appreciate and develop dynamic forms, because we work under dynamic laws as well as those, which are static. Now it is important to give some action and life to the portrait. This as you now see it the form is very static. It is just as stiff and immovable as an Egyptian statue.

Egyptian Art and the Law of Frontality

Egypt was a strong nation and its armies captured many slaves. The laws were strict and the punishment was severe, resulting in a rigid aspect to their culture. Their artists created many large and imposing statues, and some magnificent colossal statues carved in stone still stand. The sculptors were skillful and the features were powerful, yet they worked with a static style. The Egyptians learned about the geometric pattern involving the vertical and horizontal lines and carved very fine and great statues. Their early carvings were in stone, a material with limitations. This determined the structures they could carve.

They later carved in wood, but in much the same manner. They were also very conscious of symmetry. Whenever they made something on one side, it was always the same on the other side. All of their statues stand stiff, just as stiff as a poker. As a result, they always look directly forward. Their figures don't look down, or to one side or the other or even up. They always look directly in front. This is called the law of frontality. Presently in the beginning of this portrait it is very similar to Egyptian sculpture, very strong but static. Some Egyptian artists did learn to put one foot forward, and sometimes an arm indicated action. This was a great advance.

The earliest Egyptian art was made prior to the Old Kingdom. It was characterized by unsophisticated art with relatively crude craftsmanship. The sculpture of that time which has been found is carved in stone. During the Old Kingdom, they began to conventionalize the

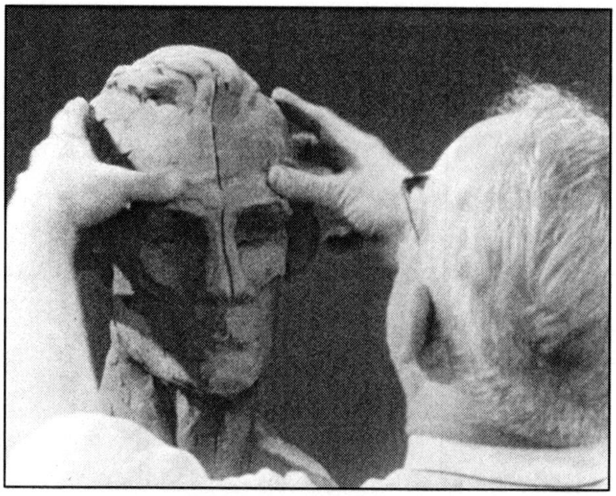

Fig. 73. Lines over the forehead are also erased.

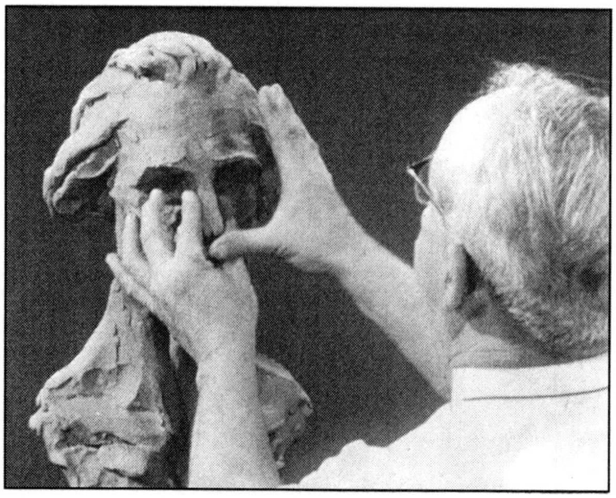

Fig. 74. Attention to the nose to the nose improves its form.

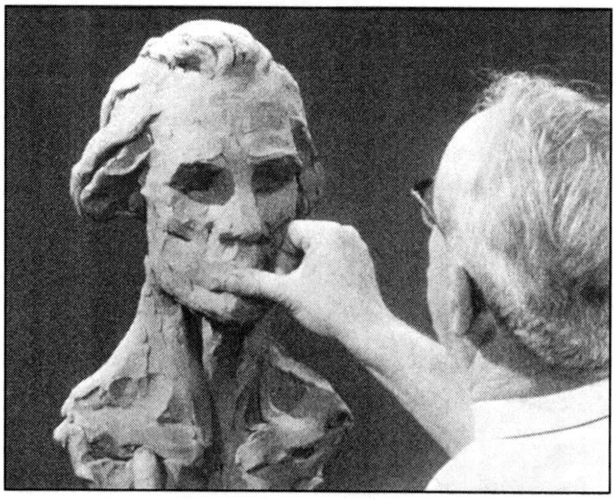

Fig. 75. There is additional smoothing of the lips.

statues, which were very static and stiff. They had stylized almond eyes. The form of frontality was the standard representation. The figures faced forward and were expressionless. During the Middle Kingdom, whose capital was at Thebes, Egyptian artists developed marvelous techniques with fine details. They had conventionalized eyes and lips but the bodies were thinner. There was no action in free standing figures but action was portrayed in the decorative reliefs.

In the New Kingdom or period of the Empire, there was more action but statues still appeared stiff. In this period, Egyptian artists did occasionally put one foot forward and sometimes an arm was extended. An indication of action was a great advance in their art, but most of their figures had a stiff appearance.

Greek Sculpture with Freedom and Dynamics

The Greeks learned an informal symmetry and greatly improved on the art of sculpture; not only did they put one foot forward, but they also rested on one foot. This allowed the forward foot to move about more freely. The Greeks stressed athletics, and had a love for nature, as evidenced by their study of science and philosophy. They had a love of beauty manifest by their development of the arts. They also had a love for individuality and of individual liberty. Their sculpture therefore expresses this sense of freedom and dynamics. The graceful beauty of the Greek statues is largely due to this freedom of movement. They also recognized that with the weight on the right foot, if one steps forward with the left foot, initiating motion, the left shoulder swings up and forward. We first have a formal symmetry followed by an informal symmetry, then by a dynamic symmetry. The next law after symmetry is balance. When one rests on the left leg, the pelvis tilts and the right leg drops as the knee bends. The right shoulder tilts up and forward while the left shoulder moves down and back.

You may note that when I am standing like a soldier at attention, I am stiff. However, when I put the weight on one foot, I can move the other around. When we walk we put our weight alternately on one foot and then the other. When I change my weight from one foot to the other, my whole body moves, and in that action there is motion. When one puts the right foot forward, the left shoulder moves forward and up, and the right hip also moves forward and up. The right shoulder moves down and back, while the left hip moves down and back. This is called *contraposto* or counterpoise (see Appendix).

This form alternates while walking. It is interesting that the British soldiers are trained, while shouldering a rifle, to throw one hand forward and then back as they march. They are taught to do that because it improves balance and makes it easier for them to move. When we appreciate the effect of motion and the alternating activity, we may understand the next law, after symmetry is balance and a third law is rhythm. Then alternating rhythms are the rhythms of movement.

Action and Life Added to the Portrait

Before continuing with refinement of features, this is a good time to give the portrait some action and life. At present it is stiff and unbending. George Washington, however was a man who could act, who could move, who could make changes and direct the affairs of men.

I am going to do something with this head; this is like an Egyptian statue. I am not an Egyptian artist and I am not working in an Egyptian fashion. I have learned more than just to make static figures. I model in a dynamic manner and therefore, action will be incorporated into this work. The head will be twisted moderately either right or left, and it can also be bent forward or back (Fig. 76, 77). At this time, the head is twisted a little to the left, but it must not look sentimental (Fig. 78). There is a less formal appearance with this slight torsion The head is bent slightly to the left in a natural pose and the shoulders are adjusted In this manner (Fig. 79-81). The head may be lifted slightly to give him some dignity, a quality that Washington possessed. If we consider actions in which George Washington might

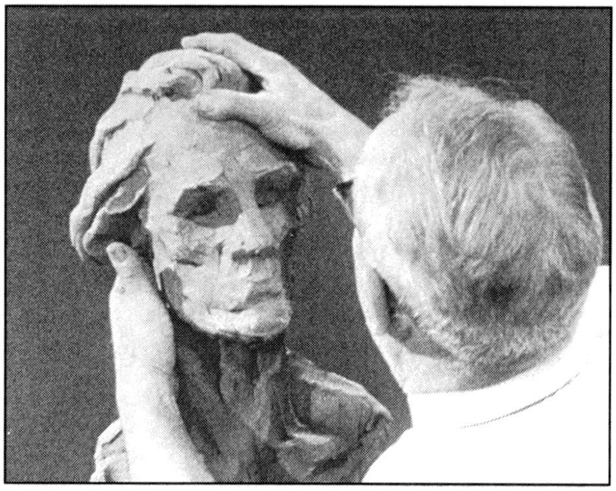

Fig. 76. In order to demonstrate action, the head is turned to the left.

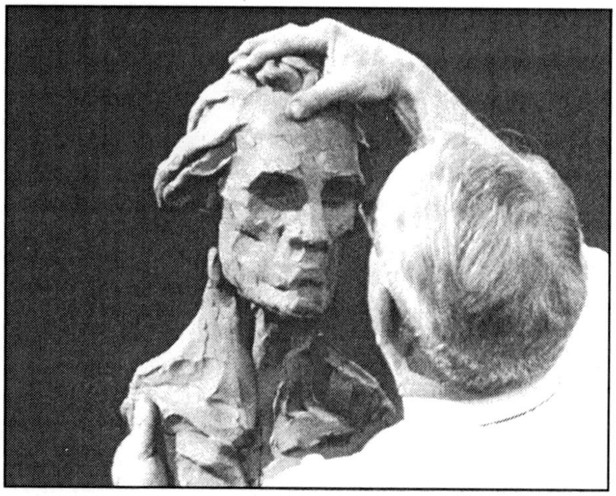

Fig. 77. The head is next tipped to the left by bending the neck.

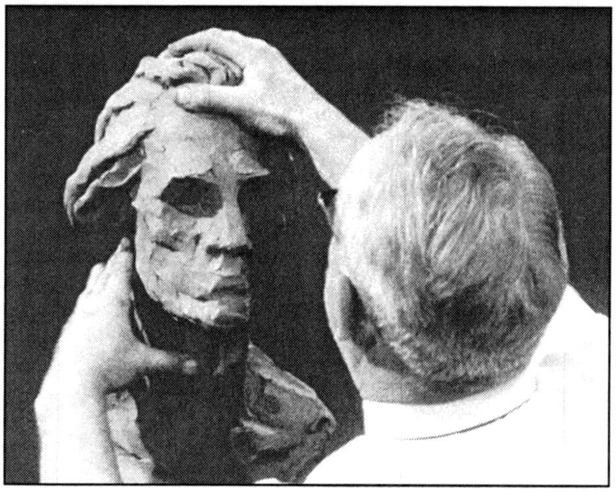

Fig. 78. The head is then straightened with a slight turn to the left.

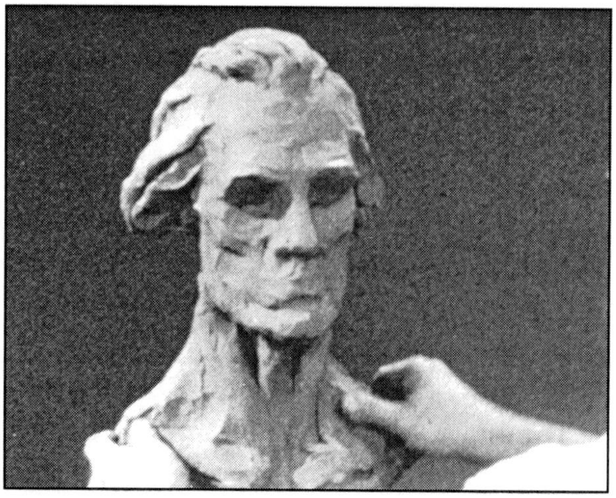

Fig. 79. Additional action is achieved by moving the right shoulder down and elevating the left shoulder.

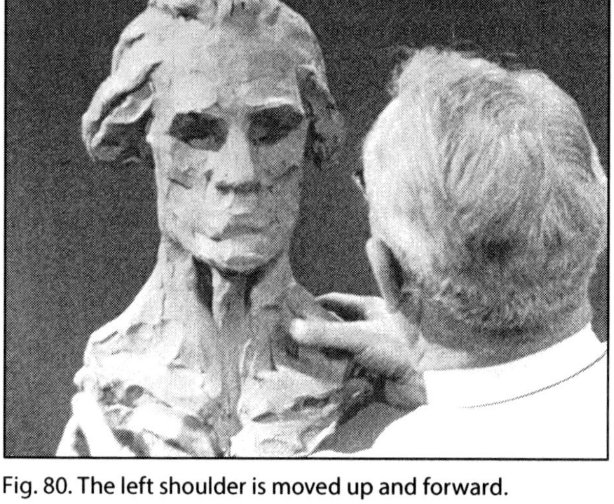

Fig. 80. The left shoulder is moved up and forward.

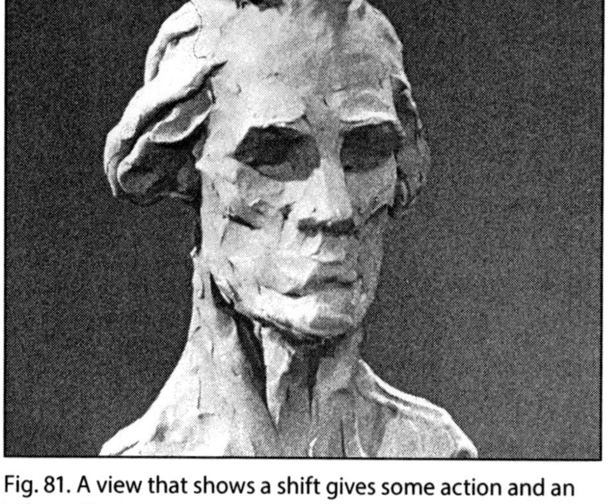

Fig. 81. A view that shows a shift gives some action and an informal balance.

be involved, as reaching for his sword, writing at his desk or reflecting over the problems at Valley Forge, it will help to lend a natural and appropriate attitude to this portrait. The left shoulder is moved forward and elevated and the right is moved slightly down and posterior. In this manner I may give him a more natural quality. And now, it is possible to bestow on this clay some action and life. He was like an Egyptian statue, stiff and unbending, but now his head was bent . The shoulders were also be adjusted. In this way the sculptor can give more life to the character, which is being portrayed. You will now begin to notice more resemblance to that famous and revered person in our nation's history, our first President, George Washington.

The Eyes

This portrait still has empty sockets for the eyes and now I begin to make the features for the eyes. I will make the eyes with lids on them. A little ball of clay is first placed in each socket (Fig. 82). First the lower lid is formed by a small roll, about the size of a match stick (Fig. 83). Another is placed to form the upper lid (Fig. 84, 85). Finger strokes smooth the borders (Fig. 86-88).

The upper lid covers over an arc of the iris down to the pupil, except when a person is startled, while the lower arc of the iris is tangent to the lower lid. It is like a tire rolling along the pavement. The lower eyelid is larger when we look up or straight ahead, while the upper eyelid is larger when we look down. The upper eyelids cross over the lower eyelids at the lateral corners.

The Nose

Up to this point a generalized type of face has been modeled. The application of smaller details, the eyes, nose and mouth begin to form particular characteristics of an individual. After adding a little more to the hair, the form of the nose will be improved. Presently the nose is a little stubby. Washington had a prominent nose, so this nose will be modeled larger. Washington's nose appeared wider than average in most of the portraits available, particularly those made by

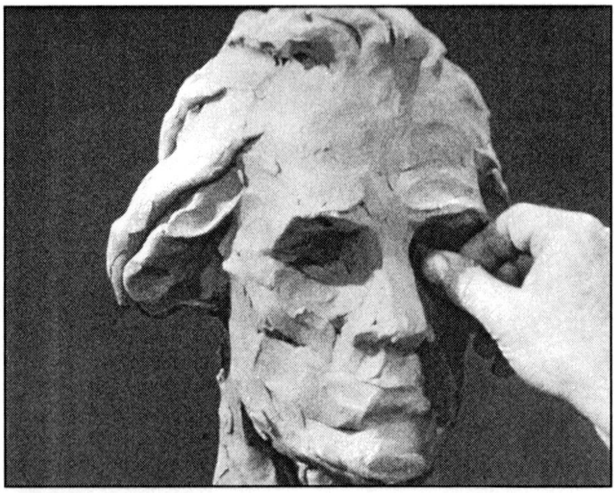

Fig. 82. A small roll of plastiline is placed on the left lower eyelid.

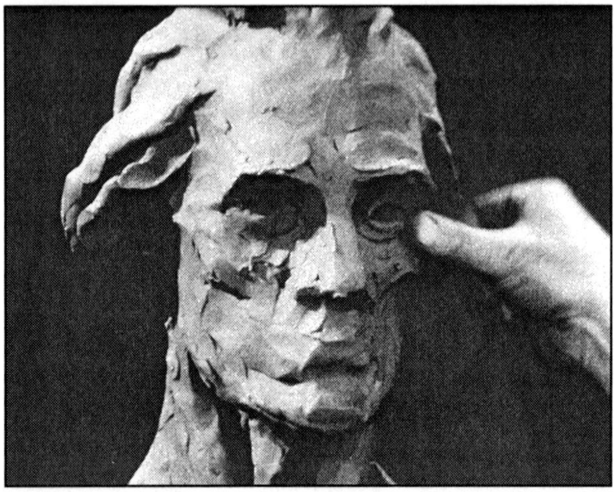

Fig. 83. A roll is applied beginning the left lower eyelid.

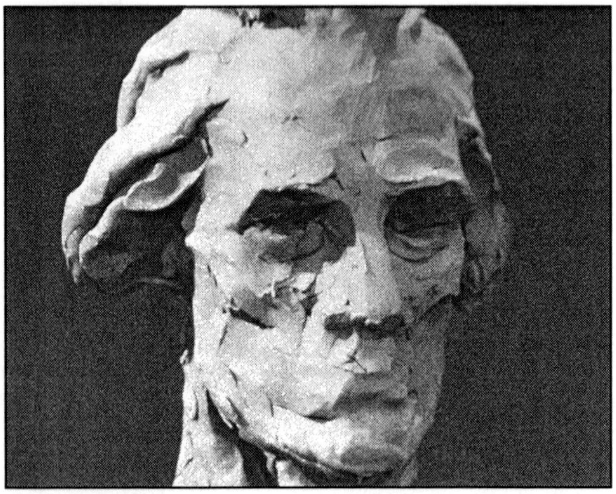

Fig. 84. A view demonstrates left eyelid progress.

Gilbert Stewart. In order to accurately portray him, it is essential to study of the portraits of him, created by his contemporaries. They had an

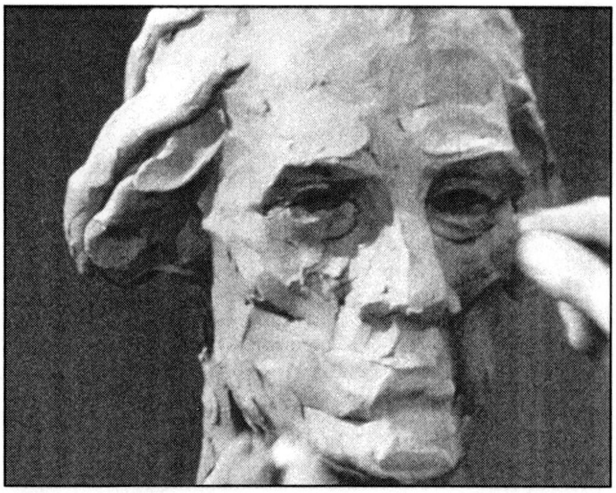

Fig. 85. A small roll of plastiline is applied to the left upper lid.

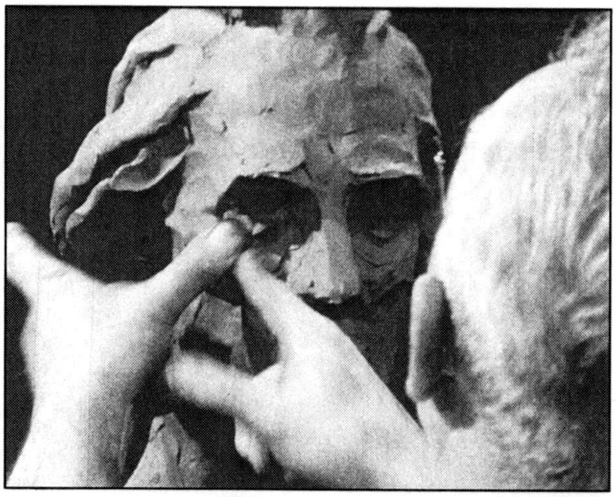

Fig. 86. A small roll of plasteline is added to the right lower eye lid.

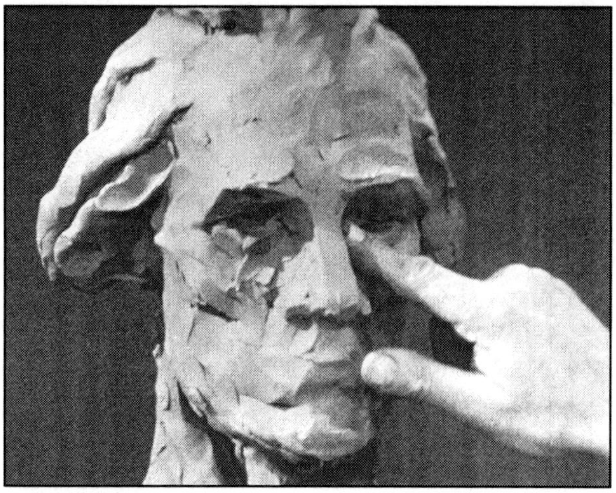

Fig. 87. The contours of the left lower lid are improved by a finger stroke.

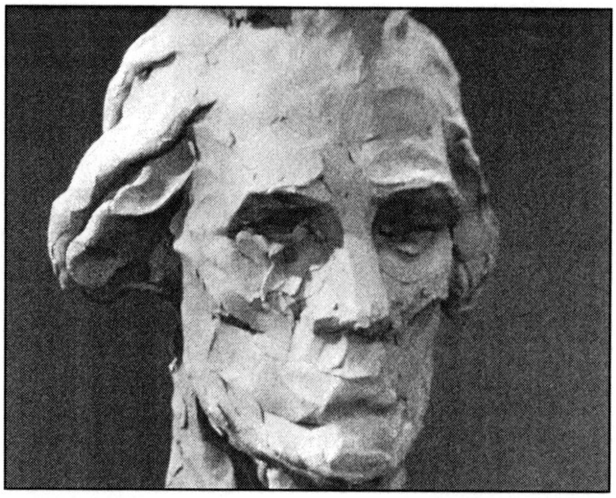

Fig. 88. A view demonstrates the preliminary eyelid development.

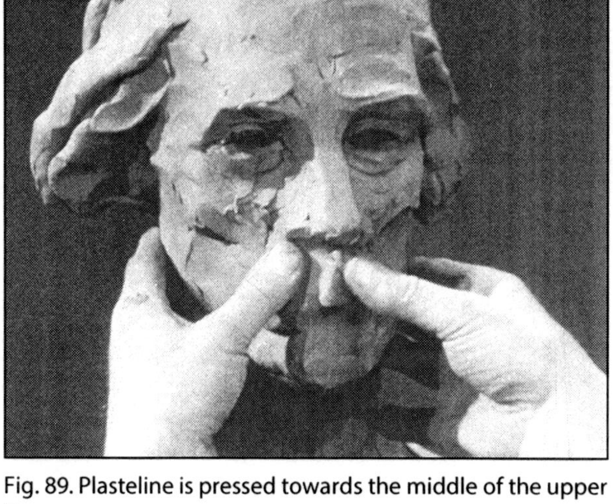

Fig. 89. Plasteline is pressed towards the middle of the upper lip.

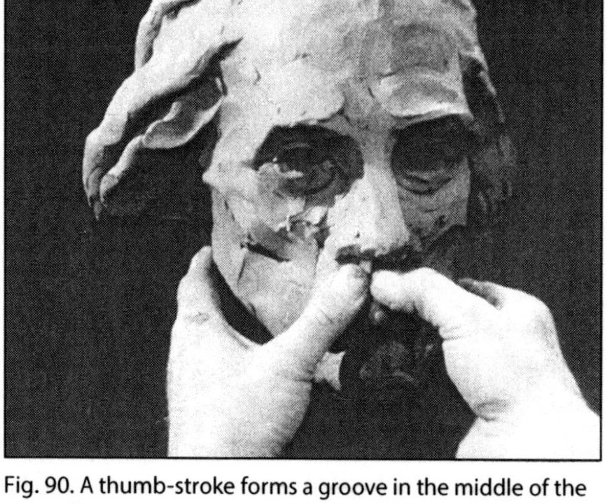

Fig. 90. A thumb-stroke forms a groove in the middle of the upper lip.

opportunity for close observation, to have him pose for portraits in person. The nose modeled therefore will closely resemble the nose features frequently portrayed. (See article about Washington portraits.)

Noses are usually nearly flat on the anterior or leading border below the bridge of the nose. The general form is improved by adding clay and some strokes of the finger, but the rough contours will wait for more detailed modeling.

The Lips

The form of the mouth was modeled by spreading a roll of clay across where the teeth would be on a skull. A vertical stroke of a finger or a tool in the midline under the nose is followed by gentle pressure medially on both sides of the upper lip forms vertical ridges representing the columella and the hollow between that represents the philtrum (Fig. 89-91). These features of the upper lip develop in everyone during embryonic growth. A midline structure grows down from the nose while the lateral portions of the upper lip grow medially from the cheek area. The junctions are the two columella manifest as vertical ridges under the nose. (A failure of fusion in early embryonic life results in a hare lip. Note the illustration on embryonic development in the Anatomy section.)

See how simple it is to model a mouth. First, with a wire loop tool I cut in to make the corners of the mouth. I do this making an up-curved and medial-slanting stroke that incises the left one third of the mouth (Fig. 92). An upward and inward curved stroke of the tool incises the right third of the mouth. After another curved stroke with apex down is made in the middle third of the mouth (Fig. 93-95). The lip aperture resembles a Grecian bow.

Then I will cut into the hollows below the upper lip and then the hollows above the lower lip. After developing these hollows, I make the ridges of the lips (Fig. 96, 97). After forming the ridges, a shallow concavity is incised for corners at the lateral thirds of the upper lip (Fig. 98, 99). A curved transverse cut is then made, apex up,

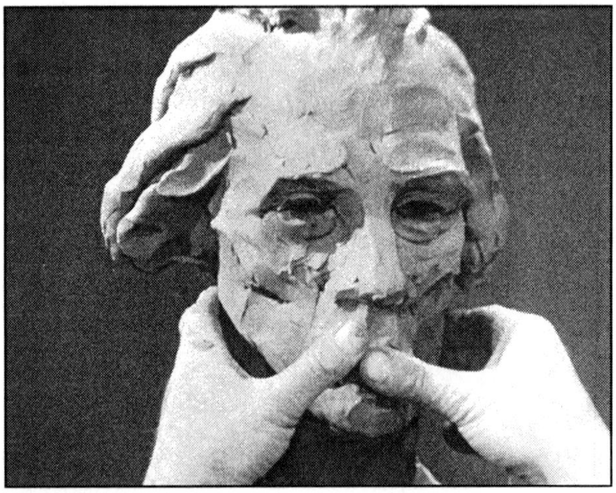

Fig. 91. Upward pressure is applied by a thumb towards the upper lip.

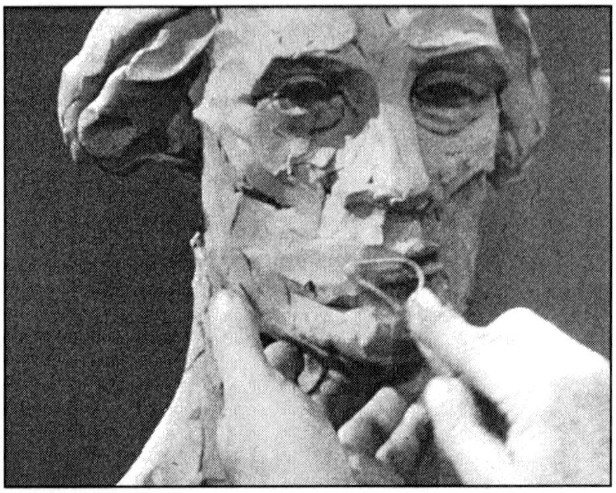

Fig. 92. An upward and inward stroke with a wire loop tool initiates the left corner of the mouth.

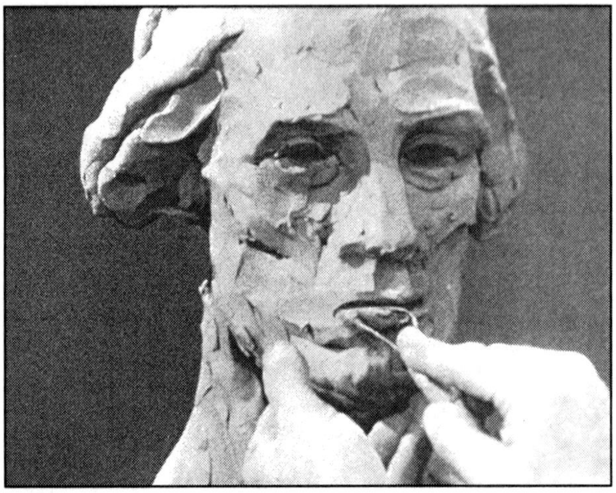

Fig. 93. The wire loop tool stroke initiates separation of the lips in the middle of the mouth.

creating a hollow under the lower lip representing the sublabial crease (Fig. 101). A more definite philtrum is formed with bilateral pressure

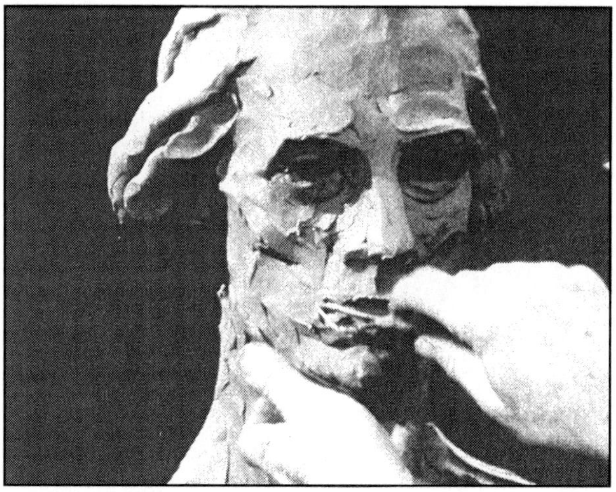

Fig. 94. The right mouth corner is refined by tool strokes.

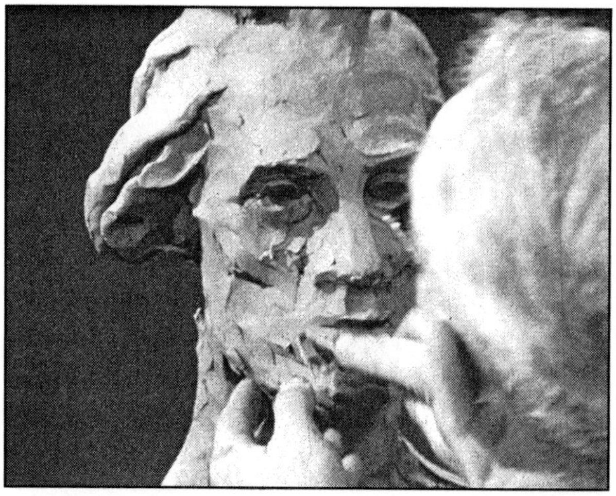

Fig. 95. An upward and inward tool stroke initiates the right corner of the mouth.

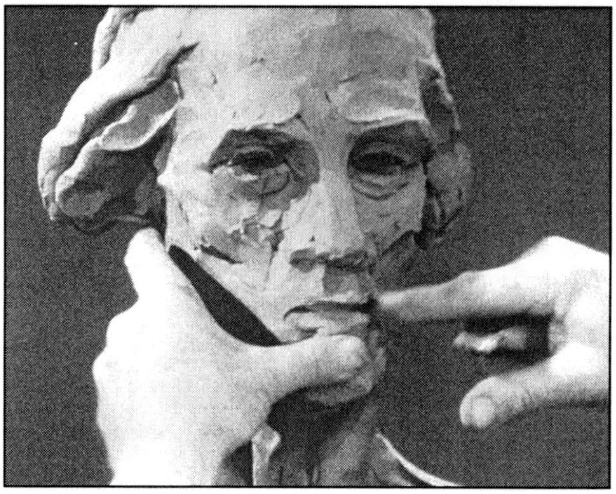

Fig. 96. The lips are improved with gentle strokes of a finger.

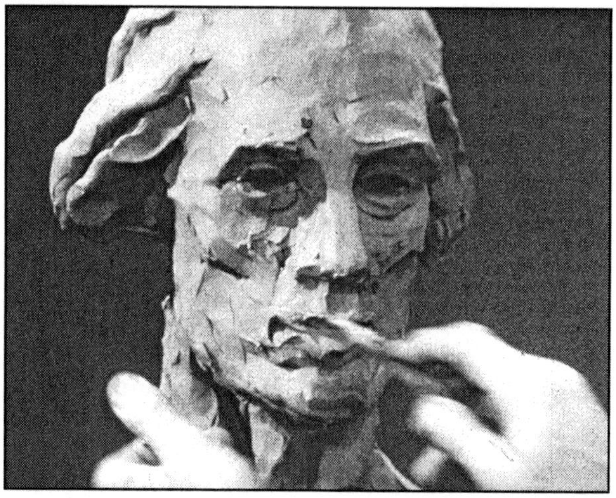

Fig. 97. The right corner of the lips are accentuated by strokes of the tool.

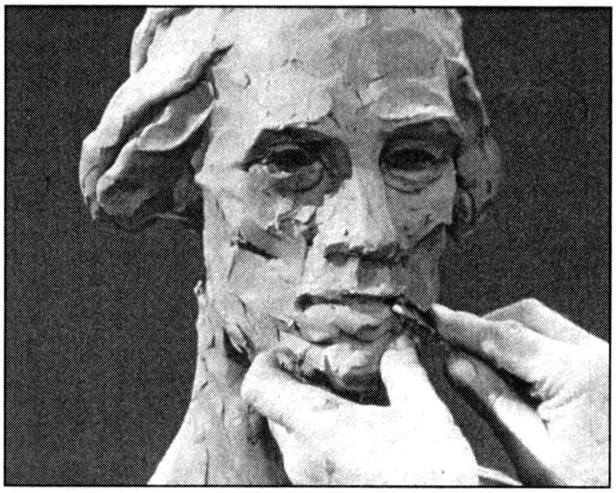

Fig. 98. The left corner of the lips are accentuated by strokes of the tool.

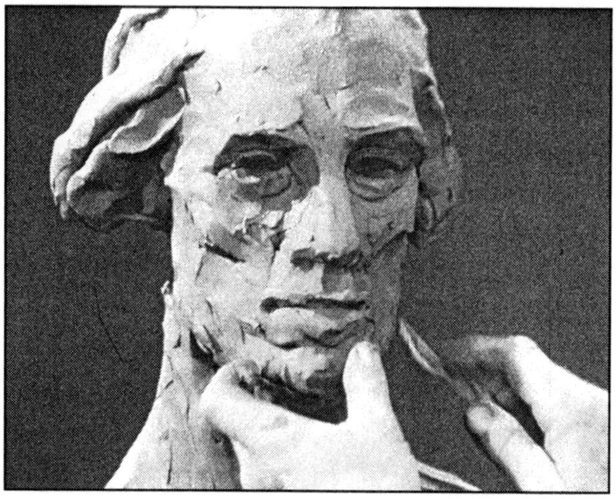

Fig. 99. The mouth form becomes more evident.

toward the middle of the upper lip (Fig. 102, 104).

Considering the ridges of the lips, called the vermilion borders, they are more carefully modeled with gentle strokes of a sculptor's finger or a modeling tool (Fig. 103). There are hollows at the corners of the mouth with a fullness around and above the hollows. The vermilion borders of the lips approach the corners of the mouth and turn into the mouth. They do not end in an sharp, acute angle. The upper lip at the corners usually covers over the lower lip (see detailed illustration).

The chin and lower lip are also formed in embryonic life by lateral tissues growing medially until they fuse. There is a midline seam in the lower lip where a person may occasionally develop a cracked lip. There may also be a slight midline prominence at and below the vermilion border, especially on those with prominent lips, but this is seldom noticed. Yet these small details are important when an artist strives to make a portrait both expressive and realistic. Therefore one may recognize the two seams, the columella, above the upper lip, one obscure seam in the lower lip, a concavity below the nose, the philtrum between the columella, and a concavity below the lower lip, the sublabial crease (Fig. 104).

Modeling the Cheeks

Following formation of the lips, the cheeks need attention and individual characteristics to be added. There are still hollows where there should be cheeks and these should be filled. Therefore, I add clay to fill in more form to the cheeks, (Fig. 105, 106). Cheeks contain fatty tissue, which serves to beautify the face. However if one has a lot of fat, one does not have a lot of beauty. Fat fills the intermuscular spaces in various places of the face. Actually fat is a type of connective tissue and is therefore important in the construction of the body.

The face, then, deserves a more gently rounded contour. Plasteline is added to fill out the left cheek (Fig. 105). A better form of the right cheek is then modeled with finger strokes (Fig. 106). So far features have been modeled of an adult male resembling George Washington. The characteristics, of a definite individual, need to be developed early as the modeling progresses.

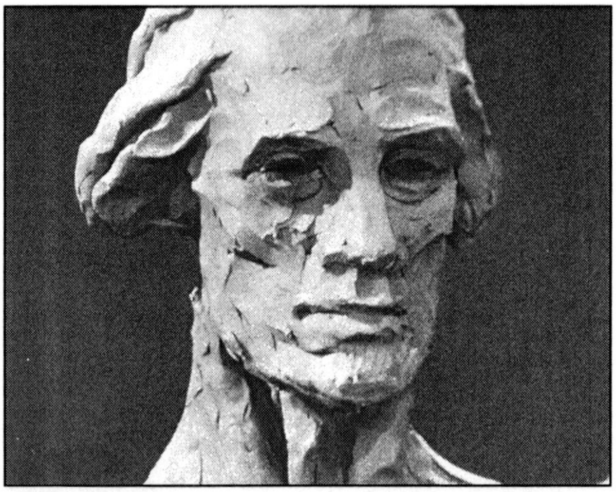

Fig. 100. A view demonstrates the preliminary mouth modeling.

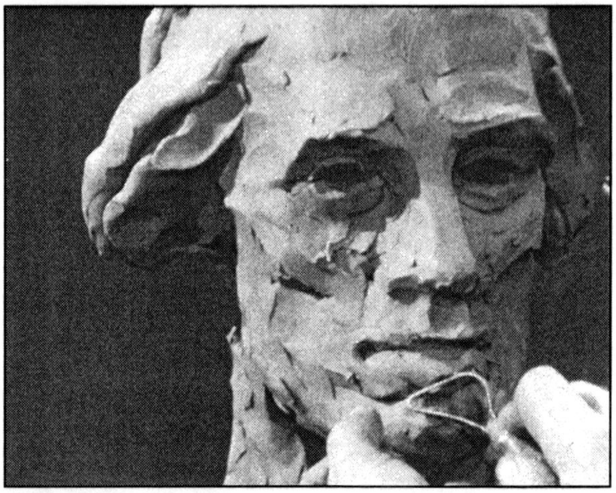

Fig. 101. The left lower lip margin is defined with a modeling tool.

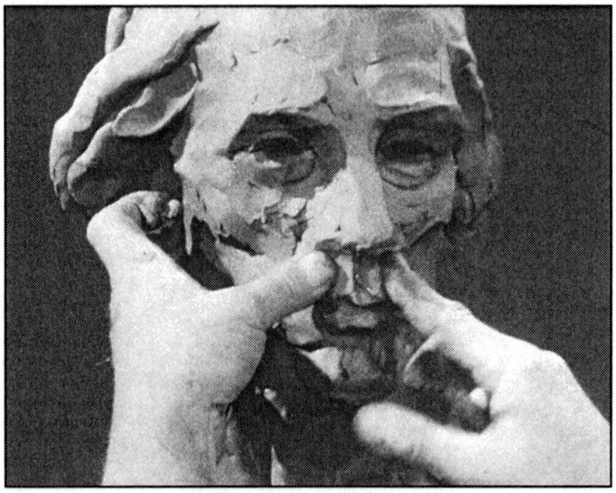

Fig. 102. Pressure applied to each side narrows the philtrim of the upper lip.

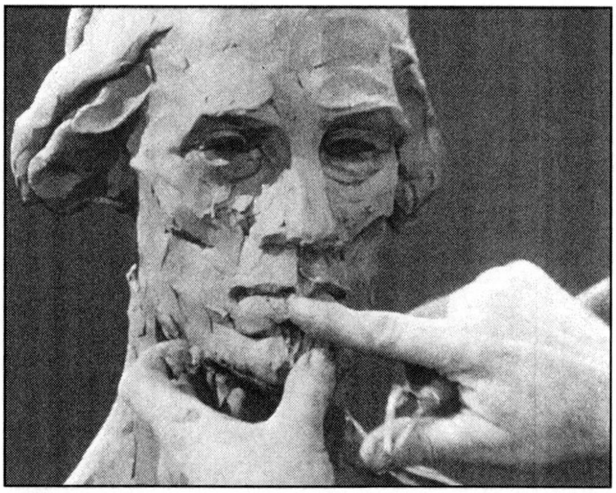

Fig. 103. The lip margin is improved with gentle finger strokes.

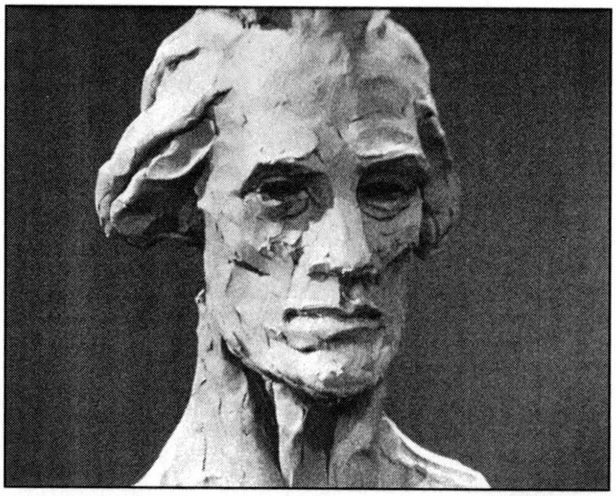

Fig. 104. A view demonstrates an improved preliminary form of the lips.

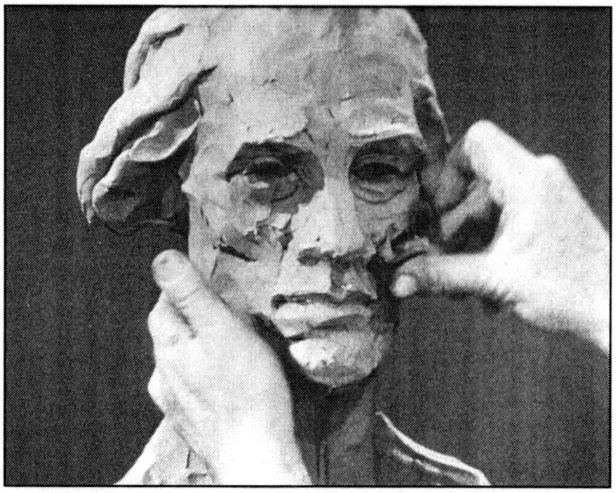

Fig. 105. Plasteline is added to fill in the void of the left cheek.

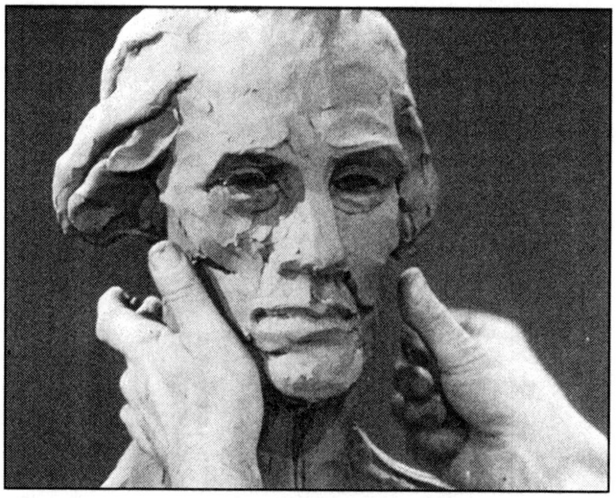

Fig. 106. The plasteline is smoother with a thumb stroke.

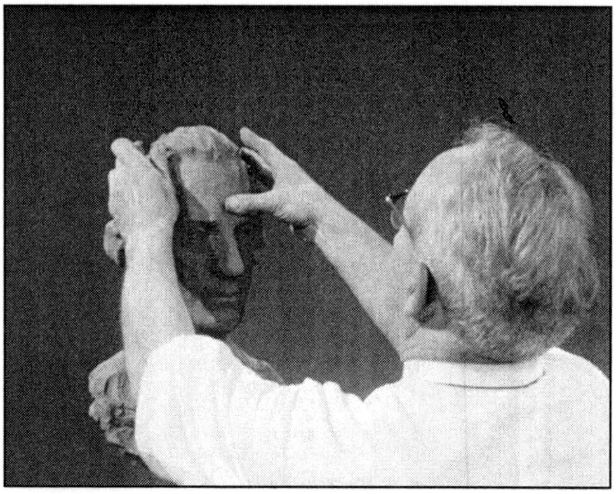

Fig. 107. Plasteline is added to prominences over the frontal sinuses.

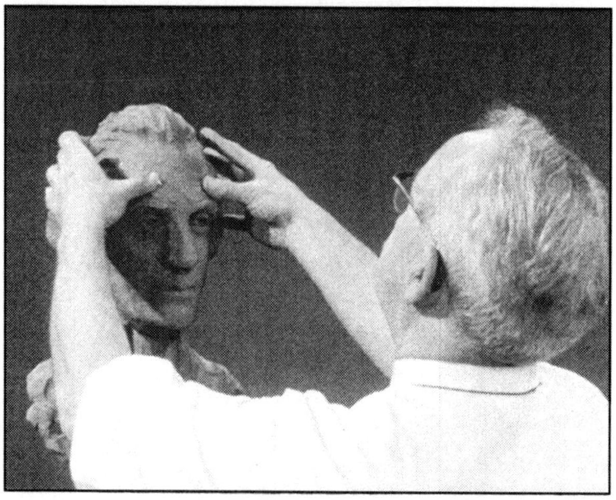

Fig. 108. Forms of the frontal eminences are improved by smoothing with a finger.

Refining Details

The face has been refined with gentle strokes of the wire loop tool, to create the preliminary representative features. I have brought it to the point where it needs additional attention. Each detail requires considerable careful modeling. More clay is added above each brow representing prominences over the frontal sinuses (Fig. 107-109). Now that the modeling has progressed from basic construction to a more personal resemblance, it is at a point of making more refinements. The face is more finished than other features as hair, neck and shoulders. The eminences of the frontal bones of the forehead as well as the middle forehead ridge must be neither too prominent nor obscure One may palpate these prominences on one's own forehead. The lateral aspect of the male brow ridge is rather prominent. This is necessary to shield and protect the eye.

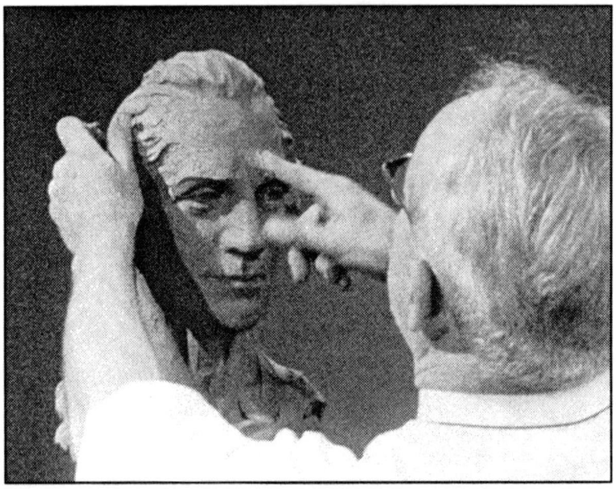

Fig. 109. Additional refinement to the forehead is made with finger strokes.

Refinement of Eye Lid Details

Attention is again directed towards the eyes. They need a little more form under the eyes. After applying a small roll of plasteline, more careful form is modeled with a tool. The right lower lid needs more definition and a careful stroke of the finger sharpens the border (Fig. 110). The same careful stroke is given the left lower eyelid (Fig. 111, 112). The cheeks have plasteline added to fill out contours (Fig. 113, 114). Some texture is noted on the face where modeling has been affected by the serrated edge of the wire loop tool. Some of these marks are not smoothed over as they impart a texture giving character and strength to the subject.

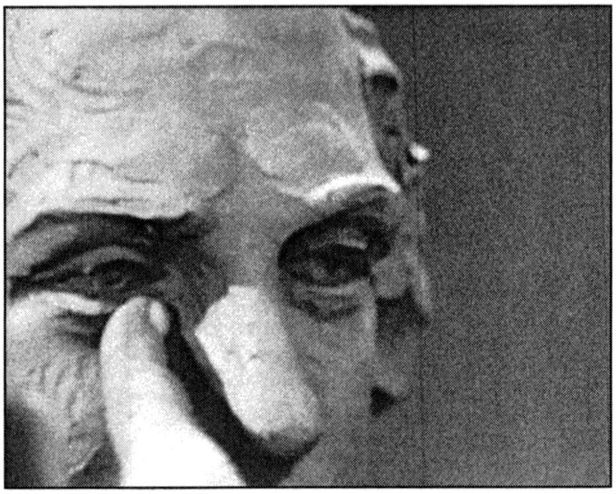

Fig. 110. The right lower eyelid is refined with finger strokes.

If I had modeled George Washington as a younger man in the times of his early career when he was a surveyor, his face would be more oval with softer features. He was first a surveyor and engineer in the Ohio Territory. George Washington knew our country from first hand experience. He knew the frontier of the West and also the cities of the East. He was a man of rare ability and broad understanding.

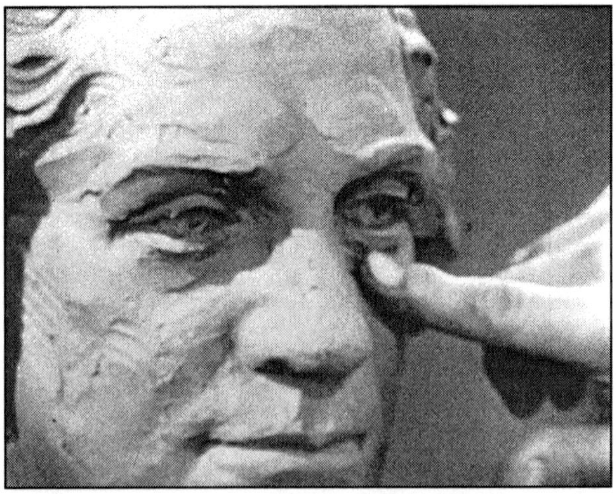

Fig. 111. Left lower eyelid is also refined with finger strokes.

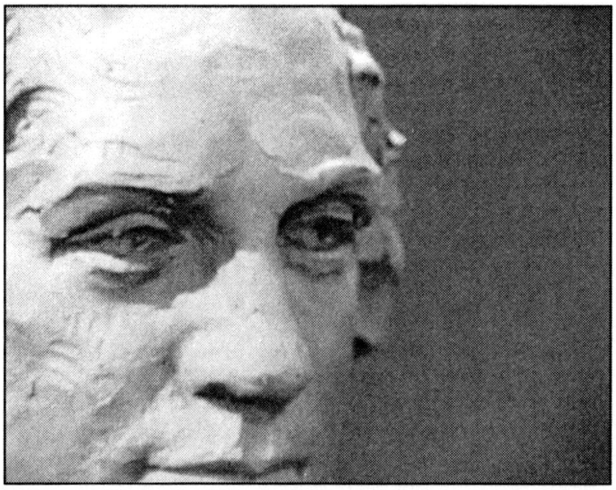

Fig. 112. View of both eyelids reveals improvement after fine gentle finger strokes.

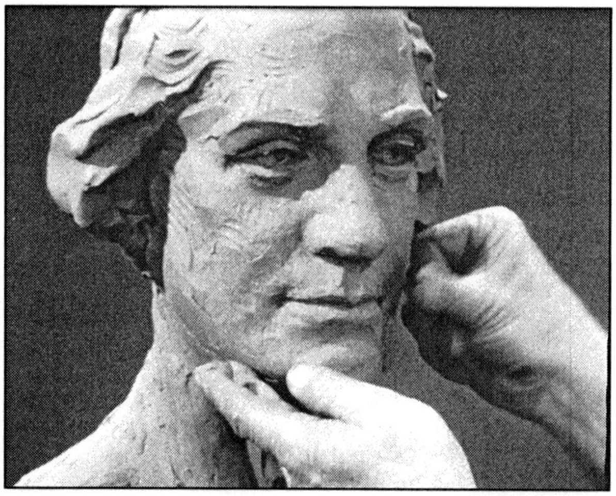

Fig. 113. Additional plasteline is added to improve the left cheek.

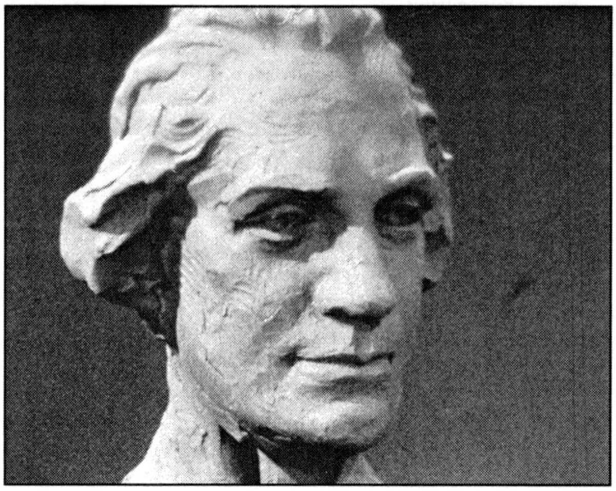

Fig. 114. View of face after careful modeling demonstrates the improvement.

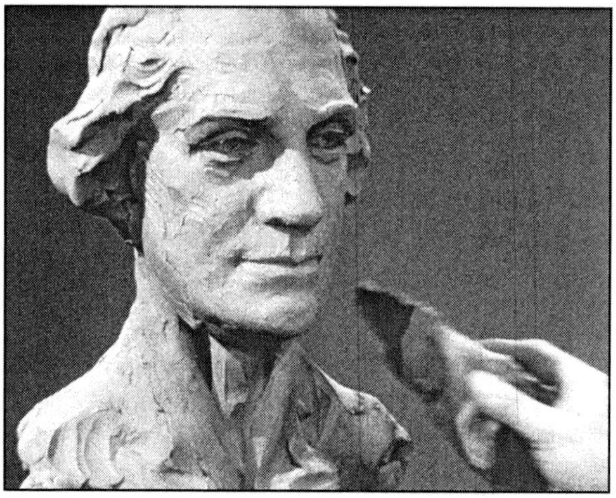

Fig. 115. A roll of plasteline is prepared for the left collar.

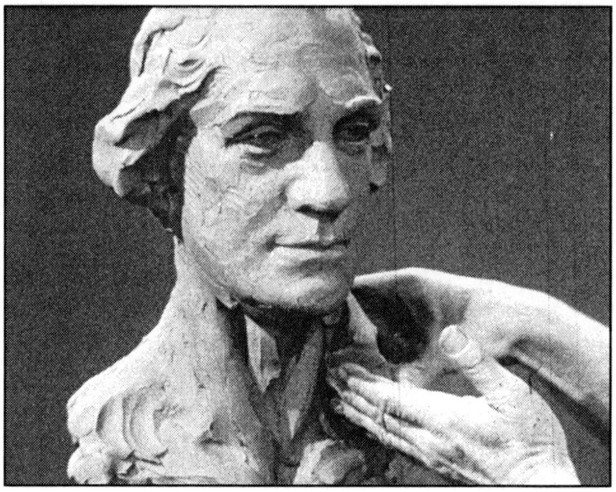

Fig. 116. The plasteline is firmly applied for the left collar.

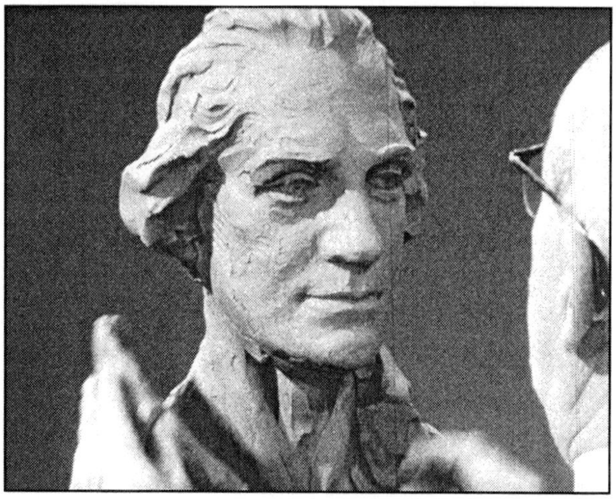

Fig, 117. A roll of plasteline is prepared for the right collar.

Uniform

Clothing now needs to be added so that he will appear as an individual of the Colonial Period. I now place upon him a collar of a uniform and so I begin to make him an individual of the American Revolution. First a collar on the left side (Fig. 115, 116), and then on the right side (Fig. 117, 118). The style of the times is hereby shown, now as a soldier and then later as a private citizen. It would seem more appropriate to model a military uniform for this portrait.

Flowing lines of the collar are modeled as it conforms to the contours of the person (Fig. 119). More plasteline is added to form the lapels on each side of his uniform (Fig. 120). A cravat or neck wrap in the style of the times is modeled on the neck (Fig. 122). The frilled or ruffled linen shirt front, a jabot, is modeled in the period style (Fig. 123-125). The costume is modeled over the previously modeled muscles and larynx of the neck. Fine details of a neckpiece and shirt are de-emphasized as they may detract from the more detailed and animated face.

As we know from his history, Washington was a great frontiersman. He was an engineer, an officer under General Braddock, and he saved the day at that time. He was the man of the hour at the time of the Revolution and he was a great citizen. He renounced the opportunity to be king, which had been offered to him, because he was concerned that the United States should become a great republic. As a private citizen he was the American who deserves the honors and praise given to him.

Additional Refinements, Lips

After the primary features of the face have been modeled, the texture of the face is smoothed by gently stroking with fingers or a wire-loop tool. Considerable refinements to facial features have been done. A better contour of the chin has been developed. The lips have been rounded more distinctly and the ridges, the vermilion borders, are more definite. The mouth aperture is refined using a modeling tool (Fig. 126). By giving a slight upturn to the right corner of the

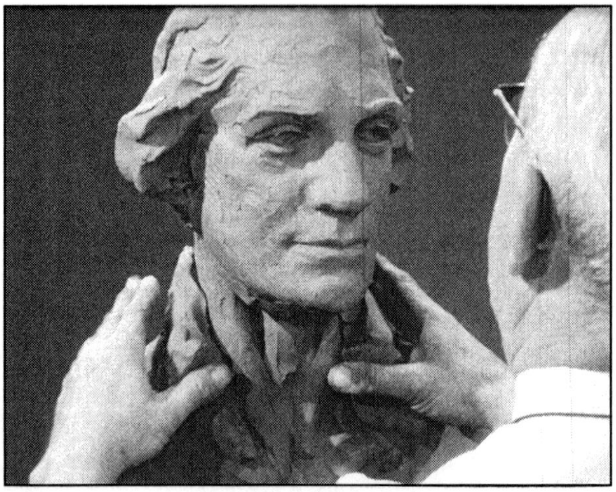

Fig. 118. The roll of plasteline is firmly applied for the right collar.

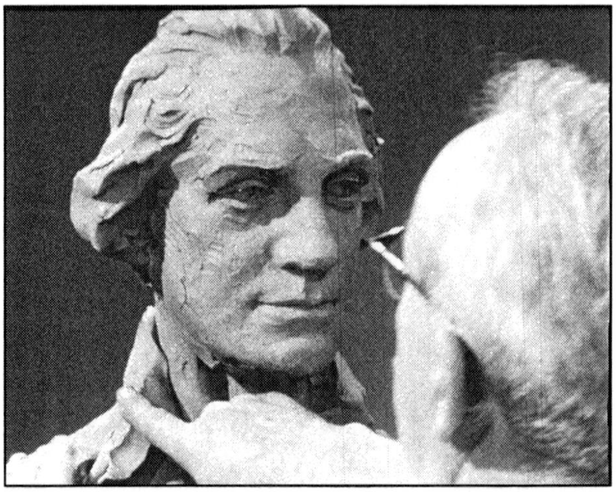

Fig. 119. Additional shape is applied to the right collar.

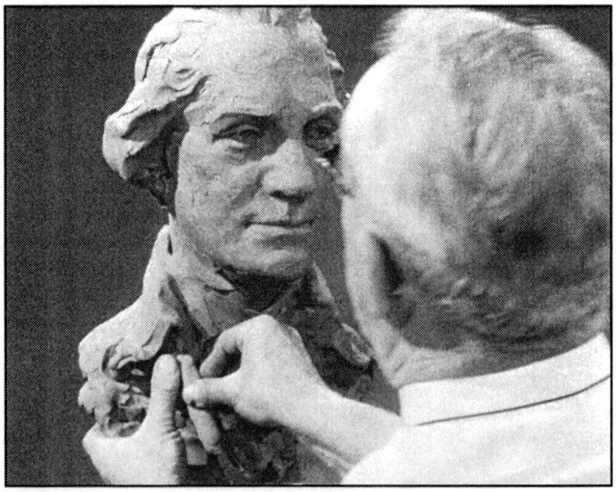

Fig. 120. A roll of plasteline is applied to improve the form of the right collar.

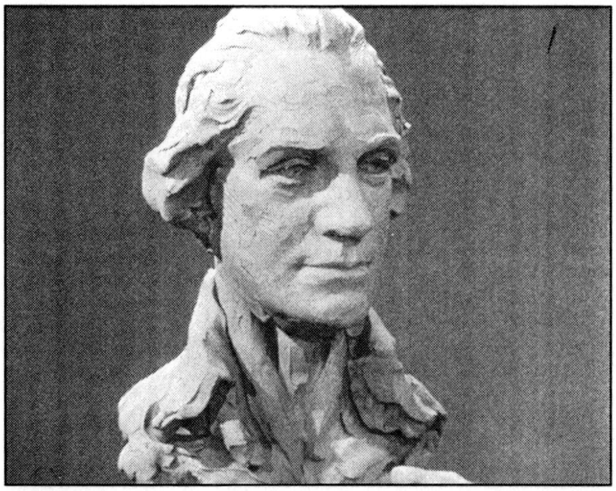

Fig. 121. Progress is demonstrated in the forming of the of the collar.

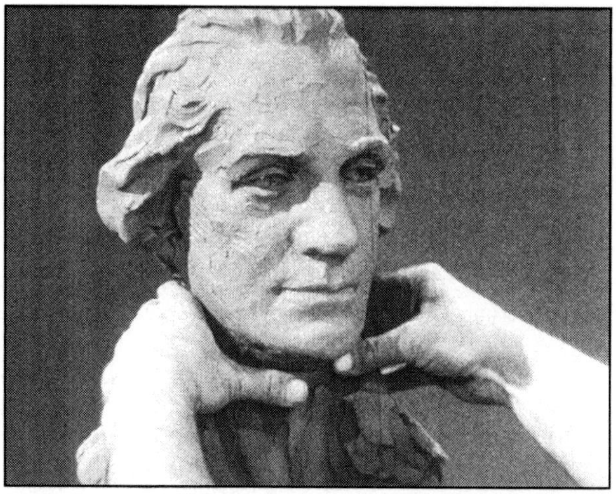

Fig. 122. A neck band of the shirt is applied below the chin.

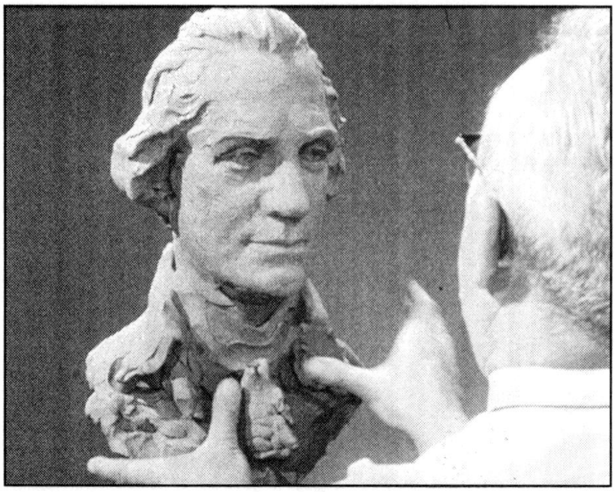

Fig. 123. The jabot, a frill on the shirt, begins to develop.

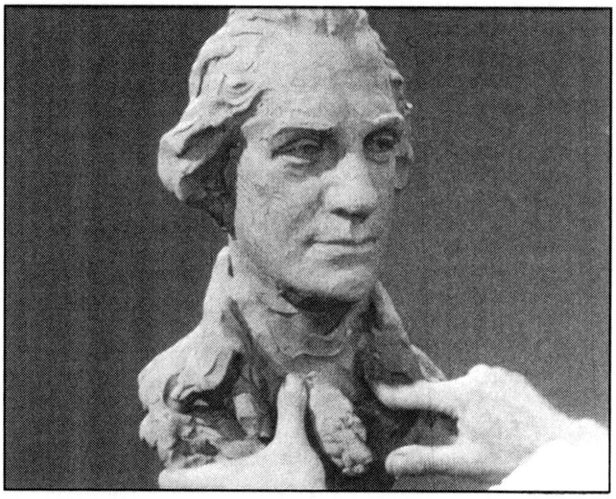

Fig. 124. More form is modeled into his shirt.

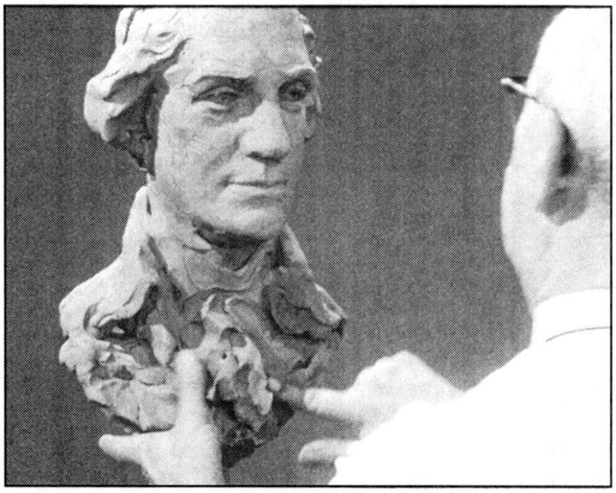

Fig. 125. More details develop into the shirt and the jabot.

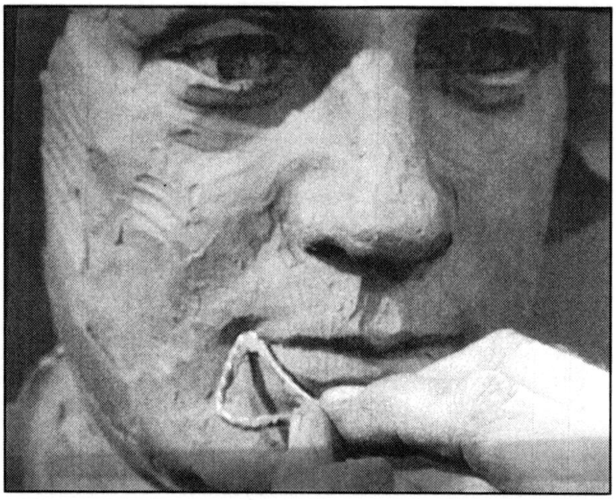

Fig. 126. Form of the lip is improved on the right corner of the mouth.

mouth , there is an expression of a faint smile (Fig. 127). The form of the lower lip is improved (Fig. 128, 129). A slight upturn is also given to the left corner of the mouth (Fig. 130). George Washington, in spite of all the hardships, was a very pleasant fellow. During many times of struggle and times of discouragement he could maintain good composure. Moreover, he was not without a sense of humor. Close friends have related instances when he laughed hilariously at funny incidents.

Washington had rather thin lips and they were moderately tightened. He had to tighten them sometimes when his generals did not do what he had wanted them to do. He often tightened his lips; sometimes he wouldn't say anything. Other times he would give very direct orders. He was not known to make ungentlemanly expressions, except on one occasion when one of his generals disobeyed his orders in battle. It is interesting that even though he commanded an army, and even though times were very difficult, Washington didn't use terms that were improper. He was disciplined; he had an attitude of reserve. He found power in dignity.

Improvement of Details, Eyes

The portrait now requires modeling of more minor details. Attention is given to the form for a fullness below the lower eyelids (Fig. 131). You may notice small rolls were placed for the eyebrows. A few strokes are made by a tool represent hair of the eyebrows (Fig. 132, 133). Near the midline these short brow hairs first point up, then angle laterally along the middle third and then down on the lateral eyebrow. The eyebrows are not arched, nor are they straight. There is a gentle curve above the eye to the corner of the brow ridge. Here an eyebrow angles down, laterally and back.

Attention is again directed to the eyes. By cutting a small circular excavation in the eye, a concavity is created which really gives color and life to this piece of sculpture (Fig. 134). This shallow excavation, made with a wire tool in a twisting motion, represents the iris and pupil,

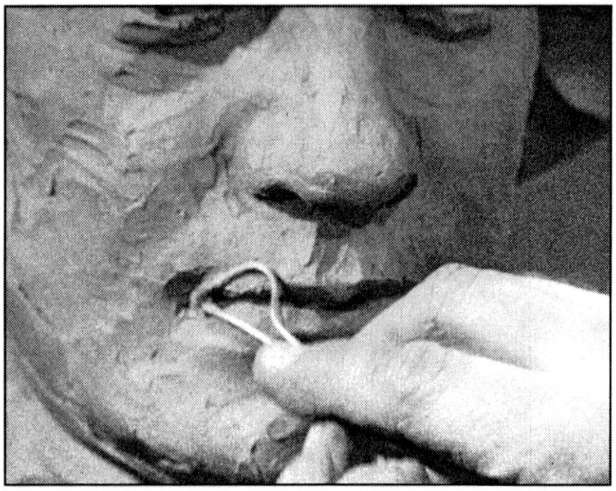

Fig. 127. A slight upturn to the right corner of the lips gives a gentle smile.

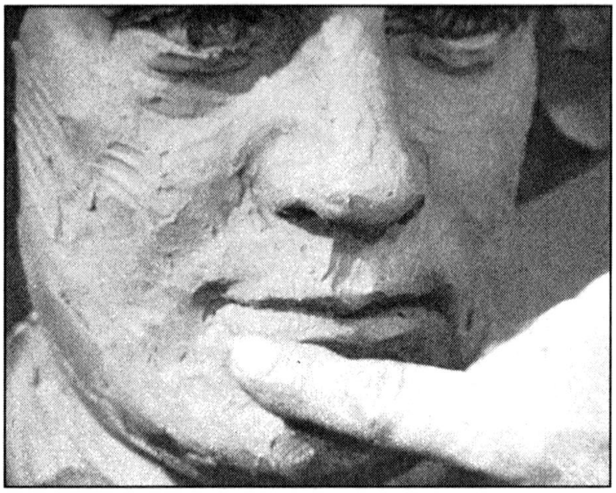

Fig. 128. The vermillion border of the lower lip is given more definition.

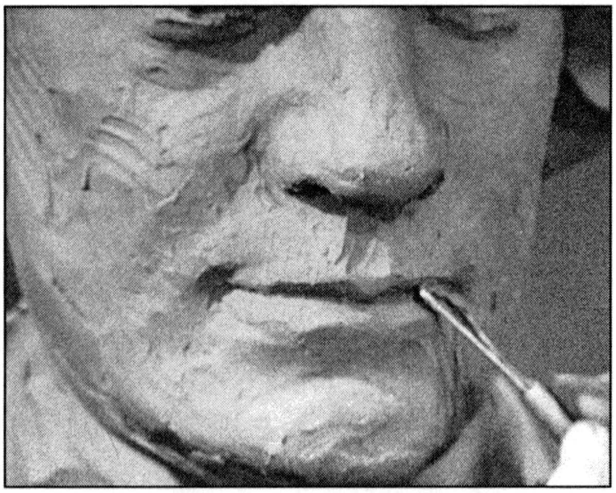

Fig, 129. A tool stroke to the left corner of the mouth renders better definition.

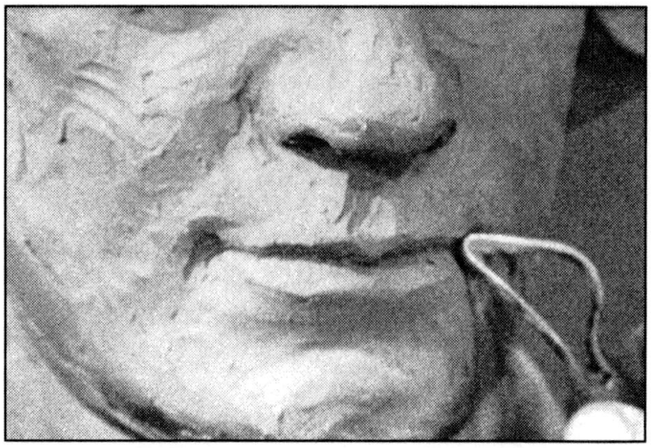

Fig. 130. An upturn tool stroke to the left corner of the mouth adds a gentle smile.

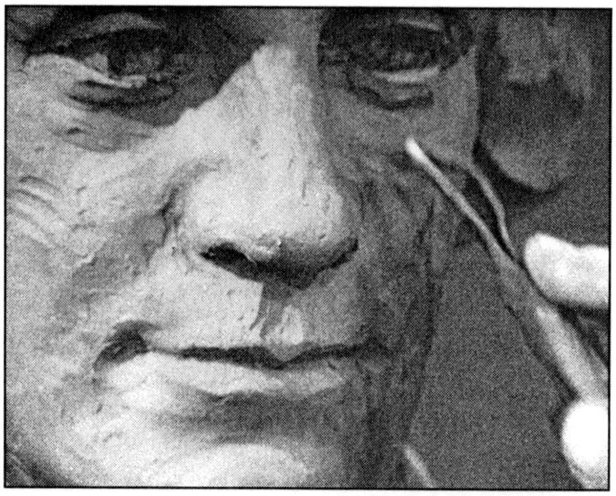

Fig. 131. Contours of the left cheek are improved with gentle tool strokes.

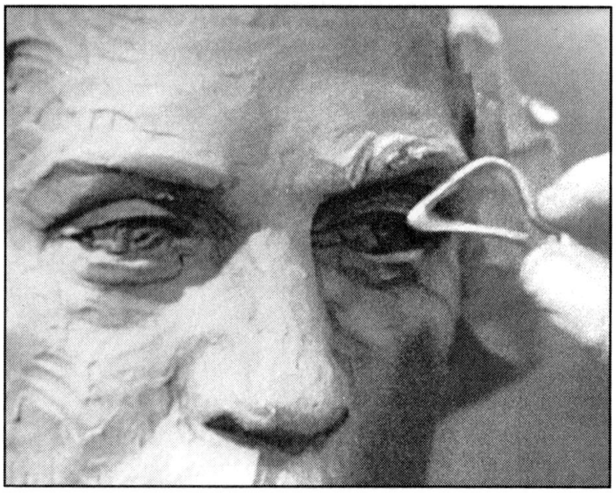

Fig. 132. The appearance of hair in the left eyebrow hair is made with tool strokes.

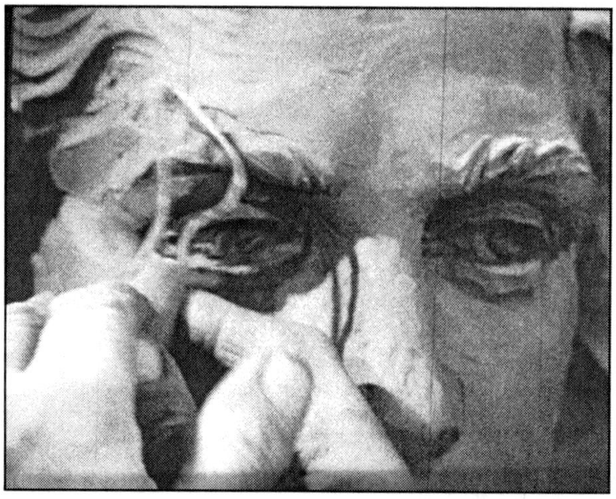

Fig. 133. Tool strokes applied to the right brow indicates eyebrow hair.

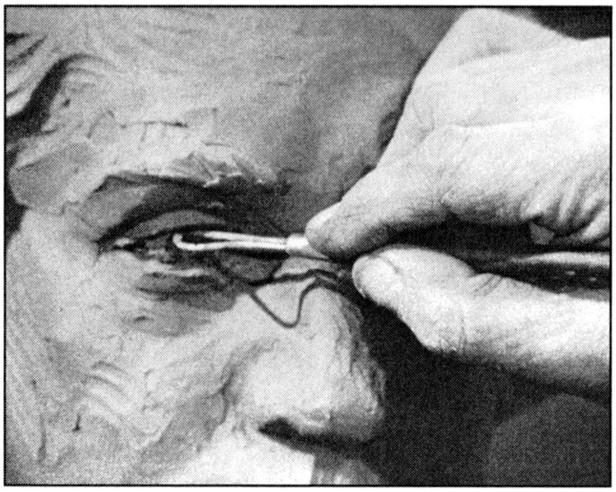

Fig. 134. The cornea and a light reflex of the right eye is made with a twist of the wire tool.

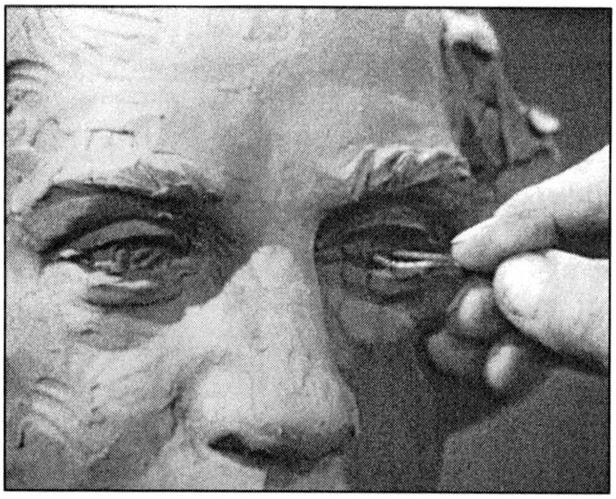

Fig. 135. A similar twisting tool stroke creates the cornea and the light reflex to the left eye.

but an incomplete excavation leaves a prominence to represent the light reflex (reflection) from the cornea of the eye. The same stroke is applied to the other eye (Fig. 135). Greek sculptors left holes for the cornea and put semiprecious stones in their bronze statues to represent the iris and pupil, but robbers soon stole them. The Romans modeled the eyes as spheres, anatomically correct but unanimated, giving the portrait a blank stare. The shallow concavities should be symmetrical and the light reflexes should point in the same direction. Here he is looking in a definite direction, slightly to one side.

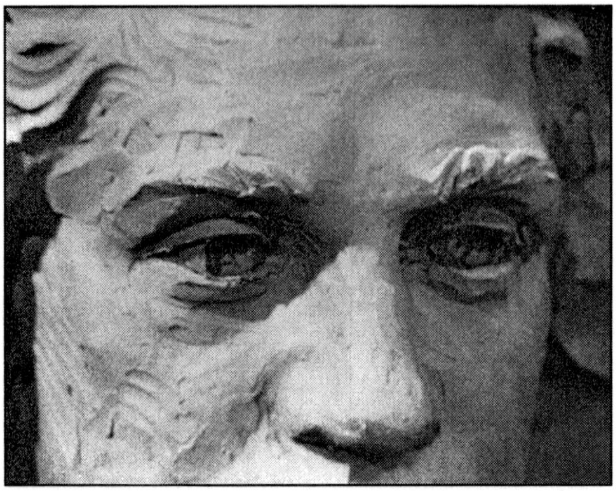

Fig. 136. Both eyes look slightly to the left in an animated appearance.

Nose Details

A better form is applied to the nose with a modeling tool, particularly to the nostrils. The central column or septum is more carefully modeled (Fig. 139). The nostrils are supported by a central cartilage and cartilages forming the ala or wings. The nostrils are not circular but somewhat oval, resemble teardrops, angling down laterally. A fullness arising at the bridge of the nose and extending down and laterally to the cheeks has been modeled. The form of the nose has been improved. A curved groove at the border of the ala or wings of the nose has been defined with the wire loop. The ala may need refinement and the outline of the sulcus or groove between the ala of the nose and the cheek needs better definition. This sulcus intercepts a diagonal crease between the upper lip and cheek, which extends down laterally beyond the corners of the mouth.

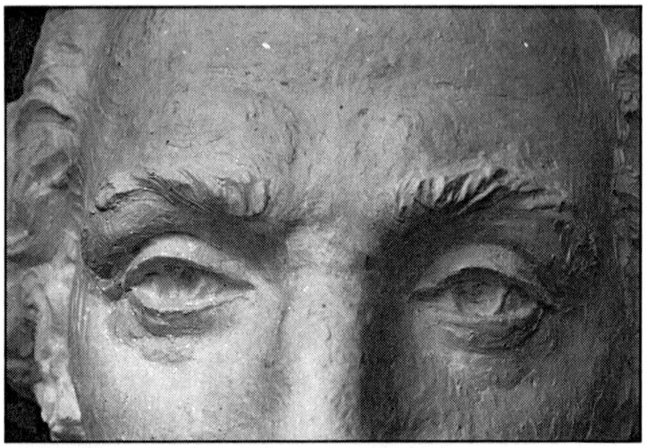

Fig. 137. A frontal view of the eyes is presented for details in a finished cast.

There are many individual variations in noses and attention to details are important in portraiture. Washington had a large straight nose. The leading ridge of a nose is nearly flat on top, and the sides slope laterally at about a 60 degree angle. The tip is slightly bulbous, and the width of the nose at the ala is as wide the space between the eyes, which is equal to the width of an eye.

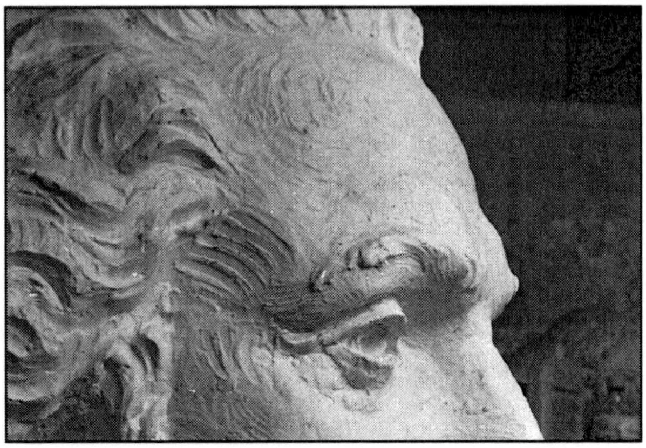

Fig. 138. A lateral view shows details of the right eye is presented in a finished cast.

Hair Details

Attention is again directed toward the hair in order to model it to conform to the style of the colonial period (Fig. 140-142). Gentlemen of those times combed their hair back. It was held in place at the back of the neck by a bow called a perruque (peruke) a French word derived from perruquier, a man who styled hair. The hair needs modeling on both sides. Hair flows in locks and tresses with curved lines in an informal pattern. Light hair has little texture applied, but the illusion of dark hair is accomplished by strong texture applied with a serrated tool.

Expression

Now, to give a greater impression of life to the character we are portraying, we must indicate the effect of muscles at the side of the eyes, which pull the corners of the eyes. These are muscles, which cause the eyes to smile along with the mouth. Besides the upturned corners of the mouth, a little added detail is modeled lifting the corners of the eyes (Fig. 143). This gives greater life and character to the portrait. Along with this appearance of composure there is concern for the troubles, which beset the army. Therefore a few horizontal strokes give a furrowed forehead indicating worries (Fig. 145, 146).

More details are again added to the hair in curved lines, representing locks and tresses rather than strands, to manifest the natural curl or waves in flowing lines. The modeling of "S" waves and "C" curves or similar configurations renders a more natural flow to contours.

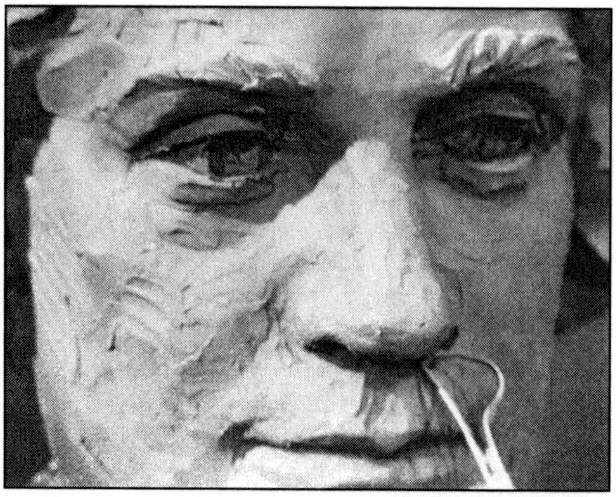

Fig. 139. A better form is rendered of the left nostril with a tool stroke.

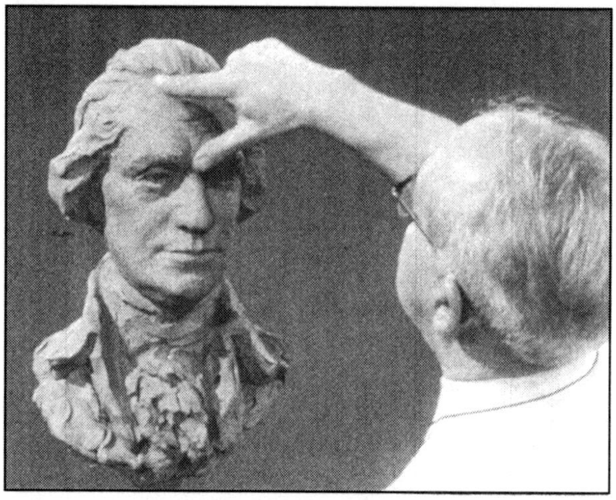

Fig. 140. A better definition is added to the right hairline by gentle finger strokes.

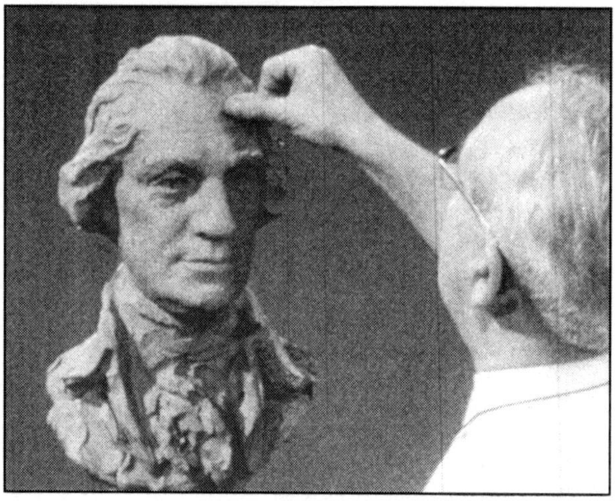

Fig. 141. Details are added to the left frontal prominence.

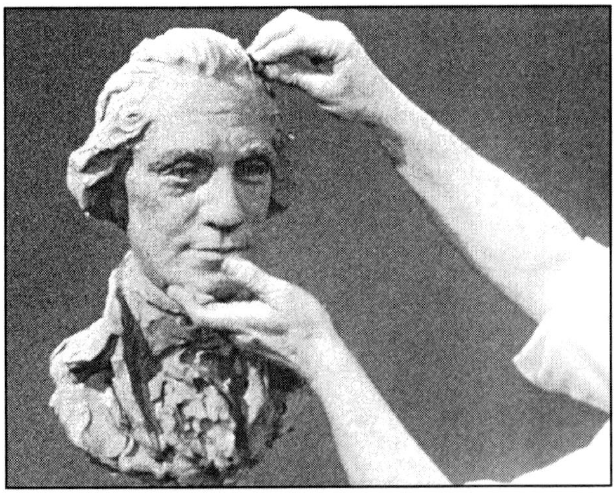

Fig. 142. A better definition is added with gentle finger strokes to the left hairline.

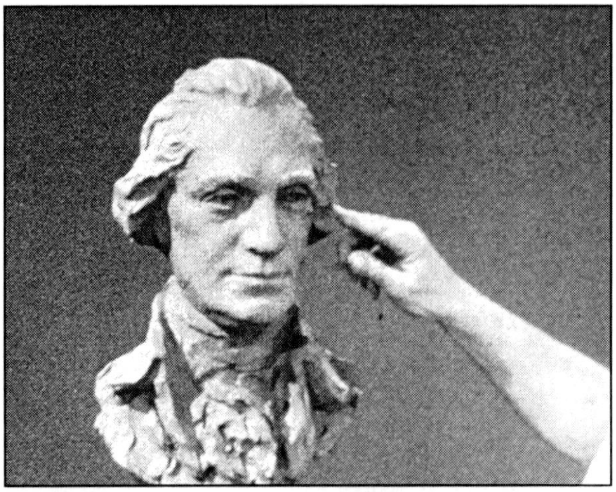

Fig. 143. Details are improved on the left temporal area.

Presently this is a sketch; to complete it would take much longer than I have here with you and time restraints, yet expectations require it to be finished enough to be presentable. When finished it must be strong, not weak, representing the character of a leader who could guide a nation to the successes that we expect of all of our leaders: A leader that would inspire a nation.

Washington was an inspiration to all our people, and I recall one boy in particular, an American boy who lived in a log cabin and who read the story of Washington's life, known as the *Life of Washington* by Parson Weems. This inspired him to so direct his life that it would be in accord with that of Washington. You may know whom I mean, Abraham Lincoln. It was the life of Washington which had such a great influence on this boy and caused him to aspire to leadership of the great nation, which he later directed. Let other young people be so inspired by the life of General George Washington to so order and direct their lives. Let those also, who are in a position to lead and have the opportunity to direct our nation, follow his example to lead our nation to a great destiny.

Avard T. Fairbanks, sculptor

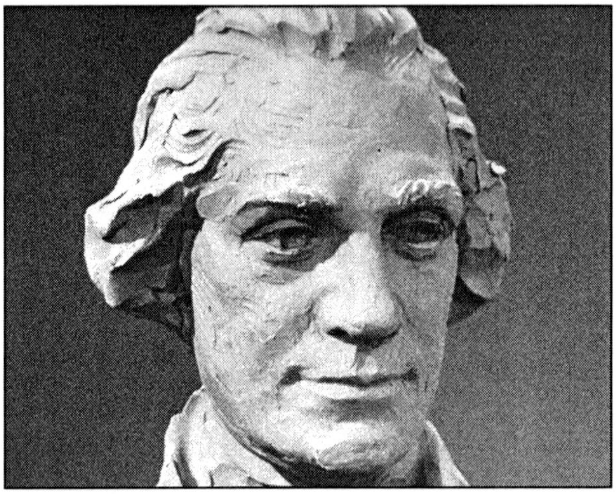

Fig. 144. A closer view is presented demonstrating improvements.

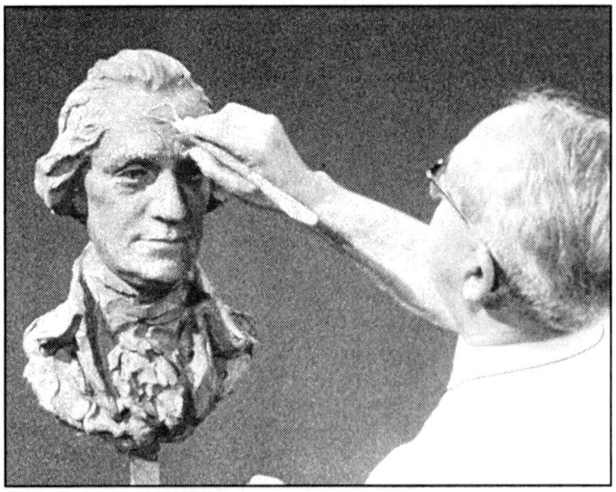

Fig. 145. Forehead creases, indicating concerns, are inscribed with a wire loop.

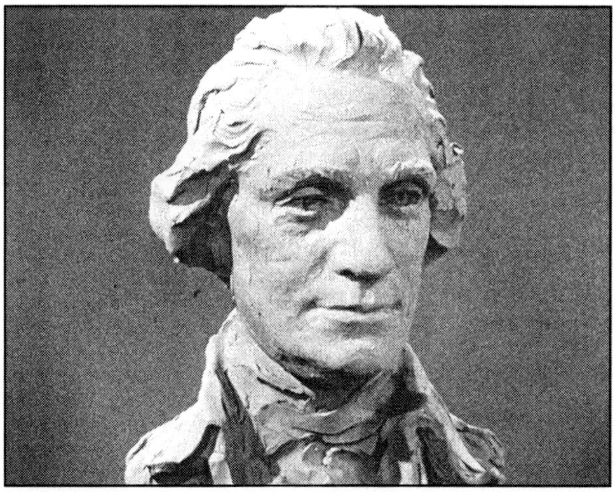

Fig. 146. A closer view demonstrates a furrowed brow.

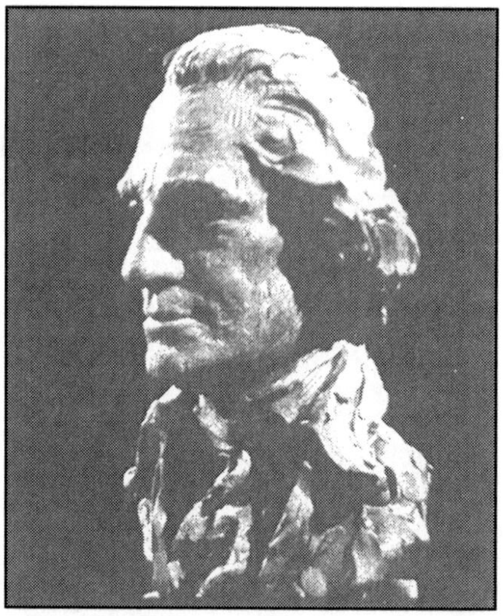

Fig. 147. A right lateral view of the face is presented at the end of this demonstration lecture.

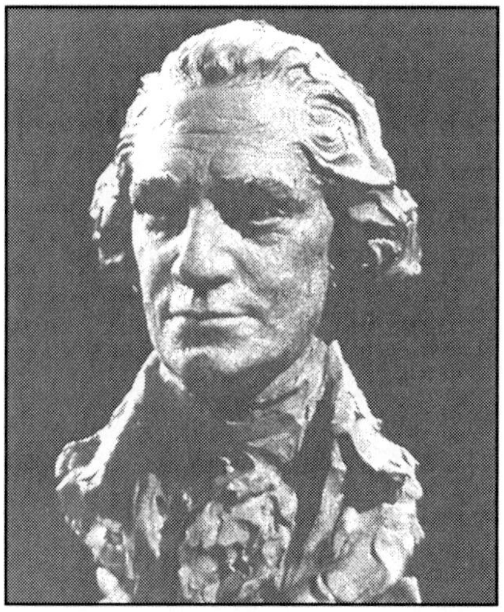

Fig. 148. A right, nearly frontal view of the portrait is presented demonstrating many details.

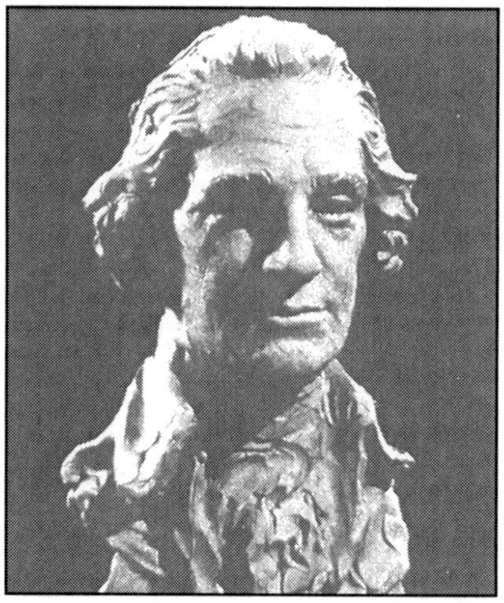

Fig. 149. A left, nearly frontal view of the portrait demonstrates other details.

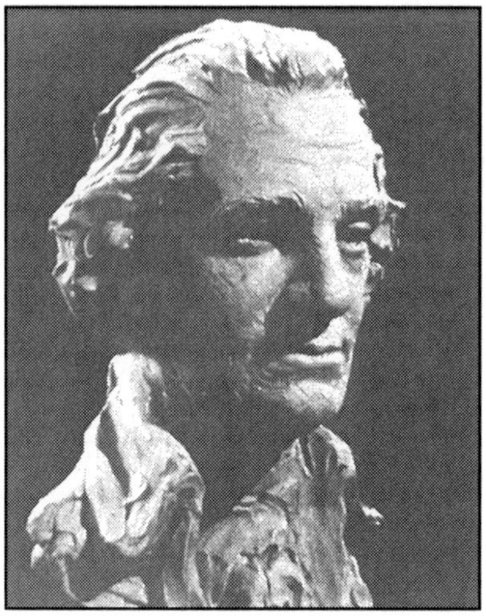

Fig. 150. A left oblique view of the face is presented.

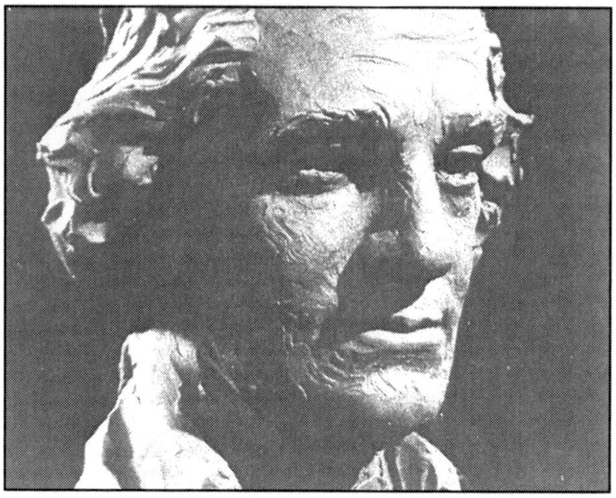

Fig. 151. A closer left oblique view of the face reveals additional details.

Locations of Colossal Bronze Portraits of General George Washington by Avard T. Fairbanks

Locations sponsored by George Washington University, Washington, DC. *On the University Campus at each corner of the campus:*

1. East side of Eye Street Mall and Eye Street NW
2. Lafayette Hall, 21st and Eye Street NW
3. Francis Scott Key Hall, 20th and F Street NW
4. The Smith Center, 23rd and F Street NW
5. At the satellite campus of Mount Vernon College of The George Washington University on Foxhall Road NW, near Washington DC.

Others

6. The Supreme Council of the Masonic Scottish Rite, 16th and T Streets, NW, Washington DC.
7. Pembroke College, Oxford, England
8. Richmond College, Surrey, England
9. Sulgrave Manor, the home of George Washington's ancestors in Northamptonshire, UK, a gift of the George Washington University
10. *USS George Washington*, Aircraft Carrier, stationed at Norfolk, VA
11. Westminster College, Salt Lake City, UT
12. Lynn College, Batesville, Arkansas
13. Peoria Civic Center, Peoria, Illinois
14. Mount Vernon Estate on the Potomac River, National Historic Site
15. The Washington State Capitol, Olympia, Washington
16. The Matheson Courthouse, Salt Lake City, UT
17. Washington City, Washington County, Utah
18. Washington College, Chestertown, Maryland
19. Sons of the American Revolution Headquarters, Lexington, Kentucky
20. The City of George, State of Washington
21. The Masonic Lodge in Houlton, Maine
22. The City and County Building in Fresno, CA
23. Washington County Museum of Fine Arts, Hagerstown, Maryland
24. Louisiana State Capitol Grounds, Baton Rouge, LA
25. The Government Center, Wayne, NJ, near the Dey Mansion, once George Washington's Headquarters of the Continental Army
26. The Campus of William and Mary College in Williamsburg, VA
27. Tufts New England Medical Center, Boston, MA
28. The Campus of Germantown Academy in Fort Washington, PA, a suburb of Philadelphia, PA
29. Beacon, New York. The monument was erected at the corner of Route 9D and Teller (Fishkill Avenue).
30. The Museum and Library of Our National Heritage, Lexington, MA, an institution of the Scottish Rite Masonic Order.
31. Utah State University campus at Logan, UT

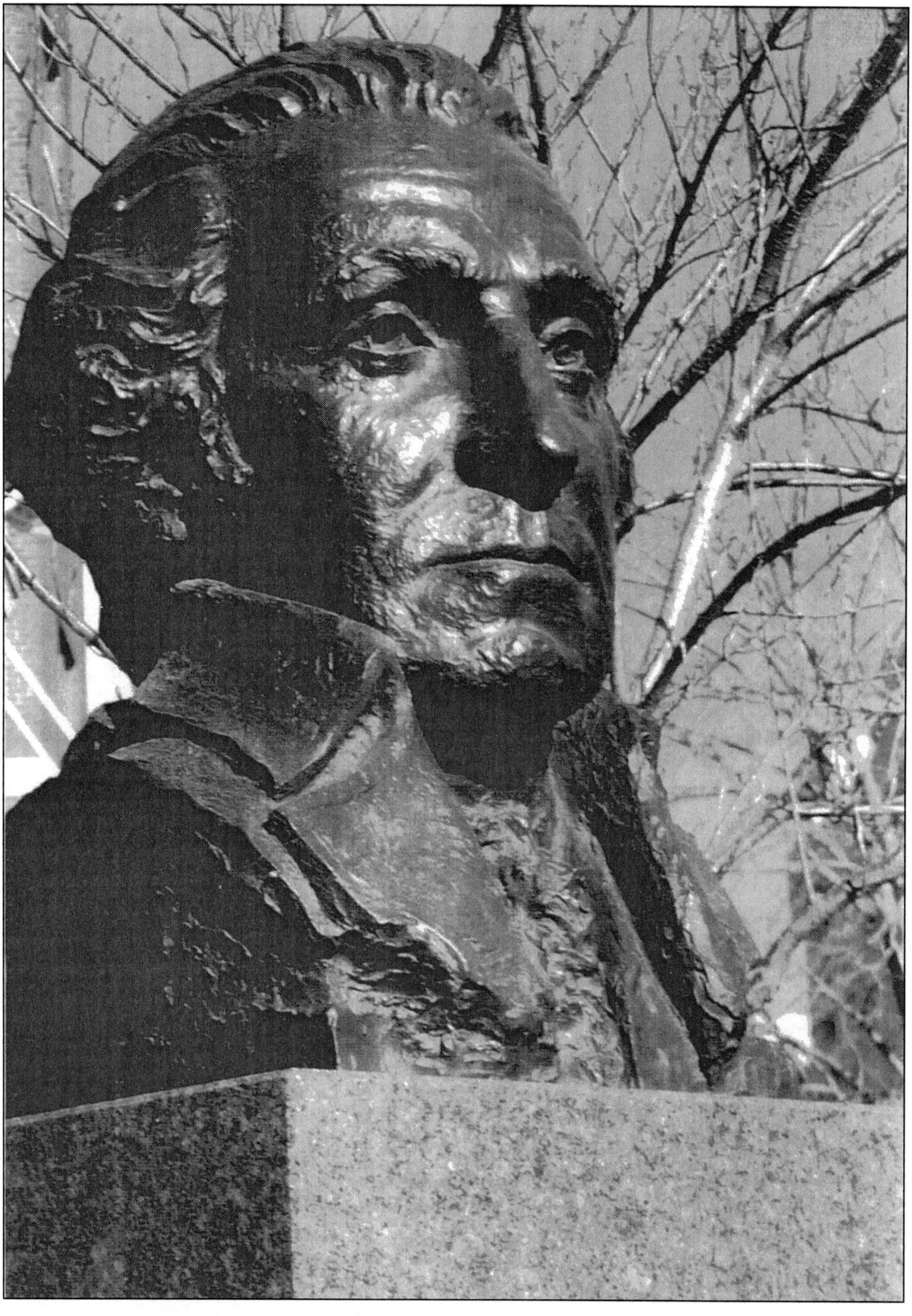

Colossal portrait bust of General George Washington by Avard T. Fairbanks, sculptor. Located at The National Headquarters, Sons of the American Revolution, Louisville, KY.

Other Statuary of George Washington by Avard T. Fairbanks

General Washington and the Express Courier

When Avard Fairbanks was commissioned to create a statue of General George Washington in which he was entrusting an urgent message to an Express, he carefully researched historical information for an accurate representation. An interesting article was found, composed later by trooper Ralph Whitney of the second Continental Light Dragoons. He copied information from a letter he was able to find in the archives of the Library of Congress. It included written orders, August 11, 1782, that were given to Lieutenant Mix to establish a line of communications from Washington's Headquarters at Newburgh on the West side of The Hudson River in New York to Boston.

Twelve dragoons were to serve as expresses and were to be stationed at intervals from Kings Ferry to Hartford, and thence to Boston. Dragoons were traditionally heavily armed cavalry soldiers, often bearing short muskets. Dragoons were selected as they were more able to protect sensitive messages from interceptions by bandits or Tories, who would convey them to the British Army. Washington's orders outline the dragoon's duties in careful detail. A part of the orders to Lieutenant Mix are copied to demonstrate, as an example, the details and thoroughness of George Washington's plans and orders:

> "To Lieut. Mix, Instructions
> Head Quarters, Newburg, August 11, 1782
>
> Sir:
> You will procure forthwith to establish a line of communication between Kings ferry and Boston; You will wait upon Col. Sheldon with the inclosed order for 12 Dragoons to form the Chain from Kings ferry to Hartford inclusive; these you will post at or in the neighbourhood of the places mentioned in the Margin (two at each), and will make effectual provision for their accommodation and subsistence.
> 1 Haight's; 2 Danbury; 3 Carletons Bridge; 4 Breakneck; 5 Southington; 6 Hartford.
>
> From Hartford to Boston you will continue the line of Expresses by persons retained for the purpose by the Qr. Mastr Department...."

General Washington also gave orders (not copied here), to Lt. Mix that contained explicit instructions to be posted for the Dragoons and Expresses about their duties on the line of communications between Kings Ferry and Boston.*

Sculptor Fairbanks carefully researched the Dragoon's uniforms, looking through books in his own studio library that also included several sets of old encyclopedias, acquired at old book sales, and by visits to a public and a university library. There are books that he studied, depicting costumes of various persons and cultures in various periods of time. A military costume of the Continental Army was chosen to represent the Express. General Washington has been portrayed in his uniform by artists during the Revolutionary War, and illustrations of these portraits were studied.

The type of horse that was chosen to be modeled was the American Quarter Horse, a colonial breed, developed to run a rapid quarter mile, since there were no mile long, oval race tracks during that period in the colonies.

* Fitzpatric, John C., Editor. *The Writings of George Washington from the Original Manuscript Sources*, 1745-1799. Publication of the U.S. Army Corps of Engineers.

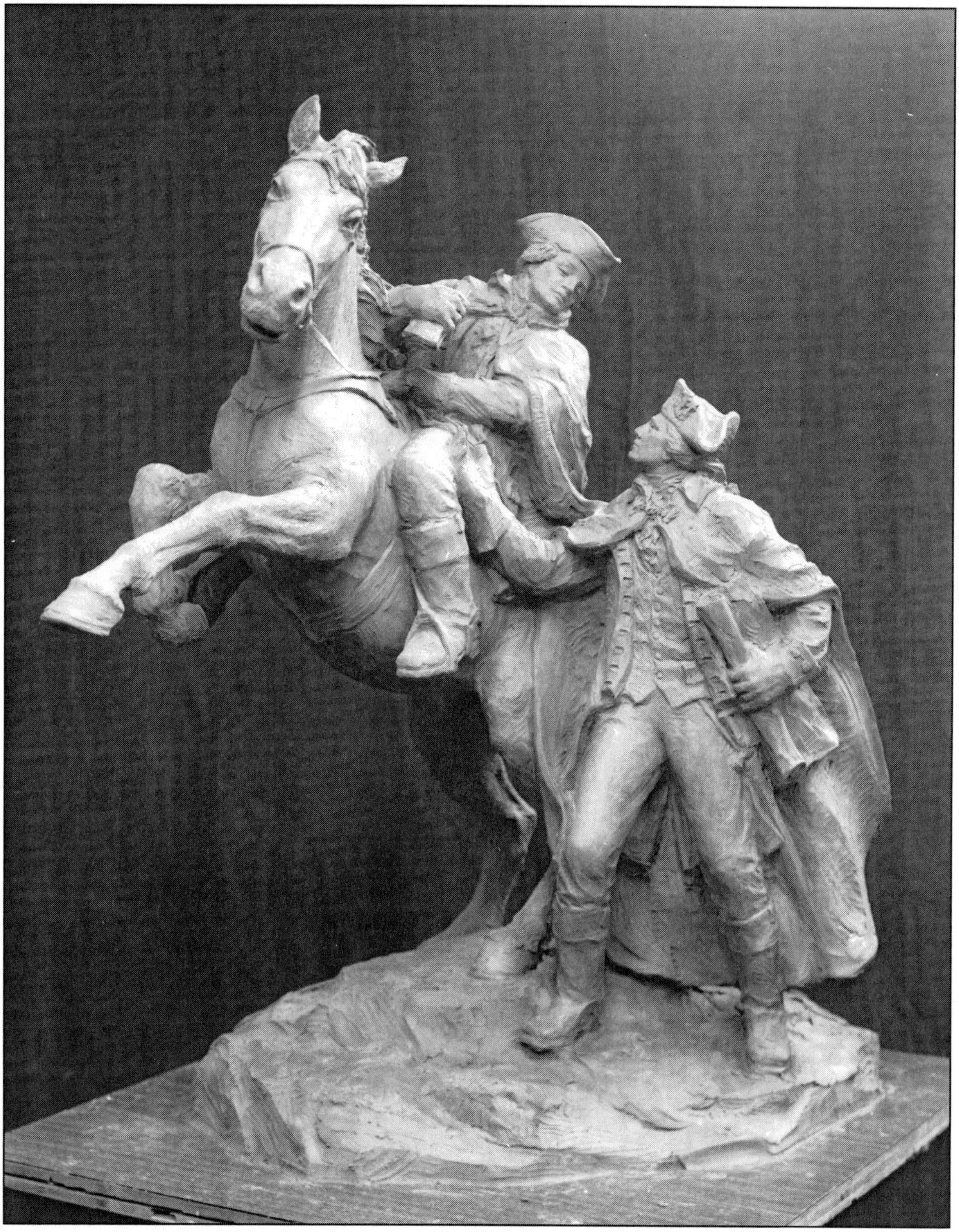

General Washington and the Express Courier.

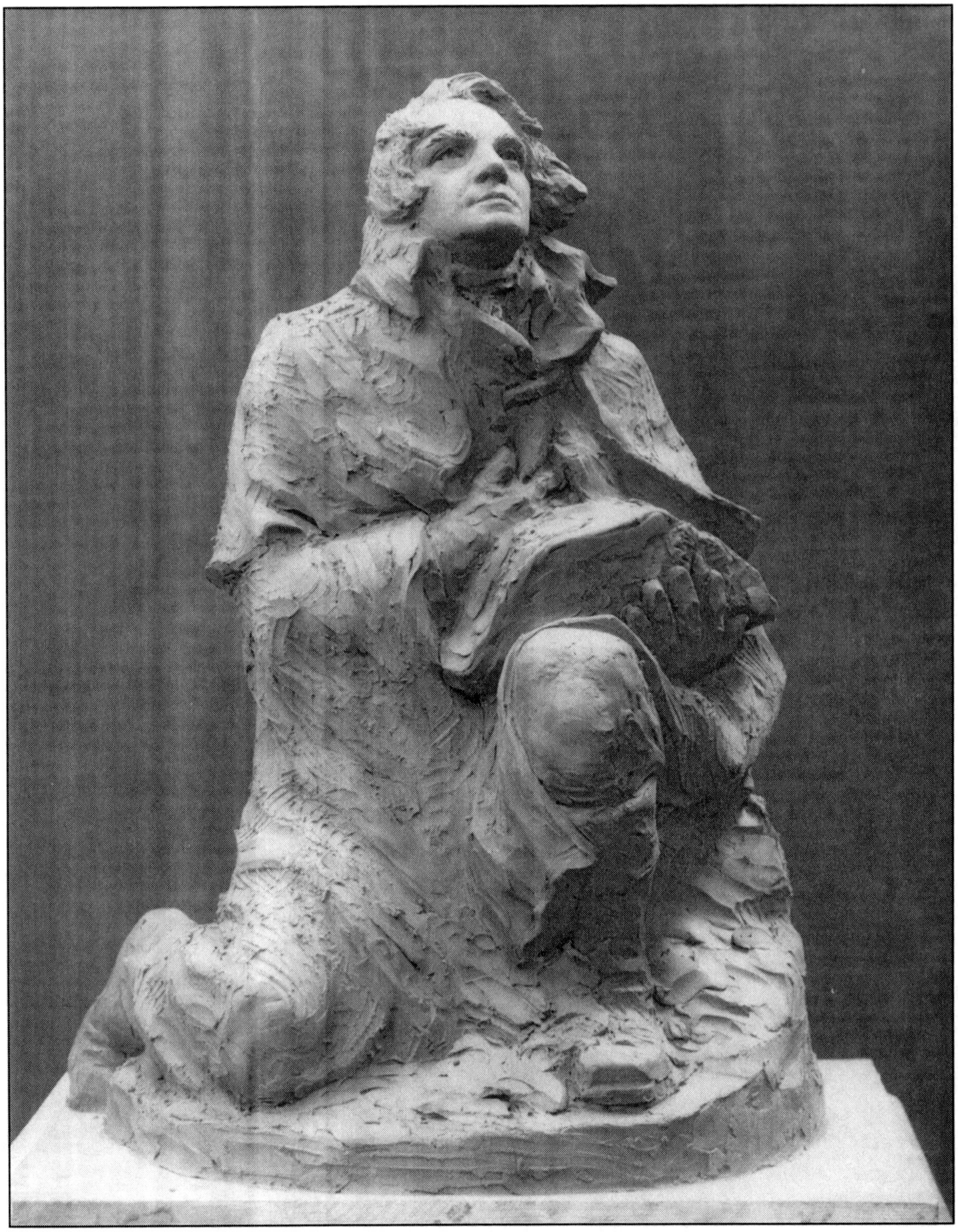

Washington's Prayer at Valley Forge.

George Washington at Valley Forge

During the winter of 1777-78, troops of the Continental army were encamped in Valley Forge, sheltered in log cabins. They suffered from lack of adequate clothing, boots, and food supplies. There had been a conspiracy by a group of incompetent generals trying to displace Washington by slanderous letters to some members of Congress. When this plot was revealed to him, he was able to expose the perpetrators and convince Congress to give him more authority.

The Quartermaster General's department was also disorganized by mistaken policies of the Continental Congress. General Washington feared that if the situation did not improve, the army would be reduced to starvation or to dissolve or disperse.

In these times of despair, it has been thought that he sought divine guidance for hope, assistance, and inspiration. This one-half life-size statuette re-creates a moment in difficult times when he sought solitude, knelt in the snow, and uttered a sincere prayer.

When he was able to induce Congress to appoint General Greene as Quartermaster General, the department improved and became more effective. Shelter in cabins, boots, clothing and food supplies for the troops became more adequate.* Without sufficient supplies of basic military needs, the Battle of Trenton could never have been planned.

* Frothingham, Thomas, G. *Washington Commander in Chief.* 1930. Boston and New York. Houghton Mifflin Company.
pp. 234-241.

Valley Forge

Away from the men he was called to lead
  Alone in the forest with his trusty steed
He quietly knelt in the snow covered sod
  To petition a blessing from his God.

His men were hungry, tired, and cold;
  There was no money for pay, I'm told;
Enlistments were up, but the war dragged on:
  The losses were many, their provisions gone.

Just a handful of men against the Crown
  How could they hope to gain the ground
To make a nation of free men sure,
  Thirteen States that would endure.

There must be a way to win the war;
  The colonists knew what the fight was for;
Freedom to worship and do as they please
  Had brought their General to his knees.

It's conquer we must; be brave and endure
  We all have our Valley Forges for sure.
Have courage and faith to do what you dare
  By finding the answer in solemn prayer.

Farrall D. Fairbanks
November 1992

Farrell Fairbanks was a younger brother of Avard Fairbanks. He wrote this poem to express the sense of despair and sacrifices during the winter at Valley Forge and to compliment the sculpture titled *Washington's Prayer at Valley Forge.*

George Washington Greeting his Revered Mother

This statuette expresses a moment in time that could have been during some of the troubled days of the Revolutionary War, or in her declining years, when George Washington visited his mother and expressed his appreciation for her parental care and guidance.

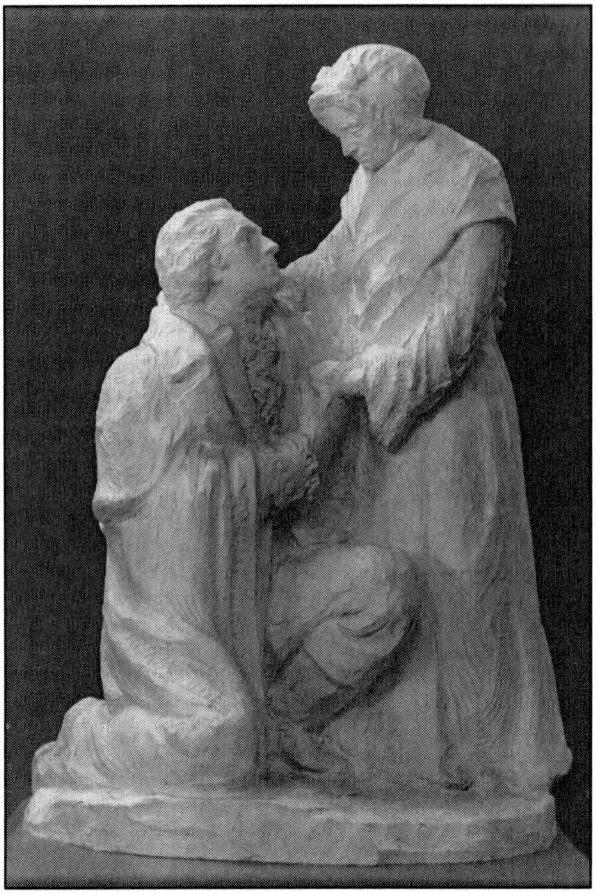

George Washington Greeting his Revered Mother.

Mary Ball Washington was a true heroine as an outstanding Mother of Men important to our national heritage. History has somewhat passively acknowledged her importance, being over-shadowed by her illustrious son.

She was born in 1708, became fatherless at the age of three and became an orphan at the age of twelve. She was placed under the guardianship of George Eskridge, a Lawyer. She married the widower, Augustine Washington, when she was twenty-three and he was thirty-seven years of age. He had four children by a previous marriage, but only two survived to adulthood. They lived at the Ferry Farm in Virginia. Together they had six children: George, Betty, Samuel, John Augustine, Charles, and Mildred.

Augustine Washington died in 1743, leaving her a widow at age thirty-five with her oldest son, George, only twelve-years old. She was organized, resourceful, and expected discipline of those on the plantation, including her family. She continued alone to rear her children and to manage the Ferry Farm until George came of age. She also continued to live at the six-hundred acre plantation for the next twenty-nine years.

George Washington was concerned for her safety living alone on the farm, and relieved her of the management demands of the Ferry Farm.

In 1772 he bought her a fine home in Fredericksburg, where she lived there until her death in August 1789. Mary Washington often visited her daughter, Betty and her husband, Fielding Lewis, at their Kenmore Plantation near Fredericksburg.

She lived to see her son become Commander in Chief of the Continental Army, and in April 1789, be elected the first President of the United States.

During Mary's declining years, she developed a breast cancer. George visited her in April 1789 and said he would eagerly return as soon as he tended to public matters that needed him in New York. She bravely told him, "This will be our last meeting in this life."

He is quoted in 1789 as having said, "All that I am, I owe to my mother." She died in August of that year and was buried on the Kenmore Plantation. The Kenmore House is now operated as a museum, open to the public. Mary is honorably remembered in Fredericksburg by the Mary Washington House, maintained as a public museum, The Mary Ball Washington Museum and Library, the Mary Ball Washington University, and The Mary Ball Washington Hospital.

* Information gathered in March 2013 from the *Wikipedia* entry on Mary Ball Washington.

The Spirit of Washington, as a Guide to Young Abraham Lincoln

Avard Fairbanks believed and taught that a master sculptor must also be an historian. When researching the life events of Abraham Lincoln for major monuments, he was impressed with recorded information about how Abraham Lincoln learned to read early, encouraged by his mother, and he became an avid reader. He borrowed every book he could in his neighborhood.

During his youth, one book he borrowed was *The Life of Washington* by Mason Locke Weems, published in Philadelphia in 1800. It became damaged and he had to pay for it by three days labor. Once it was his, he could read it often. And he was so impressed with Washington's deeds that it helped him as a guiding light in his endeavors.

Although critics have discounted this book as having no great merit as a critical biography, young Abraham Lincoln was deeply impressed.

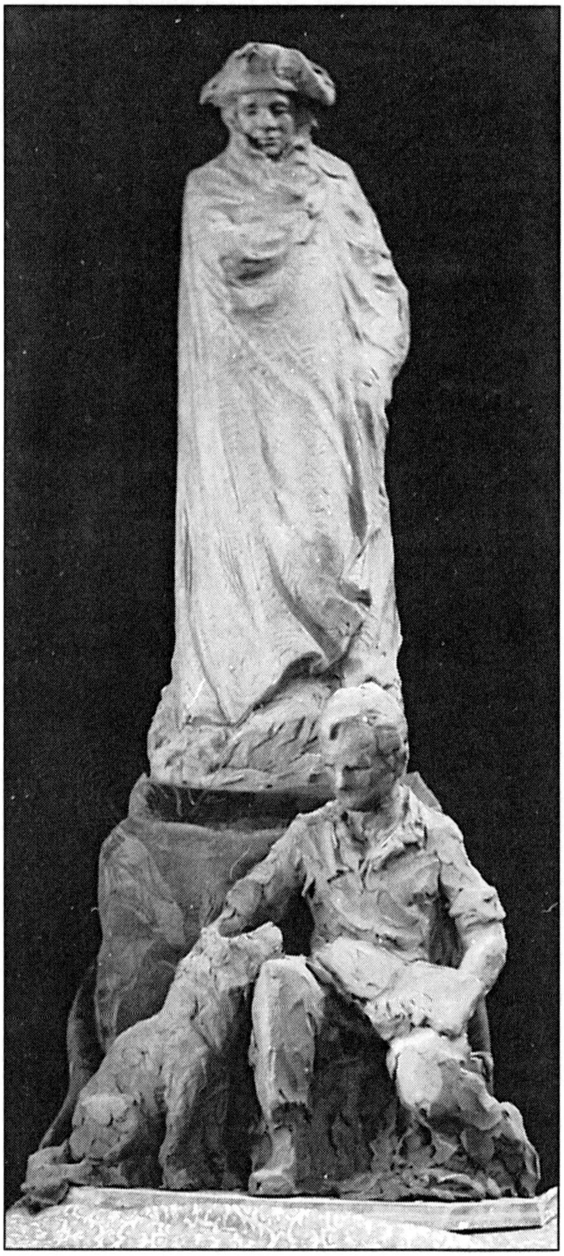

The Spirit of George Washington, roughly modeled as an idea to be expanded upon.

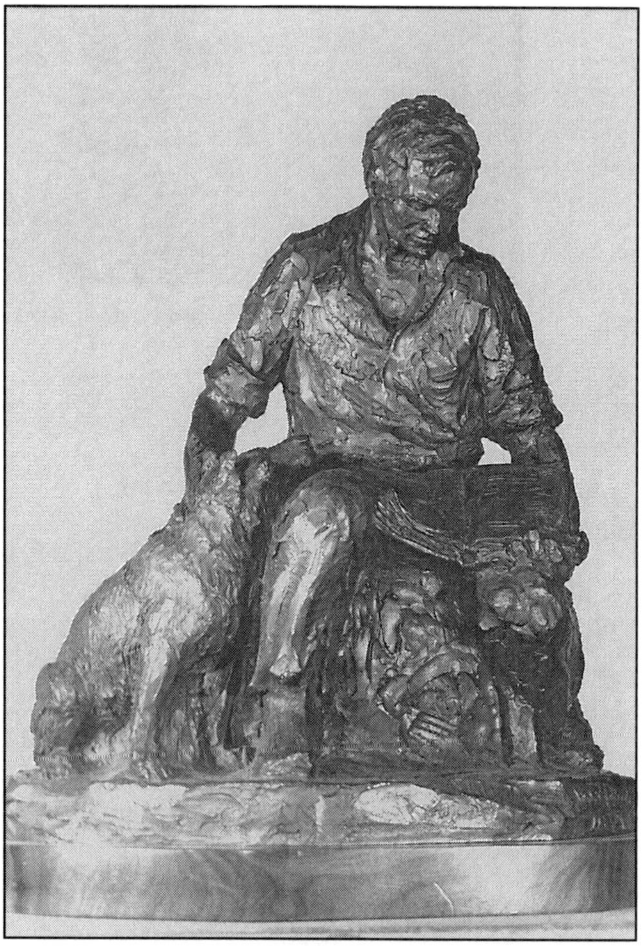

Young Lincoln Reading the Life of George Washington.

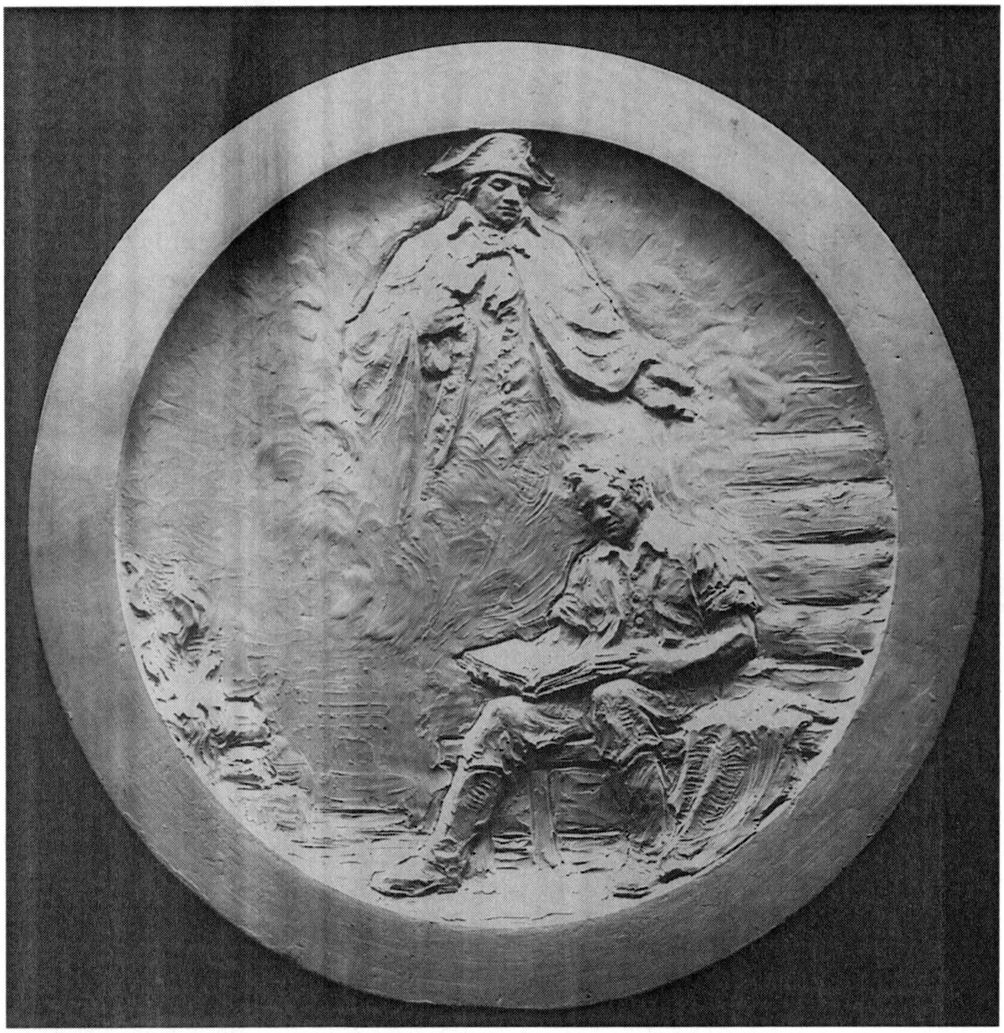

Obverse side of the medal of Abraham Lincoln Reading the Life of George Washington.

Paul Angle quotes Lincoln in his book, *The Lincoln Reader.*

"In 1861, in addressing the Senate of the State of New Jersey, he said: 'May I be pardoned if, on this occasion, I mention that away back in my childhood, the critical days of my being able to read, I got hold of a small book, such as a one as few of the younger members have ever seen—Weems' *Life of Washington*.
I remember all the accounts there given of the battle-fields and struggles for the liberties of the country, and none of them fixed themselves upon my imagination so deeply as the struggle here at Trenton, New Jersey. The crossing of the river, the contest with the Hessians, the great hardships endured at that time, all fixed themselves on my memory more than any single Revolutionary event; and you all know, for you have all been boys, how those early impressions last longer than any others. I recollect thinking then, boy even though I was, that there must have been something more than common that these men struggled for.' "*

Fairbanks envisioned an intriguing concept of a youth reading about a courageous national

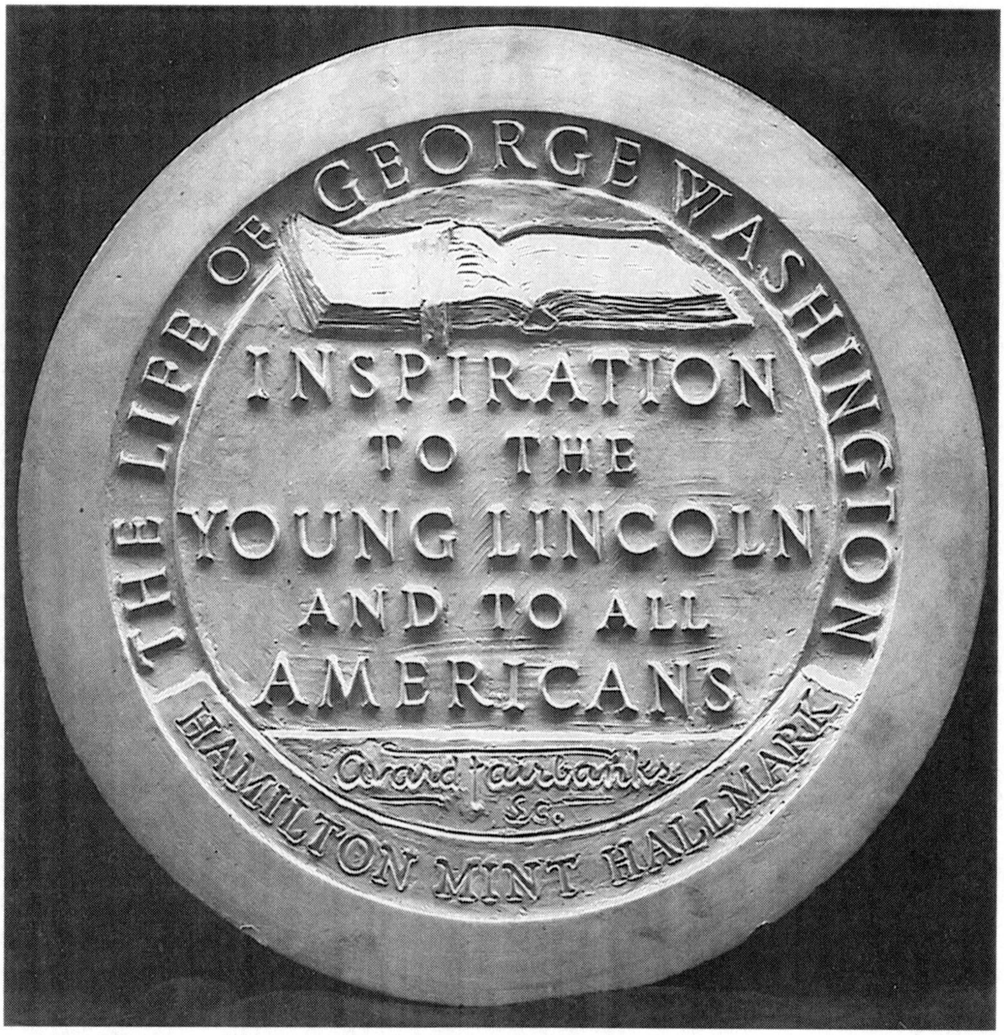

The medal of Abraham Lincoln Reading the Life of George Washington.

figure and it became the inspiration for a statuette that could be enlarged later into a heroic monument. The thought of a young Lincoln in a rustic log cabin, reading the small book, *The Life of Washington,* by the light of the rude fireplace could be a dramatic reenactment of an event in time. Standing behind the youth would be the spirit of General George Washington, an image carved in white marble, an ethereal figure like a spirit that would contrast with the bronze statue of the inspired youth. The statuettes were created. The concept was profound, almost immortal, but no individual or organization generated enough interest for the fulfillment of this grand project.

Yet the concept did not perish. Avard Fairbanks incorporated it into a medal that was struck by the Hamilton-Hallmark Mint at about the time of the Bicentennial of American Independence. The obverse depicts the youthful Lincoln exhilarated by reading of the heroic deeds before the dim light of a crackling fire on the stone hearth of the frontier log cabin. In the background an image of General Washington rises in the vapors and wisps of smoke above the blaze as though rendering counsel and guidance.

* Angle, Paul M. *The Lincoln Reader.* 1947 New Brunswick Rutgers University Press, p. 25.

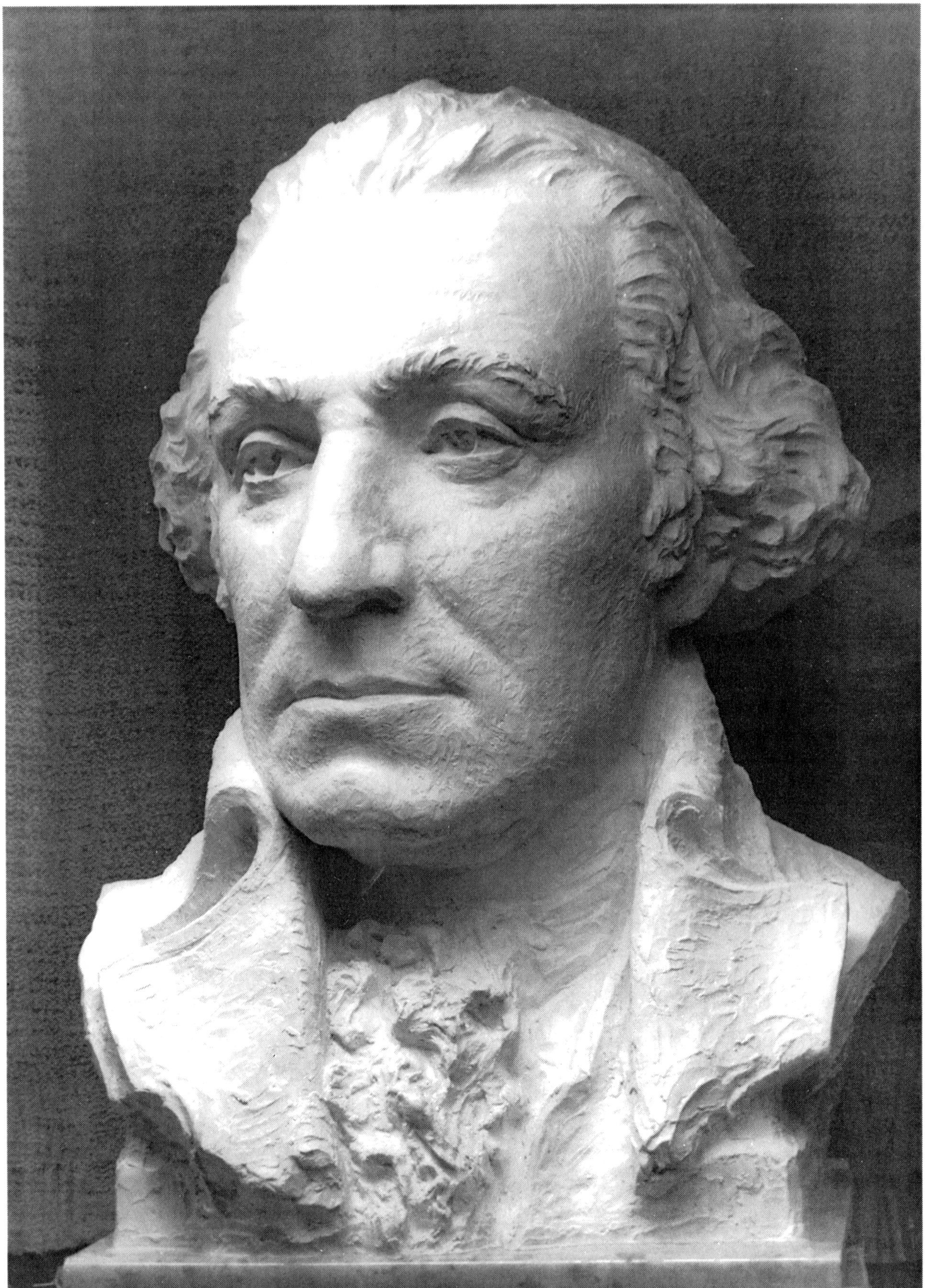

General George Washington, a colossal portrait by Avard T. Fairbanks. Placed in the reception room, Washington State Capitol, Olympia, Washington, and at Washington University Medical School, Washington, D.C.

Selected Portraits of Individuals by Avard T. Fairbanks

During his long career, over seventy years of professional sculpture, Avard Fairbanks created more than one hundred portraits of significant individuals. These include five in colossal size. There are many additional portraits of children. Many additional portraits and commemorative monuments have been made in low relief. The selection listed represents a variety of persons portrayed. The portraits follow this list.

1. Justin Fairbanks: 1928, the sculptor's fourth son as a child, carved in marble.
2. Jonathan Fairbanks: 1933, Three-week-old infant, the sculptor's sixth son.
3. Edward Sammons: 1931, a child, Portland, Oregon.
4. Caroline Fairbanks: 1968, a granddaughter, the daughter of his son Virgil. The portrait was carved in marble.
5. Mrs. Helen Gardiner Phelan and daughter, Gail: 1948, the portrait was carved in marble. Toronto, Ontario, Canada.
6. Old Bill Keddington: 1915, a character study of a western pioneer and scout, Salt Lake City, UT. This portrait was exhibited at the Pan Pacific International Exposition, San Francisco, CA.
7. Ezra Meeker: 1926, Oregon Trail Pioneer, a western pioneer financier, banker, hop farmer, and founder of the Old Oregon Trail Association. The portrait was placed in the Meeker Mansion Museum, Puyallup, Washington.
8. Albert Woolson: 1956, a Civil War Veteran at Duluth, MN. He was the last survivor of the Grand Army of the Republic. The Portrait was erected in the City Hall in Duluth, MN, 1985.
9. Carl Sandberg: 1958, Poet, journalist, and eminent Lincoln historian: His portrait was created during the Lincoln Sesquicentennial. It was cast in bronze and placed at the Chicago Historical Museum and at Knox College, his alma mater, in Galesburg, IL.
10. Brigham Young: 1977, a pioneer and leader of the Church of Jesus Christ of Latter-Day Saints in its westward migration of 1847, the portrait represents his early years.
11. Brigham Young: 1979, president of the Church of Jesus Christ of Latter-Day Saints, in his later years.
12. Right Honorable William Lyons Mackenzie-King, Prime Minister of Canada: 1943. He was one of the world's great leaders and was Prime Minister of Canada for over twenty-five years. The portrait, cast in bronze, was placed in the Parliament Building in Ottawa, Ontario, Canada.
13. Honorable Gerry G. McGreer: 1954. He was elected Mayor of Vancouver, British Columbia, and later he was elected a member of the Canadian Parliament, Ottawa, Ontario, Canada 1954.
14. Dr. Virginia Cutler, Professor and Chairperson of the Home Economics Department of the University of Utah. She developed the home living center at the University of Utah and the Brigham Young University. She was a delegate of the United States Government to Thailand to establish home living centers in Asiatic nations.
15. Dr. Clarence Cook Little: 1955, President of the University of Michigan, and then continued as an eminent mammalian cancer research scientist at Jackson Laboratory on Mount Desert Island, Bar Harbor, Maine.
16. Dr. G. Carl Huber: 1932. He was an eminent neuro-anatomist, Professor of Anatomy,

and Dean of the Graduate School at the University of Michigan.

17. Dr. Harvey Fletcher: 1955. A research physicist, he was the Director of the Bell Telephone Laboratories, "The Father of Stereophonic Sound," and the founding Dean of the College of Engineering at the Brigham Young University.
18. Rufus Von KleinSmid; 1955. After promoting and expanding the University of Arizona as its President, he was appointed President of the University of Southern California, an institution of about five thousand students. During his administration, the institution progressively expanded to have a larger campus and faculty and over twenty-five thousand students. For his many achievements, he was honored and awarded the title of Chancellor of the University for Life.
19. Kate Carter: 1977, She was a pioneer leader of the Woman's Relief Society of the Church of Jesus Christ of Latter-Day Saints. The portrait, carved in marble, was placed in the Daughters of the Utah Pioneers Museum, Salt Lake City, UT.
20. Walter P. Chrysler, 1937. He was the founder and Chairman of the Board of the Chrysler Motor Corporation, Detroit, MI. The portrait was cast in bronze and placed in the Chrysler Museum in Norfolk, VA.
21. Howard R. Driggs: 1952, an educator and historian. He was Chairman of the Department of American Literature at the New York University. He was also a successor to Ezra Meeker as President of the American Trail and Landmarks Association. The portrait was placed in Howard R. Driggs Elementary School, Salt Lake City, UT.
22. James C. Penny: 1954. A merchant, financier, founder, and President of the J.C. Penny Company. The portrait was presented on the Golden Anniversary of the founding of the company.
23. J.M. McDonald: Merchant, associate of J.C. Penny, founder of J.M. McDonald Store, Guernsey stock breeder, and philanthropist, 1955.
24. Esther Hobart Morris: 1960. While hosting a social event, she encouraged territorial legislators in Wyoming to pass women's suffrage. In 1869, Wyoming was the first state to grant women suffrage. When a Justice of the Peace resigned in protest, she was appointed Justice to replace him. She was the first woman Justice in the United States. In 1976 she served as Vice President of the American Woman Suffrage Association. Avard Fairbanks created a heroic statue of her that was placed in Statuary Hall, Washington, DC, and at the State Capitol, Cheyenne, WY.
25. Alice Paul: 1975. Founder of the National Women's Party in 1913 and author of the Equal Rights Amendment in 1923. She was a dedicated advocate for women's suffrage and organized parades, protests and pickets promoting the cause. The pendant of her necklace depicted a jail-house door, reminiscent of women jailed for promoting women's suffrage. The bronze portrait was placed in the Sewall-Belmont house, the Headquarters and Museum of the National Women's Party in Washington, DC.
26. Lott Smith: 1963. He was a western pioneer, a scout and the leader in the Echo Canyon conflict of the early Utah Territories.
27. Frederick Moench: 1964. A pioneer educator and founder of the Weber State University, Ogden, Utah. A heroic statue was erected at the campus.
28. Marshall Dana: 1955, an eminent journalist in Portland, Oregon and a leader in National Reclamation efforts.
29. Lamar Tooze: a wounded veteran of World War I. He later became a prominent attorney in Portland, Oregon. During World War II, he was called again to military service and

was progressively advanced in rank, retiring as a Major General.

30. James Madison: 1969. A president of the United States. This portrait was placed at the Madison Elementary School in Salt Lake City, UT.
31. Thomas Jefferson and the Declaration of Independence: 1982. A marble portrait was placed at the Kenmore International Center for Jefferson Studies at the Jefferson Estate, Monticello, VA. A bronze portrait was placed at the University of Virginia in Charlottesville, VA. And a bronze portrait was placed in the Jefferson Elementary School in Rochester, MN.
32. Dr. William B. Pillsbury: 1932. Professor of Psychology, and Chairman of the Department of Psychology at the University of Michigan.
33. Dr. William Hobbs: 1930. He was a Professor of Geology and Chairman of the Geology Department at the University of Michigan.
34. Dean Roscoe Pound: 1980. He was an eminent scholar in constitutional law, Professor of Law, University of Nebraska, and Dean of the Law School, Harvard University. His portrait was placed in the Nebraska Hall of Fame at the state capitol in Lincoln, Nebraska, and at the Harvard University Law Library.
35. The Sioux Warrior: 1965. The portrait was created representing "The Fighting Sioux" for the Athletic Building at the University of North Dakota.
36. Samuel Cosgrove: 1953. A jurist at Pomeroy, Washington. He was elected Governor of the State of Washington. The heroic portrait was erected at the Garfield County Courthouse, at Pomeroy, WA.
37. The Pirate: 1970, for the high school mascot. It was placed at Magna High School, Magna, UT.
38. Spencer Penrose: 1958, realtor and financier. The portrait was created and a heroic monument was erected at Broadmoor in Colorado Springs, CO.
39. John F. Kennedy: A president of the United States and the Eternal Flame.
40. George Eisenberg: 1986, a Chicago resident, a philanthropist and donor to the Mayo Foundation. The heroic bronze was placed in the Eisenberg building of the Mayo Medical School 1985. It was formerly the Methodist Hospital. This was the last major work of Avard Fairbanks.
41. A. Fairbanks modeling the portrait of George Eisenberg.

Abraham Lincoln heroic size portraits: 1959. Carved in Carrara marble, commissioned by Broadcast Music Corporation for the Lincoln sesquicentennial. Later donated to the Department of the Interior.

42. Abraham Lincoln the Youth, placed in the Ford Theater Museum in Washington, DC.
43. Abraham Lincoln the Frontiersman, placed in the Ford Theater Museum in Washington, DC. Another heroic carving in marble was placed by the Illinois Historical Society in the Lincoln House Museum, Springfield, IL.
44. Abraham Lincoln the Lawyer, prominently placed in the Temple of Justice, the Supreme Court Building in Washington, DC.
45. Abraham Lincoln, the president, placed in the Ford Theater Museum in 1959.
46. Abraham Lincoln the Youth, modeled in plasteline.
47. A colossal portrait of Lincoln the Frontiersman, 1965, cast in bronze was placed at the Lincoln High School in Seattle. WA. Another cast was placed at Utah State University at Logan, UT, along with a colossal portrait of George Washington.

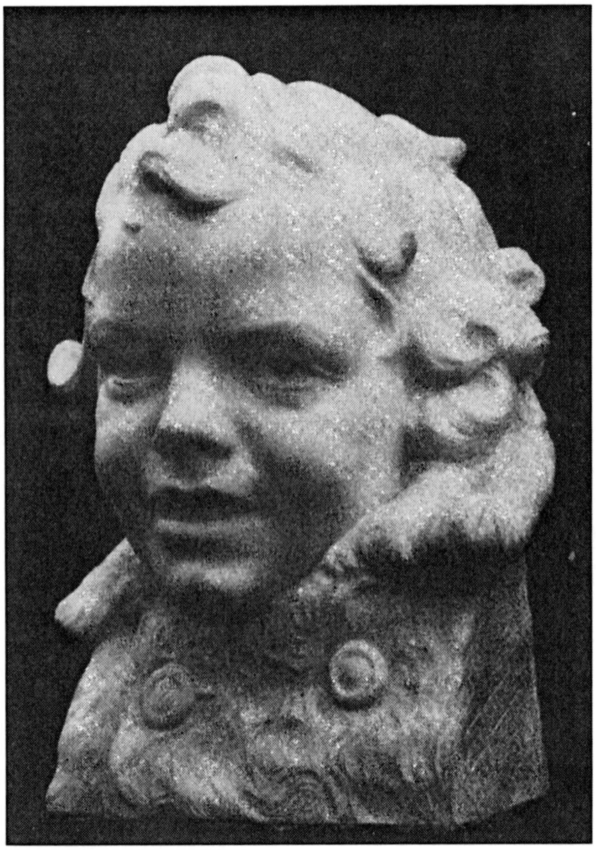

1. Justin Fairbanks: 1928, the sculptor's fourth son as a child, carved in marble.

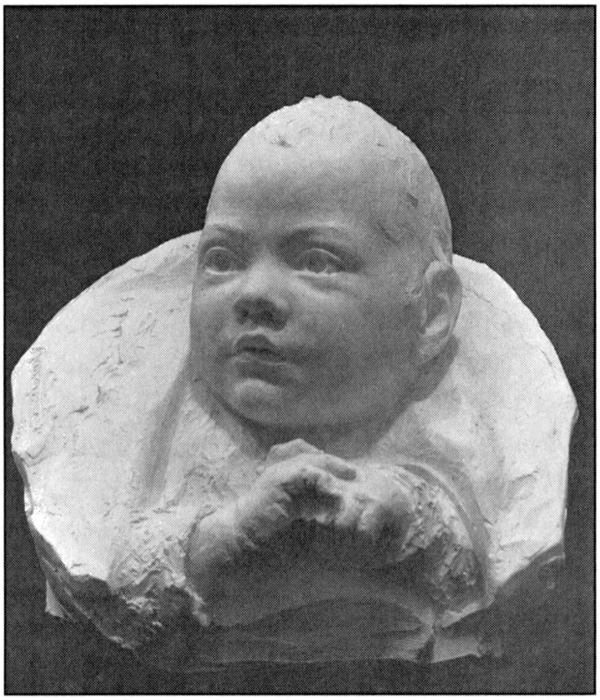

2. Jonathan Fairbanks: 1933, Three-week-old infant, the sculptor's sixth son.

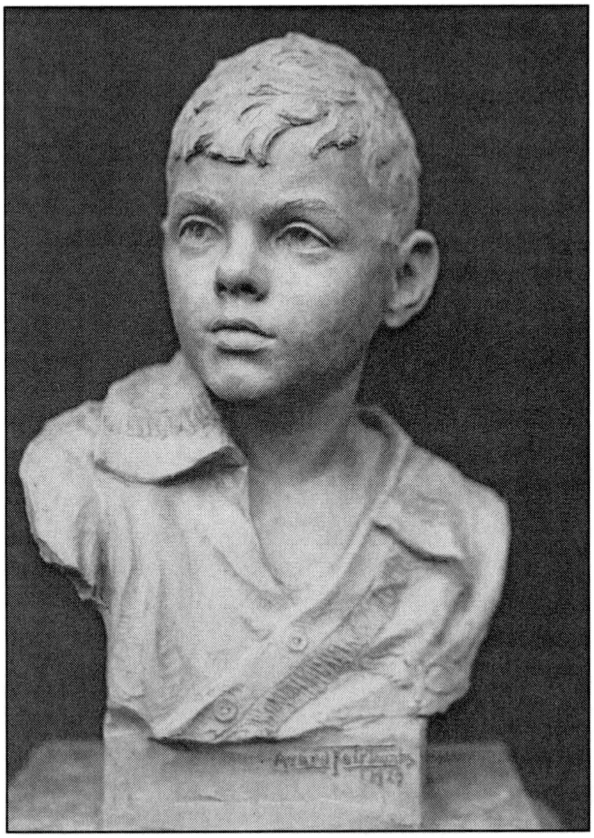

3. Edward Sammons: 1931, a child, Portland, Oregon.

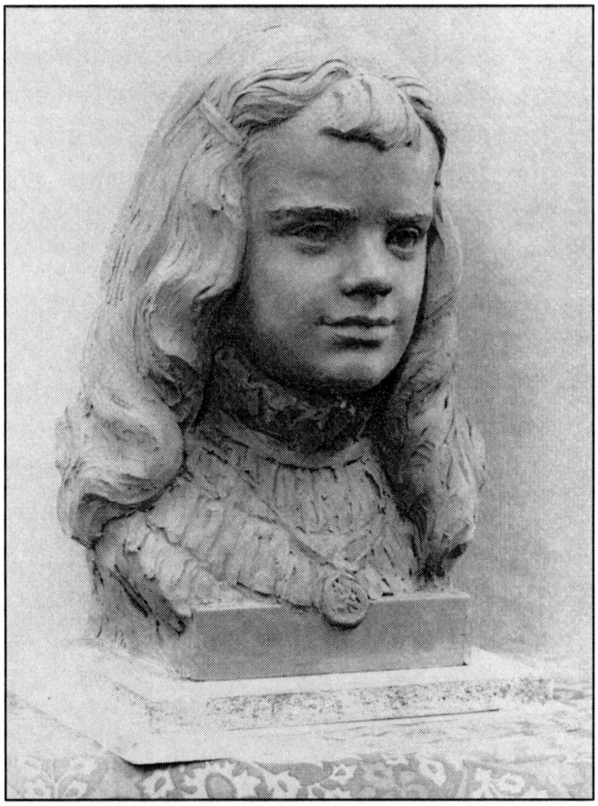

4. Caroline Fairbanks: 1968, a granddaughter, the daughter of his son Virgil. The portrait was carved in marble.

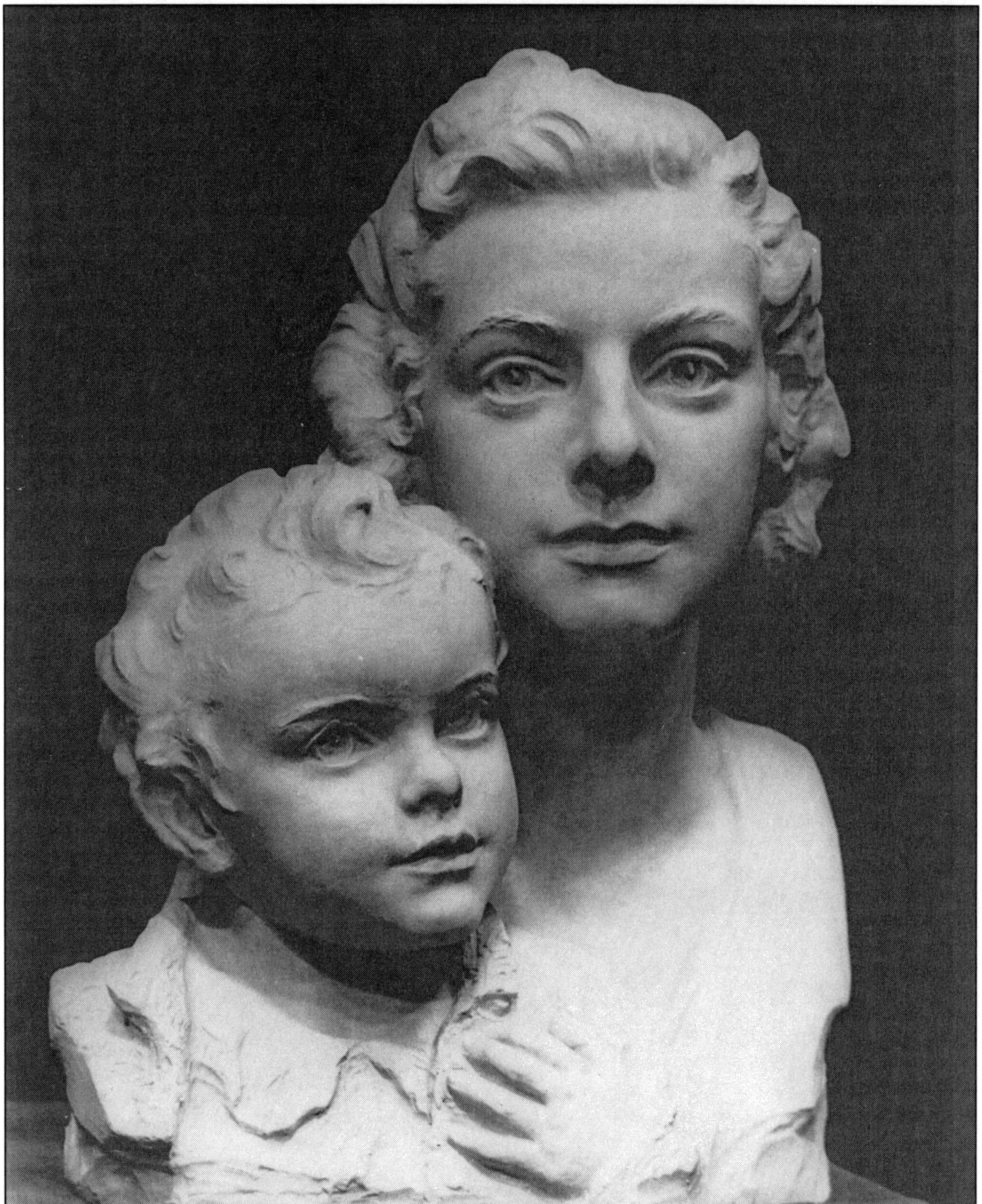

5. Mrs. Helen Gardiner Phelan and daughter, Gail: 1948, the portrait was carved in marble. Toronto, Ontario, Canada.

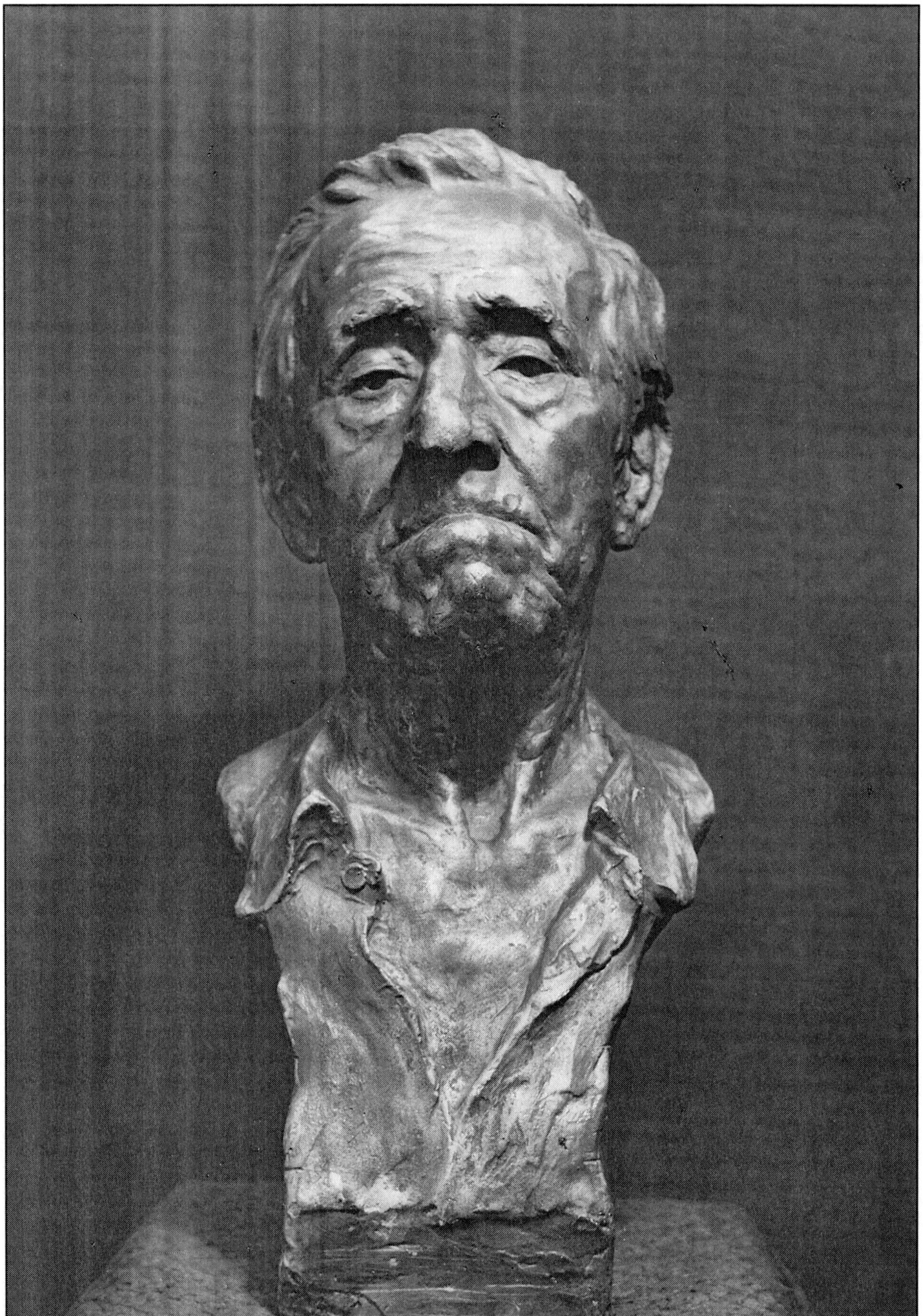

6. Old Bill Keddington: 1915, a character study of a western pioneer and scout, Salt Lake City, UT. This portrait was exhibited at the Pan Pacific International Exposition, San Francisco, CA.

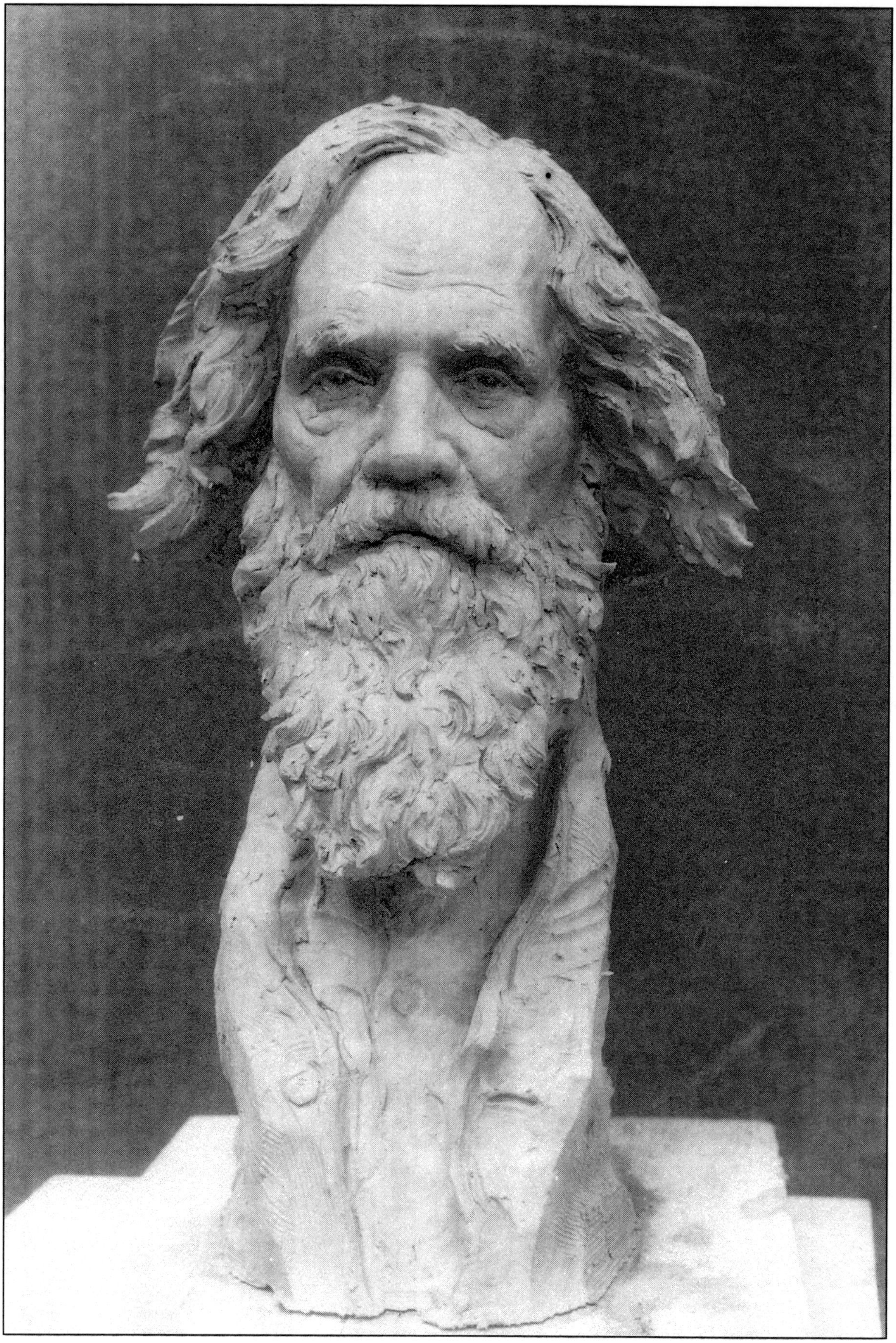

7. Ezra Meeker: 1926, Oregon Trail Pioneer, a western pioneer financier, banker, hop farmer, and founder of the Old Oregon Trail Association. The portrait was placed in the Meeker Mansion Museum, Puyallup, Washington.

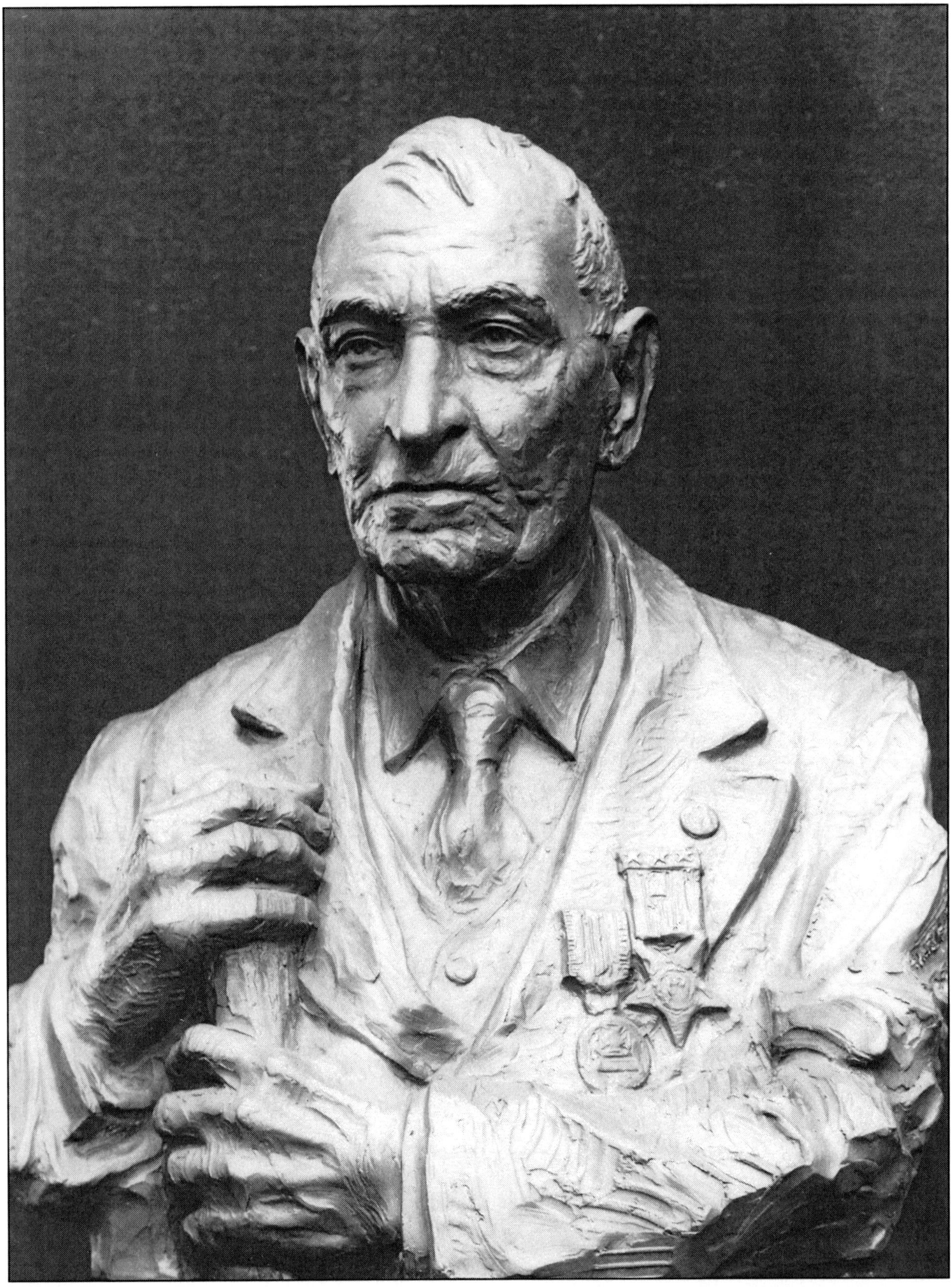

8. Albert Woolson: 1956, a Civil War Veteran at Duluth, MN. He was the last survivor of the Grand Army of the Republic. The Portrait was erected in the City Hall in Duluth, MN, 1985.

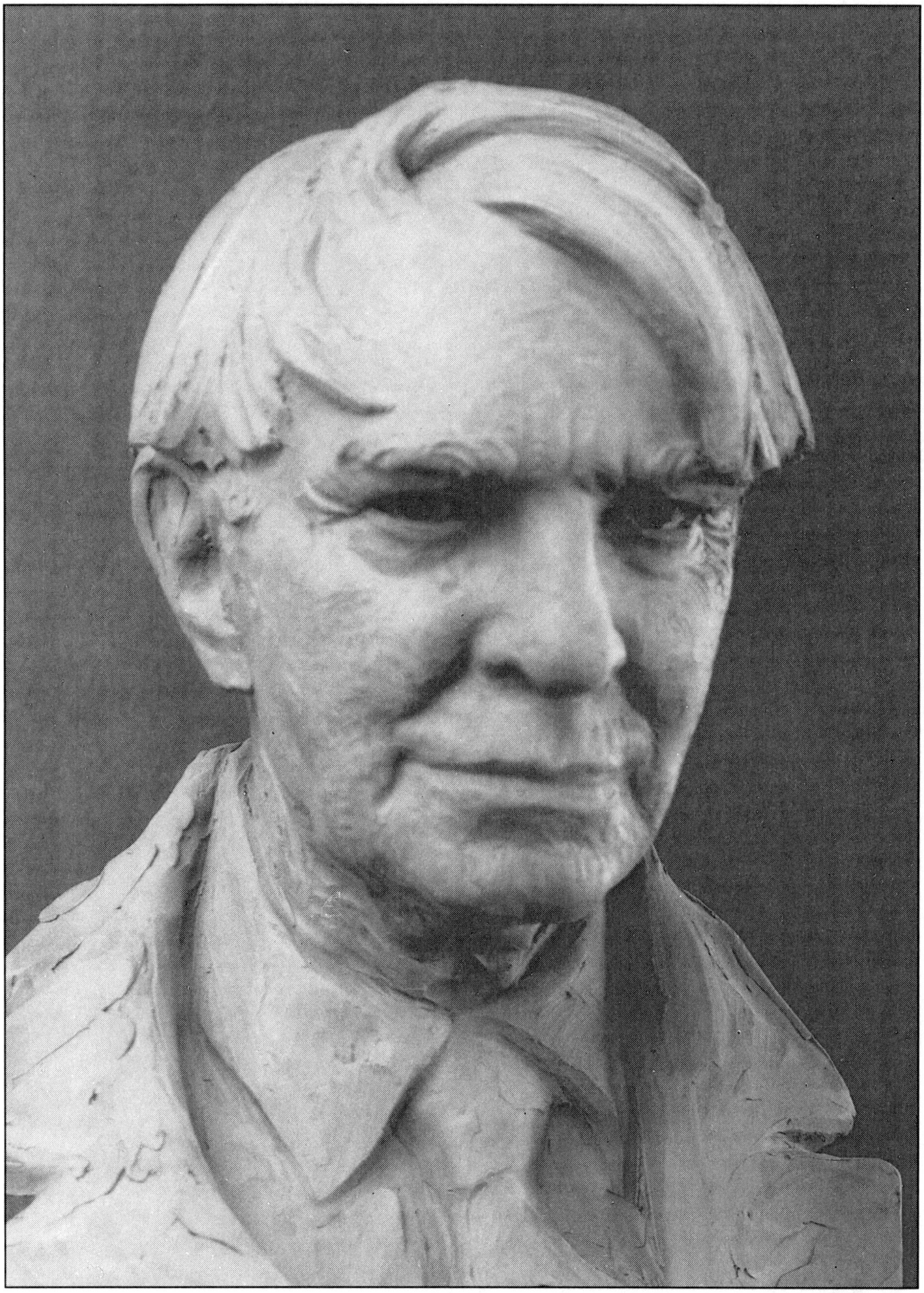

9. Carl Sandberg: 1958, Poet, journalist, and eminent Lincoln historian: His portrait was created during the Lincoln Sesquicentennial. It was cast in bronze and placed at the Chicago Historical Museum and at Knox College, his alma mater, in Galesburg, IL.

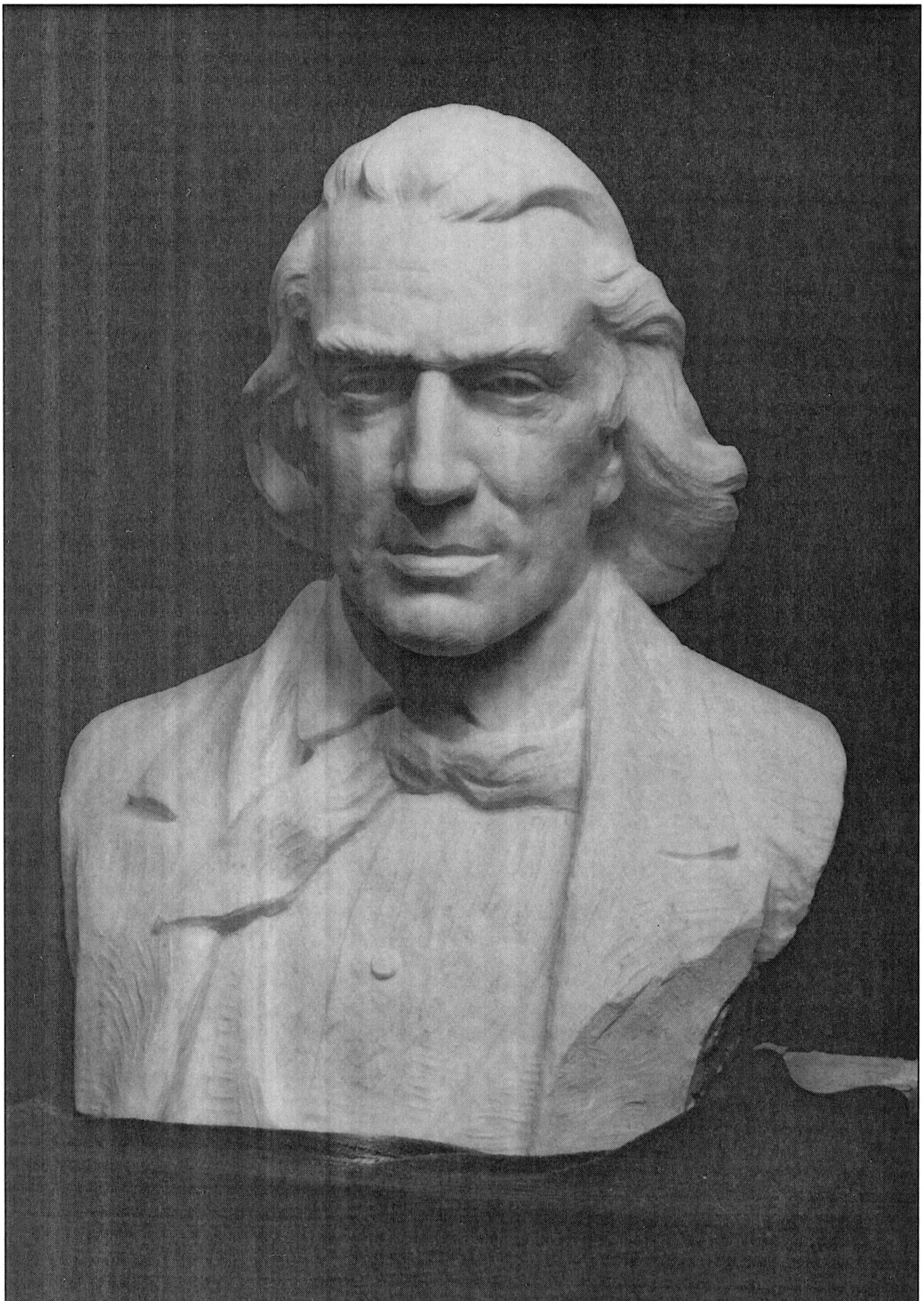

10. Brigham Young: 1977, a pioneer and leader of the Church of Jesus Christ of Latter-Day Saints in its westward migration of 1847, the portrait represents his early years.

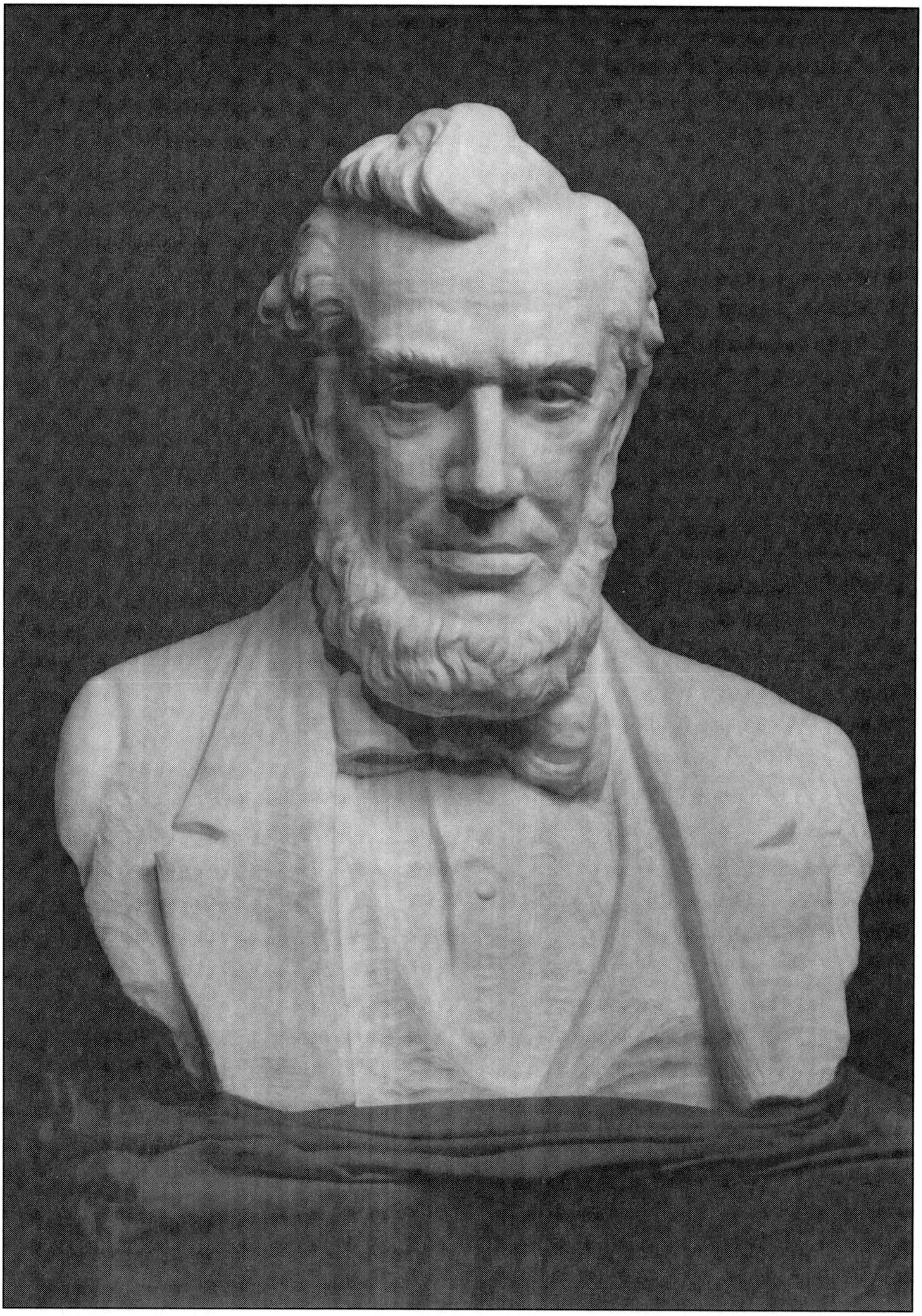

11. Brigham Young: 1979, president of the Church of Jesus Christ of Latter-Day Saints, in his later years.

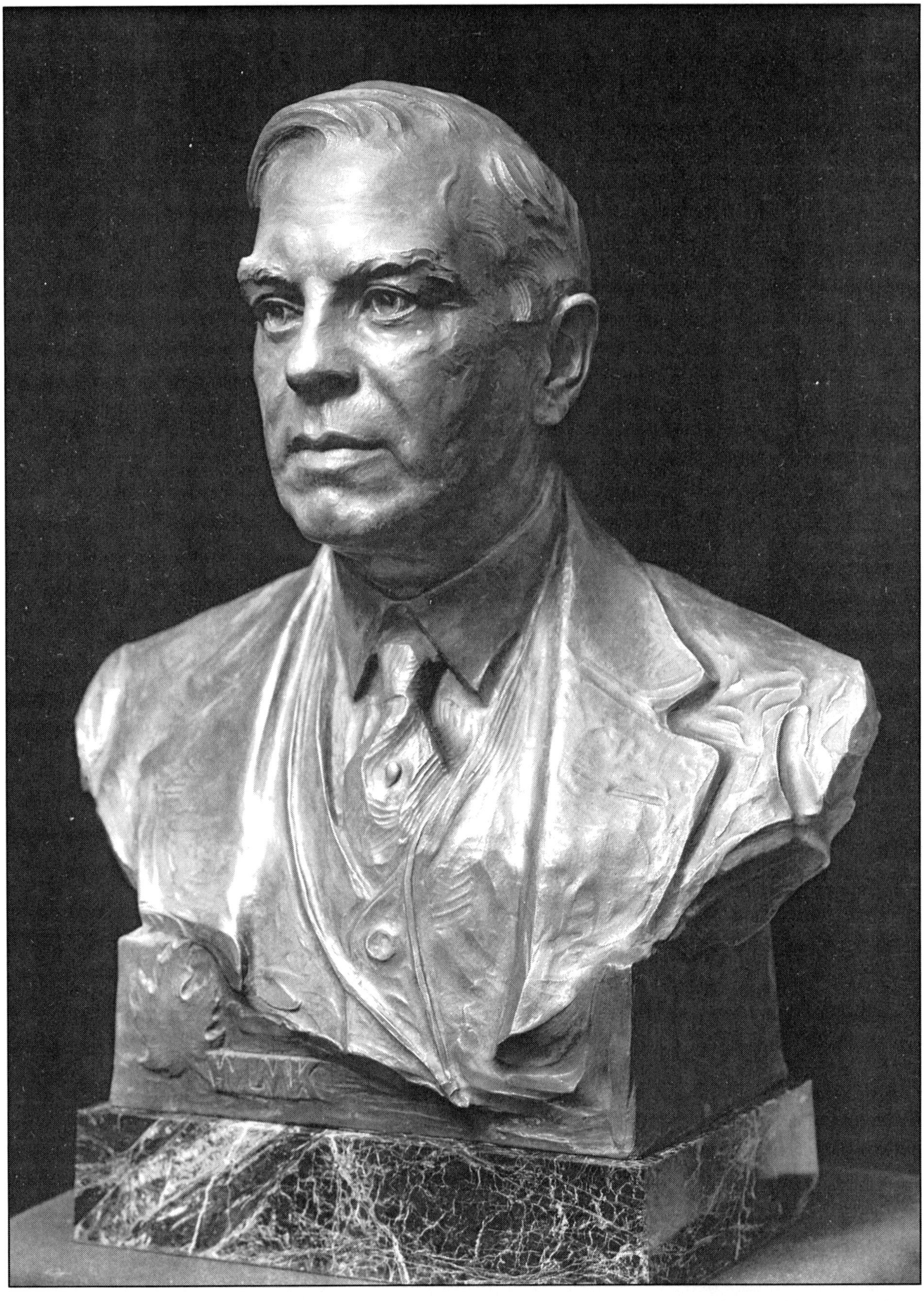

12. Right Honorable William Lyons Mackenzie-King, Prime Minister of Canada: 1943. He was one of the world's great leaders and was Prime Minister of Canada for over twenty- five years. The portrait, cast in bronze, was placed in the Parliament Building in Ottawa, Ontario, Canada.

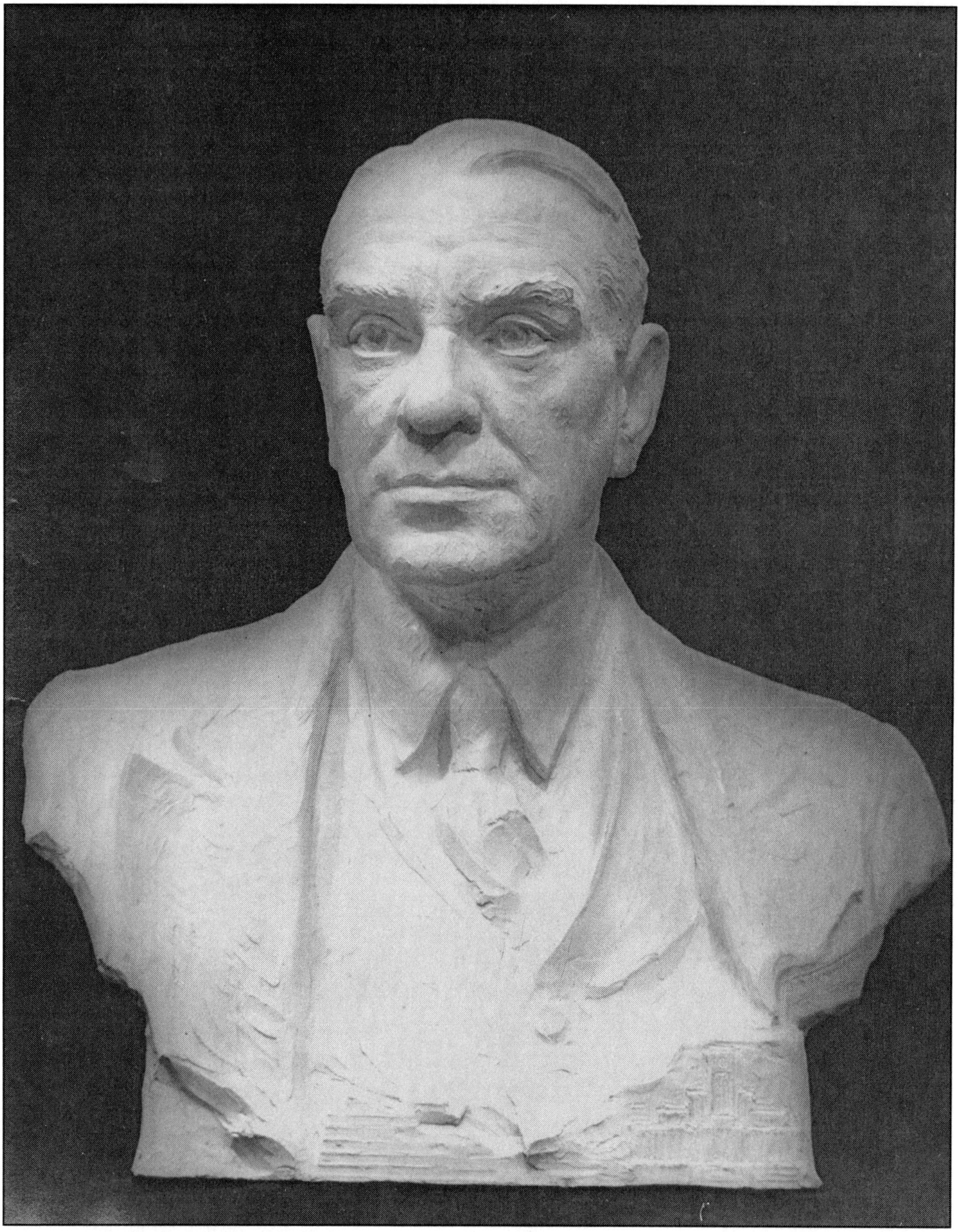

13. Honorable Gerry G. McGreer: 1954. He was elected Mayor of Vancouver, British Columbia, and later he was elected a member of the Canadian Parliament, Ottawa, Ontario, Canada 1954.

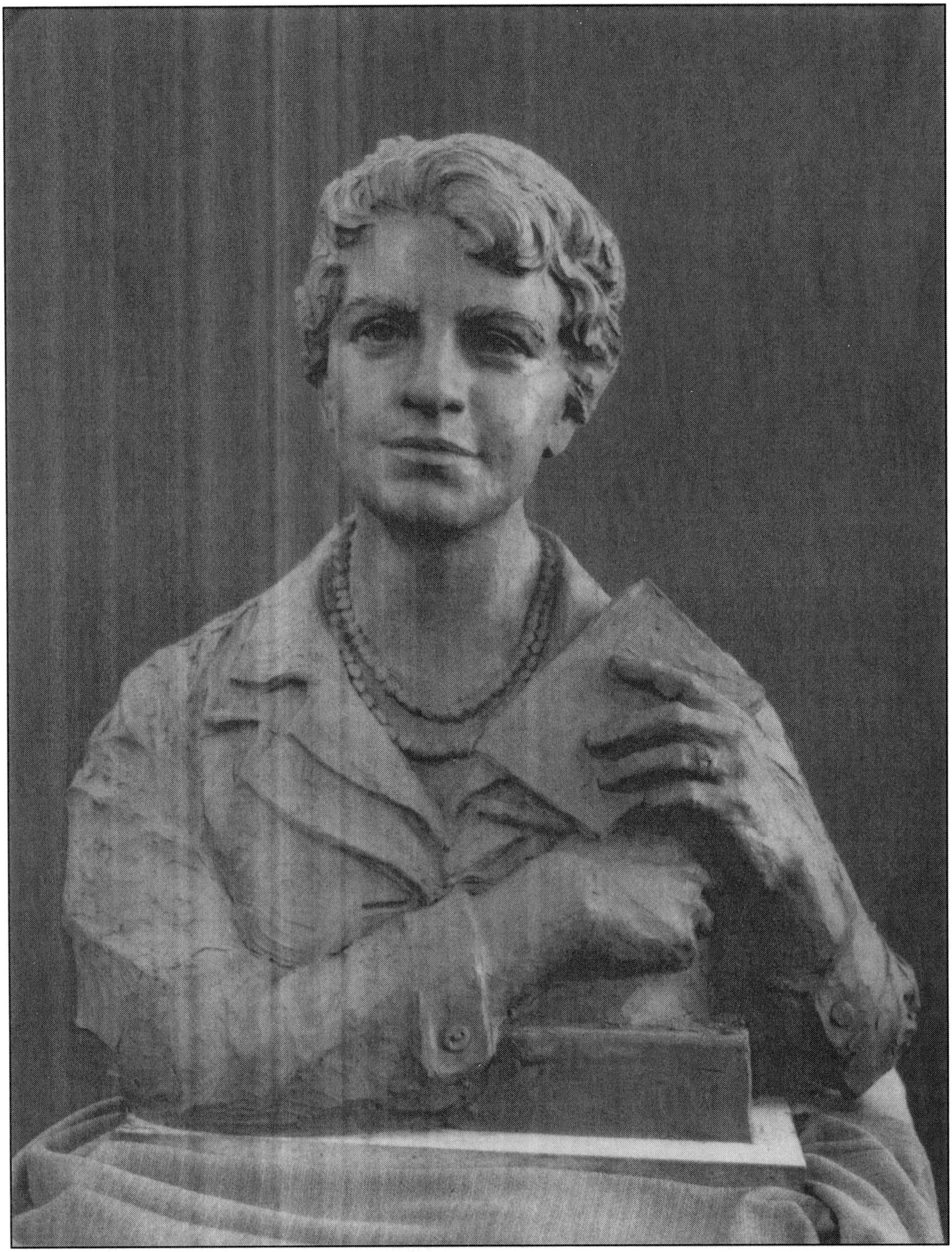

14. Dr. Virginia Cutler, Professor and Chairperson of the Home Economics Department of the University of Utah. She developed the home living center at the University of Utah and the Brigham Young University. She was a delegate of the United States Government to Thailand to establish home living centers in Asiatic nations.

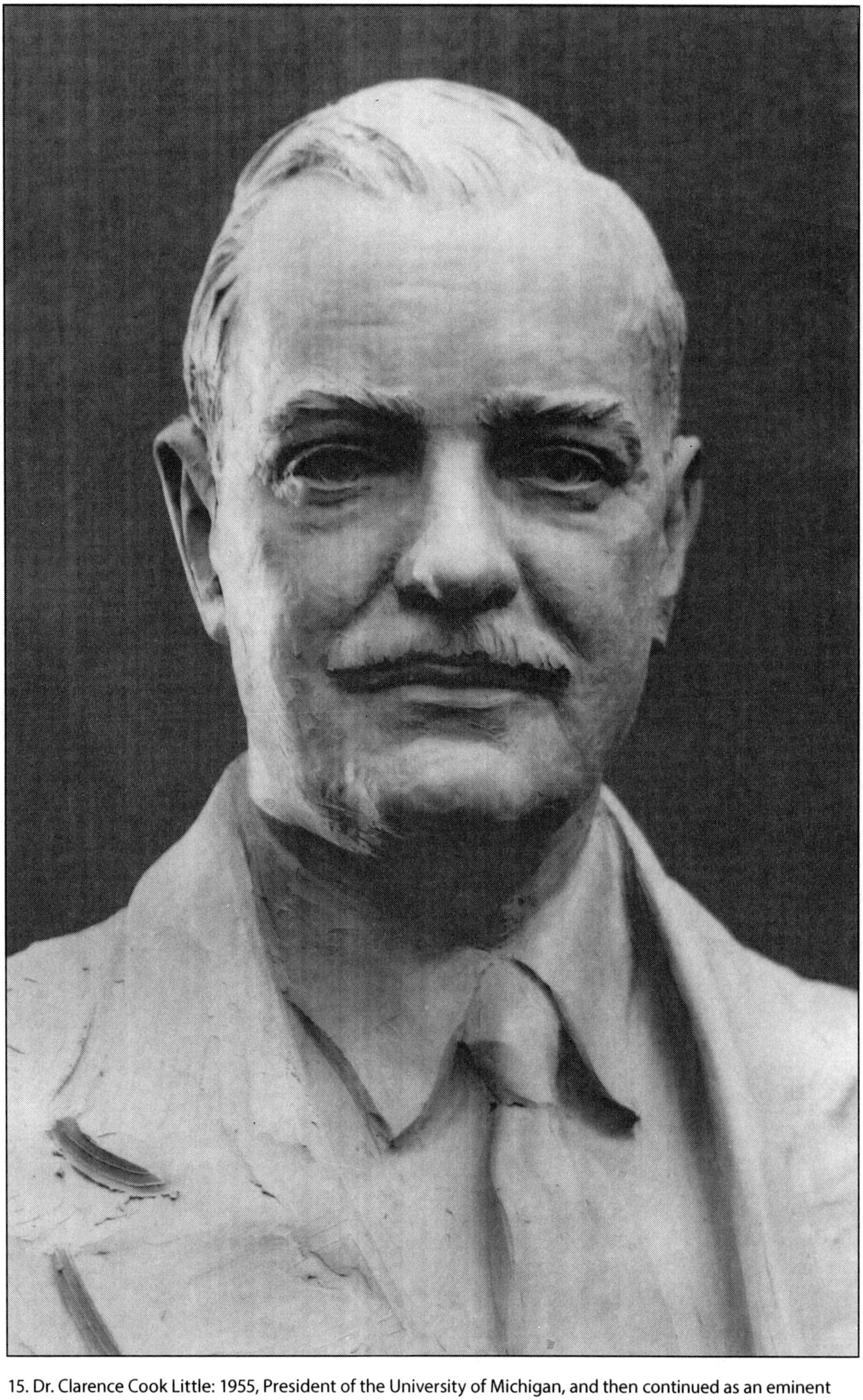

15. Dr. Clarence Cook Little: 1955, President of the University of Michigan, and then continued as an eminent mammalian cancer research scientist at Jackson Laboratory on Mount Desert Island, Bar Harbor, Maine.

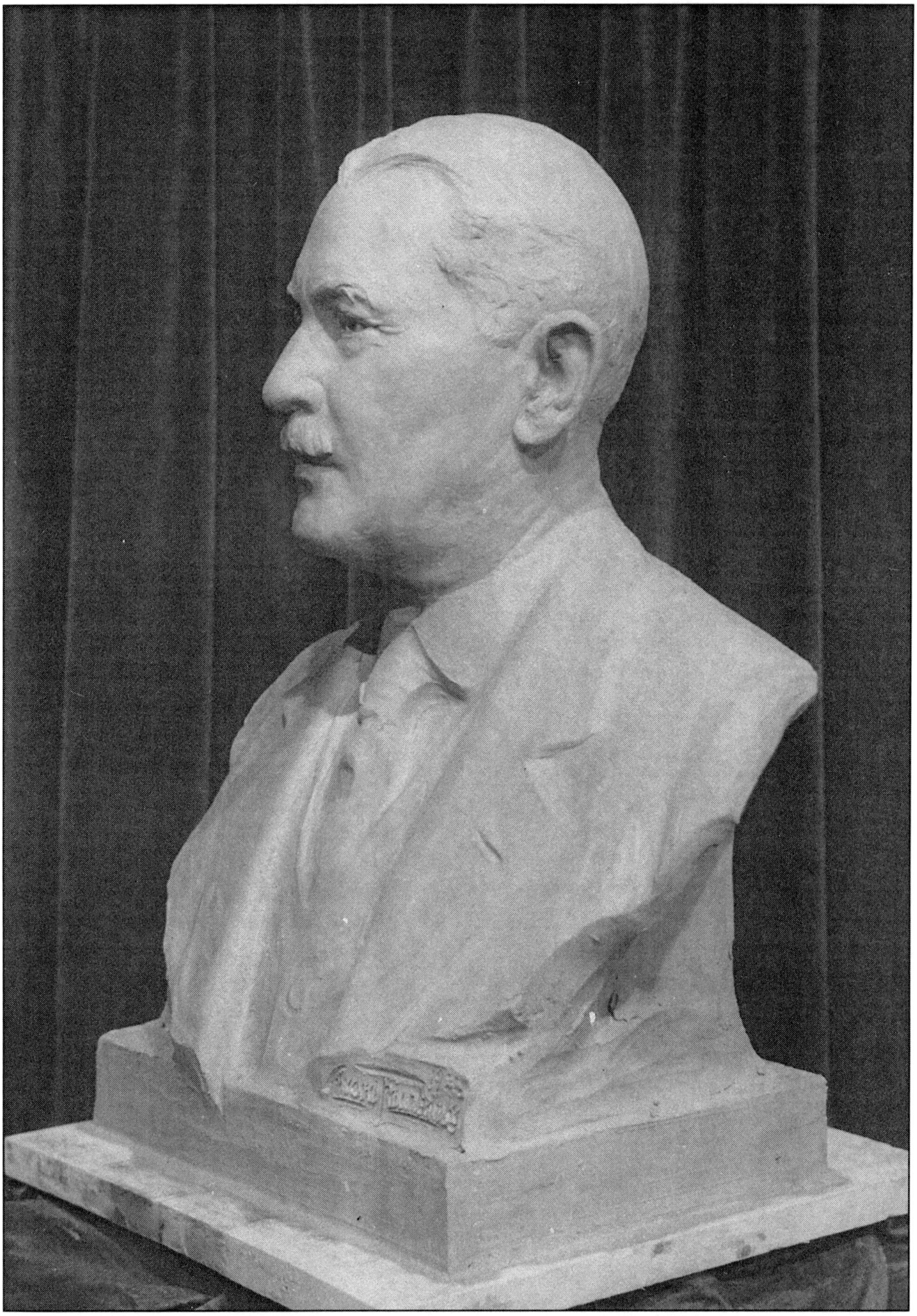

16. Dr. G. Carl Huber: 1932. He was an eminent neuro-anatomist, Professor of Anatomy, and Dean of the Graduate School at the University of Michigan.

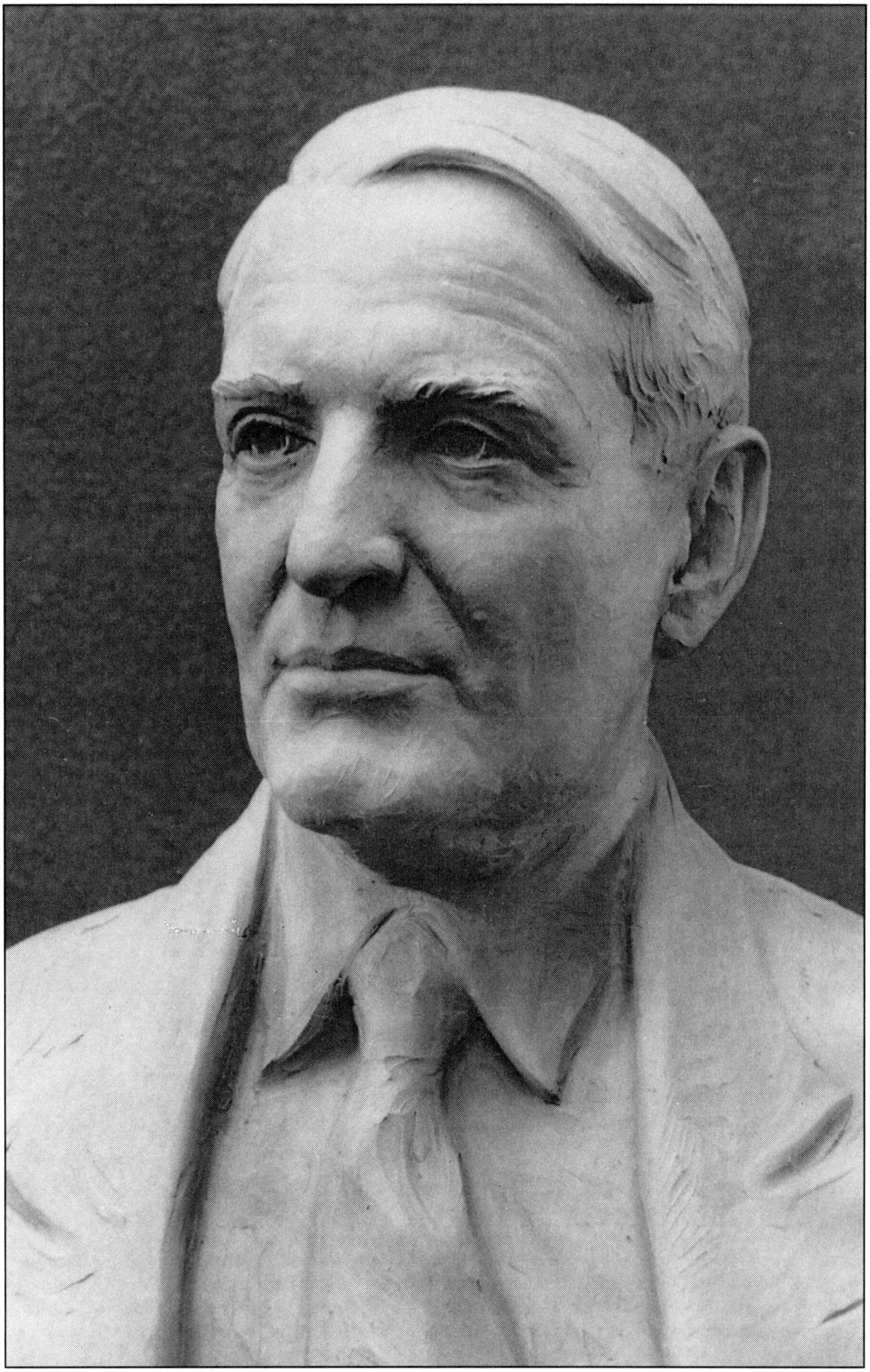

17. Dr. Harvey Fletcher: 1955. A research physicist, he was the Director of the Bell Telephone Laboratories, "The Father of Stereophonic Sound," and the founding Dean of the College of Engineering at the Brigham Young University.

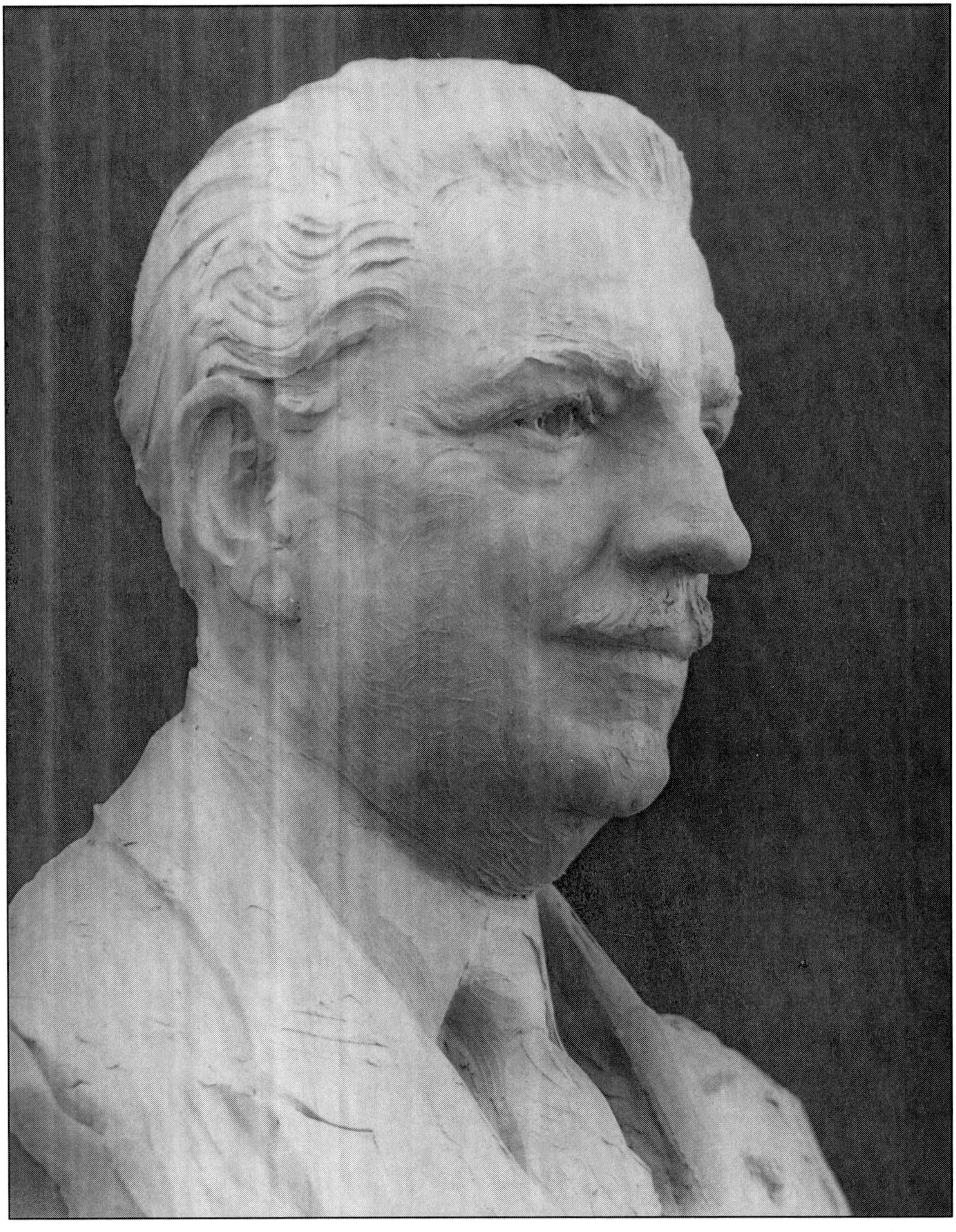

18. Rufus Von KleinSmid; 1955. After promoting and expanding the University of Arizona as its President, he was appointed President of the University of Southern California, an institution of about five thousand students. During his administration, the institution progressively expanded to have a larger campus and faculty and over twenty-five thousand students. For his many achievements, he was honored and awarded the title of Chancellor of the University for Life.

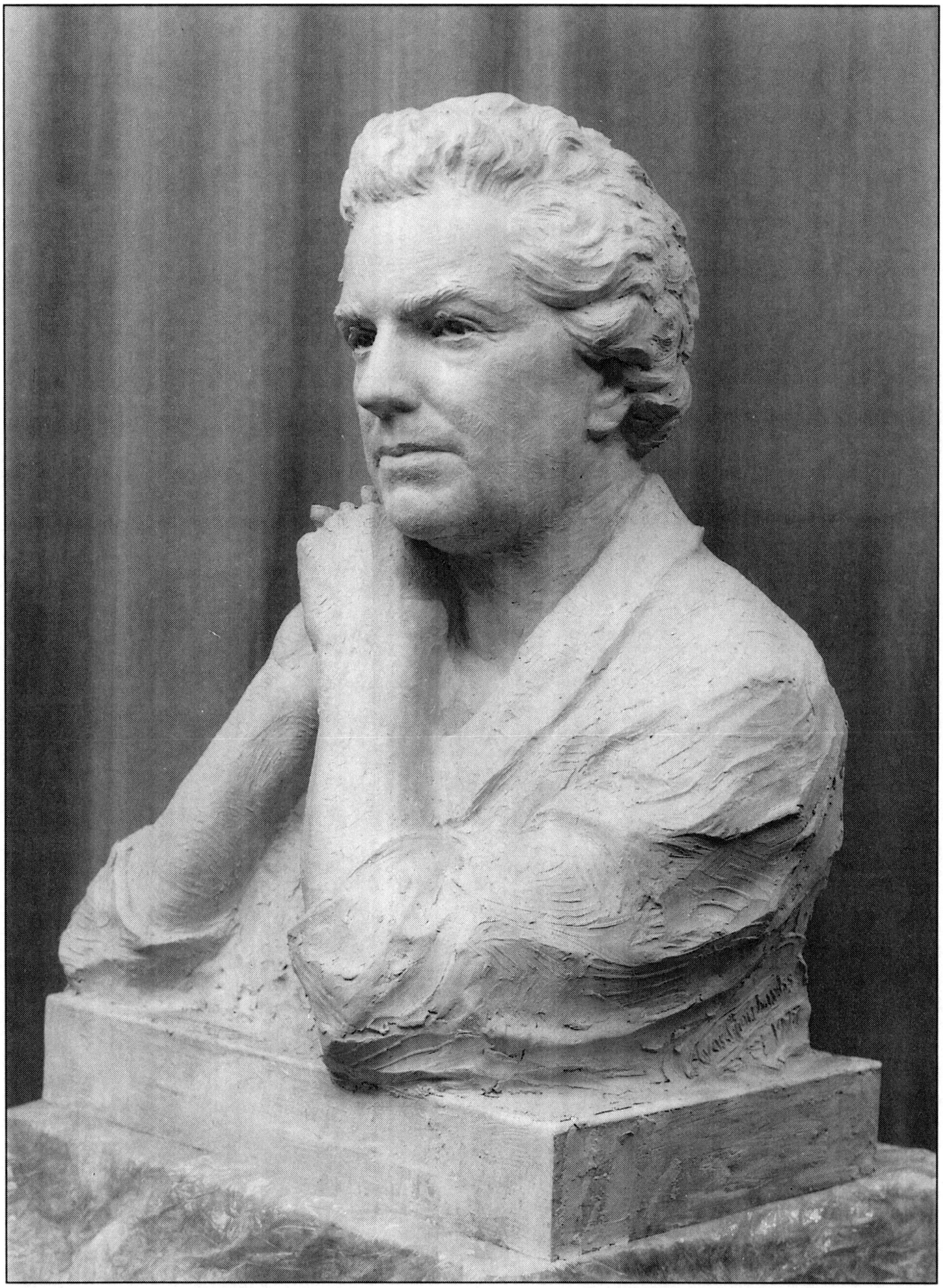

19. Kate Carter: 1977, She was a pioneer leader of the Woman's Relief Society of the Church of Jesus Christ of Latter-Day Saints. The portrait, carved in marble, was placed in the Daughters of the Utah Pioneers Museum, Salt Lake City, UT.

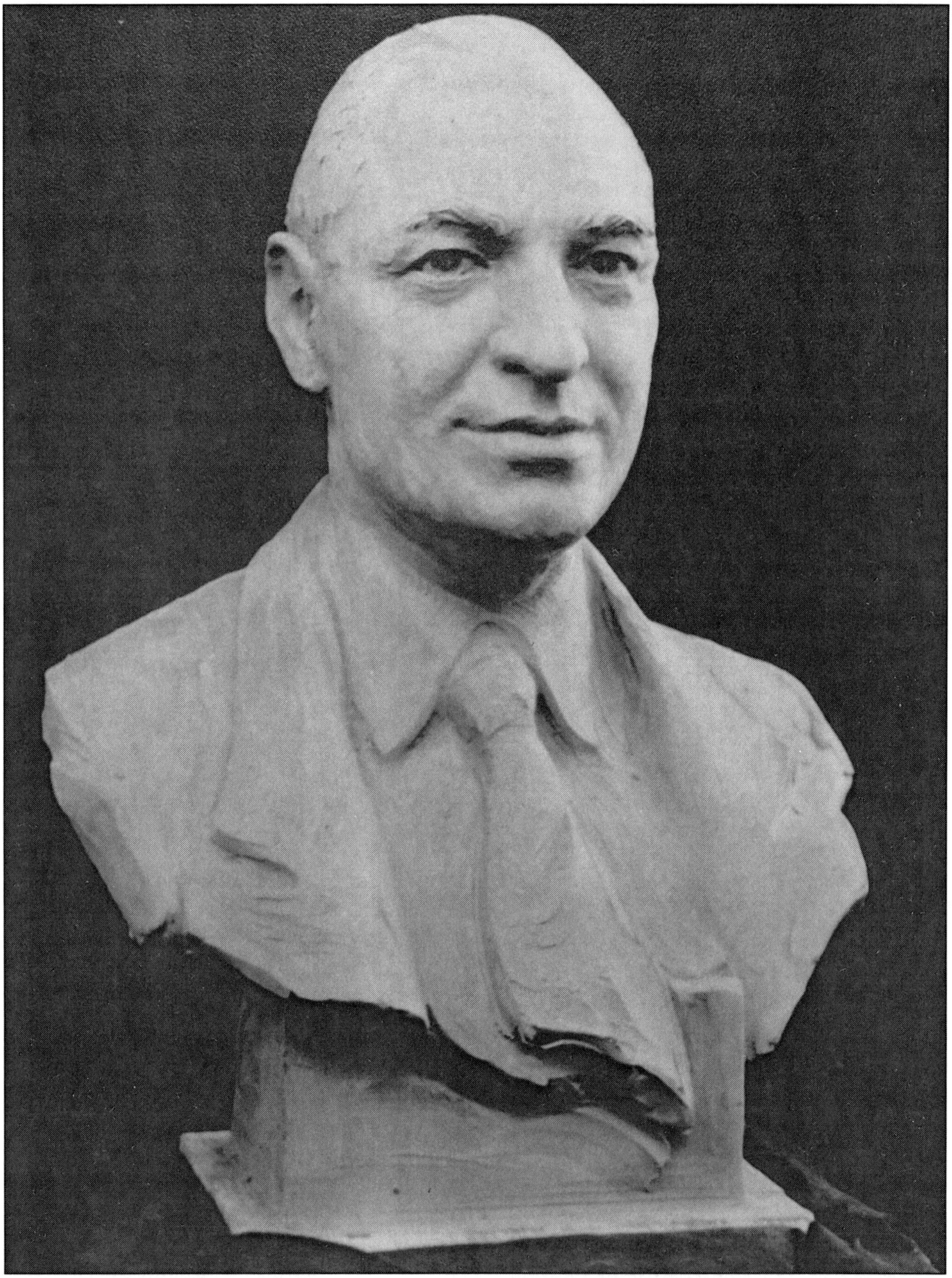

20. Walter P. Chrysler, 1937. He was the founder and Chairman of the Board of the Chrysler Motor Corporation, Detroit, MI. The portrait was cast in bronze and placed in the Chrysler Museum in Norfolk, VA.

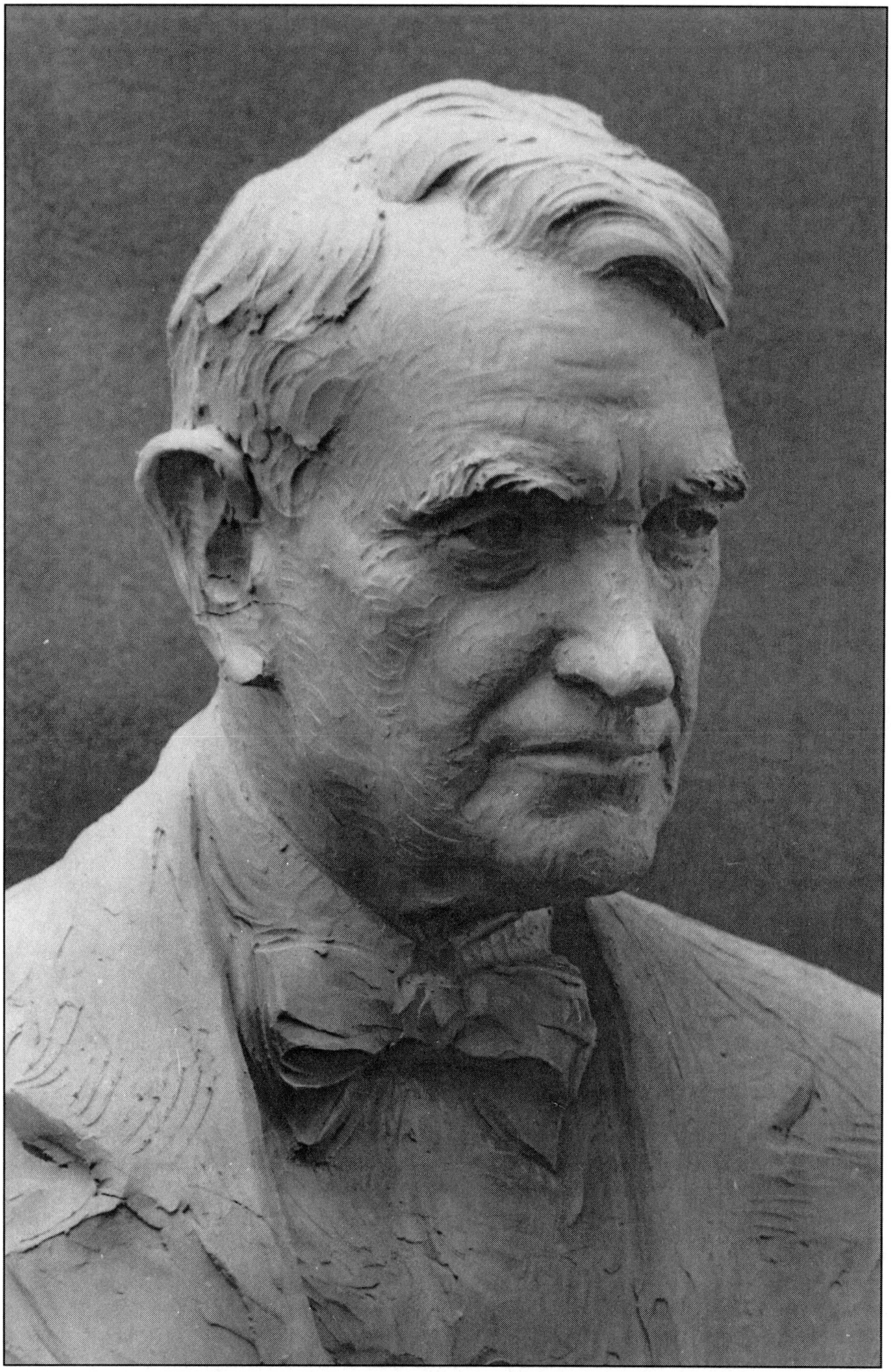

21. Howard R. Driggs: 1952, an educator and historian. He was Chairman of the Department of American Literature at the New York University. He was also a successor to Ezra Meeker as President of the American Trail and Landmarks Association. The portrait was placed in the Howard R. Driggs Elementary School in Salt Lake City, UT.

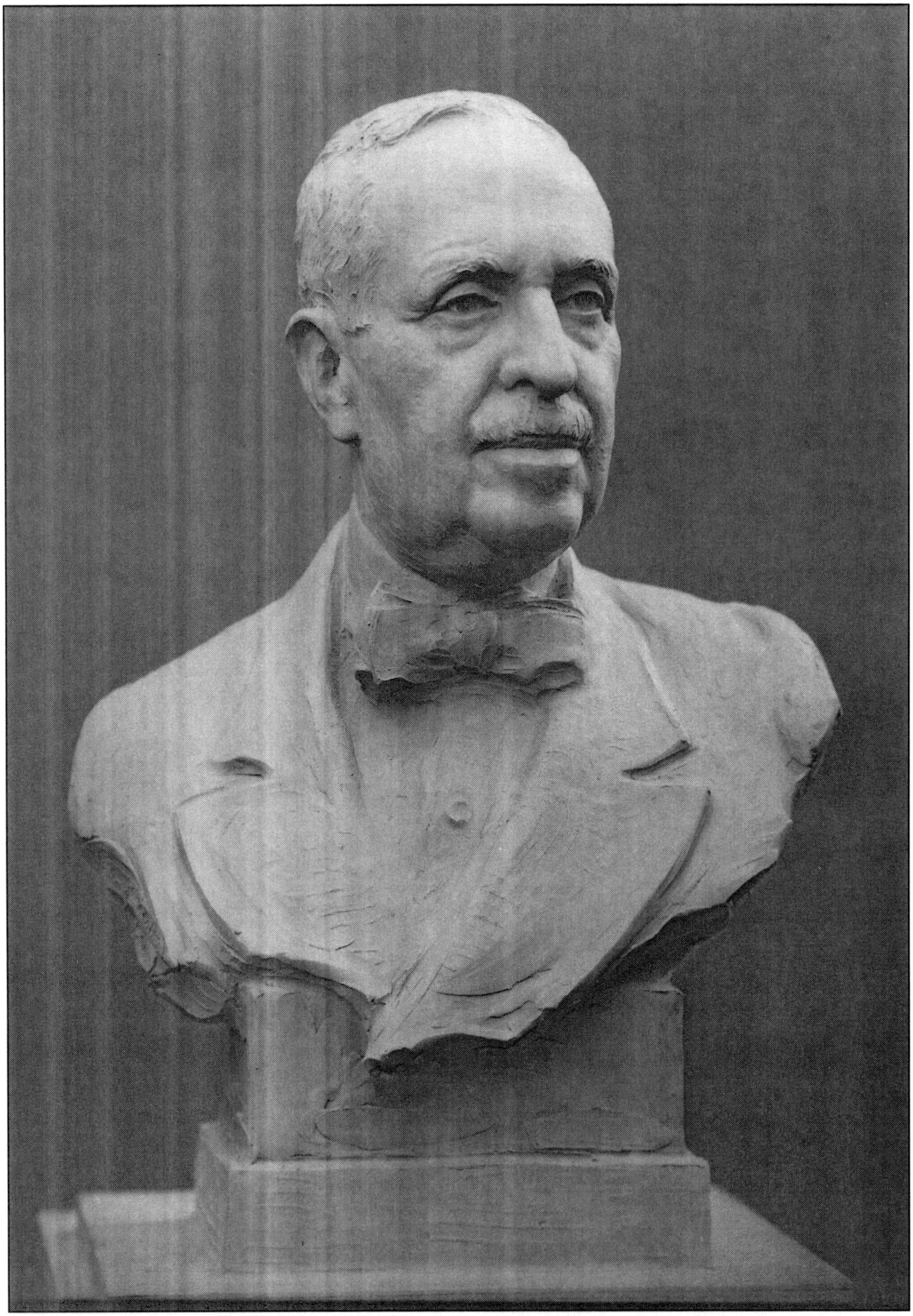

22. James C. Penny: 1954. A merchant, financier, founder, and President of the J.C. Penny Company. The portrait was presented on the Golden Anniversary of the founding of the company.

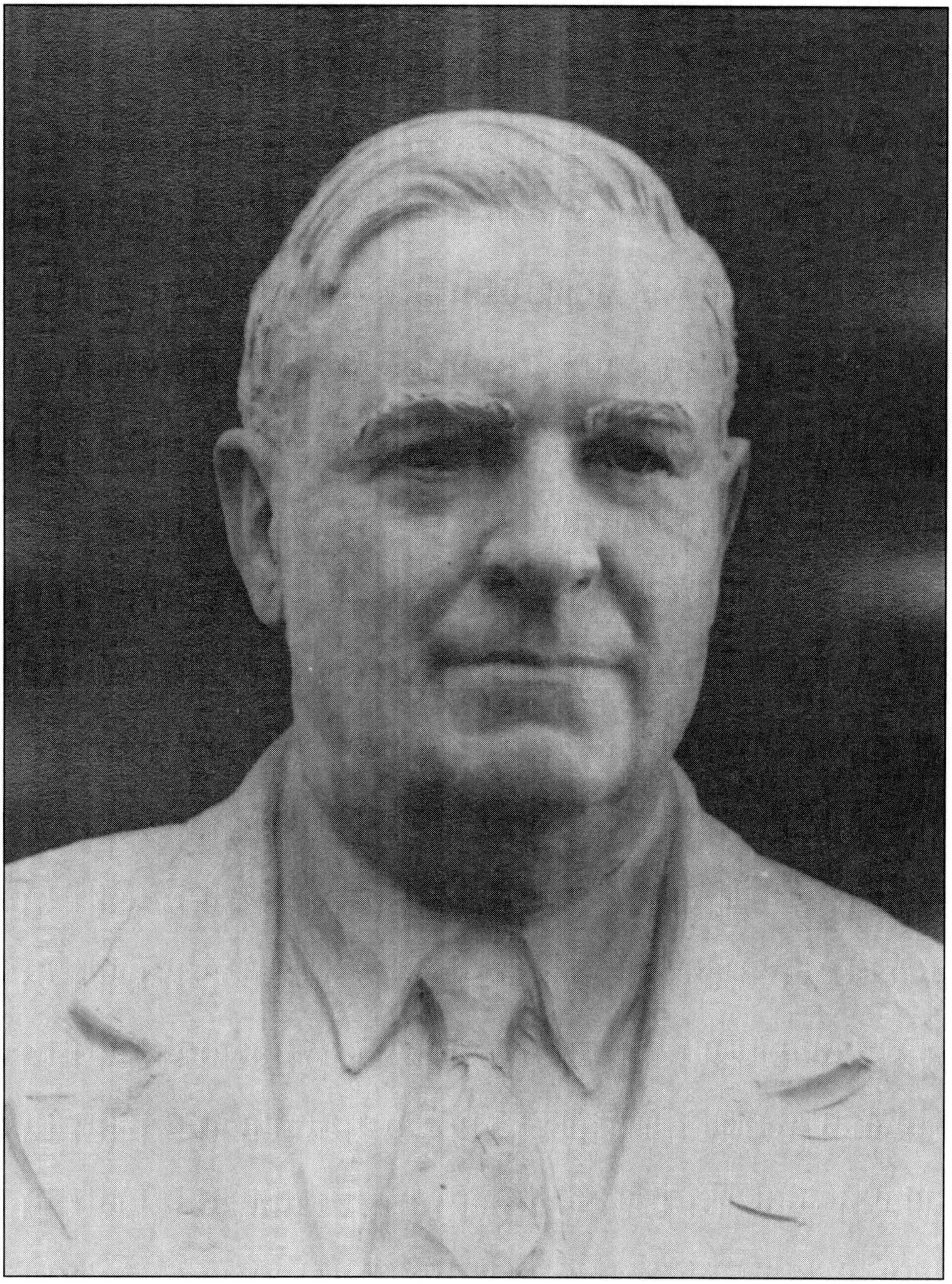

23. J.M. McDonald: Merchant, associate of J.C. Penny, founder of J.M. McDonald Store, Guernsey stock breeder, and philanthropist, 1955.

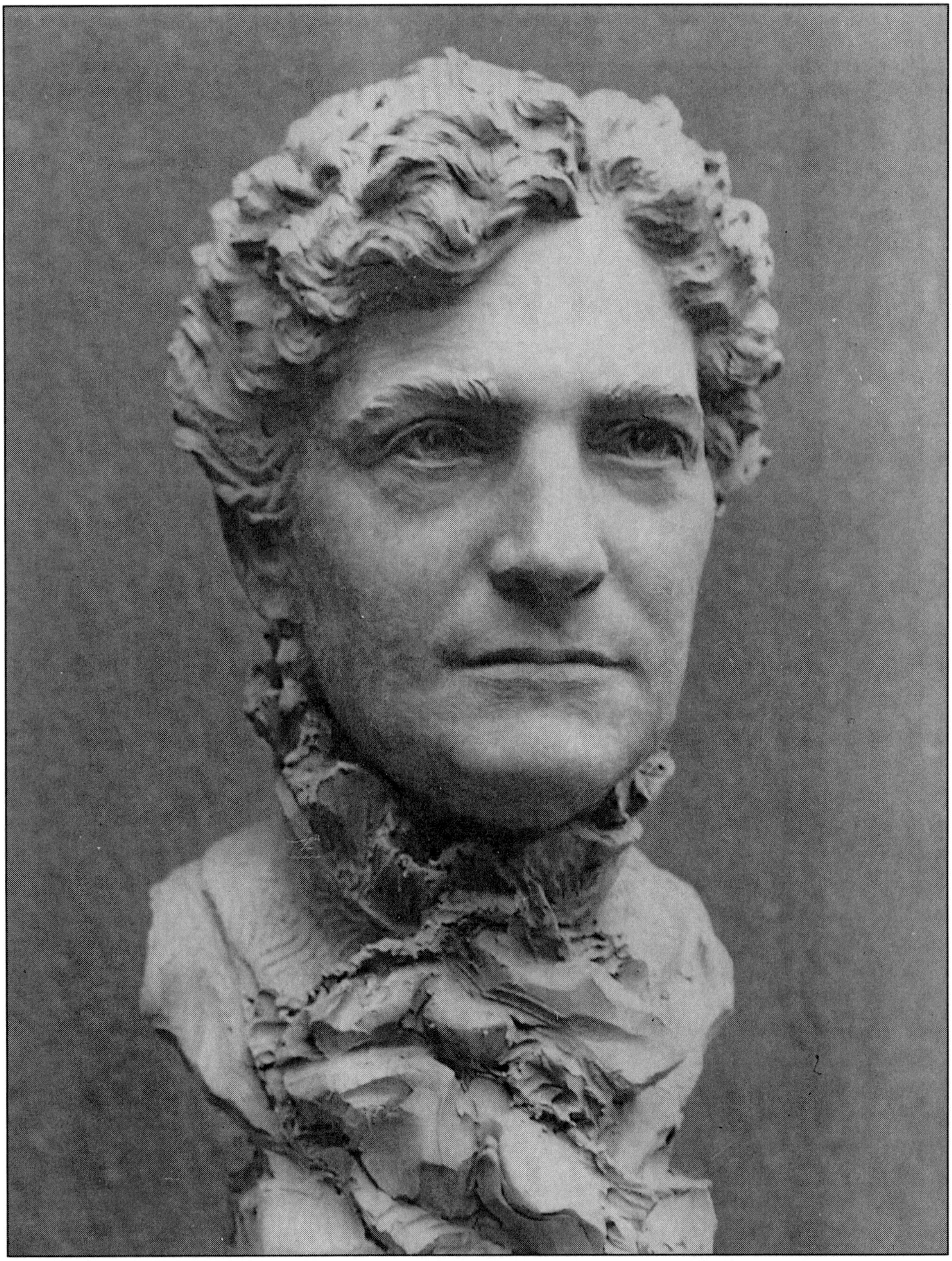

24. Esther Hobart Morris: 1960. While hosting a social event, she encouraged territorial legislators in Wyoming to pass women's suffrage. In 1869, Wyoming was the first state to grant women suffrage. When a Justice of the Peace resigned in protest, she was appointed Justice to replace him. She was the first woman Justice in the United States. In 1976 she served as Vice President of the American Woman Suffrage Association. Avard Fairbanks created a heroic statue of her that was placed in Statuary Hall, Washington, DC, and at the State Capitol, Cheyenne, WY.

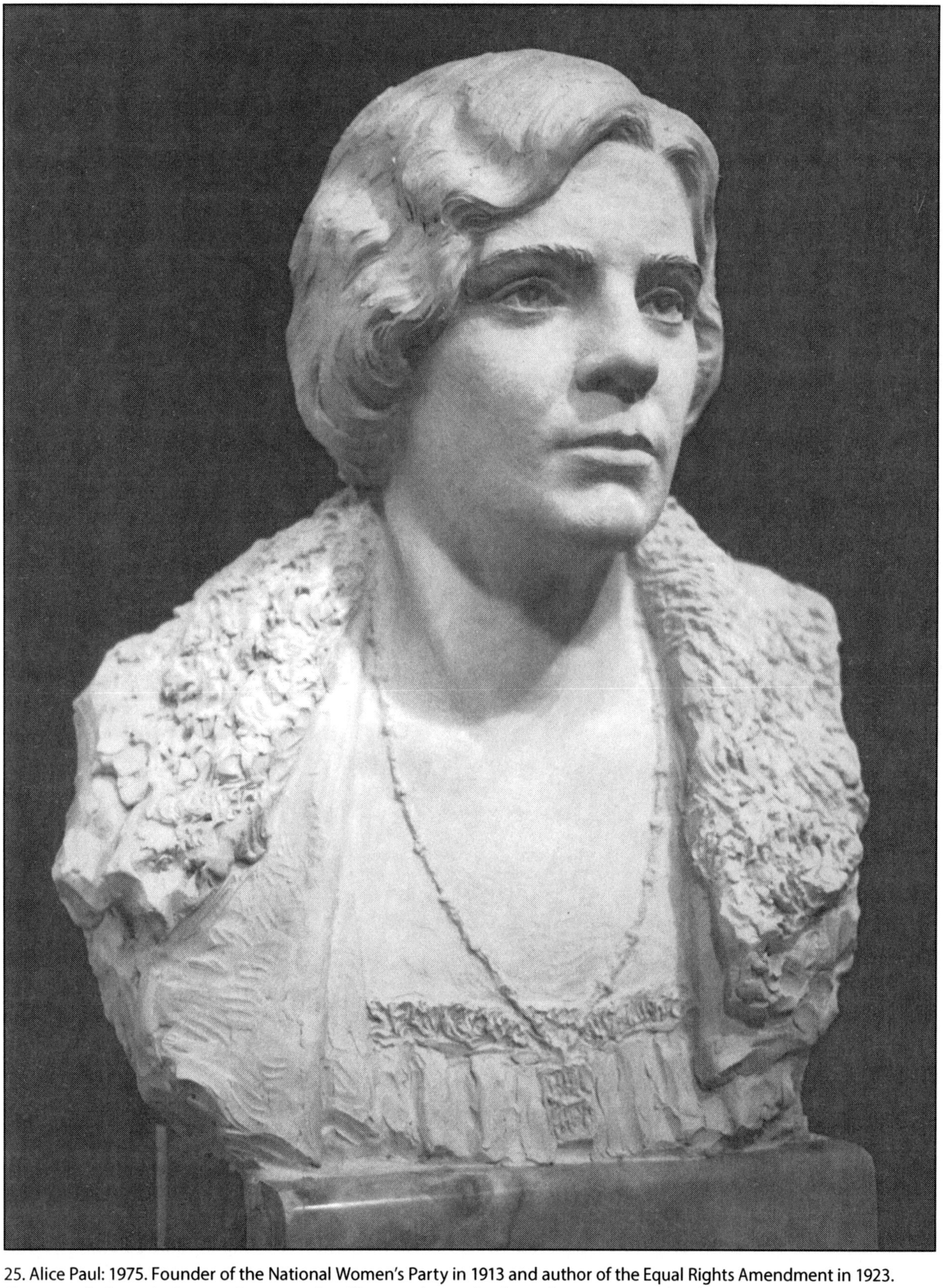

25. Alice Paul: 1975. Founder of the National Women's Party in 1913 and author of the Equal Rights Amendment in 1923. She was a dedicated advocate for women's suffrage and organized parades, protests and pickets promoting the cause. The pendant of her necklace depicted a jail-house door, reminiscent of women jailed for promoting women's suffrage. The bronze portrait was placed in the Sewall-Belmont house, the Headquarters and Museum of the National Women's Party in Washington, DC.

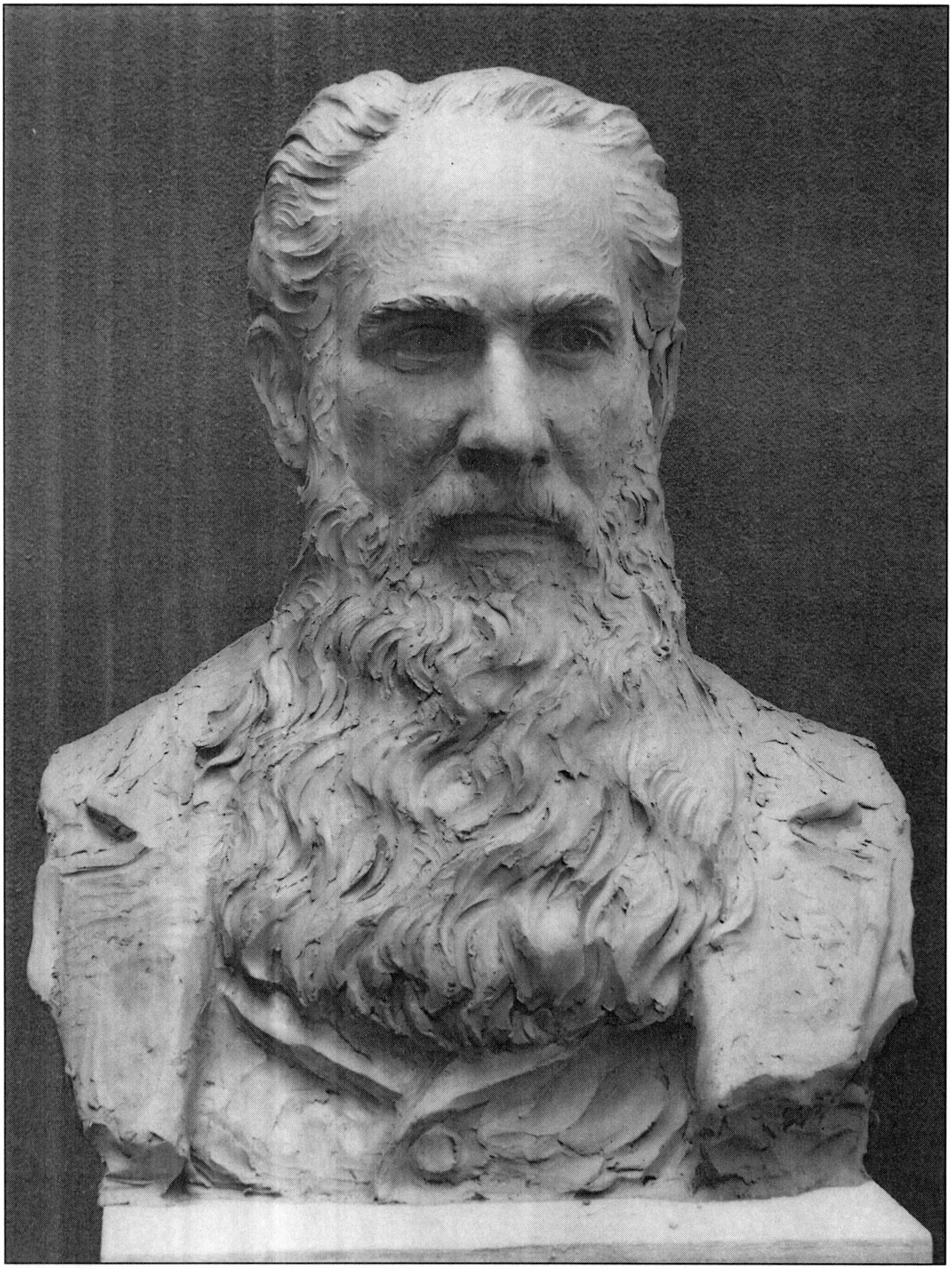

26. Lott Smith: 1963. He was a western pioneer, a scout and the leader in the Echo Canyon conflict of the early Utah Territories.

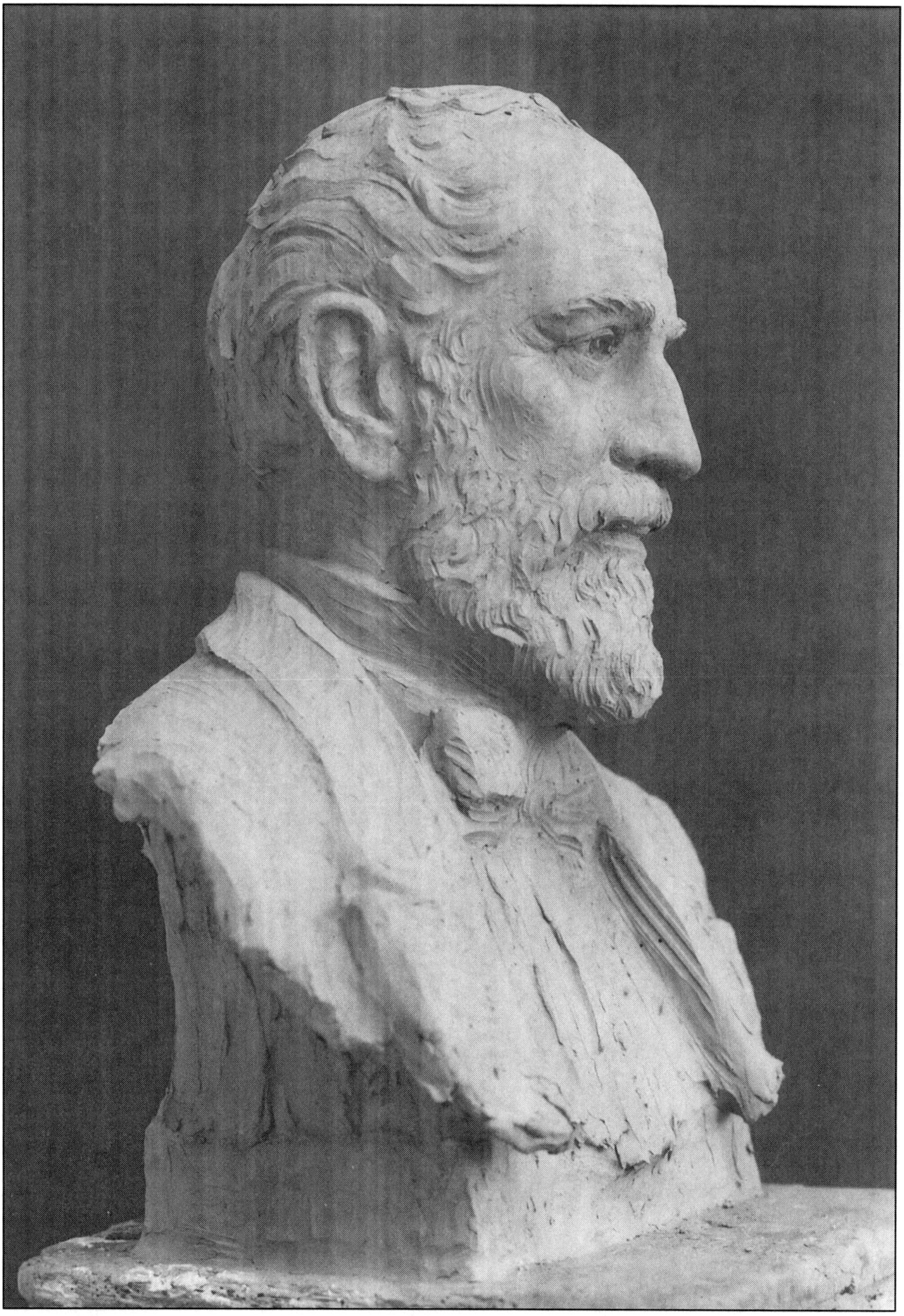

27. Frederick Moench: 1964. A pioneer educator and founder of the Weber State University, Ogden, Utah. A heroic statue was erected at the campus.

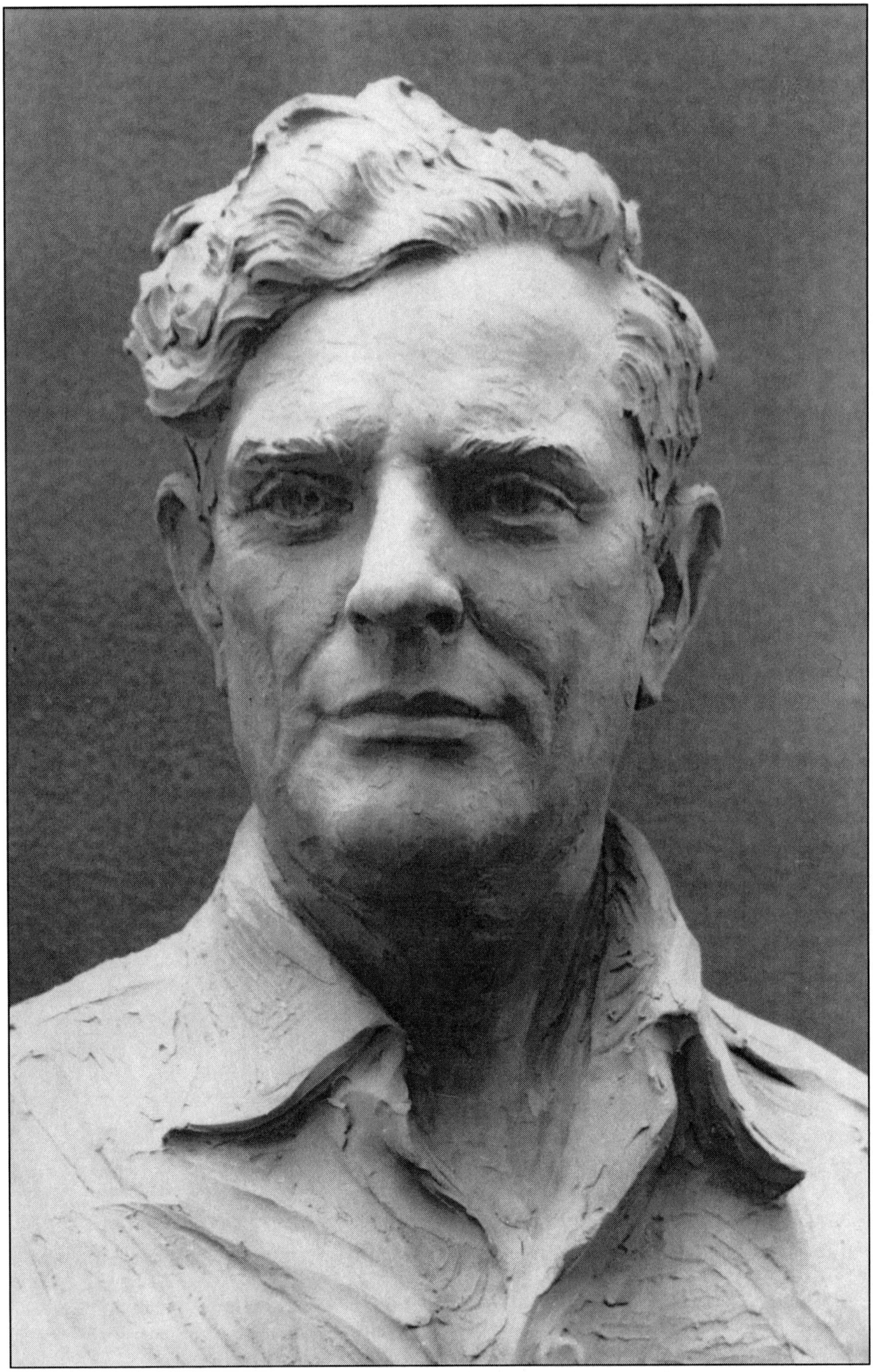

28. Marshall Dana: 1955, an eminent journalist in Portland, Oregon and a leader in National Reclamation efforts.

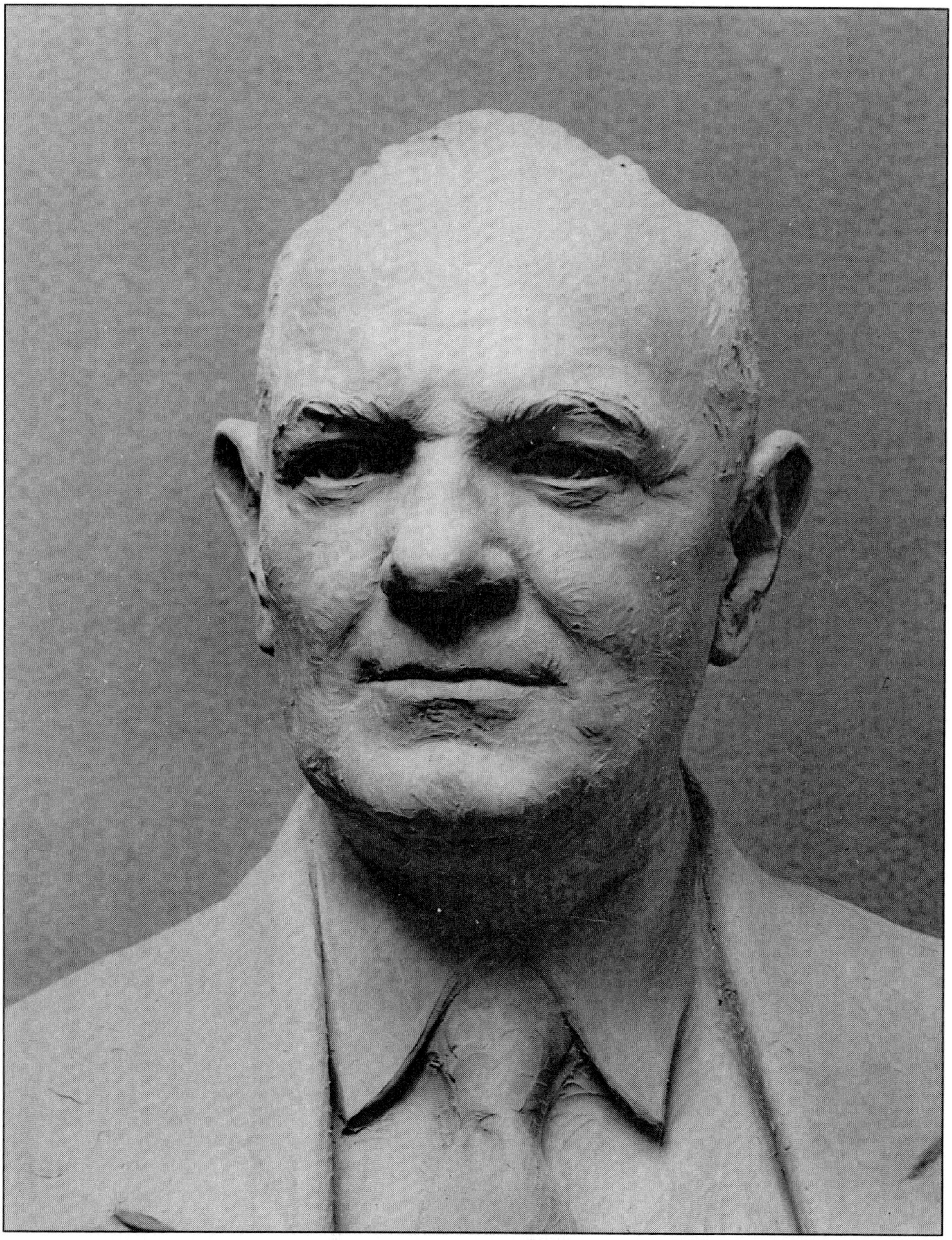

29. Lamar Tooze: a wounded veteran of World War I. He later became a prominent attorney in Portland, Oregon. During World War II, he was called again to military service and was progressively advanced in rank, retiring as a Major General.

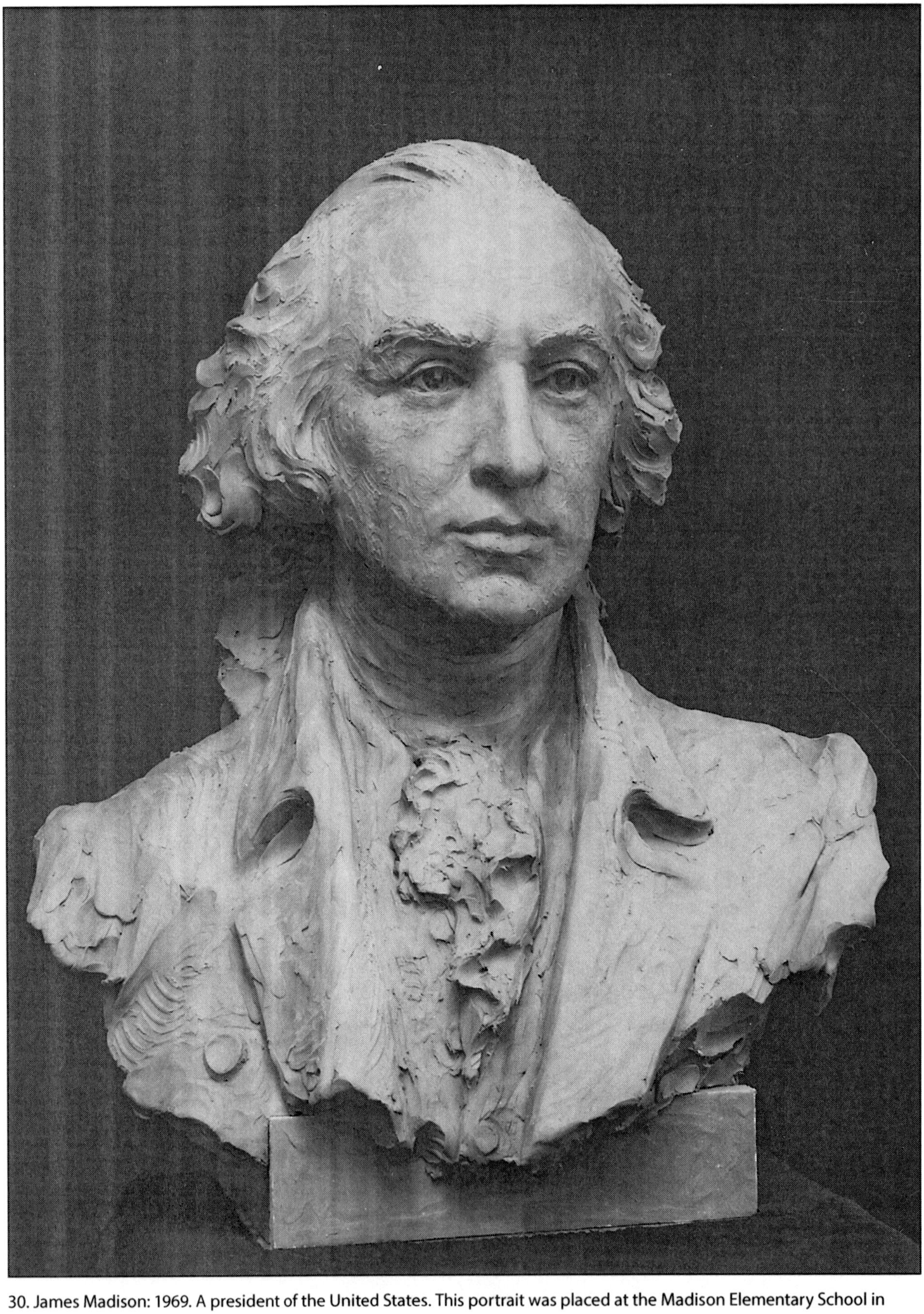

30. James Madison: 1969. A president of the United States. This portrait was placed at the Madison Elementary School in Salt Lake City, UT.

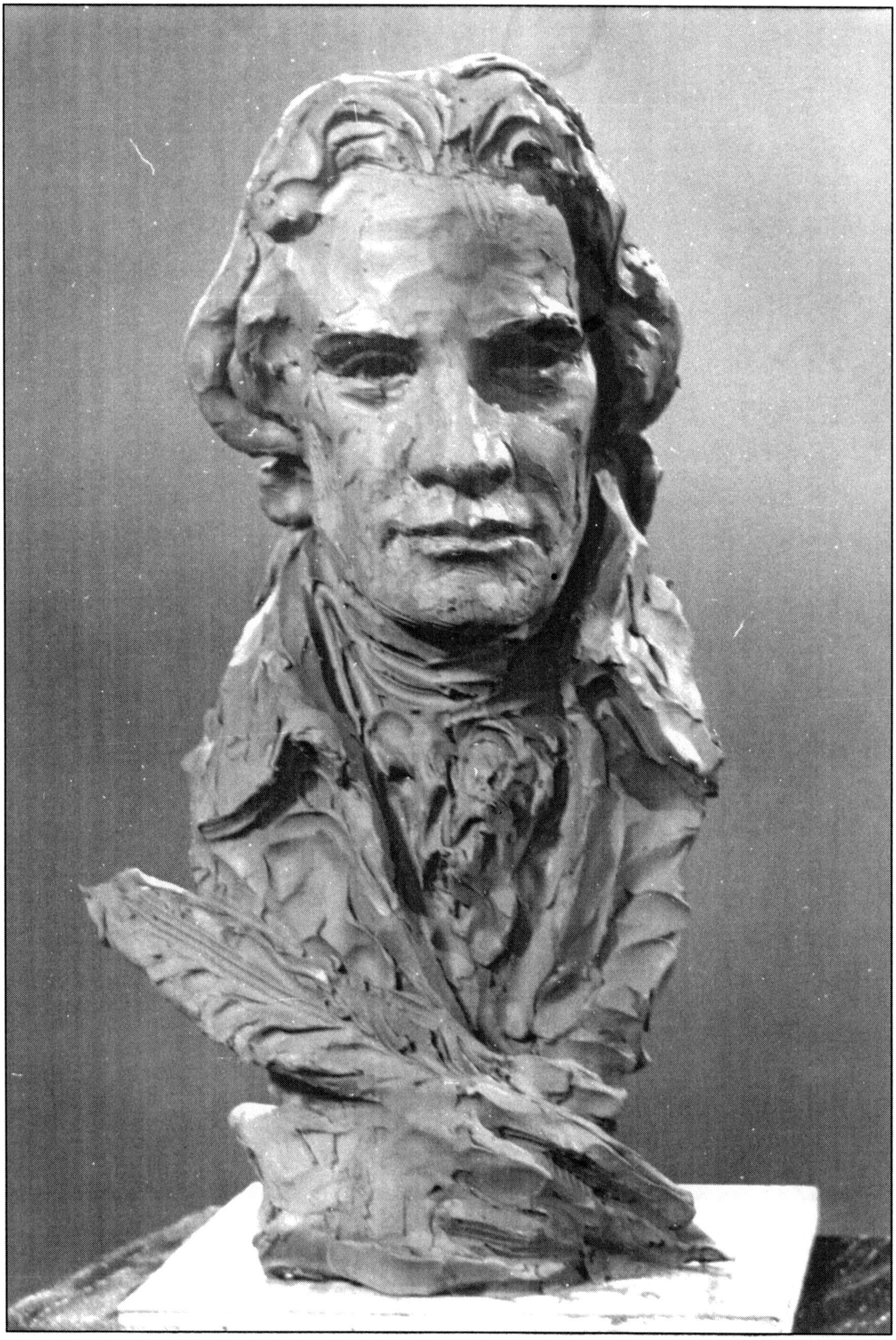

31. Thomas Jefferson and the Declaration of Independence: 1982. A marble portrait was placed at the Kenmore International Center for Jefferson Studies at the Jefferson Estate, Monticello, VA. A bronze portrait was placed at the University of Virginia in Charlottesville, VA. And a bronze portrait was placed in the Jefferson Elementary School in Rochester, MN. Shown is the beginnings of the plasteline modeling.

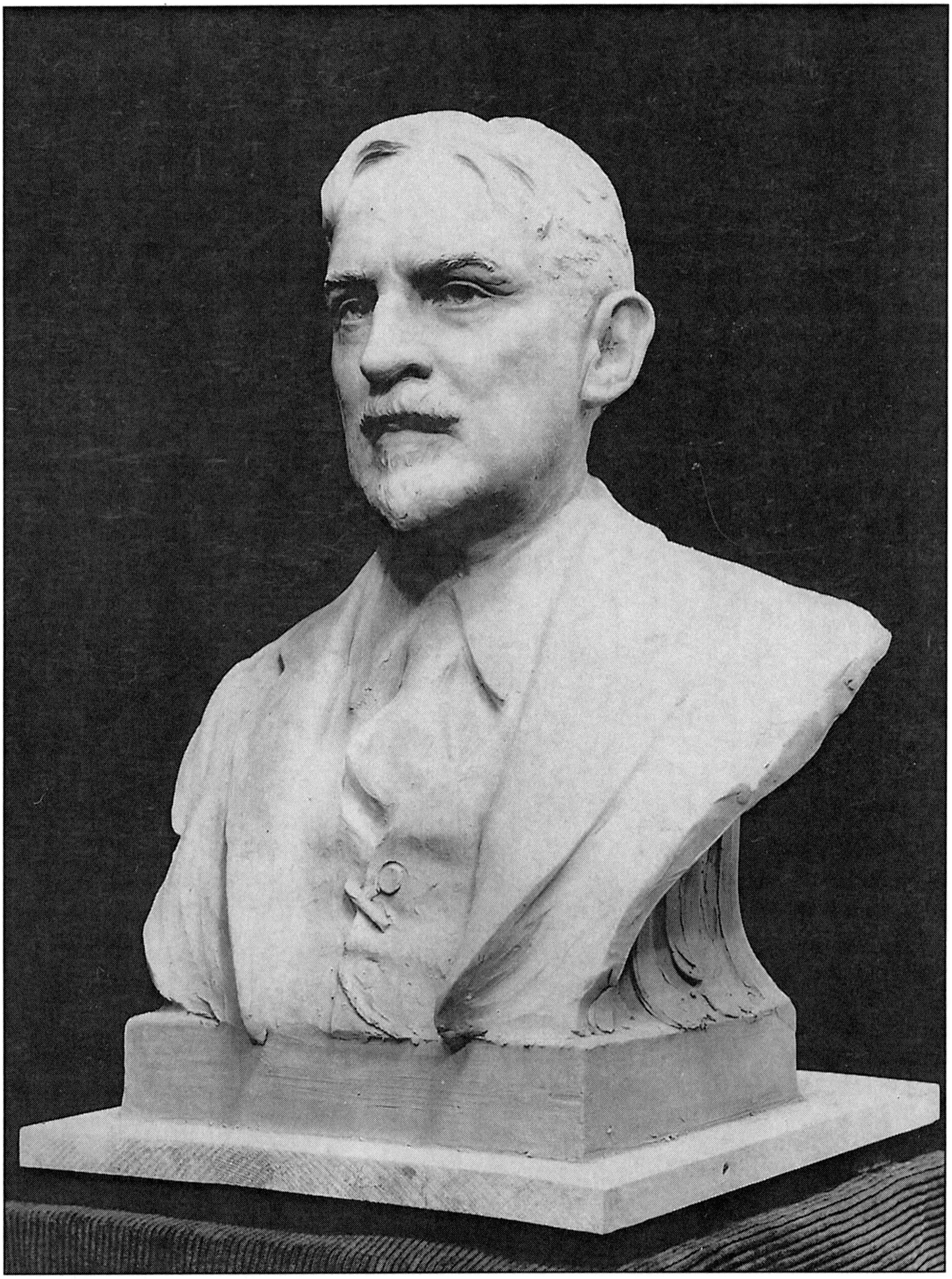

32. Dr. William B. Pillsbury: 1932. Professor of Psychology, and Chairman of the Department of Psychology at the University of Michigan.

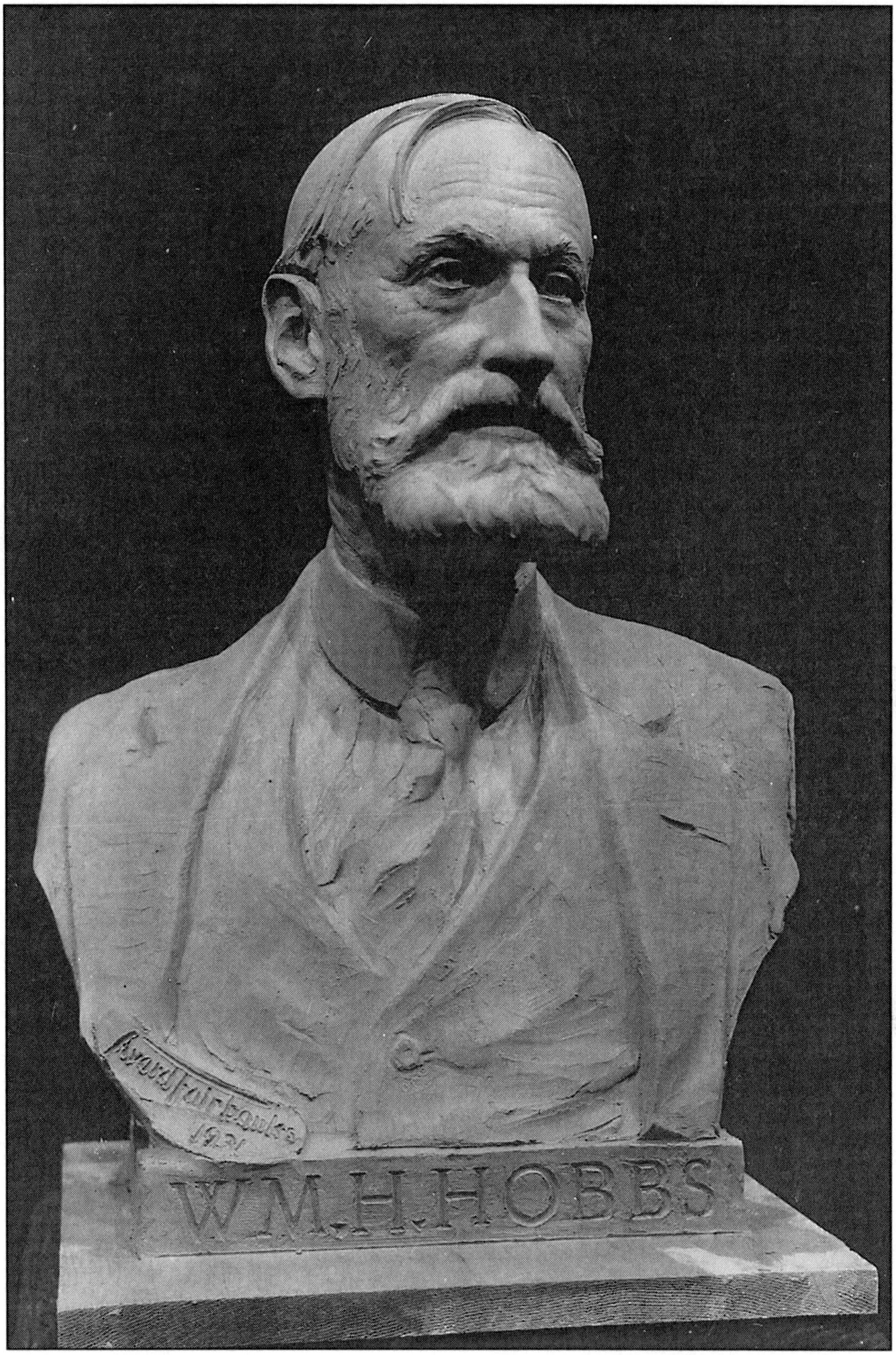

33. Dr. William Hobbs: 1930. He was a Professor of Geology and Chairman of the Geology Department at the University of Michigan.

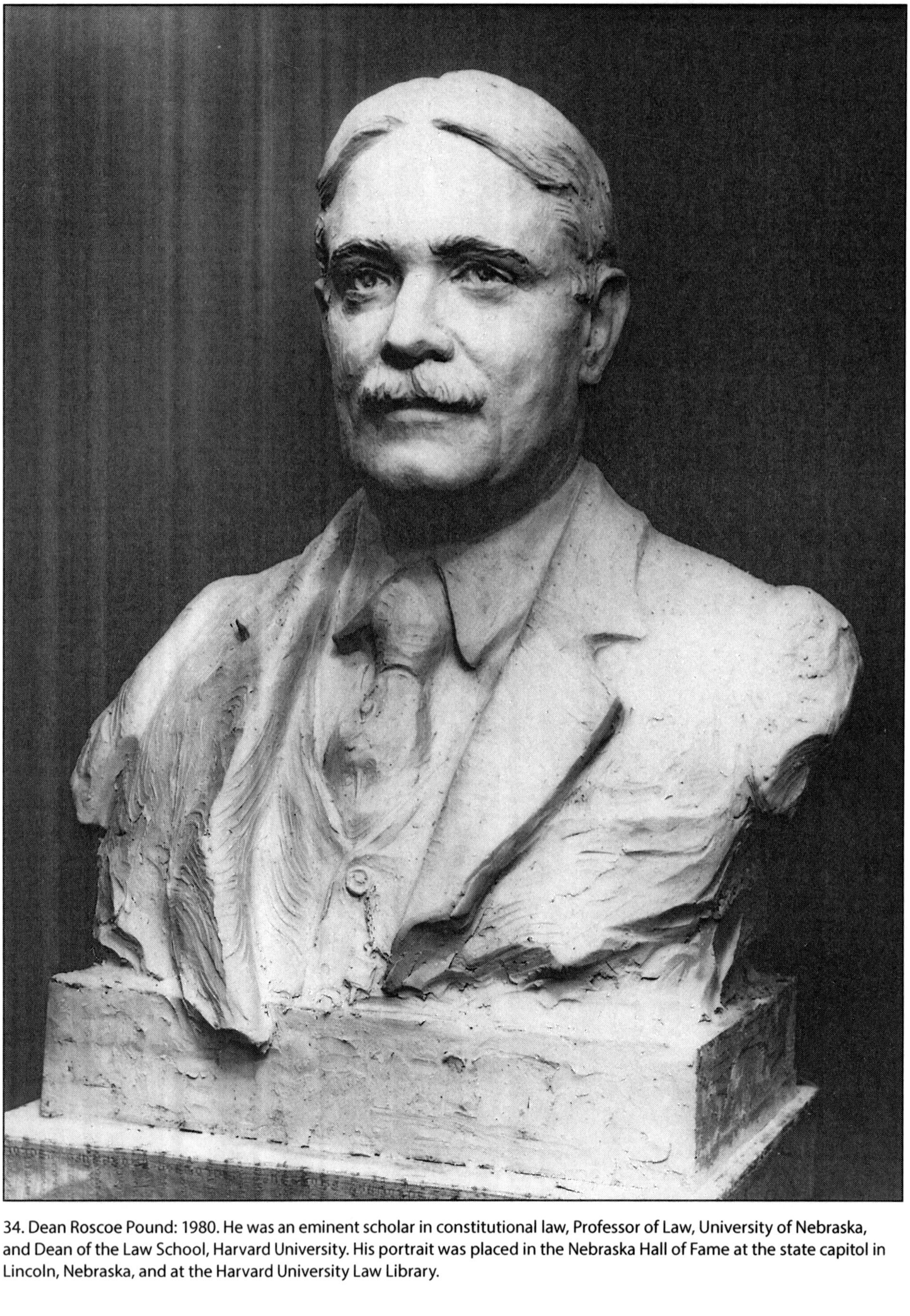

34. Dean Roscoe Pound: 1980. He was an eminent scholar in constitutional law, Professor of Law, University of Nebraska, and Dean of the Law School, Harvard University. His portrait was placed in the Nebraska Hall of Fame at the state capitol in Lincoln, Nebraska, and at the Harvard University Law Library.

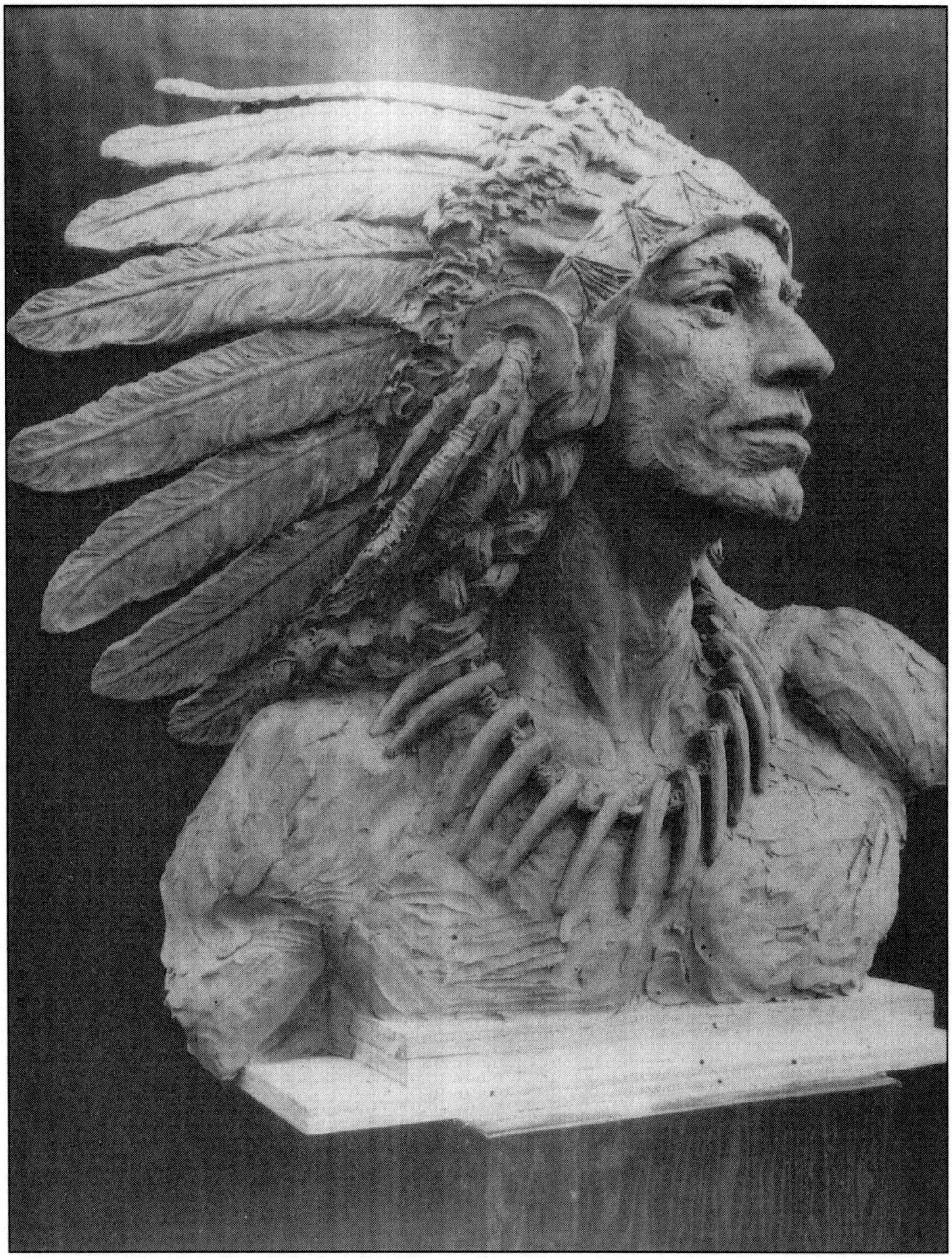

35. The Sioux Warrior: 1965. The portrait was created representing "The Fighting Sioux" for the Athletic Building at the University of North Dakota.

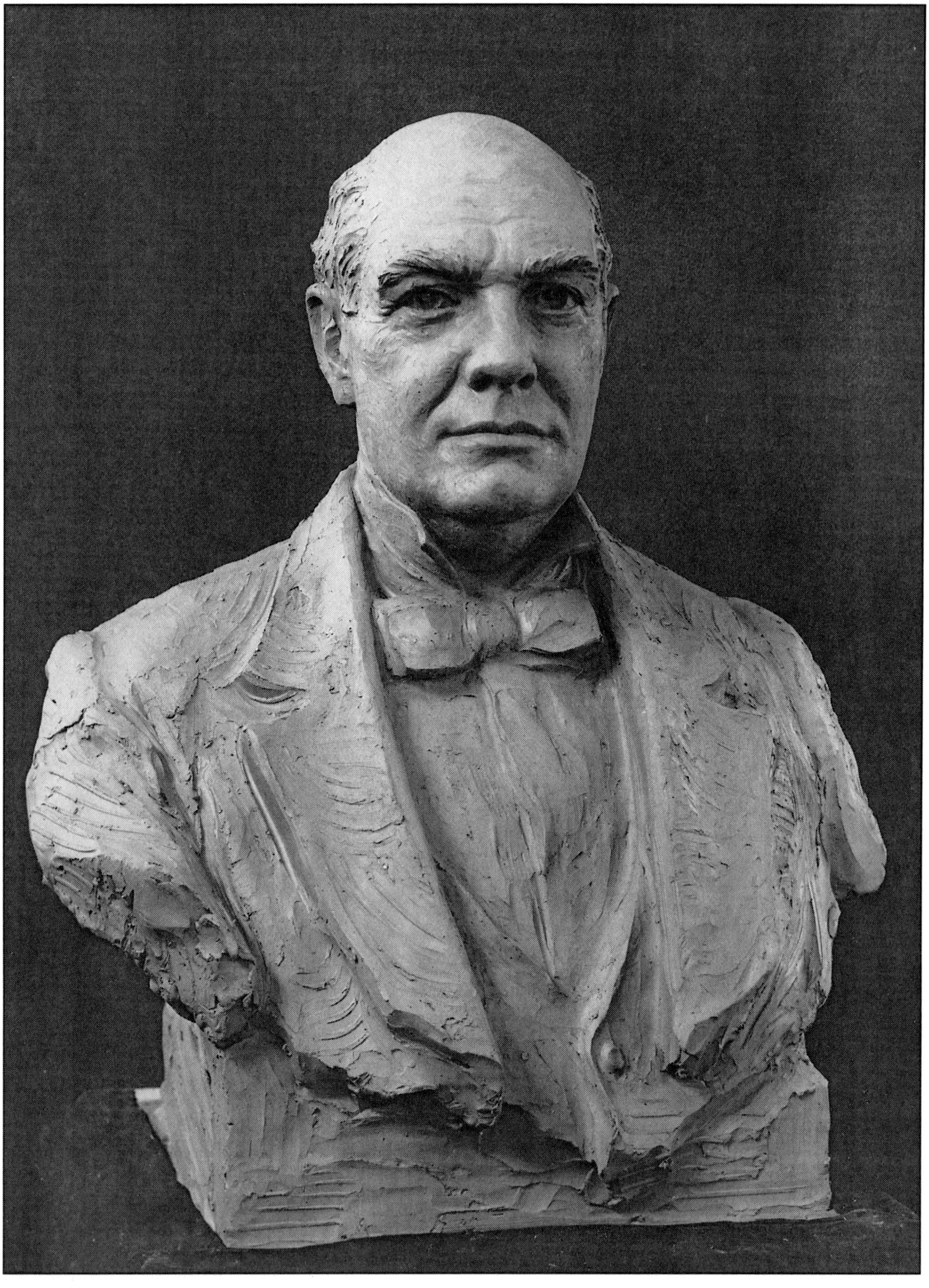

36. Samuel Cosgrove: 1953. A jurist at Pomeroy, Washington. He was elected Governor of the State of Washington. The heroic portrait was erected at the Garfield County Courthouse, at Pomeroy, WA.

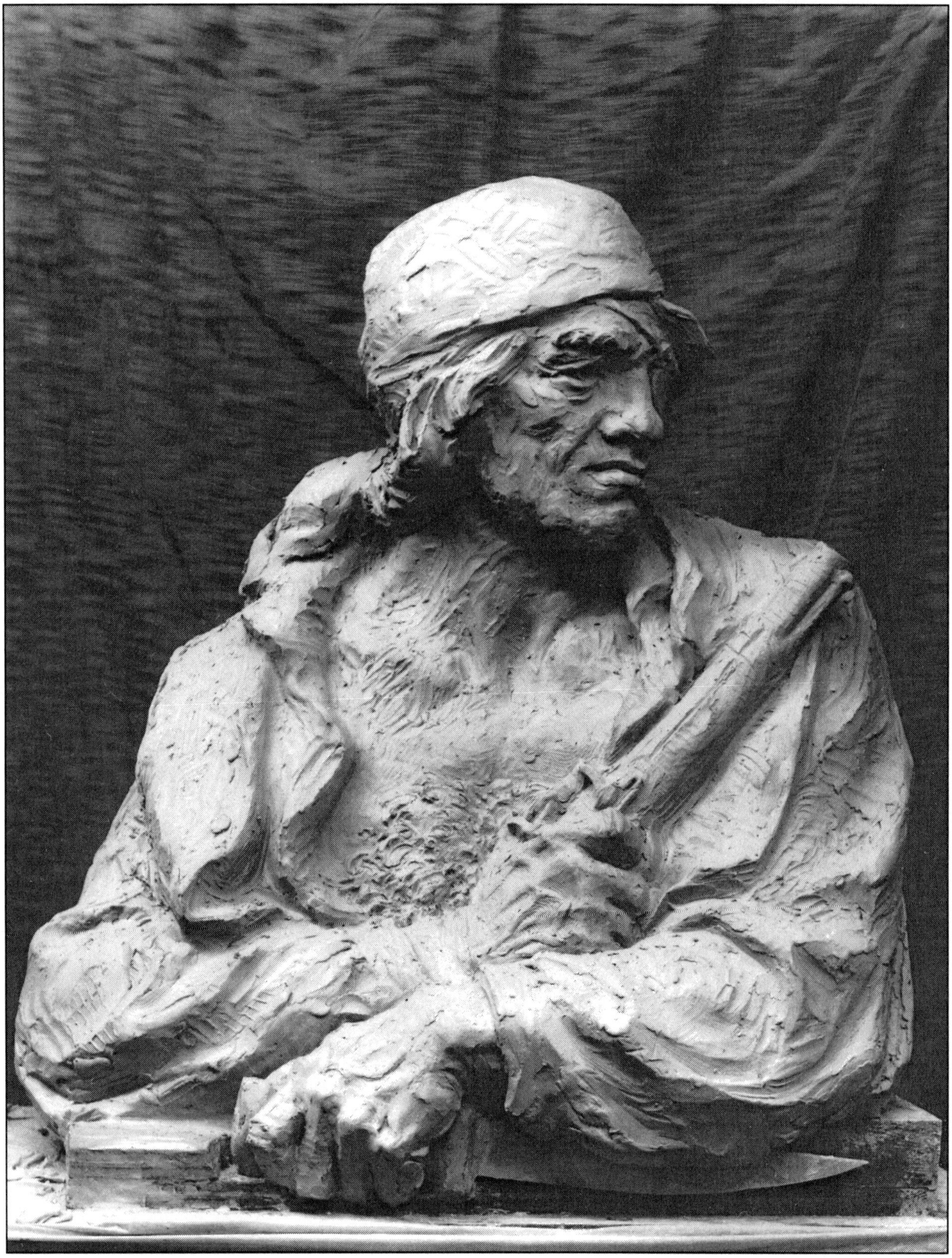

37. The Pirate: 1970, for the high school mascot. It was placed at Magna High School, Magna, UT.

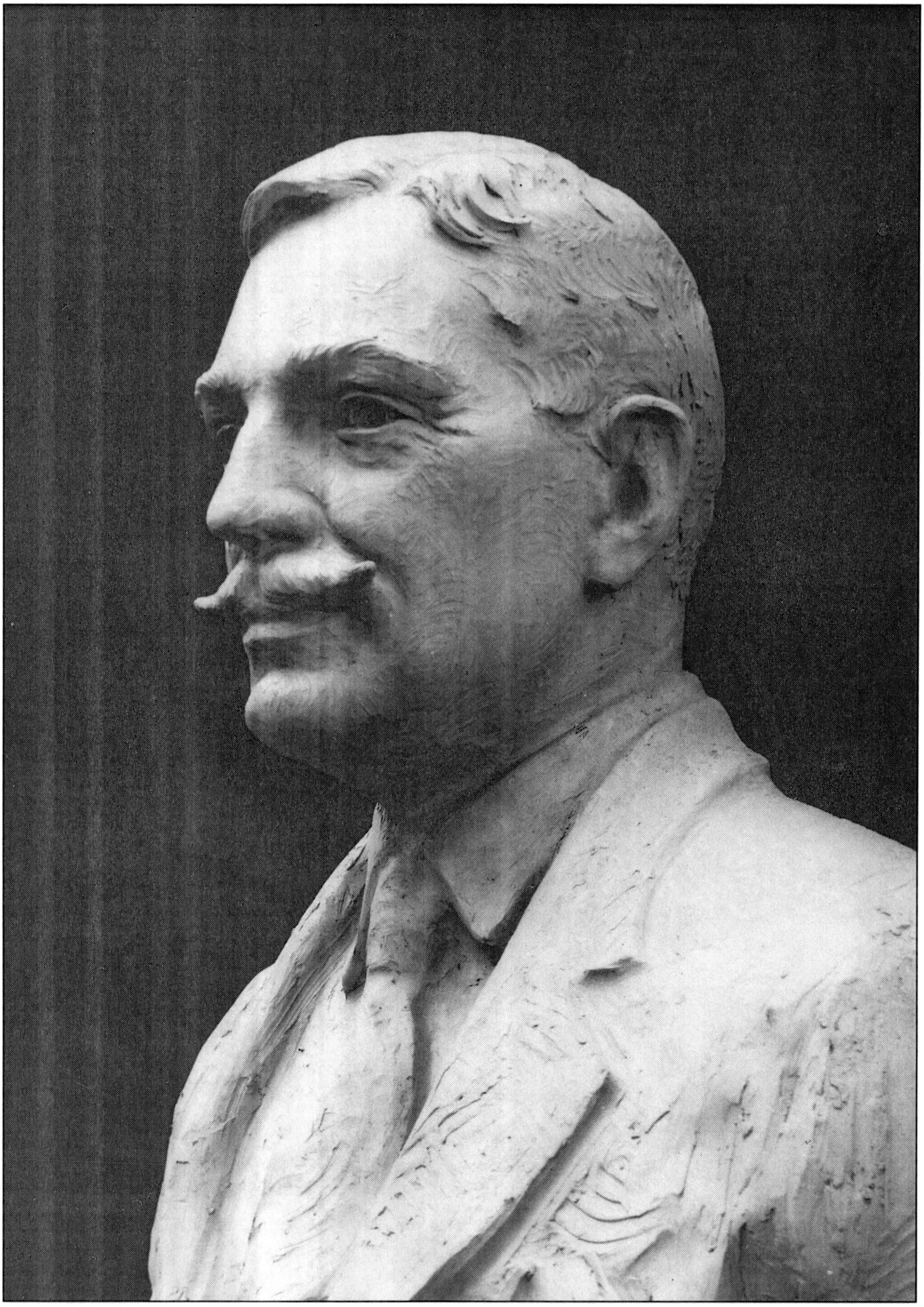

38. Spencer Penrose: 1958, realtor and financier. The portrait was created and a heroic monument was erected at Broadmoor in Colorado Springs, CO.

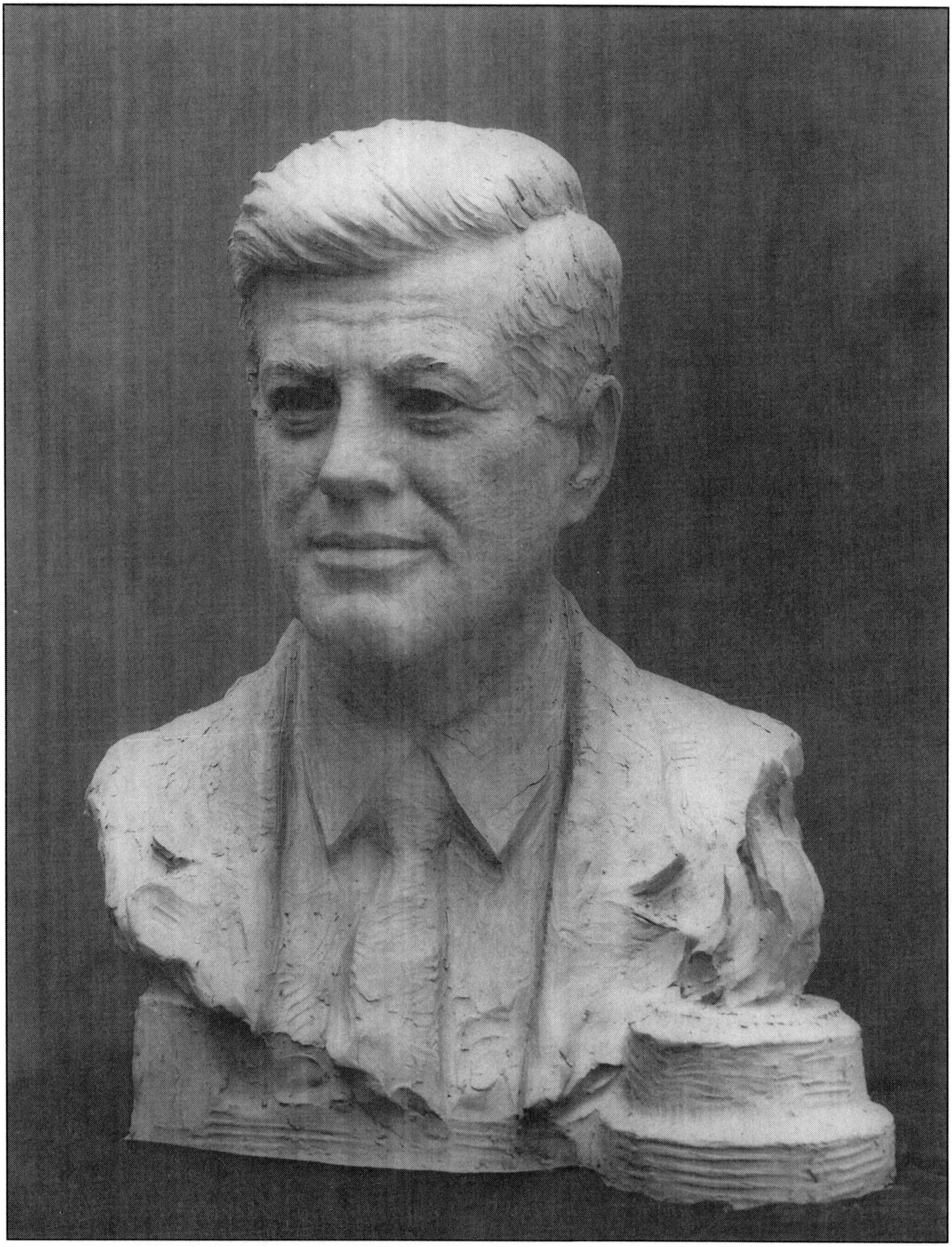

39. John F. Kennedy: A president of the United States and the Eternal Flame.

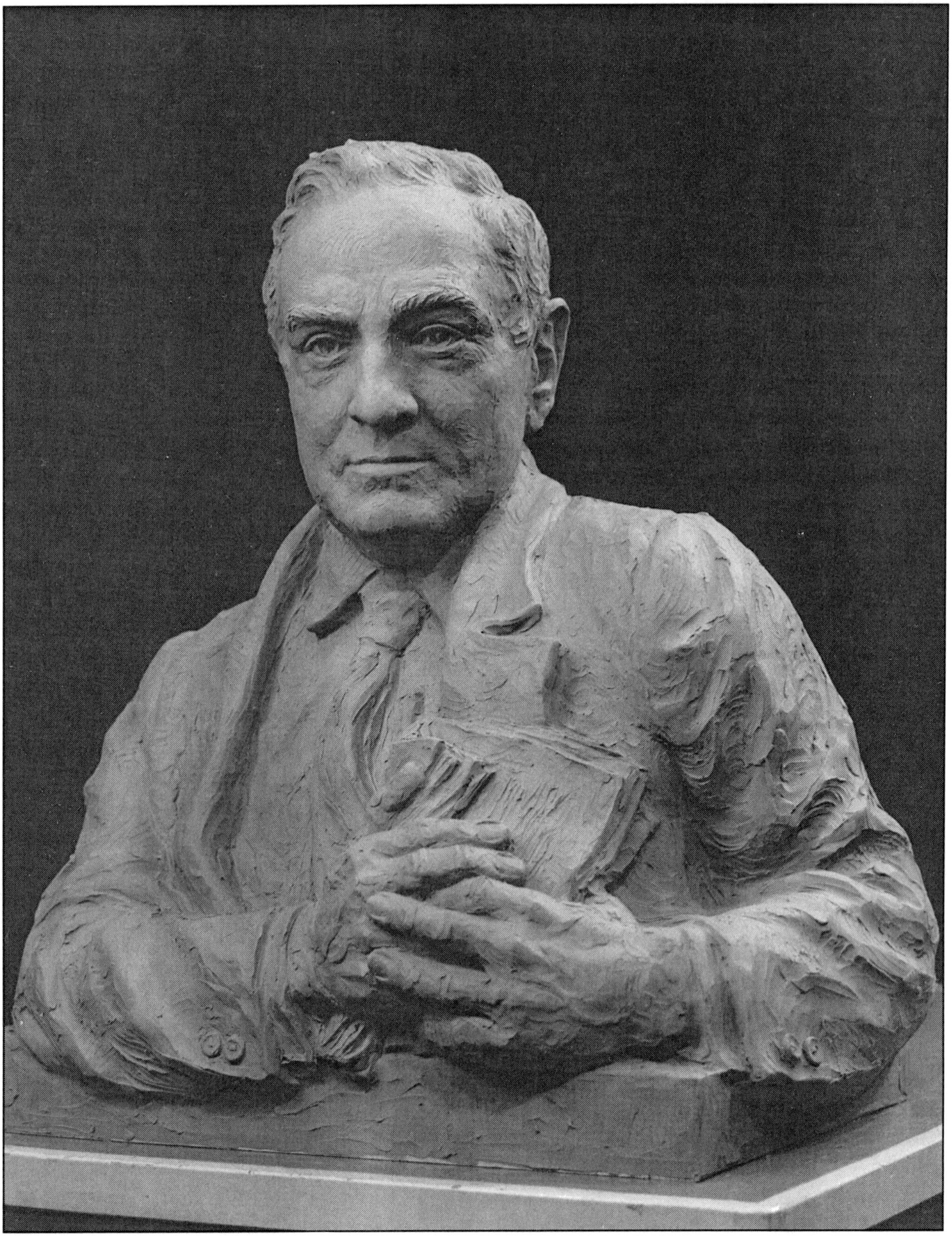

40. George Eisenberg: 1986, a Chicago resident, a philanthropist and donor to the Mayo Foundation. The heroic bronze was placed in the Eisenberg building of the Mayo Medical School 1985. It was formerly the Methodist Hospital. This was the last major work of Avard Fairbanks.

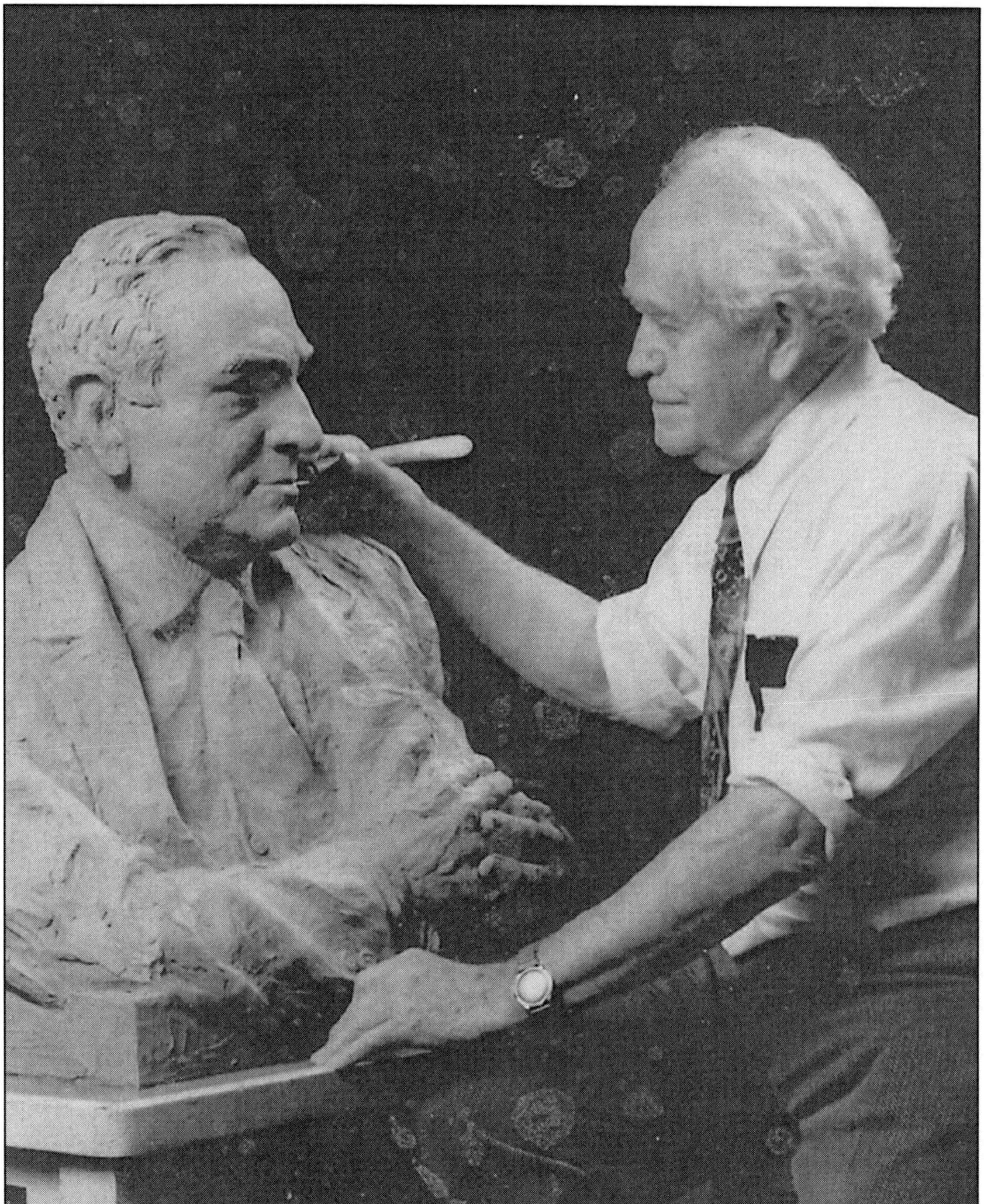

41. Avard Fairbanks modeling the portrait of George Eisenberg.

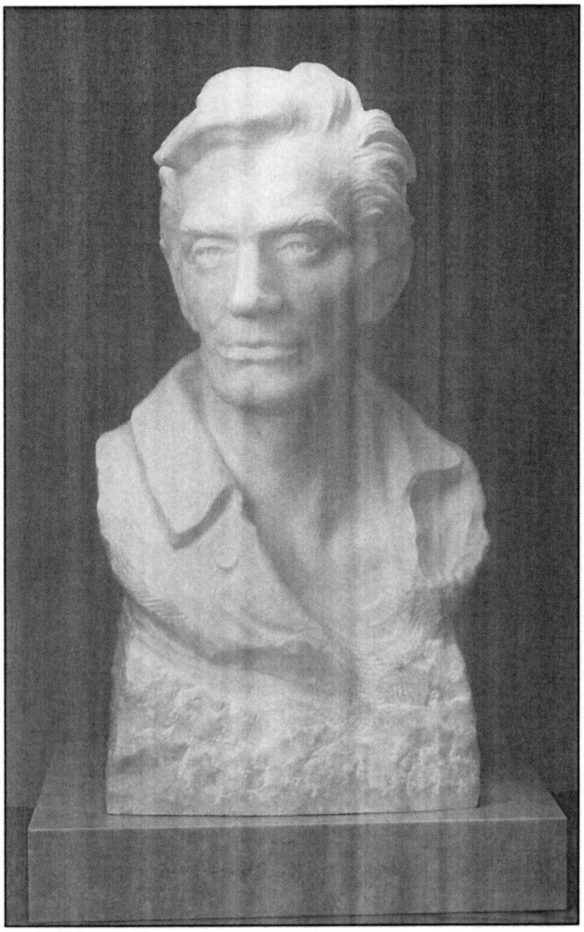

42. Abraham Lincoln, the Youth: 1959. This heroic portrait, carved in Carrara Marble, was placed in the Ford Theater Museum in Washington, DC.

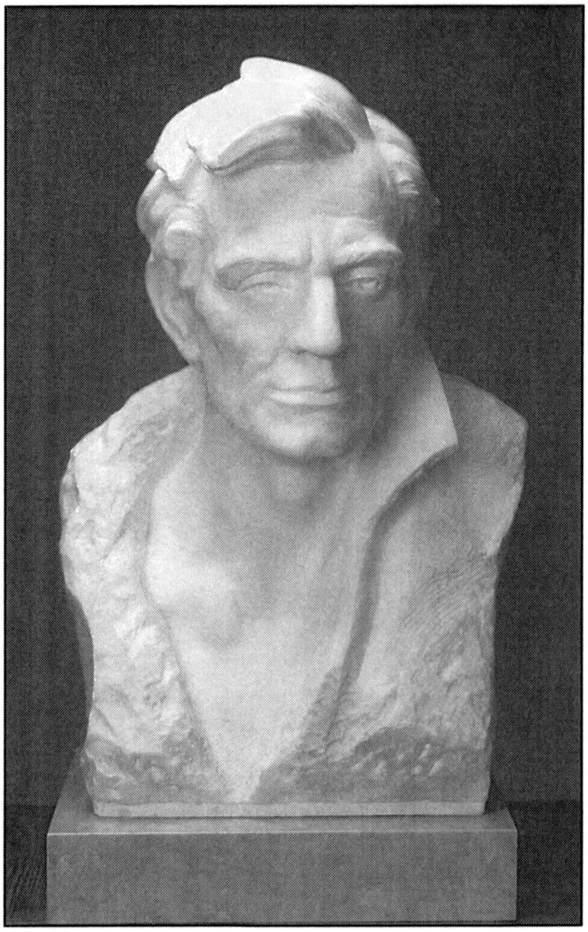

43. Abraham Lincoln, the Frontiersman, is a heroic portrait carved in Carrara Marble. It was placed in the Ford Theater Museum. Another heroic carving in marble was placed by the Illinois Historical Society in the Lincoln House Museum in Springfield, IL. Another marble carving was placed in the League of Nations Building in Geneva Switzerland. His son, Virgil, later donated a heroic carving to the Mayo Clinic in Rochester, MN.

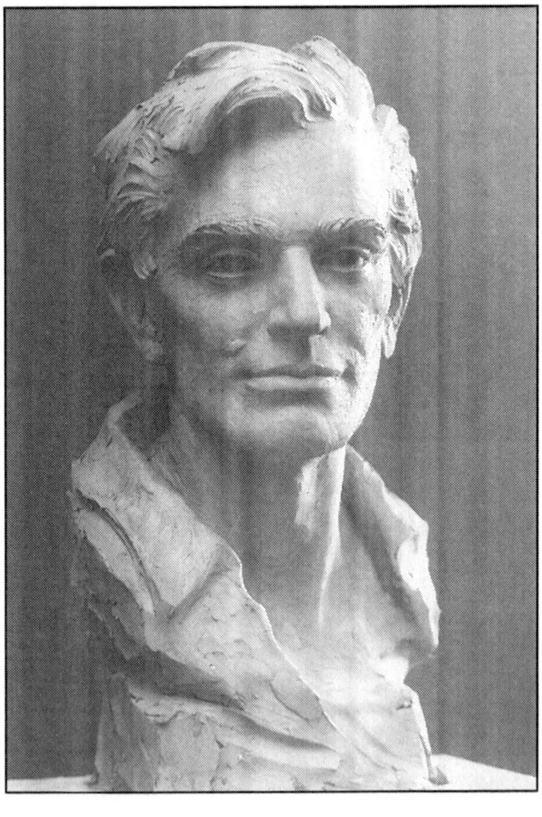

46. At left: Abraham Lincoln, the Youth, modeled in Plasteline.

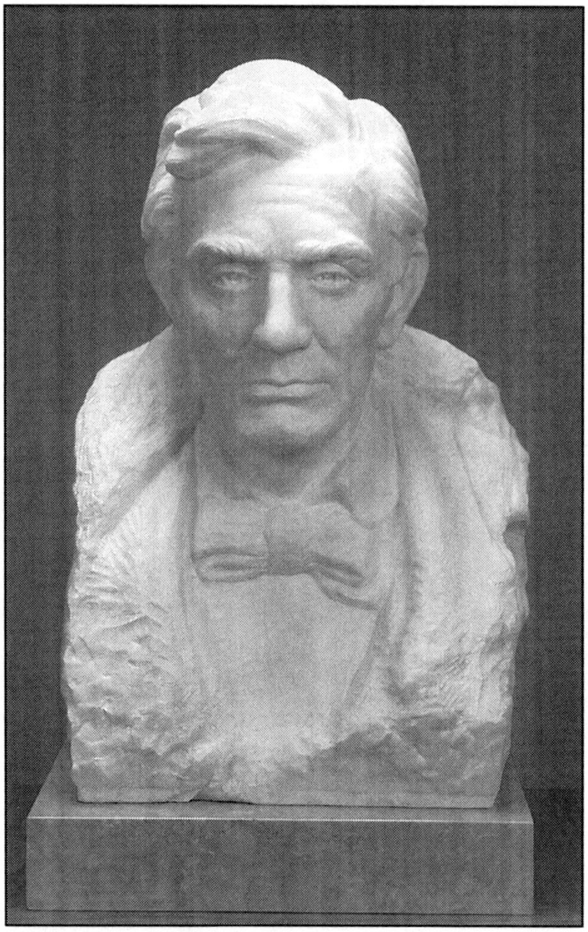

44. Abraham Lincoln, the Lawyer, is a heroic portrait carved in Carrara Marble. It was prominently placed in the Temple of Justice, the Supreme Court Building in Washington, DC.

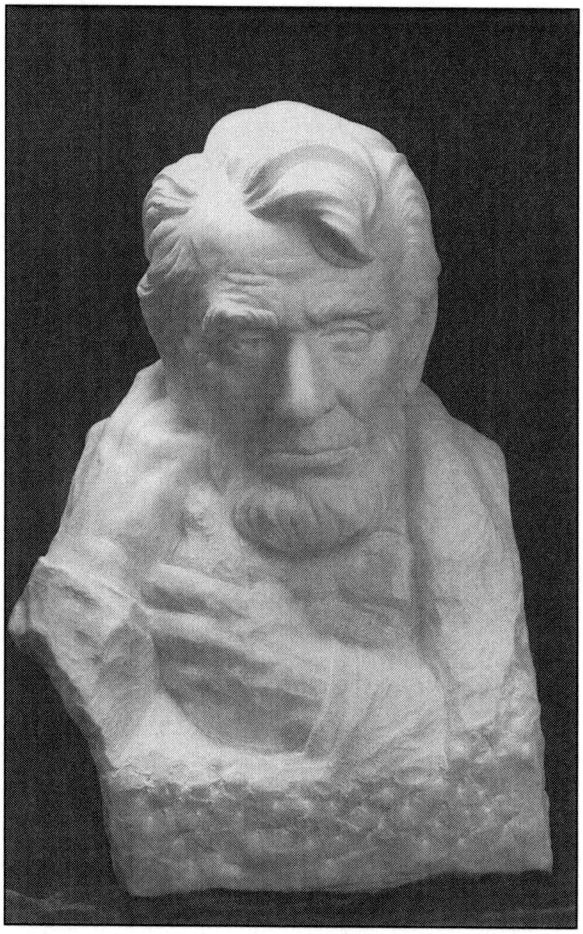

45. The fourth in the series of heroic portraits carved in Carrara Marble represents Abraham Lincoln, the President. It was placed in the Ford Theater Museum.

Abraham Lincoln Heroic Size Portraits

The Broadcast Music Corporation commissioned Avard Fairbanks to create a series of four heroic portraits representing four ages of Abraham Lincoln for the Lincoln Sesquicentennial Celebration. Each of these were to be near likeliness of his youth, his years as a frontiersman, His career as a lawyer, and his time as President of the United States of America.

Using his experience of creating portraits of persons of various ages, Avard Fairbanks was able to use information from the life mask, created by Leonard Volk, for the youth, the frontiersman and the lawyer ages. The life mask of Abraham Lincoln by Clark Mills served well for Lincoln the president.

The portrait busts were modeled in Plasteline and cast in plaster. Duplicate casts were sent to marble carving studios in Pietrasanta, Italy. He then went to Pietrasanta, Italy, and finished the marble carvings, adding life and expression to the marble. They were then shipped to Washington DC. These were donated to the Interior department in 1959 after the celebration. Three were placed in the Ford Theater Museum and one was placed in the Supreme Court Building.

Colossal Portraits

A colossal portrait of Lincoln the Frontiersman, 1965, cast in bronze was placed at the Lincoln High School in Seattle. WA. Another cast was placed at Utah State University at Logan, UT along with a colossal portrait of George Washington.

A colossal portrait of Lincoln the Legislator, carved in Portuguese rose marble was placed in the congressional Committee meeting Building in Washington, DC, in 1978.

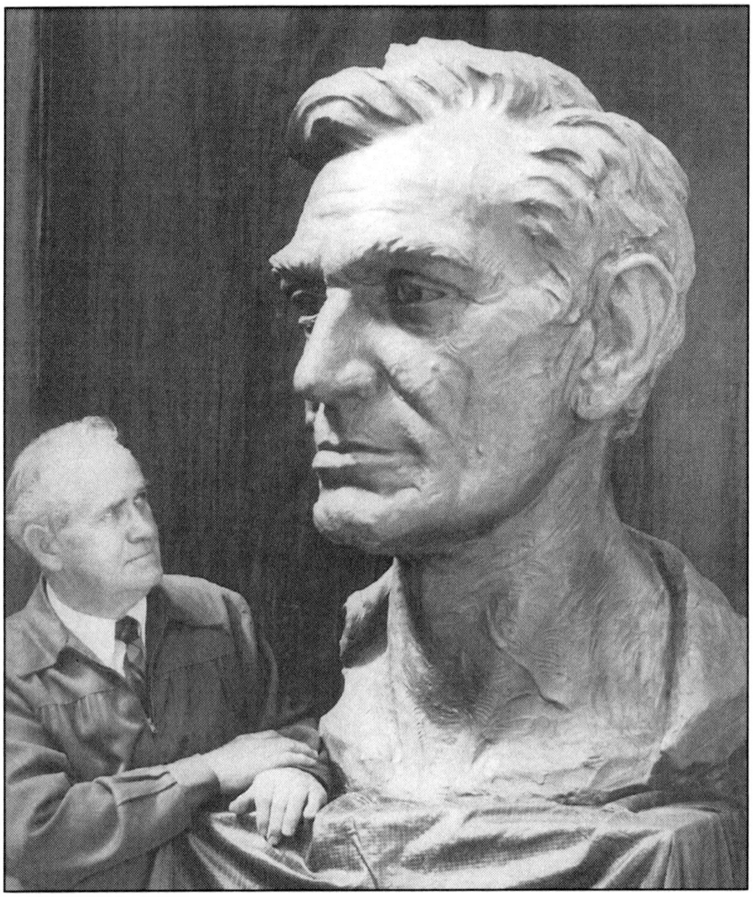

47. Avard Fairbanks reviewing his colossal portrait of Abraham Lincoln. The finished portrait was erected at Lincoln High School, Seattle, Washington.

Form is Fundamental to a Portrait

after Justin Fairbanks, July, 1970

There are four fundamental aspects of modeling a portrait:

The first consideration is **form.** This includes form of the skull and the living head.

The second aspect is **proportion** of the head, the face, the neck, and the shoulders.

The third includes the preliminary forms of various **features** of the face. Finished details of facial features soon follow.

The fourth consideration is **expression**. This last item includes how to model expression by the alterations of facial features.

Form of the Head

Form will be discussed first. The examples will be presented for an initial prototype from which later alterations and adjustments may be made to an image that is intended to resemble a personality. The form of the head including the face is determined by the shape of three different components. The hard and inflexible substance that is bone. The firm but flexible substance is the cartilage particularly of the ears and nose; both of which are attached to bone. Covering each of these are various types of soft tissues, including muscle, fibrous tissue, fatty tissue, and skin. An artist observes the surface, yet needs to understand what lies beneath the skin to render a realistic and expressive form of the head and the face.

In order to make the form of the head, which Avard Fairbanks created in his demonstration lectures, he began with a very simple armature and a supply of plastiline in rolls of various sizes. He first modeled the bony structure of the skull's cranium by applying large rolls of plasteline, about one inch diameter. These were previously formed by rotating between palms of the hands. After the initial large masses were formed, he modeled other bony structure of the face by adding more plasteline using intermediate size rolls to the cranium. The forms, supported by the cartilage, were later applied, particularly the ears and nose that attach to the bony structure. Soft tissue features were indicated by additional rolls of plasteline applied where it was appropriate to the already modeled skull. When fine details were needed, small rolls, matchstick in size, were rolled between a thumb and forefinger. Applying plasteline in small rolls resembles sketching with charcoal.

The simplest and fundamental form of the cranium is like a sphere. The first part of developing the skull, after establishing a midline, was to add layers of plasteline to represent the cranium. The second improvement was to add a brow and make the cranium in the form of an oval, like a hen's egg. The broadest portion of the skull is in the posterior aspect, above and behind where the ears will later be placed. The temporal area is anterior and is a more narrow aspect of the skull. The forward part was then flattened to represent the forehead. The brow is the lower border of the anterior cranium. The third additions were the cheekbones or maxillae. The orbits or eye sockets were then formed between the brow of its frontal bones and the maxillae of the cheek. The jaw bone, the mandible, was applied next.

The skull is composed of the cranium and the face. The cranium is technically called the *neurocranium;* it is a bony vessel that contains the brain. The bony structure of the face is anatomically named the *viscerocranium.* Although the face includes the forehead, the *viscerocranium* is essentially from the brow to the chin. Its purpose is primarily for the human physiologic needs for breathing air and eating food. The face, the vis-

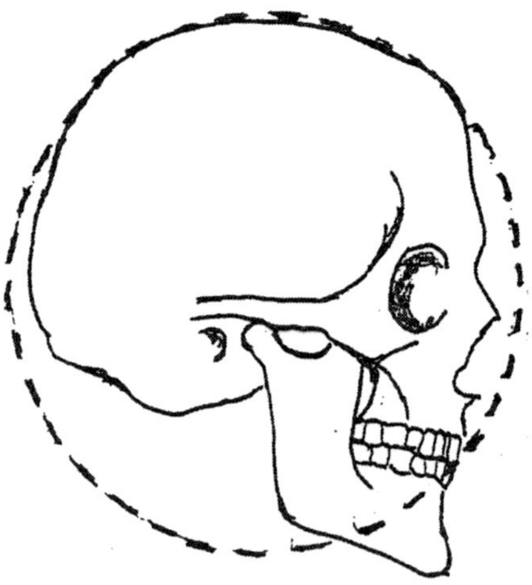

A circle has a perimeter that is equidistant from one point.

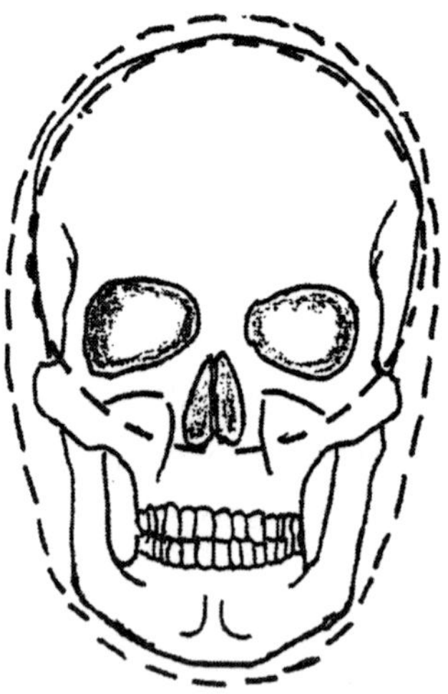

An ellipse has a perimeter that is equidistant from two points.

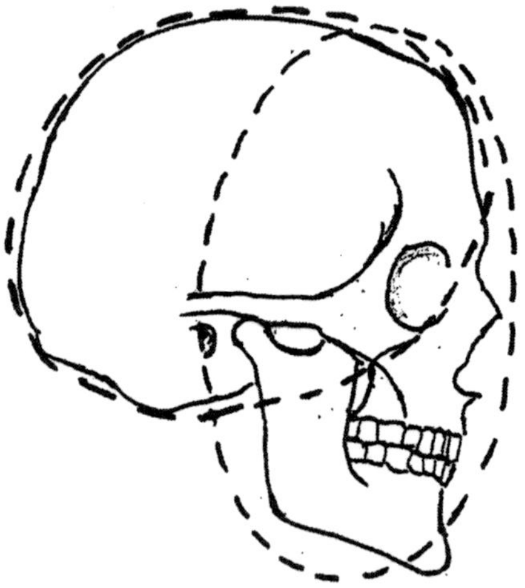

An oval has a perimeter that is equidistant from three points.

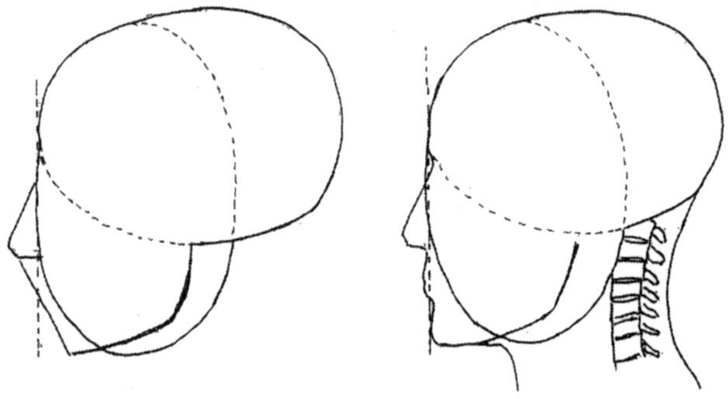

The skull's form resembles a 'P' and intersecting ellipses.

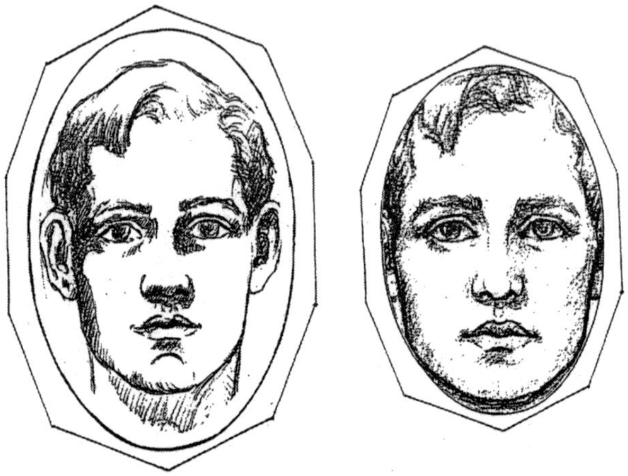

The face conforms to an ellipse and an elongated decagon.

Illustrations of geometric figures that resemble the form of the skull.

cerocranium plus the forehead, is also generally shaped like a vertical ellipse but modified slightly as a vertical oval with the broader diameter of the forehead in the upper half and the lower half that narrows toward the chin. On lateral view, the skull appears to be like two intersecting ovals that resemble broad "P." The forehead is both a part of the cranium and the upper third of the face. After rolls of plasteline were added representing the muscles of the neck, the simple "P" configuration became less apparent.

On frontal view, the face may also be considered like an ellipse that resembles an elongated octagon that becomes a ten sided figure or a decadron. One-half of an octagon, the upper half, is above the eyes, extending down to the zygomzatic arches. The lower part of the face resembles the other half of the octagon. Then consider each configuration to have rounded corners.

The fourth addition to form the skull is the mandible or jaw bone that represents two mandible bones that are fused in the midline at the chin. Each mandible has an upright portion, the ramus, attached just anterior to an ear and it extends down to the angle of the jaw. The part of each half of the mandible containing teeth extends forward at a slight obtuse angle and it curves medially to join its mate at the chin in the midline. After placement of the mandibles, soft tissues were added, representing the lips and the cheeks.

After brow ridges were improved, a roll of plastiline was added to represent the nose. The preliminary form of the nose is with a straight leading border at about thirty degree angle from vertical with a flat top and sides that angle out to the cheeks at about a sixty degrees. Distinctive details and refinements were to be added later.

The preliminary form of the lips started with a roll of modeling clay applied over the rough features representing the mandible and lower maxilla. The contours of the mouth aperture were incised with a modeling tool creating an outline of a very broad "M" that would later resemble a Grecian bow. Appropriate beveling of the lips was then applied. Refinements were delayed to a later time when other face details would be improved. Details were later refined along with other features so that they progressed relatively simultaneously.

Before refinement details were started, attention needed to be directed to the neck that both supports the head and yet allows remarkable flexibility. For the body to accomplish this there is a combination of bones (the vertebrae) and many muscles connected to the vertebrae, the thorax, or the shoulders. These muscle masses were represented by rolls of plasteline. The posterior and lateral masses were overlaid by the broad trapezius muscles. The prominent anterior muscles are the sternocleidomastoid muscles that originate on the sternum and the clavicles and angle up and laterally to insert on the mastoid processes of the skull just behind the ears. With muscular support, a rigid, front gazing portrait may be changed by a slight twist of the head and an adjustment of the shoulders into an informal posture making the individual look more animated as if in a conversation.

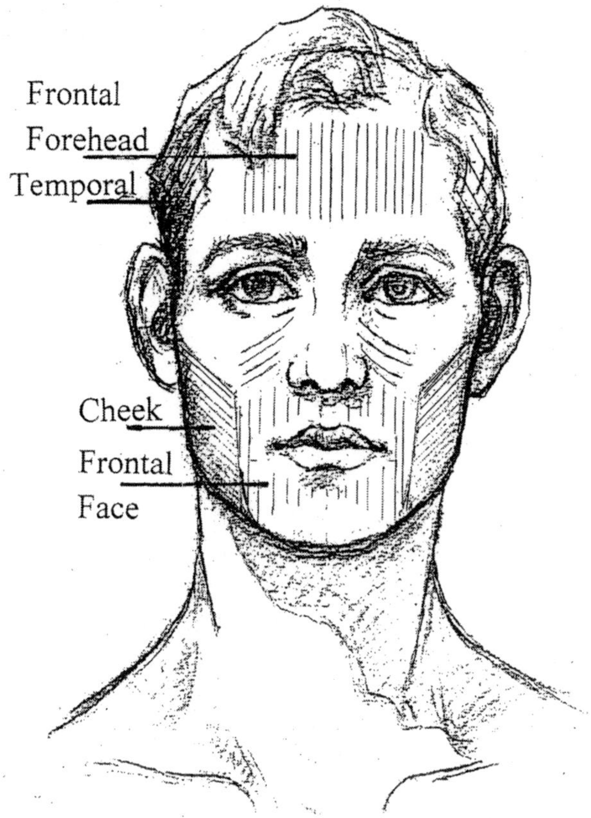

Planes of the face.

Planes of the Face

There are several planes of the face. The predominant plane is the frontal plane that starts at the forehead and extends down but narrows toward the chin. It is interrupted by the eyes, the nose, and the lips. The forehead has a distinct plane with two frontal prominences that are at about two thirds the distances from the brow to the hairline. On the sides of the forehead are temporal planes directed posteriorly and angled slightly laterally along the temporal ridges. These ridges are arcs at the origins of the temporal muscles at their attachments to the skull. These muscles lift the jaw when chewing. One can easily palpate them on one's self when biting and chewing.

The temporal bones form anterior-posterior planes that diverge moderately toward the parietal bones which are at the widest diameter of the skull. The parietal prominences are just posterior to and above apex of both ears.

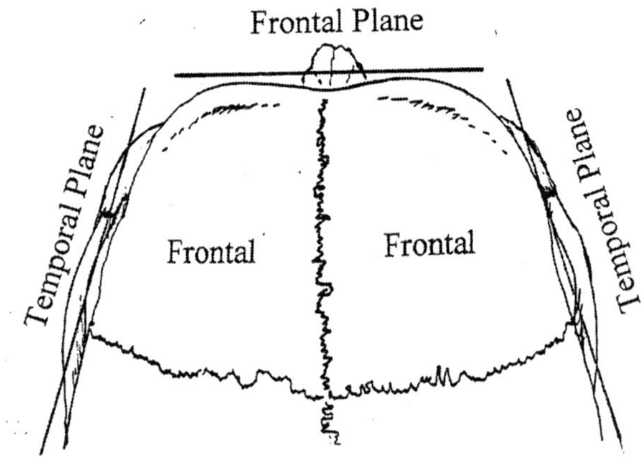

Forehead planes.

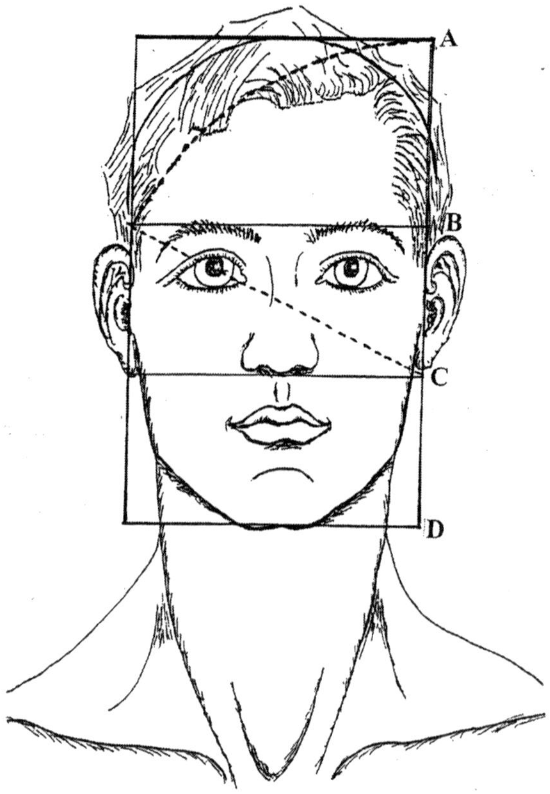

Head proportions conform to the Golden Mean.
AD ÷ AC = 1.6… = Φ

The brows are paired with obvious bony prominences near the midline of the brow. These cover the frontal sinuses that are just above the orbits or eye sockets. Lateral to the corners of the brows in the temporal area, there are also shallow concavities just posterior to the lateral border of the forehead and above the zygomatic arches of each cheekbone. These are the beginnings of the temporal planes and the temporal ridges. The horizontal zygomatic arches are at the widest diameter of the face and extend to the ears.

The lower half of the face has a pair of slightly curved planes of the cheeks, bounded by the cheekbones above and by the borders of the mandibles below, and they curve in toward the mouth and chin to a crease lateral to the lip corners. These planes are at about sixty degree angle with each other. This conforms to the angle of the two mandibular bones, or jawbones that joins at the chin. This jawbone angle of about sixty-degree divergence is more apparent when another person looks up at the ceiling. The anterior apex of the jaw angle is truncated, or squared off and rounded at the chin where it is covered by the soft fibro-fatty tissues.

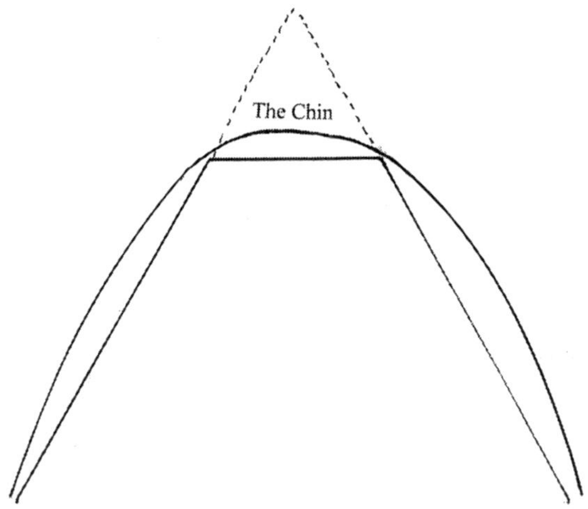

The jaw conforms to a truncated 60° angle.

The articulations or joints of the jaws are deep to the zygomatic arches and just anterior to the tragus or ear flaps of the ears. A jawbone has a vertical part connected at an obtuse angle, but resembles a right angle, to the nearly horizontal portion of the jaw that supports teeth. The shape and contour of the mouth and lips conform to arcs of the teeth which are solid structures. The upper arc of teeth is the larger arc. The ears and the nose are the semi soft features that are supported by cartilage, while the hard features are the bony portions of the skull and jaw bone or mandible.

Form and Proportions of the Human Head

An understanding of human proportions gives an artist a command of portrait fundamentals. Knowledge of the design and geometric ratios of the head and face, from a standpoint of beauty, gives insight into the pattern of forms and basic refinements. Artists and scholars have been studying human proportions for many centuries. One of the first careful analysis and documentation of proportions was made by Leonardo da Vinci. The famous sculptor, Michelangelo also contributed generously of his talents to the study of body proportions. The understanding of human proportions is basic and fundamental to skilled creations in fine art and fine sculpture.

The male vertical skull measurement of height compared to width, at the zygomatic arches of the cheeks, is a ratio of about three to two, or nine inches (22.9 cm) high to six inches (13.3 cm) wide. Leonardo da Vince taught that the face can be conveniently divided into thirds. One third is the distance of the hairline to the brow. The middle third is from the brow to just below the nose. The lower third is from just below the nose to the chin.

The ear is in the middle third; its upper pole is in line with the brow, while the lobe is on the same level as the nostrils. On lateral view, the ear canal is slightly posterior to one-half the anterior-posterior distance, brow to occiput of the skull. The ear canal is also about one-half the distance from the vertex to the lower level of the chin.

The lower third of the face, nose to chin, may be conveniently divided into three unequal measurements. The upper third consists of the nose to mouth opening. The middle third, the smallest division is measured from the mouth opening to the crease in the hollow below the lower lip. The larger lower third includes the chin from the crease to the lower border of the mandible. When modeling the portrait of a person, it is advisable to measure these details, since they vary with individuals.

The widest part of the face is just in front of the tragus of an ear where the zygomatic arch joins the temporal bone. The widest diameter of the cranium is at the parietal prominences that are above and just posterior to the ears. The facial proportions are significant considerations for artists. On frontal view the horizontal width, compared to the vertical height is a ratio of six to nine inches in male faces, or about two-thirds. In female faces, the ratio is about five to eight inches or 0.625... (nearly 2/3). The inverse ratio is 1.62... (nearly 1 2/3). This is a ratio called the Golden Mean. It is also called Phi in the Fibonacci series. It is frequently present in nature, since it is an important ratio for the growth of living organisms.

Mathematicians have shown an interest in the Fibonacci Series, a geometric progression, 1/1, 1/2, 2/3, 3/5, 5/8, 8/13, 13/21, = 0.62... to 1, or Phi, Φ. Many have recognized the resemblance of this concept and the approximate ratio to the ideal human face and other body features to the Golden Rectangle and Golden Mean with that ratio.

However, there are individual variations and variations from the usual form and there are significant differences to ethnic groups. Anthropologists have classified these types and have designated them according to ratios of head breadth divided by head Anterior to posterior length times one hundred. Dolico-cephalic, long and narrow heads are about 70 to 76; mesocephalic, medium length heads are about 76 to 81; and brachycephalic, shorter, broader heads are about 81 to 87. The face breadth-to-height ratio is similar to the breadth-to-length. Nordic types and African American descendants of forest dwellers often have dolicocephalic features. Many Caucasians have mesocephalic features, and Asians may have brachiocephalic configurations. Head shape is not necessarily associated with skin color. Tall individuals may have dolicocephalic head features, but there are exceptions.

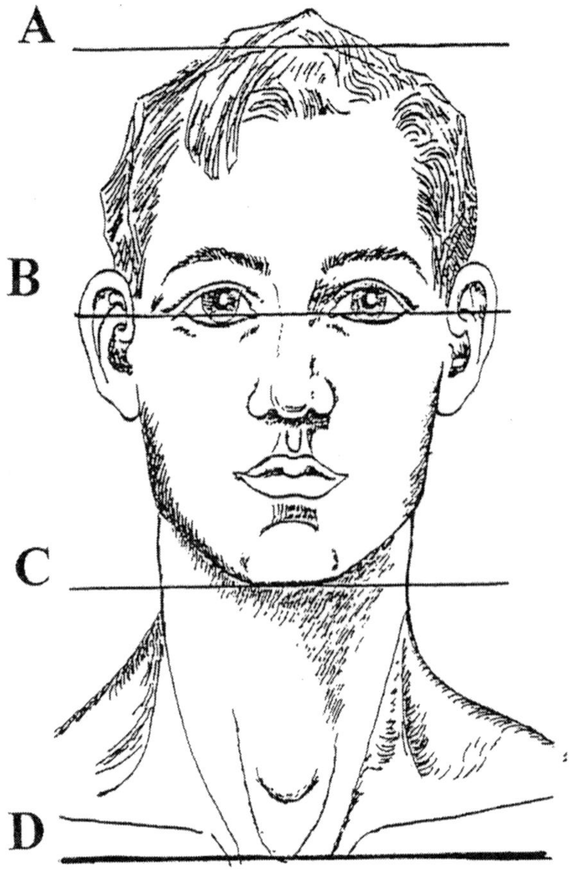

The head and neck are divided into three equal parts.

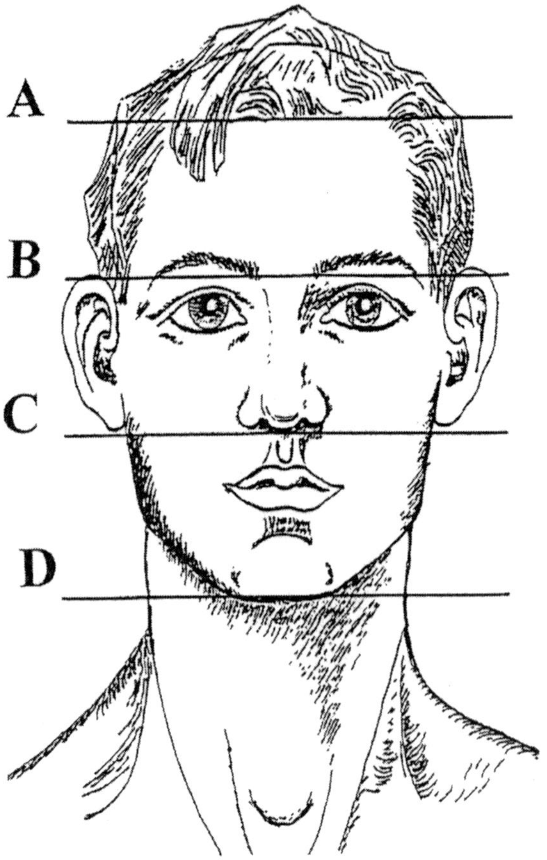

The face is divided into three equal parts.

The vertical distance of hairline to vertex is about one-eighth the distance of chin to vertex. There are many styles of hair, but when the hair is combed up and back, the top of the forelock above the hairline is about the same level as the hair at the level of vertex. The high point or vertex of the head is not at the hairline or the forehead, but it is slightly posterior to a point above on a vertical line near the tragus or flap of the ear. It is about as far posterior as the apex of the helix of an ear. (See illustration of ear proportions on page 117.)

The vertical head measurement may be divided into halves. The vertex to the eyes equals the eyes to the chin. Since the measurement from the eyes to the chin is equal to the measurement of the chin to the sternal notch or pit of the neck, there is a series of three equal measurements of head and neck: the vertex to corners of eyes; eyes to chin; and chin to sternal notch of the neck.

Certain strength is achieved by the use of halves and thirds when modeling the face. even with those having different cephalic indices. Additional subtle divisions of these major divisions of thirds and halves are less noticeable but are still important. The height of the head is divided in two parts at the eye level. The upper half is considered the cranium. The lower half is the face below the eyes. The symmetry of the face, viewed as right and left sides, divides it again into equal halves.

Since the hair, from the hairline above the forehead to the vertex, is about one-eighth the total head height. The remaining seven- eighths is face height. This can be conveniently divided into thirds. The hairline to the brow at the glabella, a palpable midline notch between the brows, is the upper third and is essentially the forehead The brow to base of the nose, the mid-face, is the middle one-third, and nose at the lip junction to the chin, the lower face, is the lower one-third.

These proportions are beautiful in effect,

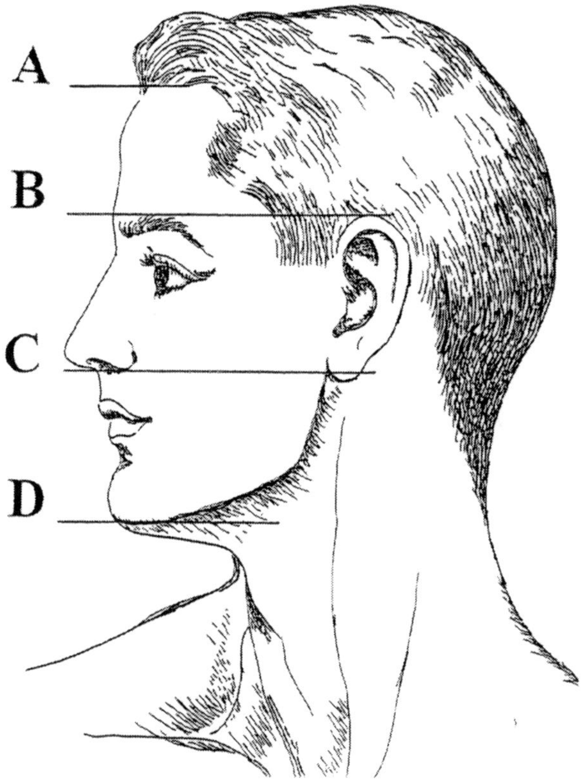

The face is divided into three equal parts.

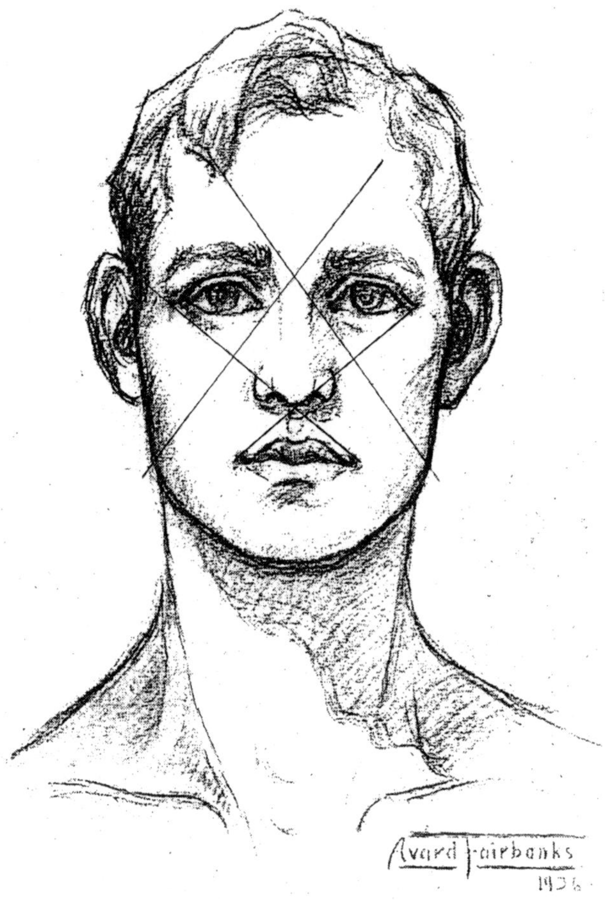

Diagonal lines of the face.

strong, yet sufficiently subtle to maintain interest. It becomes apparent that halves and thirds are quite prevalent in head and face design. They are also prevalent in body and extremity analysis.

The forehead has no special divisions in the upper one third of the face. The middle third has eyes and nose and ears. The lower third has lips, mouth and chin. Proportions and details of these are more completely discussed in the paragraphs of each feature.

Diagonal lines demonstrate interesting relationships of features. A line from the corner of right eye to the left corner of the mouth crosses a similar line from the corner of left eye to the right corner of the mouth. These lines cross at the sub nasal point, the junction of the nose and upper lip. A line from the right frontal eminence to the angle of the left mandible crosses a similar line from the left frontal eminence to the right angle of the mandible. They cross at the glabella, the mid-point of the brow

Measurements of human proportions vary with individuals. They vary with racial, ethnic, and inherited characteristics, but ratios are often similar. The skilled artist recognizes these variations and includes them when creating a portrait. Proportions vary with age; the newborn infant's face, brow to chin, is about equal to the forehead. As a child grows, for the first five years, the cranium grows faster than the face. The mid-face, brow to nose, and lower face, nose to chin, after childhood then begin to develop more to fulfill body requirements. The features approach maturity during and after adolescence. Between age fifteen and twenty-five years the female face will change less than the male face. There is a longer period of maturation in the male resulting in stronger and more angular features after the age of twenty.

One may note that young adults have a generally oval contour to the face. As a person matures into middle age at about thirty-five or forty, the face begins to assume a somewhat rectangular appearance, as the lower, lateral cheeks become more definite. There is a relaxation of the connective tissue in the cheeks that allows the fatty tissue to sag and jowls begin to develop. There is a gradual progression of changes with age at different rates in various people. The face may become even more rectangular as a person approaches age sixty. In old age, teeth may be worn down. In other persons some teeth are lost, and the alveolar ridges of both the maxilla and the mandible (upper and lower jaws) begin to resorb, the height of the lower face is diminished. Throughout later life, the mandibles become wider. These processes gradually result in the face that conforms more to a square contour.

The cartilaginous structures of the nose and the ears have been gradually growing throughout life. This results in longer ears and noses in elderly people. The cartilage also softens in time and the nose may droop slightly. The brow ridges of the older male may also become less prominent. In the very elderly, the male and female features often begin to appear similar. The wrinkles and furrows also become more apparent. Rather than deplore these changes, the artist can often use these to give greater feeling, personality, and character to a portrait. Many prefer to have aging features minimized and this should be done. However, artists, that are intending to create caricature, will often emphasize these aging features.

Representative Form and Details of Face Features

Representative forms are discussed separately with each facial feature. A discussion of proportions is included. Special details and variations to be observed and recognized are noted to be applied to the finished portrait. The separate articles are listed in the following order: the hairline; the forehead; the eyebrows; the eyes; the nose; the lips and mouth; the chin; and the neck.

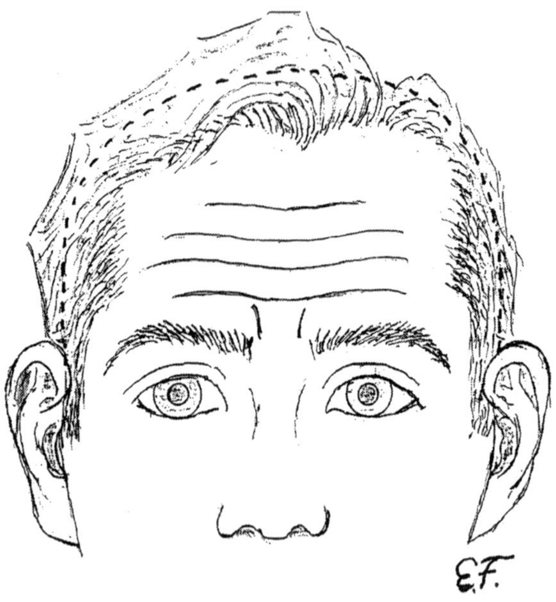

The hairline, forehead wrinkles, and eyebrows. Frontal view.

Features of the Forehead

The Hairline

The features of the upper third of the face include the forehead, the brows, and the upper border of the hair. This hairline has a distinctive, although variable outline. The superior and lateral borders of the forehead are defined by the hairline, which usually forms a characteristic pattern. In the midline of the forehead, there is a minimal to pronounced peak. The border curves gently laterally and down on both sides. It then curves posterior to a point superficial to the arc at the junction of the frontal and temporal bone of the skulls. The margin then curves anteriorly along this arc to a point about one inch above the lateral prominence of the brow. The hair margin curves back and then down to about the middle of the zygomatic arch. There is a band of down-directed hair anterior to the ear. In men, the beard begins at the zygomatic arch and continues down past the border of a mandible. The beard hair has a different texture than scalp hair, resulting in a different pattern of curl. Baldness changes the hairline, but this often deserves to be de-emphasized.

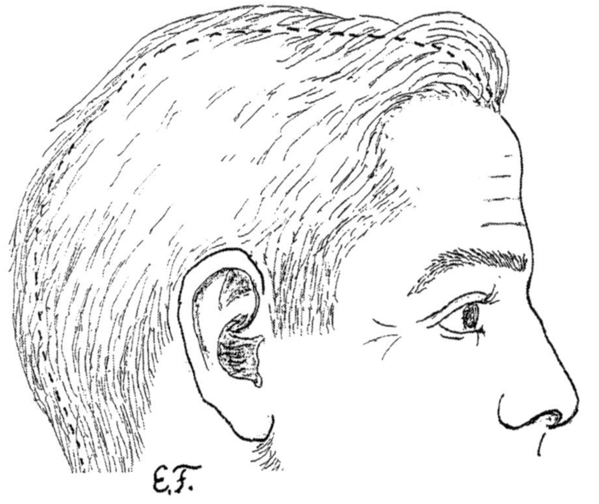

The hairline, forehead wrinkles, and eyebrows. Lateral view.

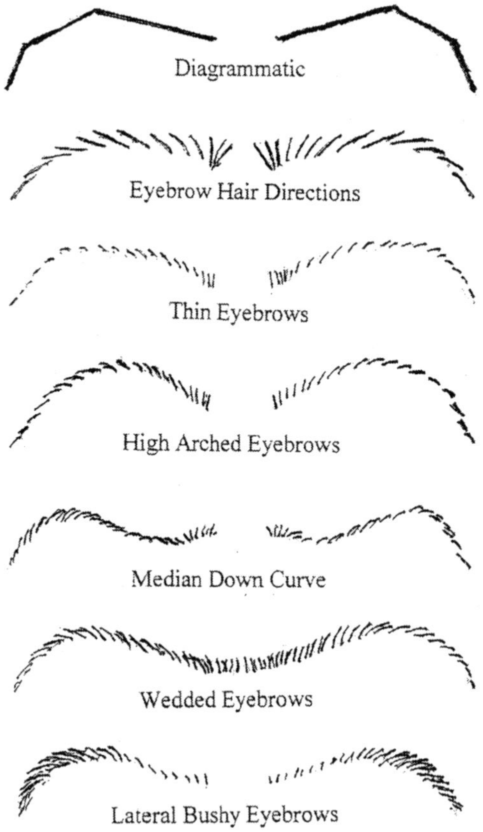

Eyebrow variations.

The Forehead

The hairless forehead has a nearly vertical frontal plane with a slight midline ridge and two frontal eminences formed by early frontal bone growth centers. The brows are more prominent in adult males than females. The forehead is often more vertical in men than women. There is a midline indentation, named the glabella, between the two brows. The bony prominences of the brows, just lateral to the midline, cover the frontal nasal sinuses. The supraorbital arch is the upper border of the orbit, or the eye socket, while above it is the supraciliary arch that is covered by eyebrows. The eyes in the orbits are protected by the brow above and by the bony ridge around the orbit.

The Eyebrows

Eyebrows are important since they represent individuality and expression. Eyebrows angle gently upward and lateral, curve and then angle downward, following the superciliary ridges of the brow. Not only are the brow ridges more prominent in adult men than adult women, but the hair of the brows is thicker and more coarse.

The usual diagrammatic form of an eyebrow can be illustrated with a line beginning at the glabella that gently angles up and lateral towards the corner of the brow where it curves down and lateral. The hair on the medial border of an eyebrow usually slants diagonally inward, then upward. Moving laterally along the eyebrow, the slant of hair progressively is more horizontal. At the lateral corner of the brow, the eyebrow hair begins to angle and point down.

There are many variations of eyebrows that deserve the artist's attention and recognition. Thin eyebrows begin with a slight tuft of hair, then follow the usual contours. These forms may vary and may be due to plucking the hairs. Some persons have high arched eye brows. Occasionally one may observe eyebrows with a medial downturn, instead of a gentle upward curve.

Hair between the brows is usually absent or thinner, but some individuals with hair between their brows have what is called "wedded brows." They are usually endowed with heavier than usual eyebrow hair. Some may have scant hair on the lateral and down-curving aspect of eyebrows, while others may have scant hair in the medial portion and bushy hair on the lateral portion. These variations add individuality and character to a person's portrait.

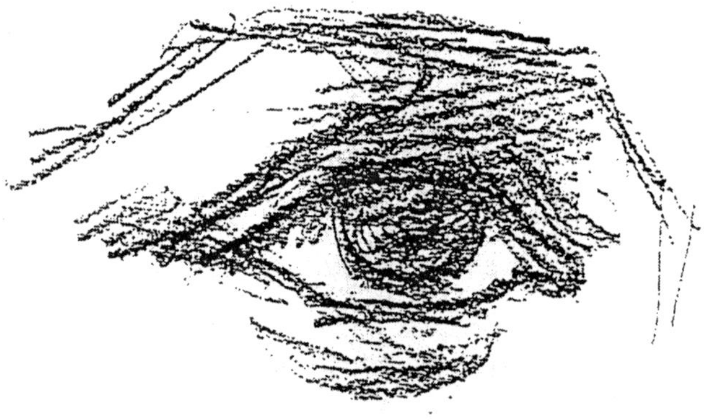

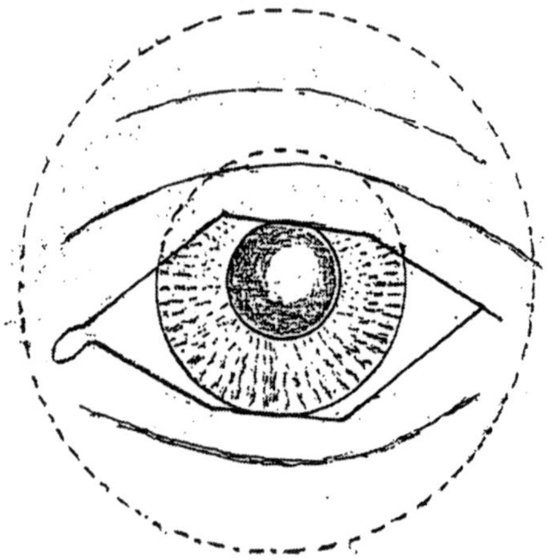

Consider a hexagon in the preliminary view and development of the eyelids.

Features of the Eyes

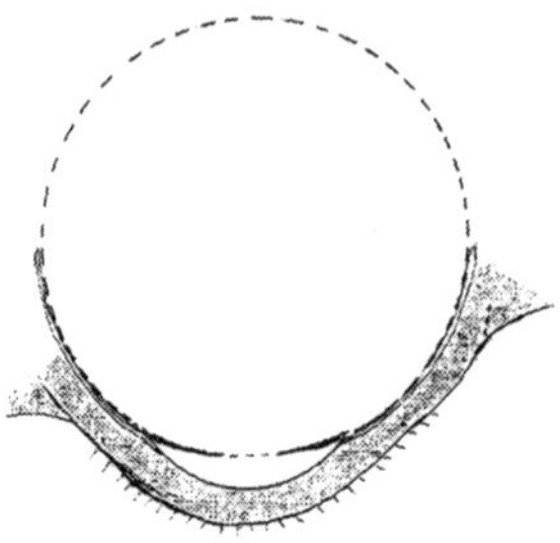

A diagrammatic view of the left eyelid is illustrated as if seen from above.

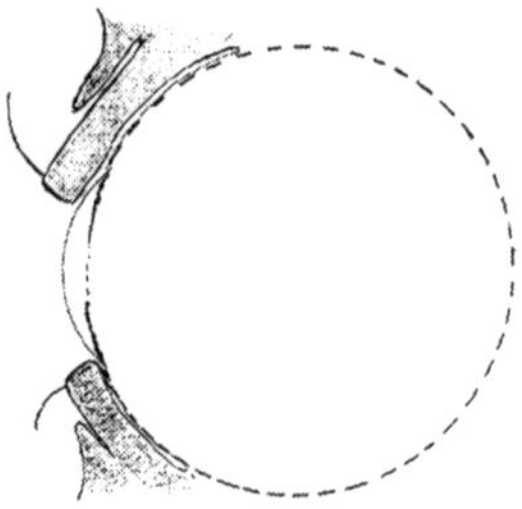

A diagrammatic view of the left eye is presented as if seen from the side.

Form of the Eyes

Recognize that the eyeballs are spheres, but most of the sphere is deep in the eye socket. Only a small section of the sphere is visible. An artist needs to demonstrate the eyelid to cover the sphere. Eyelids should not have a flattened appearance, even when the eyes are closed. Furthermore, the cornea forms a slight bulge on the anterior of this sphere. Another property to recognize is that eyelids have thickness. There are three layers: the skin on the outside, the conjunctiva lining the inside, and a tough thin fibro-cartilage membrane (tarsal plate) in between which helps protect the eye from minor impacts. This gives thickness to both upper and lower eye lids. They are not thin like paper or just a layer of skin, but are two to three millimeters in thickness.

Regarding the corners of an eye, the medial corner has a small but distinct oval notch that is directed down and medial. At the corners of this notch with the eyelids there is an upper and lower pinpoint opening (puncta) for the tear ducts. If an eye could be viewed from above, the medial corner of an eye would appear to be slightly more forward. It is also slightly lower than the lateral corner of the eyes. The lateral corner of an eye is usually more posterior and is slightly higher than the medial corner. This is not the case with all people, since some ethnic groups have slightly different configuration of eyelids, but generally speaking the outside corner, when viewed anteriorly, is slightly higher and more posterior than the medial corner. The upper eyelid is farther forward than the lower lid.

Eye Details

The eyelids appear to be intersecting arcs. The Egyptian artists created almond shaped eyes. The Greek sculptors learned to make eye more angular by modifying a hexagon. Consider the eyes first to resemble a hexagon that has rounded upper and lower corners. Then look for the high point of the upper lid and the low point of the lower lid. Sometimes the high point of the eyelid is medial to and sometimes it is lateral to the pupil. Since the cornea is a section of a smaller sphere than the eyeball, it protrudes at the anterior surface of the larger sphere. As the eye

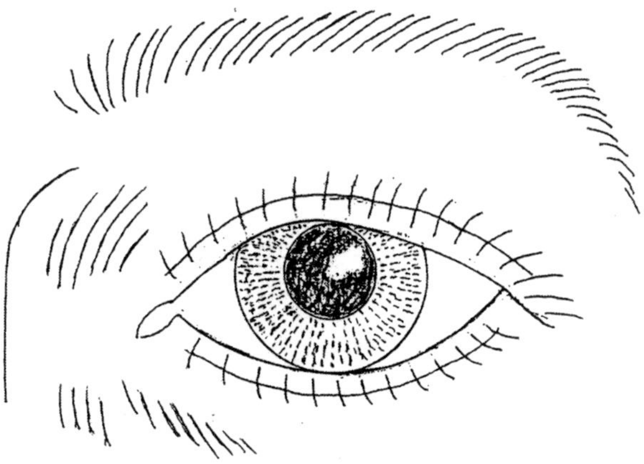

When the person is looking straight forward, the inferior arc of the iris appears along the lower lid. It seems to roll like a tire on a pavement. The upper lid covers about the upper one-third of the iris down to the border of the pupil.

moves from one side or the other, the high point of an eyelid shifts to accommodate the direction of the cornea. If the high point is indicated in the center, it may lose character for the eye.

At the lateral corner an eye, the upper eyelid crosses over the lower lid and continues down laterally past the corner. The lower lid comes up to the lateral corner like making the form of a slanted "T."

The upper eyelid is larger, and moves up and down more. The upper lid is also farther forward than the lower lid, and the lower lid is farther down on the eyeball than the upper lid. Regarding the eyeball and the iris, when the person is looking straight forward, the inferior arc of the iris appears along the lower lid. It seems to roll like a tire on a pavement. The upper lid covers about the upper one-third of the iris down to the border of the pupil. This relationship changes with expression. The sleepy eye has drooping upper eyelids, but when a person is staring or excited, the upper eyelid may be up to the border of the iris or above and even show some of the white, or sclera, of the eye. Expression from the tired to alert, or to surprised eyes may be manifest by how the upper eyelid covers the iris.

Squinting cuts down the amount of light entering the eyes. This brings up the lower eyelid more than it brings down the upper lid. This results in an increased fullness under an eye. Ranchers, cowboys, sailors, and persons habitually in the sunshine may develop a permanent squint, or called a desert squint. This adds to the character of an individual.

We very rarely put eyelashes on sculpture because one cannot have such a thin protruding structure. One can put an indication of eyelashes with some texture at the lateral edge of the upper lid curving laterally and upward pointing toward the lateral corner of the eyebrow. This may be important with women who want to have their pretty long eyelashes represented.

Make good clean lines on the eyelids. Fuzzy lines make the eye look sleepy. Look for the high spot on the upper lid and the low spot on the lower lid and model them into the portrait. The contraction of a muscle under the lateral corner of the eye lifts the corner and gives a fullness that creates a "smiling" eye. A fold over the upper eyelid, called a Nordic fold, sags with age and sometimes covers a lateral part or the entire upper eyelid.

Direct the eyes gently to one side or the other. Avoid eyes that look straight ahead as they may appear to follow an observer all around the room. A stern, sincere, wide-eyed image that appears like a holy man may render a feeling that he wishes to say, "Repent all you sinners!"

Eye Proportions

The lateral corners of the eyes are at a level of one half of the measurement from the vertex of the head to the chin. The width of an eye (palpebral fissure) or opening of the eyelids, is approximately equal to the distance between the inner corners of the eyes. It is also equal to the width of a nose at the ala and the width of the chin. The measurement between the lateral corners of the eyes is three-fourths the width of the face and is also equal to one-half of the face height, measured from the vertex to the chin. The distance between the inner arcs of the irises

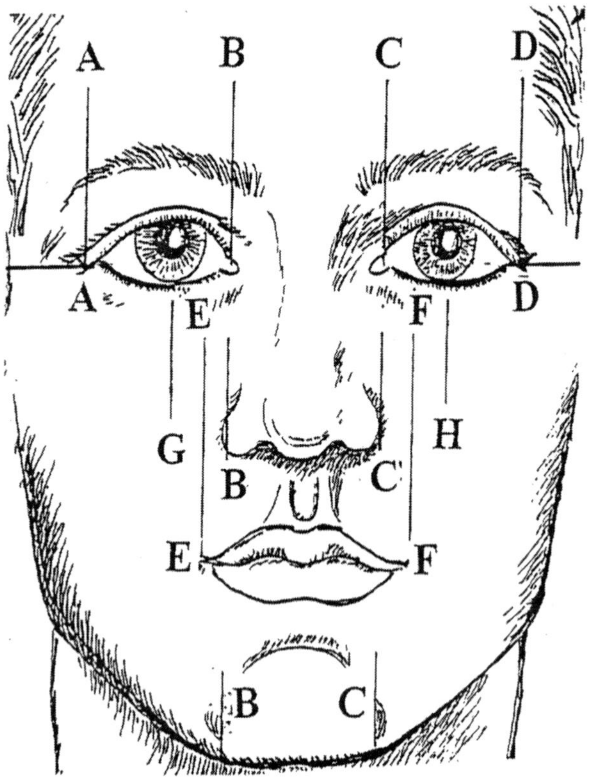

Eye proportion illustration.

The width of an eye is equal to the distance between the eyes. AB = BC = CD, and it is equal to the width of the nose at the ala, BC and the chin.

The distance between the inner arcs of the irises of the eyes, EF, equals the width of the mouth.

The distance between the pupils of the eyes, GH, equals one-third of a face height.

The distance between the lateral eye corners, AD, equals one-half of a face height.

of the eyes, equals the width of the mouth. The distance between the pupils of the eyes, equals one-third of a face height (see illustration).

There are some individual variations with these generalized proportions. Infants and young children appear to have eyes relatively larger and farther apart, because they are relatively larger. The openings of the eyelids are small so that only a small part of the sclera, or white of the eye, is exposed. Newborn infant's eyeballs are 16.5-mm anterior-posterior measurement, or 67% the size of adult eyes.

Growth of the eyes is most rapid during the first eighteen months with an average increase of 3.75-mm to 80%. By age seven years, eyes have grown to nearly adult size. They then more slowly approach adult size of 24.5-mm by age 15 to 18 years.* The portrayal of infants and children needs to indicate comparatively large eyes, because they are relatively larger. At first the color of the iris is dark blue, obscuring the circle of the pupil. Gradually the permanent color of the iris develops over several months.

Since the face of young women does not increase in height as much as men, many of them appear to have eyes slightly farther apart, and it suggests youth. This is one consideration for the choice of some actresses for dramatic productions. Youth and glamour are often expressed by facial appearance with feminine eye and nose configuration.

Face Creases Near the Eyes and Nose

A diagonal crease starts at each ala and descends to outline the junction of the upper lip with the cheeks respectively, and then blends in with them. Additional interesting, divergent geometric forms begin on each side of the nose at the junction of the nasal bones the superior lateral cartilages. They sweeps down, lateral, and spread like two fans and blend into the cheeks. The upper borders are the infraorbital margins below the eyes, and the lower borders are the creases from the ala that forms a border above the lips.

Another pair of diagonal creases begin near the corners of the mouth and descend lateral to the chin. In old age, the creases from the ala may merge with the creases descending from the mouth to form an arc lateral to the corners of the mouth.

* Faulkner, F. p. 535.

Modeling of the Nose

Nose Proportions

When an artist develops a nose for a portrait, there are proportional aspects to be considered. The nose measurement from brow to tip is nearly one third of the face height. The uppermost part is an extension of the frontal bones below the brow; it tapers from the brow at the glabella to a notch, the sellion, the saddle, or the bridge of the nose where it joins the nasal bones. There are three divisions of the nose below the sellion.

1. The bony upper portion is supported by the paired nasal bones.
2. The middle section is supported by superior lateral cartilages and septum.
3. The lower section is supported by the inferior lateral cartilages and the septum. It has a bulbous tip, the nostrils, and the ala or wings of the nose.

The distance between the inner corners of the eyes is usually the same width as an eye. The width of the ala usually equals the width between the eyes. On lateral view, the subnasal point where the nose joins the lip is usually one-half the measurement between the tip of the nose and the ala.

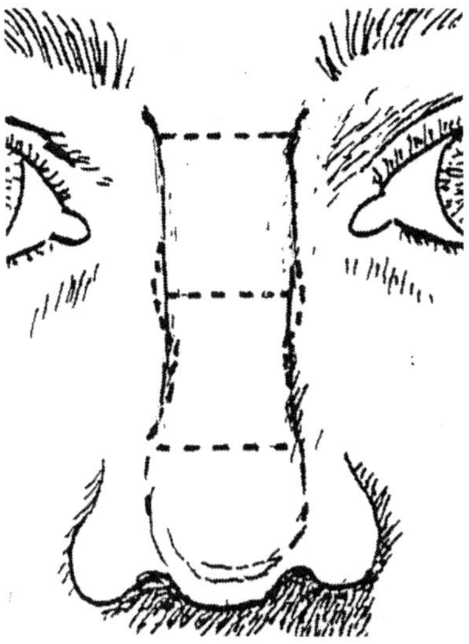

There are three segments of the nose below the sellion. Slight deviations from the usual form may need to be considered in the refinement phase.

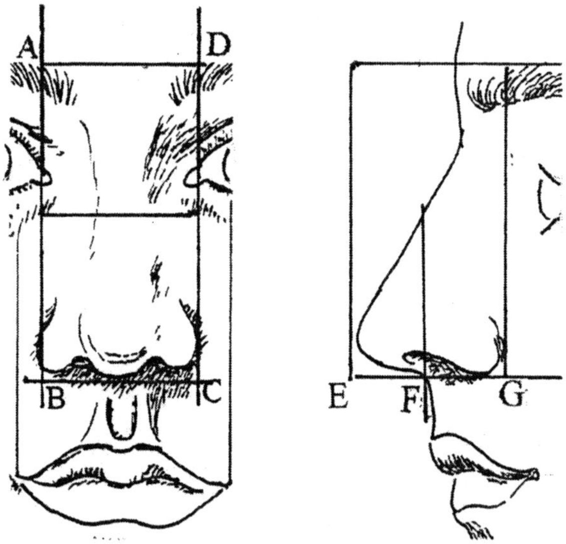

The usual nasal horizontal proportions are; the breadth of the nose at the ala, BC equals the width of an eye and equals the width between the inner corners of the eyes, AD. The height of a nose from the nose tip to the glabella of the brow equals twice the width of the ala, 2xBC. On profile, the tip of the nose to the nose-lip junction is one-half the distance of the nose tip to the lateral posterior ala, EF = FG.

Forming the Nose

After the preliminary brow and mandible have been formed, the nose needs to be added.

The beginning manner is to apply a roll of plastelline at the notch (sellion) below the brow. Make a flattened top or leading border to the nose; and then with two fingers, press down and laterally on each side to create the lateral form of the nose. The planes of the lateral sides

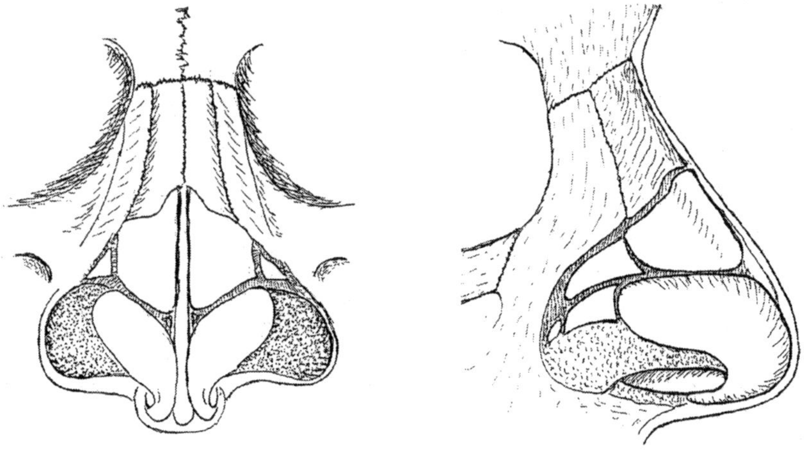

Supporting structures of the nose.

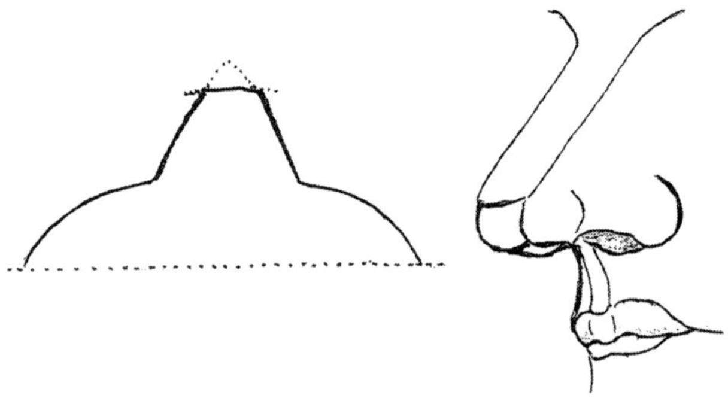

The leading border of the nose is nearly flat. Begin by modeling a flat, straight anterior border with sides sloping away at about a 60° angle. The tip resembles two angled surfaces at an obtuse angle.

of the nose diverge toward the cheeks usually at about a sixty degree angle from the nearly flat leading border. This forms the upper and middle segment of the nose.

The lower one-third segment of the nose, at the inferior lateral cartilages, has a bulbous tip and the ala or lateral wings. Small rolls of plasteline are added to represent these features. The nostrils are not just round holes. They vary depending on the shape of the nose. They are more like elongated ovals nearly tear drop shape that slope laterally downward. The width of the nose at the ala or wings of the nose is also about the same width as an eye and the width between eyes. On lateral view, the tip of the nose is blunted like two obtuse angles. There may be a slight flatness at the tip of the nose.

Preliminary lips may be added after the early nose formation. The nose to lip junction is one half the distance from the nose tip to the nose ala

After the usual nose configuration is created, adjustments need to be made for nasal contours to resemble the subject of the portrait. By understanding the proportions and the supporting structures of the nose and by recognizing how developments of the segments can vary, a more accurate and lifelike portrayal can be achieved. The variations from the usual or prototype nose are illustrated in another section of text. During later refinements, the various details can be adjusted and improved to resemble the appearance of the subject being portrayed.

Features of the Nose

In order to better understand the discussion about nose features, a review of illustrations, descriptions, and the terminology of the nose in the Anatomy Section may be helpful. When analyzing noses, there are important features to consider:

A. the width of the sellion or saddle;
B. the depth of the sellion;
C. the leading border is flat not a sharp angle;
D. the nasal slope to the cheeks in the mid portion is usually 60°;
E. the superior lateral cartilages junction with the nasal bones;
F. the configuration of the bulbous portion of the lower segment;
G. the form of the ala, or wings of the nose;
H. the angle of the nose from the tip to the ala on frontal view;
I. the breadth of the nose at the ala;
J. the nose to lip junction angle.

A. Width of the Sellion or Saddle

One of the widest appearing parts of the upper half of the nose is just below the glabella of the brow and above the sellion, or saddle. This part is supported by nasal processes of the frontal bones that taper down and in to join with the nasal bones at the sellion. This part may be broad, medium, or narrow.

During infancy the sellion is relatively broad, and the leading border is short and concave. In childhood and youth, the nose grows in length and continues to have a gentle concave leading border. By early adulthood, the leading border may become straight.

Some women continue to have a slight concave profile, but men between twenty to twenty-five years of age develop more mature and angular facial features including nose growth. With maturity, most people develop a medium width of the leading nasal border.

The noses of humans may have many variations. They all depend on the size, the prom-

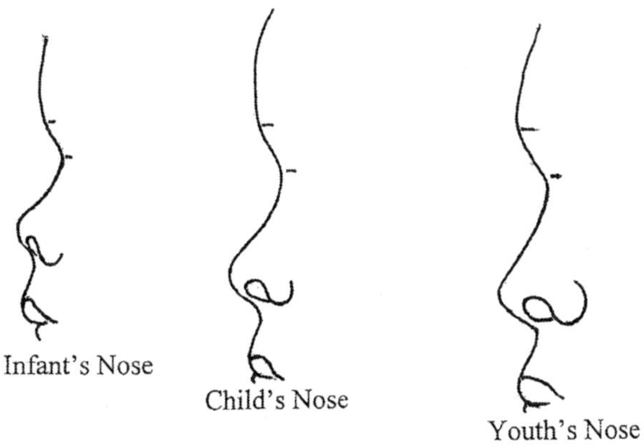

Infant's noses are short and concave with an obtuse nose-lip angle. During growth in childhood and youth, the nose becomes longer and the nose to lip angle becomes less obtuse.

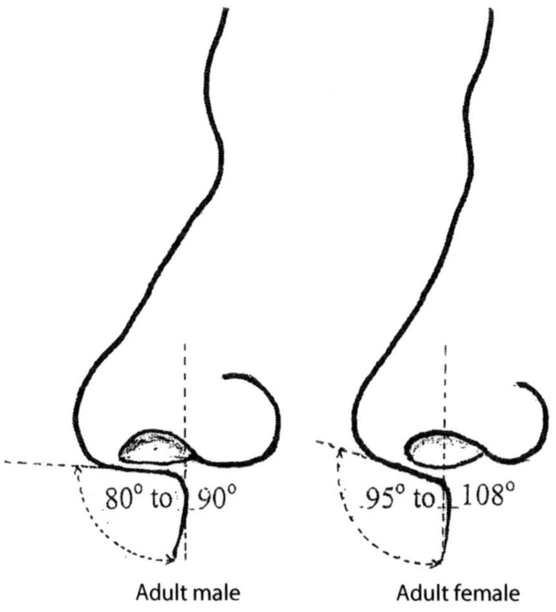

Adult nose profiles: men's noses are longer and the nose tip to the lip angle is usually 80° to 90°. Women's noses may be shorter, slightly concave, and have a nose to lip angle of 95° to 108°.

inence, and the relationship of the previously discussed elements. Some persons have a high bridge (sellion). Others have a deep notch (sellion) below the brow. Those with a humped nose have prominent nasal bones attached to the lateral superior nasal cartilages. A saddle or concave nose has less development of nasal bones and superior lateral cartilages.

Others with a prominent tip of the nose have more development of the inferior lateral cartilages. A sinuous hooked nose has prominent nasal bones, less development of superior lateral cartilages and greater development of the inferior lateral cartilages. A small nose may have all small elements. A very large nose may have all elements exaggerated. Various ethnic groups may have nasal features according to their inheritance.

B. Depth of the Sellion

Some ethnic groups with high narrow noses that deviate from the usual width. The sellion or bridge may be high, starting at the brow, but

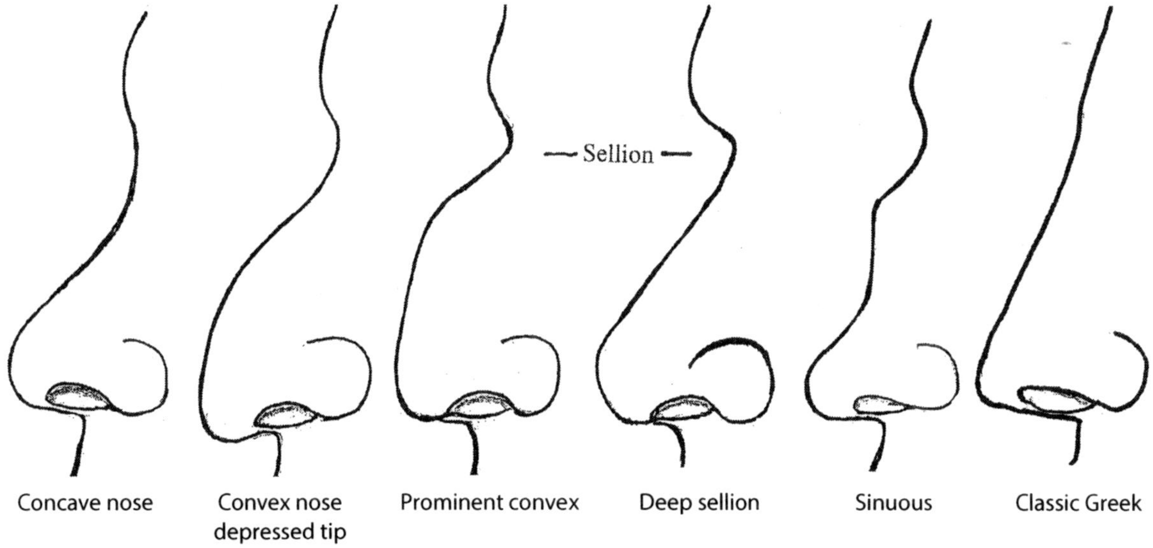

Several nose contours in profile are illustrated to demonstrate a variety that an artist may recognize and modify while applying finishing details.

rarely above it, with a nearly inconspicuous notch, as seen in the classic Greek statuary. This was typical of the Athenian and Spartan people of that era and may be seen today in their descendants. A moderate sellion is present in many people today, but some ethnic groups, as the native Australian, Papua-New Guinean, and Polynesian, may have a deep sellion that is often associated with a more pronounced brow.

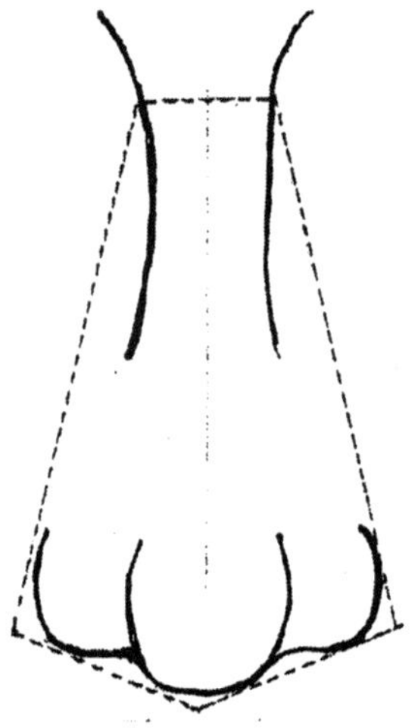

Some may wish to compare the nose outline on frontal view to a geometric figure. An elongated pentagon has a fair resemblance to the outline. The sellion serves as a horizontal top side; two elongated sides border the lateral cartilages; and short lines from each ala, converging at the tip resemble lower short angled sides.

C. Leading Border

The leading border of the nose needs to be considered broad and flat at first, and may later be gently rounded. Too many amateurs model a narrow ridge for the leading border of the nose. The initial stroke makes a flat top because these lateral supporting structures come up and join together to form a flat ridge. There is actually a palpable groove between their junction, and one can feel this groove, by stroking one's own nose with a finger. Between the lateral cartilages there is a groove that is filled with cartilage of the nasal septum and soft tissue. One of the common problems is the desire to make a sharp ridge down along the nose, (like a Halloween Jack-O-Lantern nose) and it is not like a sharp ridge. It is nearly flat. Some incorrectly think that the bone at the notch between the eyes is a pointed ridge that continues down as a sharp ridge to the tip of the nose. It is nearly flat at the nasal bones, and it is only slightly rounded for the full distance in most people.

D. Nasal Slope

At the junction of the upper nose segment and, the middle segment, (the nasal bones and the superior lateral cartilages) there may be a slight hump or prominence and a slight to definite flare. but it less often seen in women. Men may have a more definite prominence that develops following maturation in their twenties, and sometimes it is pronounced. These features may need to be adjusted later to be either more or less prominent. A concave nose may have had less development as one matured. The contours of the leading border of the lower third of the nose may continue down straight and flare to a bulbous form, depending on the development and shape of the inferior lateral cartilages.

E. Superior Lateral Cartilages

The slope of the nose on each side toward the cheeks at the mid portion, or superior lateral cartilage level, is usually about a sixty-degree angle. A narrow nose may have a more acute angle and a broad nose may have a wider angle.

F. Lower Bulbous Segment

The lower segment consists of the bulbous tip and the ala or wings of the nose. The inferior lateral cartilage supports the bulbous portion and the ala conforms to a lateral dense fibrous tissue formation. The tip of the nose may range from an inconspicuous flair, to a pronounced bulbous enlargement. A notched nose tip is often associated with a dimpled chin.

G. Ala

The outline of an ala has a definite "S" curve that starts at the top of a nostril. The line moves down, and then continues up and around, forming a lateral groove at the side of the nose.

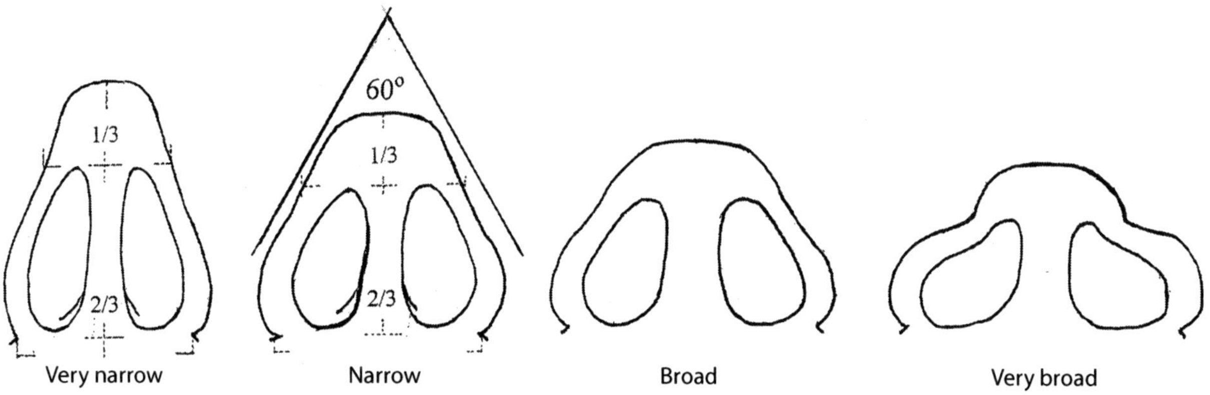

Nose widths vary from narrow to broad. Details need refinement during finishing stages. Many people have from slight to pronounced convex nasal profiles. The classic Greek nose has a high, barely perceptible sellion. Some noses have a pronounced concave profile, and others have a convex profile with a depressed nasal point. Some men have a pronounced prominence at the nasal bone and superior lateral cartilage junction. Some noses have a deep sellion with pronounced brows. A sinuous nasal profile is seldom seen. This nose has had a prominent nasal bone development, a diminished superior lateral cartilage development and a pronounced inferior lateral nasal cartilage growth.

This groove generally fans and fades out midway up toward tip of the nose. It may be inconspicuous, or it may be pronounced and curve up and forward towards the nostril, forming a slight notch at the bulb and ala junction, as is seen occasionally in some older people. There is also a diagonal crease between the cheek and the upper lip that starts at the ala groove and descends lateral to the mouth corner and then fades into the lower cheek.

H. Angle from Tip to Ala

The usual angle between the nose tip and both ala borders is about sixty degrees. The angle may be less, as fifty or forty degrees in high narrow noses. It may be a wider angle in broad noses. The width of the septum between nostrils corresponds to the width of the nose. The nose width at the apex of the nostrils is about one-third of the width of the nasal ala at the level of the sub-nasal point. The apex of the nostrils is at about one-third of the measurement from the nose tip to subnasal point.

I. Breadth of Nose at Ala

The breadth of the nose has been classified by anthropologists into a nasal index of one hundred times the breadth divided by the nasal height, similar to a percentage. There are five specific classifications to the index. Most noses are in classifications of Leptorhine, Mesorhine, and Platyrhine.

- Hyperleptorhine, a very narrow nose is 40 to 54.
- Leptorhine, a narrow nose is 55 to 69, is seen in many Caucasians;
- Mesorhine, a medium nose, is 70 to 84, is often seen in Asians;
- Platyrhine, a broad nose, is 85 to 99 is often observed in some African Americans and Polynesians. However, nasal configuration is independent of skin color.
- Hyperplatyrhine, a very broad nose, is 100 to 115.*

The paired nostrils conform to the midline septum and to the ala. The nostrils may be narrow, medium, round, or oval. Infant's nostrils are usually round. Narrow nostrils are associated with high narrow nose configurations. Median nostrils are usually oval, often with a pear shaped outline. Broad noses may have round or oval nostrils with a nearly horizontal axis. Nostrils are usually de-emphasized in sculpture unless a caricature is intended.

* Oliver, George. *Practical Anthropology.* (Springfield, IL: Charles C. Thomas. 1960) p. 58.

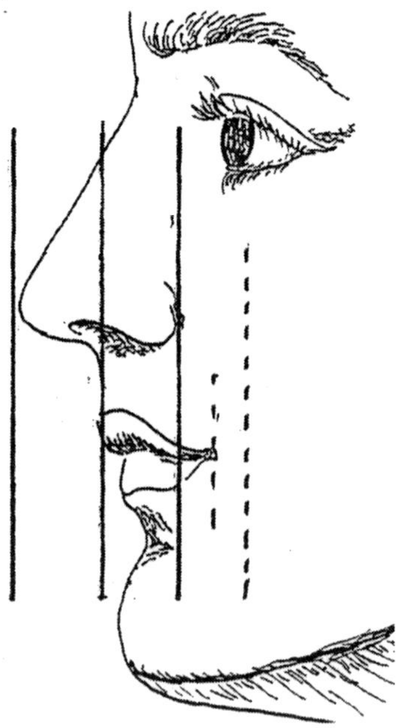

On profile, the tip of the nose to the nose-lip junction is one-half the distance of the nose tip to the lateral posterior ala.

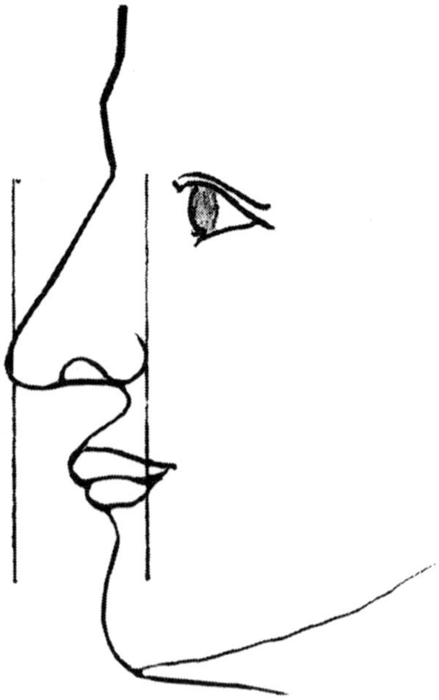

Avoid placing the subnasal point of the nose just below the ala. It may make lip appear puckered.

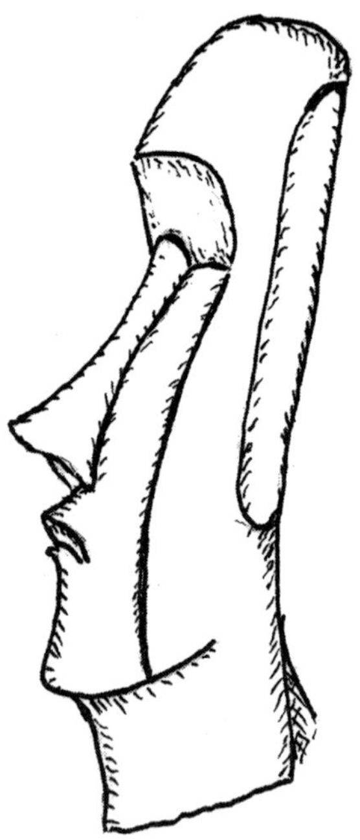

Primitive art, like the effigies of Easter Island, have a lip-nose junction at the ala with a protruding upper lip.

J. Nose to Lip Junction Angle

The nasal septum is between the nostrils. The angle that the septum meets the upper lip on profile varies with age and sex. Infants have a wide obtuse angle. As a child grows, the nose and the face lengthen, and the angle is reduced. When viewing the nose on profile, a short, slightly concave nose suggests youth, especially in women. The nose to lip angle in young women may vary between ninety-five and one-hundred-eight degrees. In men, whose noses are usually longer and are more prominent, the angle can vary from eighty to ninety-five degrees. Elderly persons of both sexes may have decreased angles of incidence, since the cartilages of the nose continue to grow with age and droops as it becomes more soft and flexible.

The attachment of the nose to the upper lip is at the subnasal point. As seen on profile, it is about one half the distance from the tip of the nose to the posterior border of an ala.

There is a very small curve up from the lip to the septum of the nose. The corner of the mouth is nearly an equal distance past the ala. This aspect of lip and nose relationship is often ignored in primitive art, like the Easter Island effigies, where on profile; the anterior border of the upper lip is placed just below the ala of the nose. The work by some amateurs have the subnasal point just below the ala. This configuration makes an upper lip protrude and appears puckered.

The configuration of a nose profile depends on the development of its three segments and their relationship to each other. A concave nose has less development of the superior lateral cartilages, while a humped nose has increased development of the lower portion of the nasal bones and the superior lateral cartilages. A large nose may have increased development of all segments. As people age, the cartilages continue to grow slowly and soften, allowing the nose to become longer and more convex. Structure and form of the nose is more thoroughly discussed and illustrated in the Anatomy Section of this book. By understanding the anatomy of the nose and its development during maturation, the form of the nose can be more accurately developed in a portrait.

Formation of the Lips and Mouth

After Avard Fairbanks developed a skull in clay, it was necessary to add soft tissues, particularly the lips and then cheeks. A couple finger-sized rolls of plasteline were pressed in, covering the area superficial to the two arcs of teeth, which are the upper teeth of the maxilla and the lower teeth in the mandible. Rolls were then placed in other areas of the face, like the cheeks, to represent other soft tissue so that the whole portrait would develop orderly and nearly simultaneously.

When early representations of other features were added, the next step for the lip formation was appropriate. He said, "See how easy it is to make the lips." With four deft strokes, using the wire loop of a modeling tool, he incised grooves that resembled a broad letter "M," that formed the opening of the mouth. With additional strokes, using the broad wooden blade of the modeling tool, he quickly rounded the plasteline adjacent to these grooves to form the mucous membranes of the lips.

Using two fingers to press the sides of the upper lip towards the center, the philtrim,and the two columella were formed. The sublabial crease, an indentation below the lower lip and above the chin, was also formed with a tool stroke.

Additional refinements, especially defining the vermillion borders of the lips, were delayed until the refinements of other facial features were in progress.

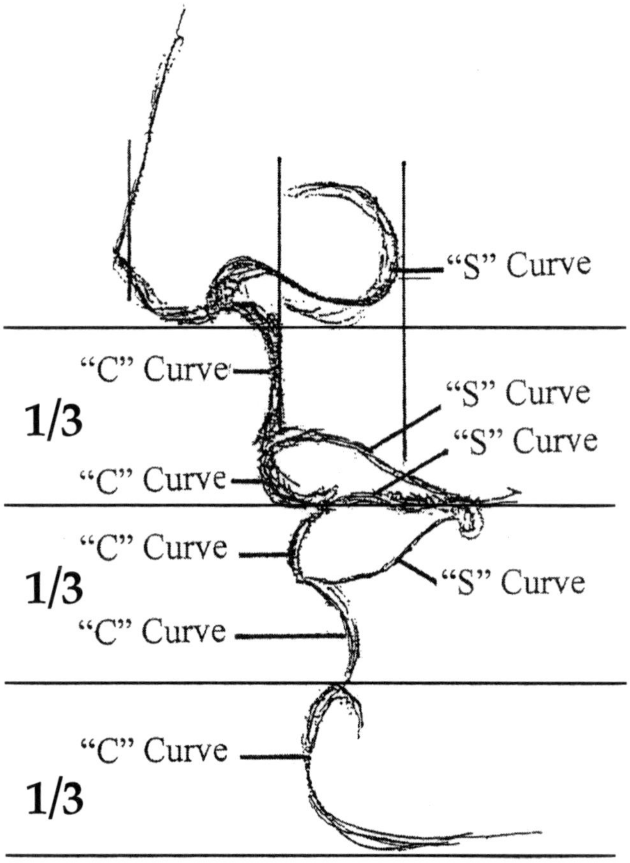

The lower face in profile, from A.T. Fairbanks' sketchbook.

Lip and Mouth Proportions

The lips, being soft tissue, have some variability. The features of the lower third of the face may be divided into three unequal vertical measurements.

1. The upper third is from the nose junction with the upper lip, essentially the subnasal point, to the mouth aperture.
2. The middle portion, the smallest third, is from the mouth to the sub labial crease that is an inverted arc above the chin.
3. The sub labial crease to the chin is the lower and largest third.

The chin to the mouth is almost two-thirds of the distance to the nose, a manifestation of the golden ratio of 0.62... The width of a mouth is usually equal to the distance between the medial arcs of the iris of each eye.

Refinements of the Lips

The vermillion borders of the lips are where the skin and the pink mucous membranes meet. Some people have more prominent vermillion borders than others. The upper lip border resembles a broad "M" configuration. The lower lip border may resemble a very broad "W" configuration.

There are variations in lip forms. Lips vary from thick to thin. The upper lip, from nose to mouth, may vary from short to long. Those with short upper lips cannot smile without exposing incisor teeth. Those with long upper lips can hardly show teeth when they smile. Men with long upper lips will often grow a mustache.

The lips cover the teeth and conform to the arcs of teeth, yet they may vary in breadth. The arc of the lower teeth is the lesser arc and the lower lip is usually less prominent. The upper lip is usually forward of the lower lip.

Illustrations of early development in the first few weeks of embryonic life are included with the anatomy to demonstrate the development of the lips. The central part of upper lip and the two central upper incisor teeth are formed by tissue growing medially and down. This frontonasal process later forms the septum of the nose. It grows down in early embryonic life between the lateral tissues, the maxillary processes, to which it joins.

The two vertical ridges of the upper lip (the columella) are below the nose where they represent the fusion of maxillary components on each side to the midline septum of the nose to develop the middle segment of the upper lip. There is a concave groove between these two ridges called the philtrum. In the center of the vermillion border of the upper lip there is an inverted notch between the columella. There is a resulting fullness or prominence in the mid portion of the upper lip. Just lateral to this are slight concavities or hollows on both sides of the central prominence, and beyond these are convexities representing the maxillary components of the mid-lateral upper lip.

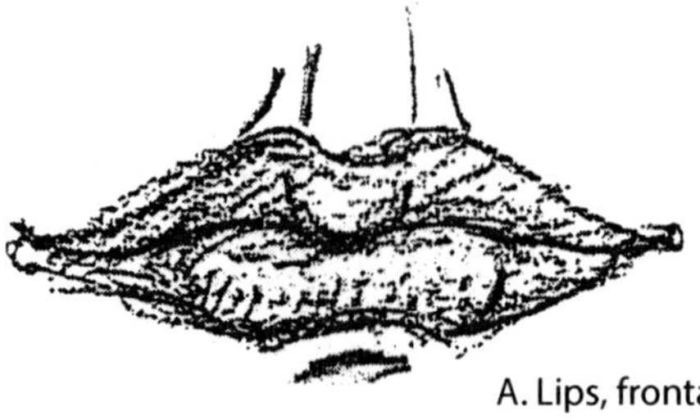

A. Lips, frontal view.

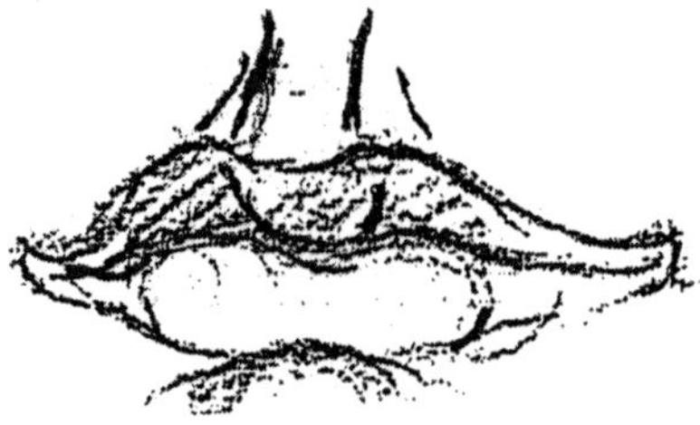

B. Lips, slightly oblique.

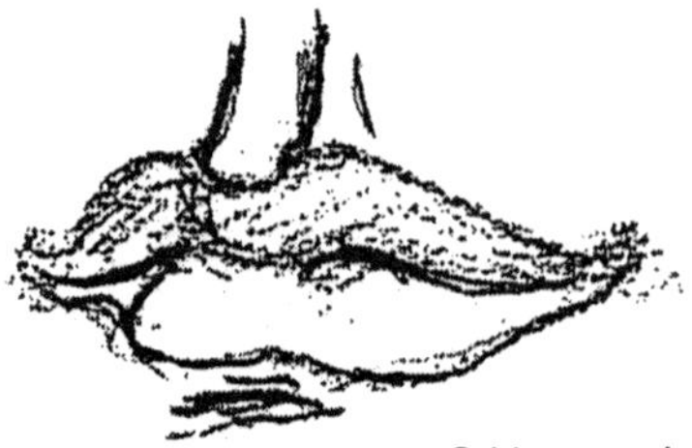

C. Lips, moderately oblique.

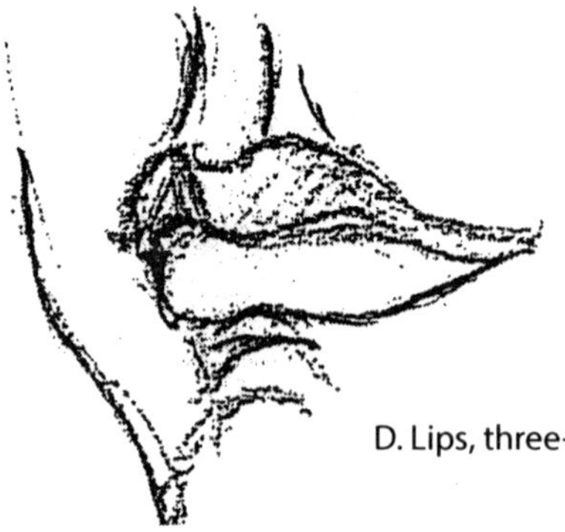

D. Lips, three-quarter view.

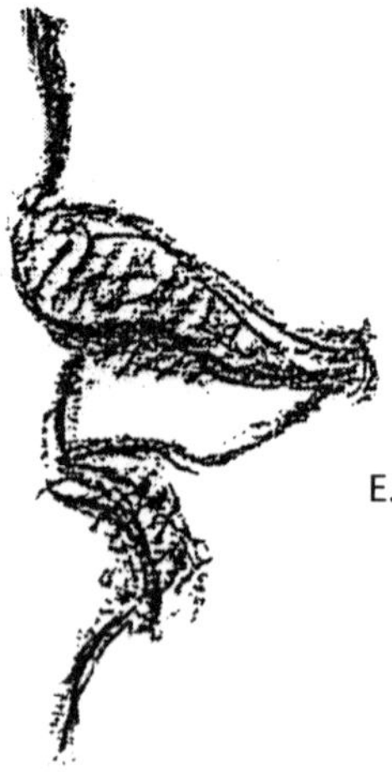

E. Lips in profile

From the sketch pad of Avard T. Fairbanks.

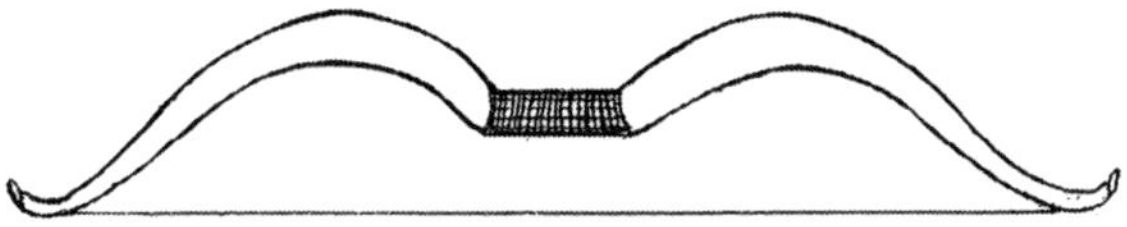

The vermillion border of the upper lip resembles a Grecian bow.

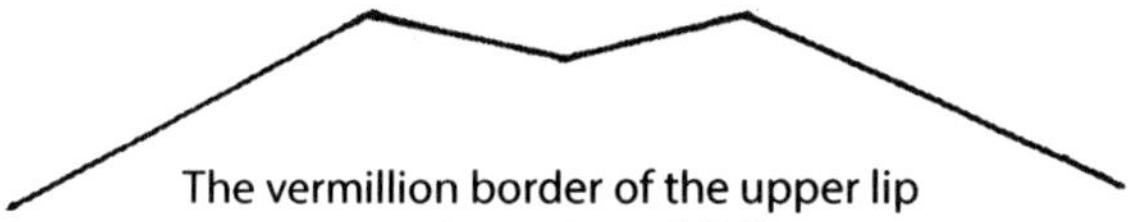

The vermillion border of the upper lip resembles a broad "M".

The mouth opening resembles a broader "M".

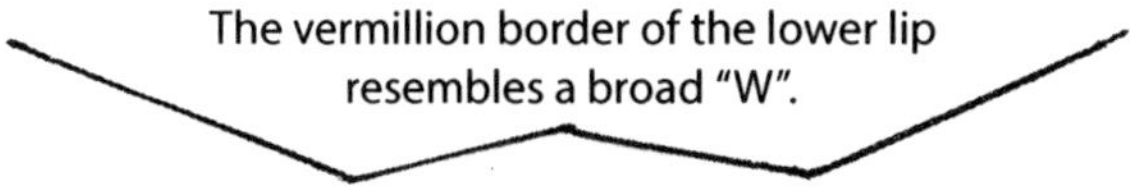

The vermillion border of the lower lip resembles a broad "W".

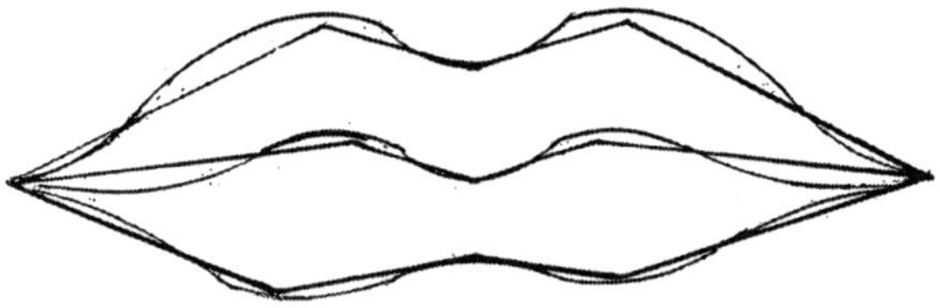

The lips, represented by straight lines with superimposed curved lines.

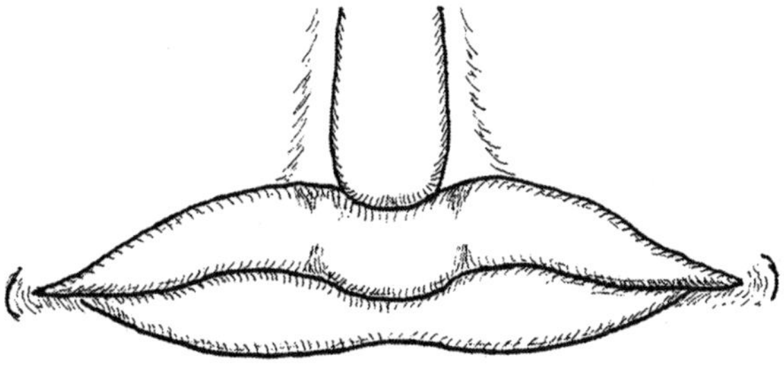

Medium Lips

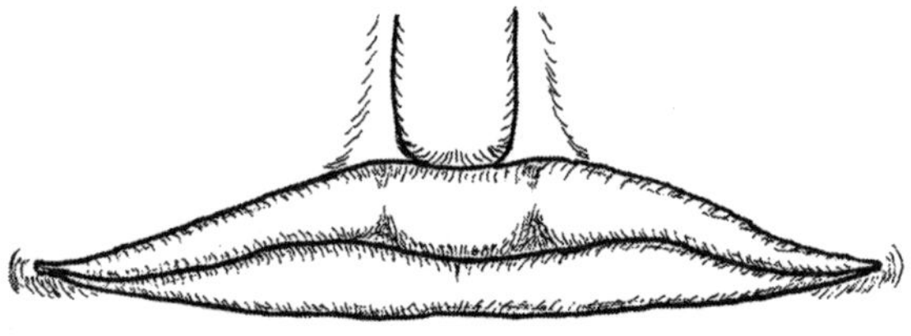

Thin Lips

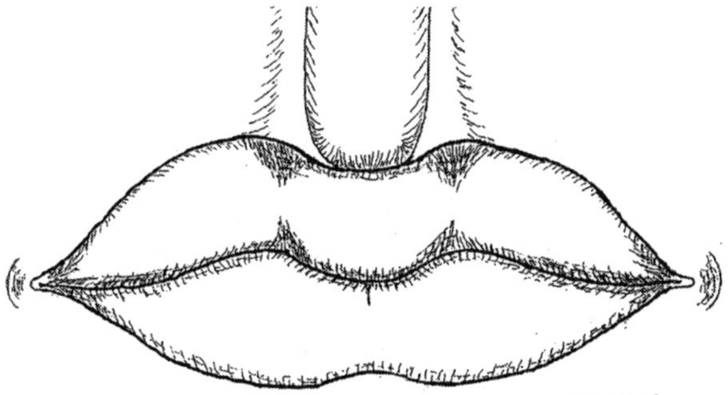

Thick Lips

E.F.

The lower lip is formed by the mandibular processes joining in the center line. In the center of the lower lip is a slight concavity which matches the convexity below the philtrum. On both sides of the central concavity of the lower lip, there are convexities that match the shallow concavities of the upper lip. Lateral to these convexities of the lower lip, there are shallow concavities that match the convexities of the upper lip. They match just as the mucous membranes of both lips join, turn up and in at the corners of the mouth. In modeling the lips, one should make these convexities match the concavities.

The upper lip had three convexities and two concavities which match the central concavity and the two lateral convexities of the lower lip. This results in a configuration of the upper vermillion border that resembles a Grecian bow or a broad "M." The mouth aperture has a similar but less pronounced but a more broad "M" configuration, and the vermillion border of the lower lip resembles a broad "W."

When viewed on profile, the upper lip is usually forward of the lower lip, and both lips have rounded anterior surfaces. The mucous membranes of the lips are the same tissue as in the mouth; it is rolled out forming the pink part of the lips. If we understand that it is rolled out, it helps us to understand the form of the corners of the mouth.

When the vermillion borders of the lips come to the corners of the mouth, they join and roll into the mouth with the upper lip slightly overlapping the lower lip. They do not come to points at the corners. There are indentations and small arcs at the mouth corners. Some want to make a point for the mouth corners. It should be curved, like very small semicircles, into the corners of the mouth, unless it is hidden as the upper lip folds over the lower lip.

Both of the lip ridges (vermillion borders) merge at the corners and the mucous membrane disappears into the mouth. The upper lip corner often folds over the lower lip which then appears to terminate in a slanted "T" configuration, but not out to a point.

The shape of the lips varies in depth from full or thick to medium, and to thin. The form of the lips is important to recognize for a person's individuality. The mouth may vary from narrow to wide, but usually mouth corners are directly below the medial arc of the iris of the corresponding eye.

If the lips were to be viewed from above, they would appear to curve laterally in an arc from the midline around to follow the curvature of the teeth. There is a fullness, lateral to the mouth corners, representing the orbiculalis oris muscle, which is a broad thin muscle that goes around the mouth to tighten or pucker the lips.

There is a pair of muscles on each side going up and laterally. There is also a pair going down and laterally from the orbiculalis oris corners towards the mandible, creating fullness on either side. This leaves a slight lateral concavity just above and lateral to the chin on each side.

NOTE: the muscles of expression are illustrated in muscles of the face in the Anatomy Section.

Anterior to the chin, there is a fibrous fatty pad, a cushion that serves as protection. Above this is a semicircular crease, the sublabial crease, an inverted arc pointing down on both sides. There is a diagonal crease on each side of the mouth that begins at the corners and progresses laterally toward the borders of the jaw. These occasionally merge with diagonal creases from the ala, especially in older persons.

There are other muscles of expression that activate the lips, which are illustrated in the section about anatomy.

In adults, the two mandible bones diverge at an angle of about sixty degrees, but are truncated, or squared-off at the chin, instead of coming to a sharp point. They are fused at the chin in the midline and function as a single bone.

The Ear Details

The Form of an Ear

The general form and outline of an ear is like a question mark, a typographical character that was apparently formed to resemble an ear. The outer border is a geometrical spiral. When it is viewed from above, the helix is slanted outward at a small angle from the temporal anterior-posterior plane of the head. An anterior view reveals that the apex of the ear has a lateral tilt of about twenty degrees from vertical. As the helix descends, it curves slightly inward as the anti-helix curves slightly outward barely obscuring the lower half of the helix. The ear's interesting shape improves hearing of various sounds.

Proportions of an Ear

The anterior border of the ear is slightly posterior to a point halfway from the brow to occiput. The slant of the ear from vertical is nearly parallel to the posterior border of the mandible above the angle of the jaw, and it also resembles the slant of the forehead. The vertical measure is one third of the face height, the same as the brow to the nose-lip junction. The anterior-posterior width is one-half of its height. The highest point of an ear, in teens and adults, is nearly the same level as the brow. The lobe and lower border is usually on the same level as the subnasal point.

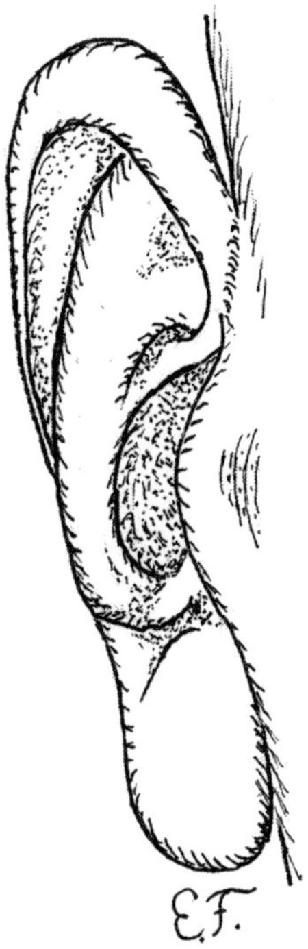

Right ear, anterior.

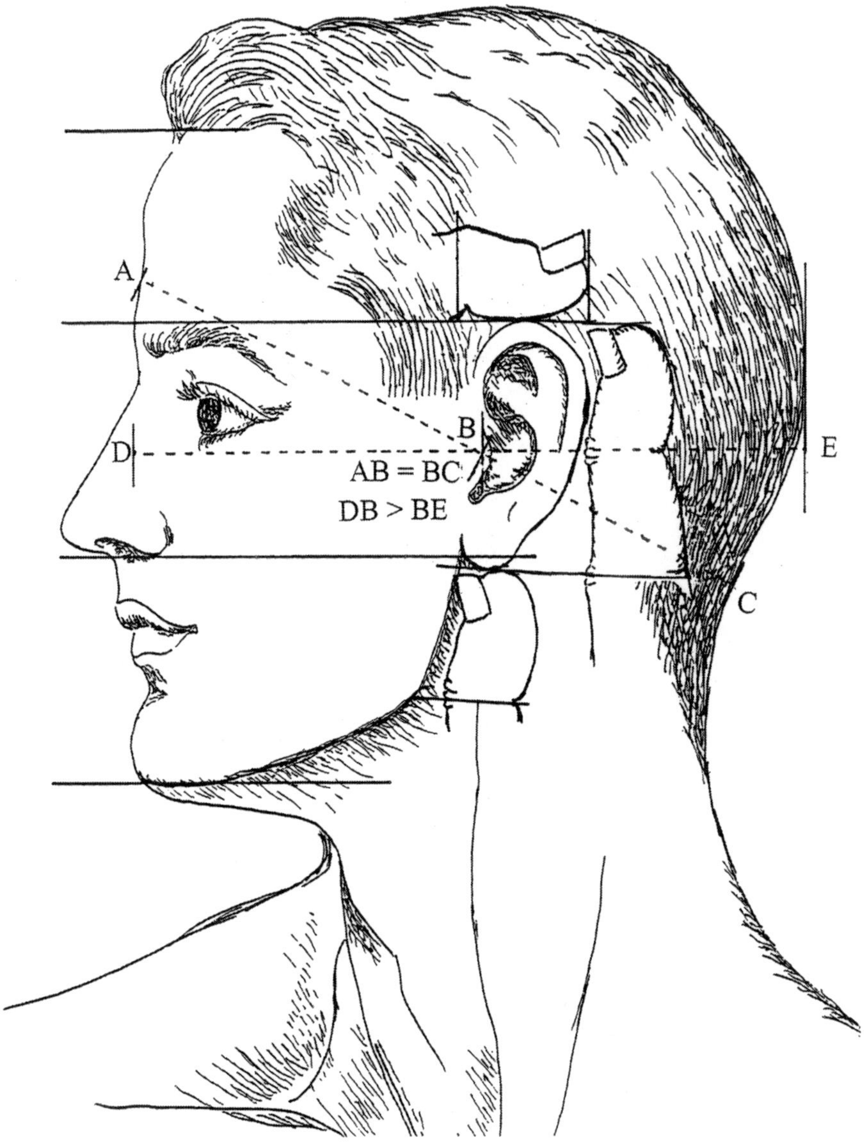

Proportions of an ear.

Preliminary Modeling of an Ear

After the preliminary modeling of other facial features, an ear can be fashioned in a sculptor's hands with two coils of clay. An inner circle represents the antihelix, and the outer coil for the helix is formed in a geometric spiral like the shape of a question mark.

The ear canal (porion) of a skull is half the distance of the brow to the occiput. Therefore the ear is placed so that the ear canal is half the distance from the forehead to occiput, and half-way between the level of the brow and nose to the lip junction. The vertical slant of an ear away from the head is usually at a twenty degree tilt at the apex from the temporal plane.

Details of the ear are to be modeled in later as other features are being refined.

Additional details and illustrations about the ear are in the Anatomy Section of this book.

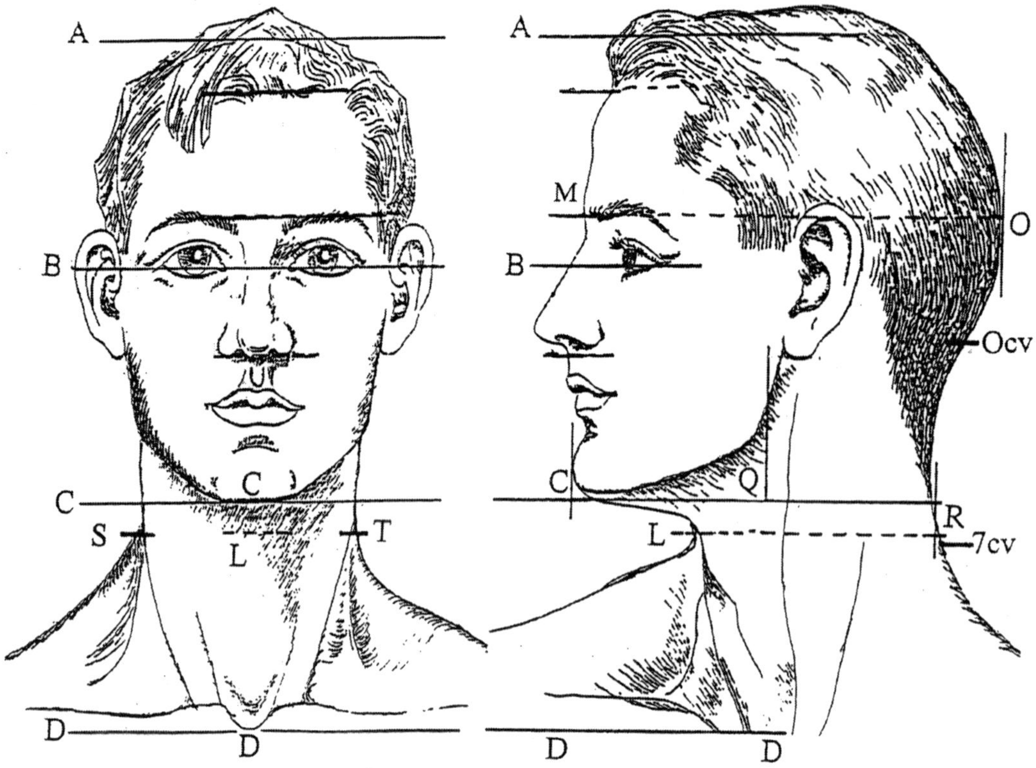

Proportions of the neck.

Proportions of the Neck

The illustrated anterior neck height, C D is equal to one-half of a head height: (C D = A B = B C). The posterior neck height is the occiput to the spine of the seventh cervical vertebra (Ocv to 7cv). The transverse diameter of the neck, S T, is equal to the anterior-posterior measurement of the neck at the level of the larynx, L R: as shown (S T = L R).

The chin to the angle of the mandible, C Q is nearly equal to the thickness of the neck (C Q ± L R). The anterior posterior measurement of the neck is nearly equal to one-half of the brow to occiput measure (L R ± M O ÷ 2).

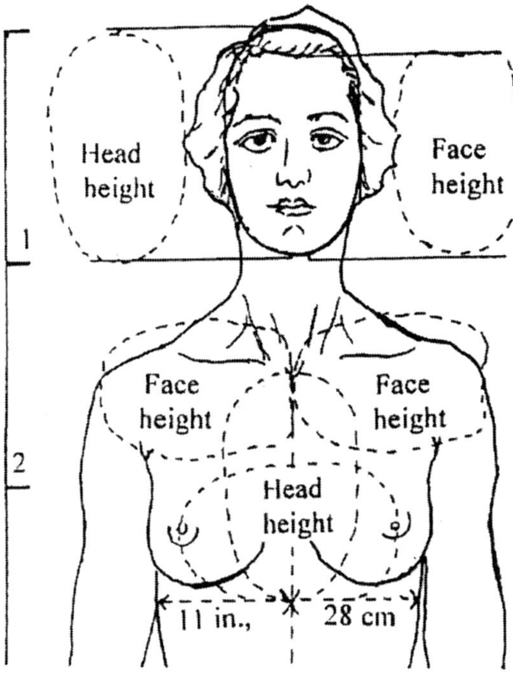

Female shoulder width is two face heights or 2.6 head widths.

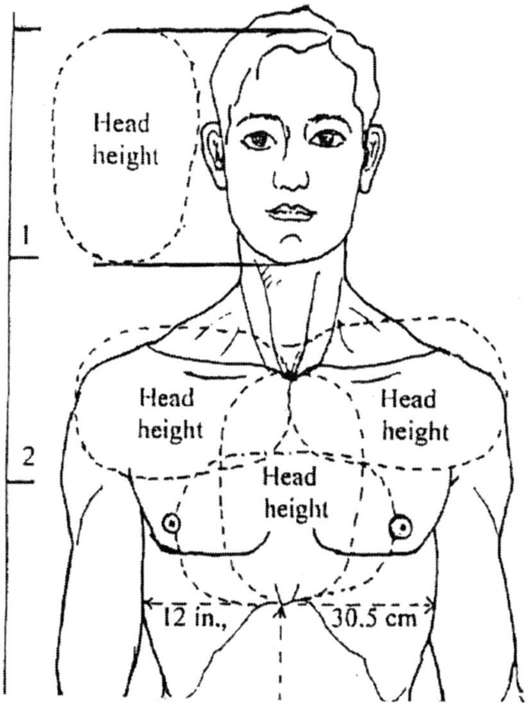

Male shoulder width is two face heights or three head widths.

Form of the Neck

Rising as a pedestal from the thorax, the neck resembles the geometric form of a curved cylinder. It is modified at both the upper and lower ends. On cross section, the neck, at the level of the Larynx, is nearly circular, and the anterior to posterior and lateral diameters are nearly equal. However, the anterior and posterior proportions are different. The upper posterior neck measurement is from the occiput of the skull, which is nearly at the level at the nose-to-lip junction. It is higher than the anterior neck measurement that begins at the chin. The posterior base of the neck is at the spine of the seventh cervical vertebra, which is at the level of the larynx in the anterior neck. The posterior base is higher than the base of the anterior neck which is at the sternal notch. The measurement of the anterior neck is from the chin to the sternal notch, which is at the level of second thoracic vertebra. It is lower than the posterior neck base. The posterior neck is mostly vertebrae and the muscle masses which slope down and laterally toward the shoulders.

The anterior neck contains muscles and physiological organs. These organs include the esophagus for eating, the trachea for breathing, large blood vessels for circulation, nerves for muscular control, and the larynx (also called the Adams apple) for vocalizing and separating swallowing from breathing. The prominent anterior muscles are the paired sternocleidomastoid muscles that slope down and inward from the mastoid processes behind the ears and attach to the sternum at the sternal notch.

On profile, there is an anterior and a posterior "C" type curve. The anterior curve is from the chin to the sternal notch. The posterior curve starts at the occiput and blends into the shoulders at the spine of the seventh cervical vertebra, the longest spine in the neck. The neck contours spread at both upper part of the neck toward the head, and at the lower part toward the thorax.

Creases of the Face Show Expression

Expression is a significant part of communication that adds animation, courage and the vibrant impressions of life. It is an important manifestation of emotions, of thoughts and feelings that help to create a great masterpiece. Various wrinkles in the face and subtle changes of face features and contours assist to demonstrate a dramatic response to a situation.

Horizontal furrows of the brow curve longitudinally upward and inward from the sides of the forehead, then gently dip in the center. These are present when one is worried, concerned, or frowning. They are accentuated when brows are elevated, but less apparent when smiling. They do not appear above the hairline, or above from where the hairline has receded. This is most obvious when a bald man frowns. These wrinkles are created or accentuated by contraction of the frontalis muscles.

Vertical wrinkles between the brows extending upward from the bridge (sellion) of the nose are also present on frowning or squinting. These are due to the contraction of corrugator muscles. These are vertical muscles at the inner aspect of the brow. The wrinkles that occur, lateral to the lateral corner of eye openings when a person squints, smiles, or laughs, is due to contraction of the orbicularis oculi muscles that encircle both eyelids. An actor's makeup includes a "crow's foot" lateral to the eye to accentuate these wrinkles, especially when he is portraying an older person. When there is a partial closing of the eyes, a pressure develops that produces a slight bulge in the soft and fatty tissue below and lateral to both lower eyelids.

The contour of the eyelids assumes its shape from a protective shield. A convex thin layer of cartilage, called the tarsal plate, is the supporting structure of the eyelid. This conforms to the spherical contours of an eyeball. Above the eyelid is a fold that is more apparent when one is looking up. When one looks down or closes his eyes, the loose skin is unfolded. A similar fold is present on the lower lid, which unfolds when one looks up, the lower lid moves upward. Below the lower eyelid there is soft tissue that extends down to the infraorbital ridge. This is not usually obvious in young people, but becomes more apparent with advancing age. (In less scientific circles, these are called bags under the eyes.) The sculptor may find it advantageous to de-emphasize this feature.

An additional interesting geometric form begins on each side of the nose at the superior lateral cartilages. These sweeps down and lateral like two fans and blend into the cheeks. The upper borders are the infraorbital margins below the eyes, and the lower borders are the diagonal creases that start at each ala and descends diagonally to outline the junction of the upper lip with the cheeks then they blend into the cheeks. This crease is less apparent in young people except when laughing or crying.

Another crease begins at the corner of the mouth and descends laterally to the chin. In older men these creases may join. Portrayal of this may give a person character. There is a crease under the lower lip, the sublabial crease that is an inverted arc above the mentalis muscles and a fibrous-fatty pad. This pad resembles a small hemisphere and is flanked by prominences of the anterior chin.

A transverse crease is often noted below the chin, just superficial to the attachments of the mylohyoid muscle to the mandible. This partial cone-like muscle is directed downward to the hyoid bone, which in turn is connected to the larynx or voice box. Increased fatty tissue deposits in this area give a prominence in some people which is called a double chin. This feature may also be de-emphasized.

---

after lecture notes of Avard T. Fairbanks

Proportional Measurements for a Portrait

The charts and images on these next pages are gathered from information in two books on human proportions for artists by Avard T. Fairbanks and Eugene F. Fairbanks. For more detailed information and illustrations, the books are available from the website shown below.

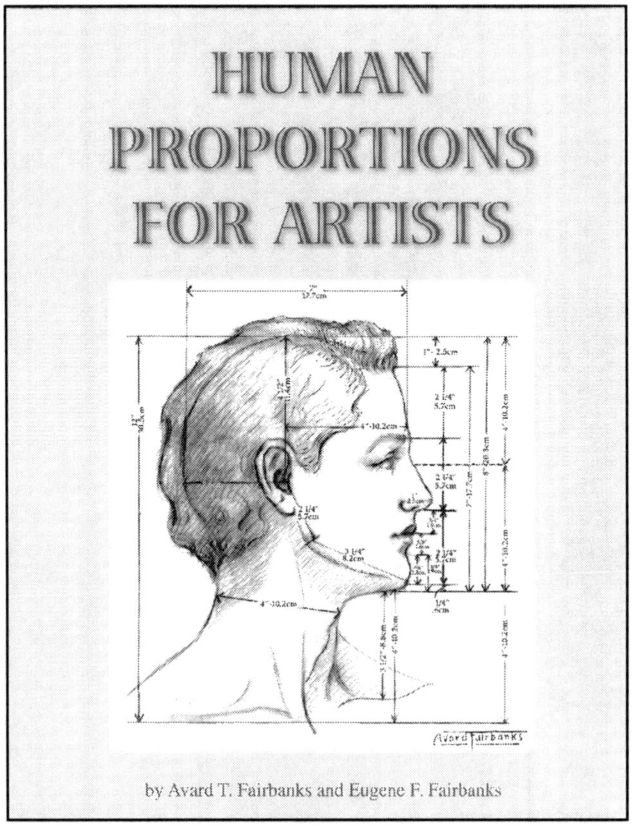

This book will be of particular interest to art students and serious amateurs. It discusses human proportions and includes profuse illustrations and tables of about 120 representative human measurements of both male and female figures in both inch and metric dimensions.

ISBN 978-1467901871

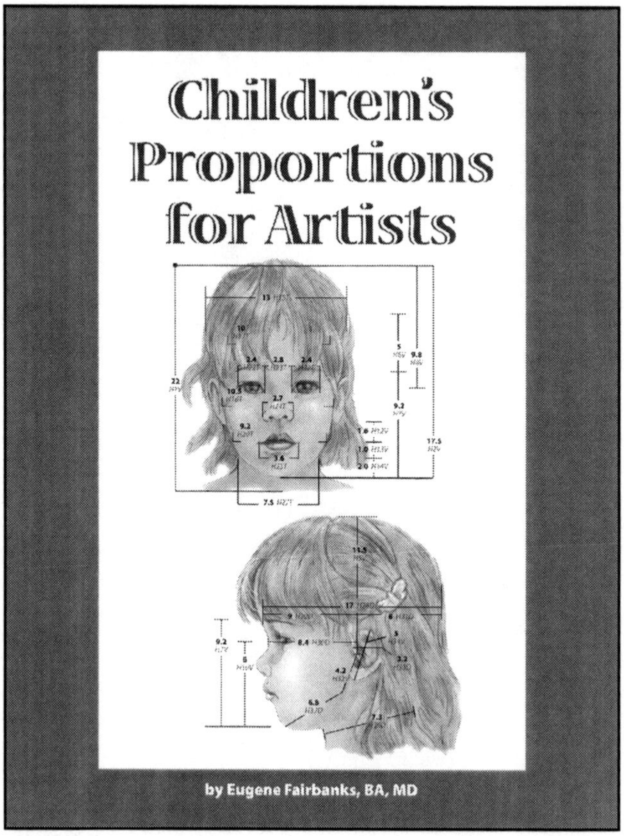

Studies are presented for figurative artists about the yearly growth and development of children of each gender from infancy to young adulthood. Illustrations are included with charts of about 130 representative measurements and proportions.

ISBN 978-0-9725841-2-8

To learn more about these two books or to purchase,

please visit www.FairbanksArtBooks.com

Masculine Head, Length 9 inches

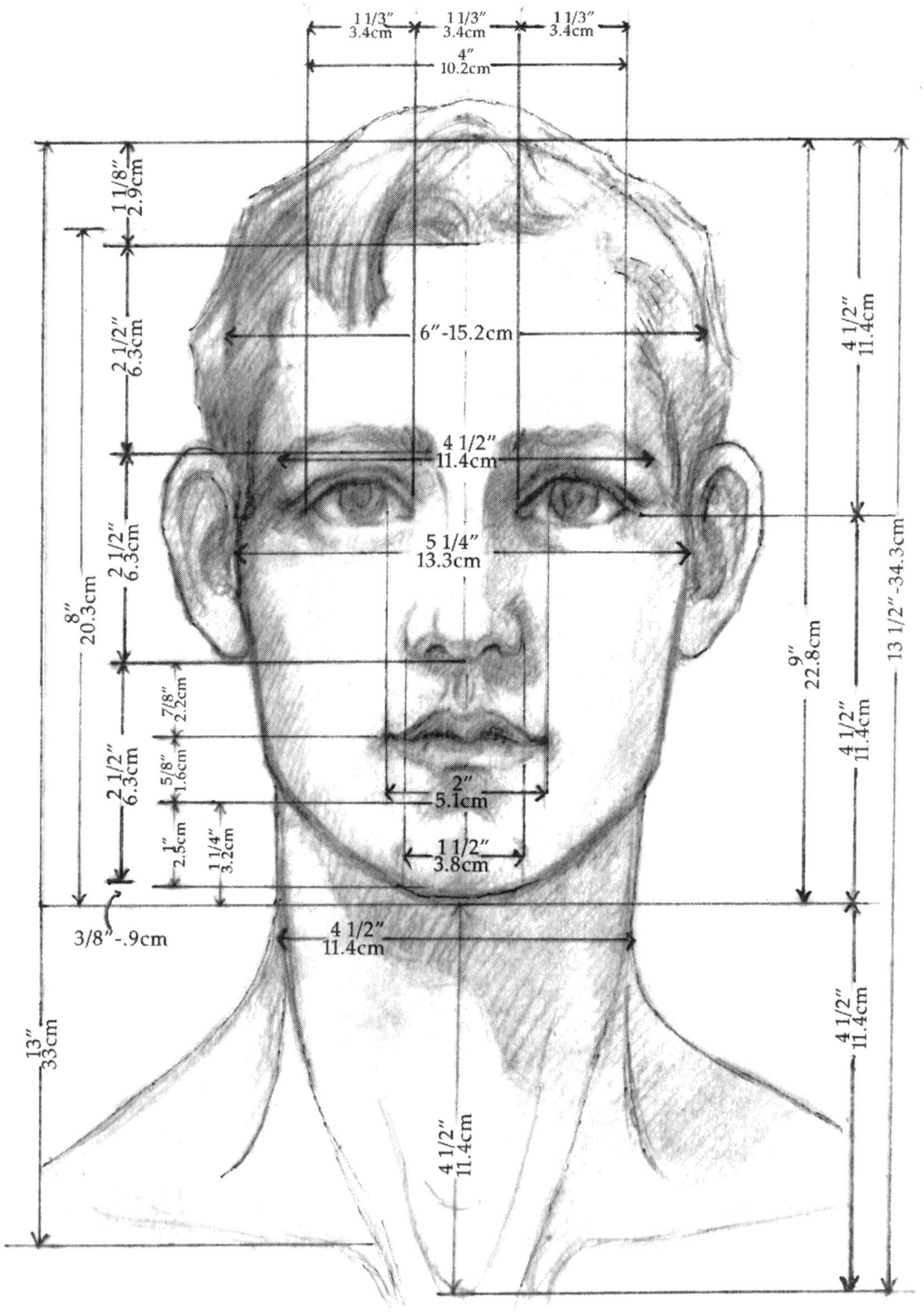

The masculine head, detailed proportions, anterior view. The head is divided in two at the level of the eyes. One half face height = distance between lateral corners of eyes. The mouth width = one half distance between the lateral corners of eyes.

Masculine Head, Length 9 inches

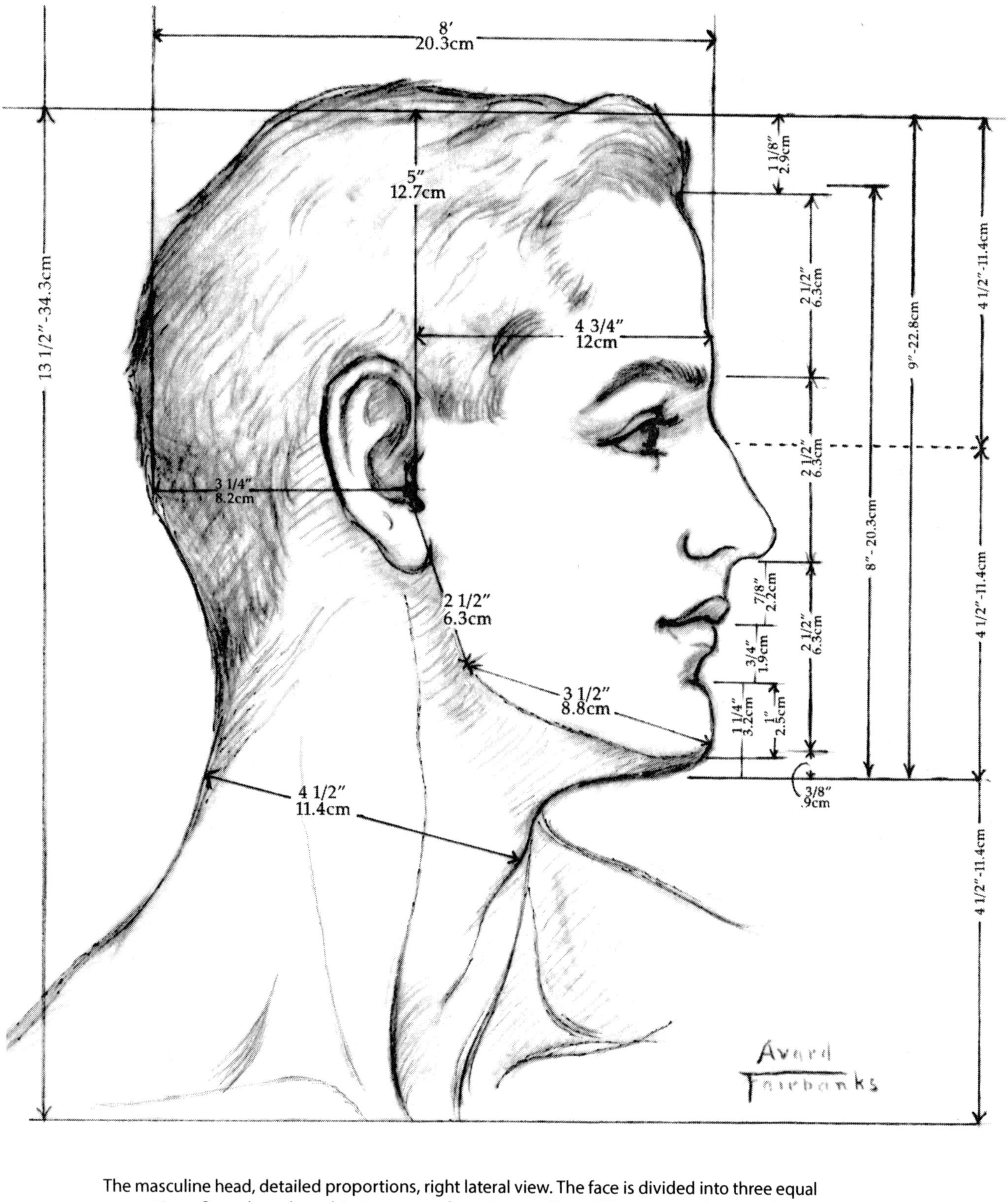

The masculine head, detailed proportions, right lateral view. The face is divided into three equal proportions: Sternal notch to chin; to corner of eye; to top of head. The ear is on the same horizontal level as the nose and length is equal. The eye is one half the distance from the top of the head to the chin.

	Fraction of Life Size			ADULT MALE PROPORTIONS Inch Measurements	Fraction of Life Size		
Life size	3/4	2/3	1/2		1/3	1/4	1/8
				VERTICAL MEASUREMENTS			
inch	inch	inch	inch		inch	inch	inch
72.0	54.0	48.0	36.0	Stature, Height, Vertex to Sole	24.0	18.0	9.0
58.5	43.9	39.0	29.3	Shoulder at Acromion to Sole	19.5	14.6	7.3
42.0	31.5	28.0	21.0	Ant. Sup. Spine of Ilium to Sole	14.0	10.5	5.3
37.4	28.1	24.9	18.7	Symphysis Pubis to Sole	12.5	9.4	4.7
32.69	24.5	21.8	16.4	Crotch to Sole	10.9	8.2	4.1
21.0	15.8	14.0	10.5	Knee to Sole	7.0	5.3	2.6
13.5	10.1	9.0	6.8	Head & Neck, Vertex to St. Notch	4.5	3.4	1.7
16.5	12.4	11.0	8.3	St. Notch, Shoulder – Ant. Sup. Sp.	5.5	4.1	2.1
26.8	20.1	17.9	13.4	Sternal Notch to Crotch	8.9	6.7	3.4
21.0	15.8	14.0	10.5	Ant. Sup. Spine of Ilium to Knee	7.0	5.3	2.6
54.0	40.5	36.0	27.0	Kneeling Height	18.0	13.5	6.8
38.0	28.5	25.3	19.0	Sitting Height	12.7	9.5	4.8
42.5	31.9	28.3	21.3	Buttock, Straight Leg to Sole	14.2	10.6	5.3
24.7	18.5	16.5	12.4	Buttock to Flexed Knee	8.2	6.2	3.1
23.6	17.7	15.7	11.8	Flexed Knee to Sole	7.9	5.9	3.0
				VERTICAL HEAD MEASUREMENTS			
inch	inch	inch	inch		inch	inch	inch
9.0	6.8	6.0	4.5	Vertex to Chin	3.0	2.3	1.1
8.0	6.0	5.3	4.0	Hairline to Chin	2.7	2.0	1.0
4.5	3.4	3.0	2.3	Vertex to Lateral Corner of Eye	1.5	1.1	0.6
5.5	4.1	3.7	2.8	Vertex to Tragion of Ear	1.8	1.4	0.7
2.5	1.9	1.7	1.3	Hairline to Brow	0.8	0.6	0.3
5.0	3.8	3.3	2.5	Hairline to Infranasal	1.7	1.3	0.6
2.5	1.9	1.7	1.3	Brow to Infranasal	0.8	0.6	0.3
2.13	1.6	1.4	1.1	Sellion to Infranasal	0.7	0.5	0.3
5.13	3.9	3.4	2.6	Sellion to Chin	1.7	1.3	0.6
2.5	1.9	1.7	1.3	Infranasal to Chin	0.8	0.6	0.3
0.88	0.7	0.6	0.4	Infranasal to Lip Aperature	0.3	0.2	0.1
0.75	0.6	0.5	0.4	Lip Aperat. to Sublabial Crease	0.3	0.2	0.1
1.25	0.9	0.8	0.6	Sublabial Crease to Chin	0.4	0.3	0.2

Fraction of Life Size				ADULT MALE PROPORTIONS Inch Measurements	Fraction of Life Size		
Life size	3/4	2/3	1/2		1/3	1/4	1/8
				TRANSVERSE HEAD MEASUREMENTS			
inch	inch	inch	inch		inch	inch	inch
6.0	4.5	4.0	3.0	Bi-Parietal	2.0	1.5	0.8
5.3	3.9	3.5	2.63	Bi-Zygomatic	1.8	1.3	0.7
4.5	3.4	3.0	2.25	Bi-Fronto Temporal	1.5	1.1	0.6
4.3	3.2	2.8	2.13	Inter Brow Ridge	1.4	1.1	0.5
5.3	3.9	3.5	2.63	Inter Tragion of Ears	1.8	1.3	0.7
4.8	3.6	3.2	2.38	Inter Angle of Mandible	1.6	1.2	0.6
4.0	3.0	2.7	2.0	Inter Lateral Corners of Eyes	1.3	1.0	0.5
1.3	1.0	0.9	0.67	Width of Eye	0.4	0.3	0.2
1.3	1.0	0.9	0.67	Inter Inner Corner of Eyes	0.4	0.3	0.2
1.5	1.1	1.0	0.75	Breadth of Nose	0.5	0.4	0.2
2.0	1.5	1.3	1.0	Breadth of Mouth	0.7	0.5	0.3
1.5	1.1	1.0	0.75	Breadth of Chin	0.5	0.4	0.2
4.5	3.4	3.0	2.25	Breadth of Neck	1.5	1.1	0.6
				ANTERIOR-POSTERIOR HEAD			
inch	inch	inch	inch		inch	inch	inch
8.0	6.0	5.3	4.0	Brow to Occiput	2.7	2.0	1.0
4.8	3.6	3.2	2.38	Brow to Tragus	1.6	1.2	0.6
4.5	3.4	3.0	2.25	Sellion to Tragus	1.5	1.1	0.6
3.3	2.4	2.2	1.63	Tragus to Occiput	1.1	0.8	0.4
2.5	1.9	1.7	1.25	Tragus to Angle Mandible	0.8	0.6	0.3
3.5	2.6	2.3	1.75	Angle of Mandible to Chin	1.2	0.9	0.4
2.9	2.2	1.9	1.44	Length of Ear, Vertical	1.0	0.7	0.4
1.5	1.1	1.0	0.75	Width of Ear, Anterior-Posterior	0.5	0.4	0.2
4.5	3.4	3.0	2.25	Anterior to Posterior of Neck	1.5	1.1	0.6

Conversion scale of inches to centimeters:

inch x 2.54 = cm cm x 0.39 = inch

See Appendix for other measurement conversions.

	Fraction of Life Size			ADULT MALE PROPORTIONS Metric Measurements	Fraction of Life Size		
Life size	3/4	2/3	1/2		1/3	1/4	1/8
				VERTICAL MEASUREMENTS			
cm	cm	cm	cm		cm	cm	cm
183.0	137.3	120.8	91.5	Stature, Height, Vertex to Sole	60.4	45.8	22.9
148.6	111.5	98.1	74.3	Shoulder at Acromion to Sole	49.0	37.2	18.6
106.7	80.0	70.4	53.4	Ant. Sup. Spine of Ilium to Sole	35.2	26.7	13.3
95.0	71.3	62.7	47.5	Symphysis Pubis to Sole	31.4	23.8	11.9
83.0	62.3	54.8	41.5	Crotch to Sole	27.4	20.8	10.4
53.3	40.0	35.2	26.7	Knee to Sole	17.6	13.3	6.7
34.3	25.7	22.6	17.2	Head & Neck, Vertex to St. Notch	11.3	8.6	4.3
41.9	31.4	27.7	21.0	St. Notch, Shoulder – Ant. Sup. Sp.	13.8	10.5	5.2
68.1	51.1	44.9	34.1	Sternal Notch to Crotch	22.5	17.0	8.5
53.3	40.0	35.2	26.7	Ant. Sup. Spine of Ilium to Knee	17.6	13.3	6.7
138.0	103.5	91.1	69.0	Kneeling Height	45.5	34.5	17.3
96.2	72.2	63.5	48.1	Sitting Height	31.7	24.1	12.0
108	81.0	71.3	54.0	Buttock, Straight Leg to Sole	35.6	27.0	13.5
63.0	47.3	41.6	31.5	Buttock to Flexed Knee	20.8	15.8	7.9
59.0	44.3	38.9	29.5	Flexed Knee to Sole	19.5	14.8	7.4
				VERTICAL HEAD MEASUREMENTS			
cm	cm	cm	cm		cm	cm	cm
22.9	17.2	15.1	11.5	Vertex to Chin	7.6	5.7	2.9
20.3	15.2	13.4	10.2	Hairline to Chin	6.7	5.1	2.5
11.4	8.6	7.5	5.7	Vertex to Lateral Corner of Eye	3.8	2.9	1.4
13.8	10.4	9.1	6.9	Vertex to Tragion of Ear	4.6	3.5	1.7
6.4	4.8	4.2	3.2	Hairline to Brow	2.1	1.6	0.8
12.7	9.5	8.4	6.4	Hairline to Infranasal	4.2	3.2	1.6
6.4	4.8	4.2	3.2	Brow to Infranasal	2.1	1.6	0.8
5.4	4.1	3.6	2.7	Sellion to Infranasal	1.8	1.4	0.7
12.0	9.0	7.9	6.0	Sellion to Chin	4.0	3.0	1.5
6.4	4.8	4.2	3.2	Infranasal to Chin	2.1	1.6	0.8
2.2	1.7	1.5	1.1	Infranasal to Lip Aperature	0.7	0.6	0.3
1.6	1.2	1.1	0.8	Lip Aperat. to Sublabial Crease	0.5	0.4	0.2
2.5	1.9	1.7	1.3	Sublabial Crease to Chin	0.8	0.6	0.3

Life size	3/4	2/3	1/2	ADULT MALE PROPORTIONS Metric Measurements	1/3	1/4	1/8
				TRANSVERSE HEAD MEASUREMENTS			
cm	cm	cm	cm		cm	cm	cm
15.2	11.4	10.2	7.6	Bi-Parietal	5.0	3.8	1.9
13.3	10.0	8.9	6.65	Bi-Zygomatic	4.4	3.3	1.7
11.4	8.6	7.6	5.7	Bi-Fronto Temporal	3.8	2.9	1.4
10.7	8.0	7.2	5.35	Inter Brow Ridge	3.5	2.7	1.3
13.7	10.3	9.2	6.85	Inter Tragion of Ears	4.5	3.4	1.7
12.1	9.1	8.1	6.05	Inter Angle of Mandible	4.0	3.0	1.5
10.2	7.7	6.8	5.1	Inter Lateral Corners of Eyes	3.4	2.6	1.3
3.3	2.5	2.2	1.65	Width of Eye	1.1	0.8	0.4
3.3	2.5	2.2	1.65	Inter Inner Corner of Eyes	1.1	0.8	0.4
3.8	2.9	2.5	1.9	Breadth of Nose	1.3	1.0	0.5
5.1	3.8	3.4	2.55	Breadth of Mouth	1.7	1.3	0.6
3.8	2.9	2.5	1.9	Breadth of Chin	1.3	1.0	0.5
11.4	8.6	7.6	5.7	Breadth of Neck	3.8	2.9	1.4
				ANTERIOR-POSTERIOR HEAD			
cm	cm	cm	cm		cm	cm	cm
20.4	15.3	13.7	10.2	Brow to Occiput	6.7	5.1	2.6
12.1	9.1	8.1	6.05	Brow to Tragus	4.0	3.0	1.5
11.8	8.9	7.9	5.9	Sellion to Tragus	3.9	3.0	1.5
8.4	6.3	5.6	4.2	Tragus to Occiput	2.8	2.1	1.1
6.5	4.9	4.4	3.25	Tragus to Angle Mandible	2.1	1.6	0.8
8.6	6.5	5.8	4.3	Angle of Mandible to Chin	2.8	2.2	1.1
7.3	5.5	4.9	3.65	Length of Ear, Vertical	2.4	1.8	0.9
3.7	2.8	2.5	1.85	Width of Ear, Anterior-Posterior	1.2	0.9	0.5
11.5	8.6	7.7	5.75	Anterior to Posterior of Neck	3.8	2.9	1.4

(Header spans: "Fraction of Life Size" over 3/4, 2/3, 1/2 and over 1/3, 1/4, 1/8.)

Conversion scale of inches to centimeters:

inch x 2.54 = cm   cm x 0.39 = inch

See Appendix for other measurement conversions.

Feminine Head, Length 8 inches

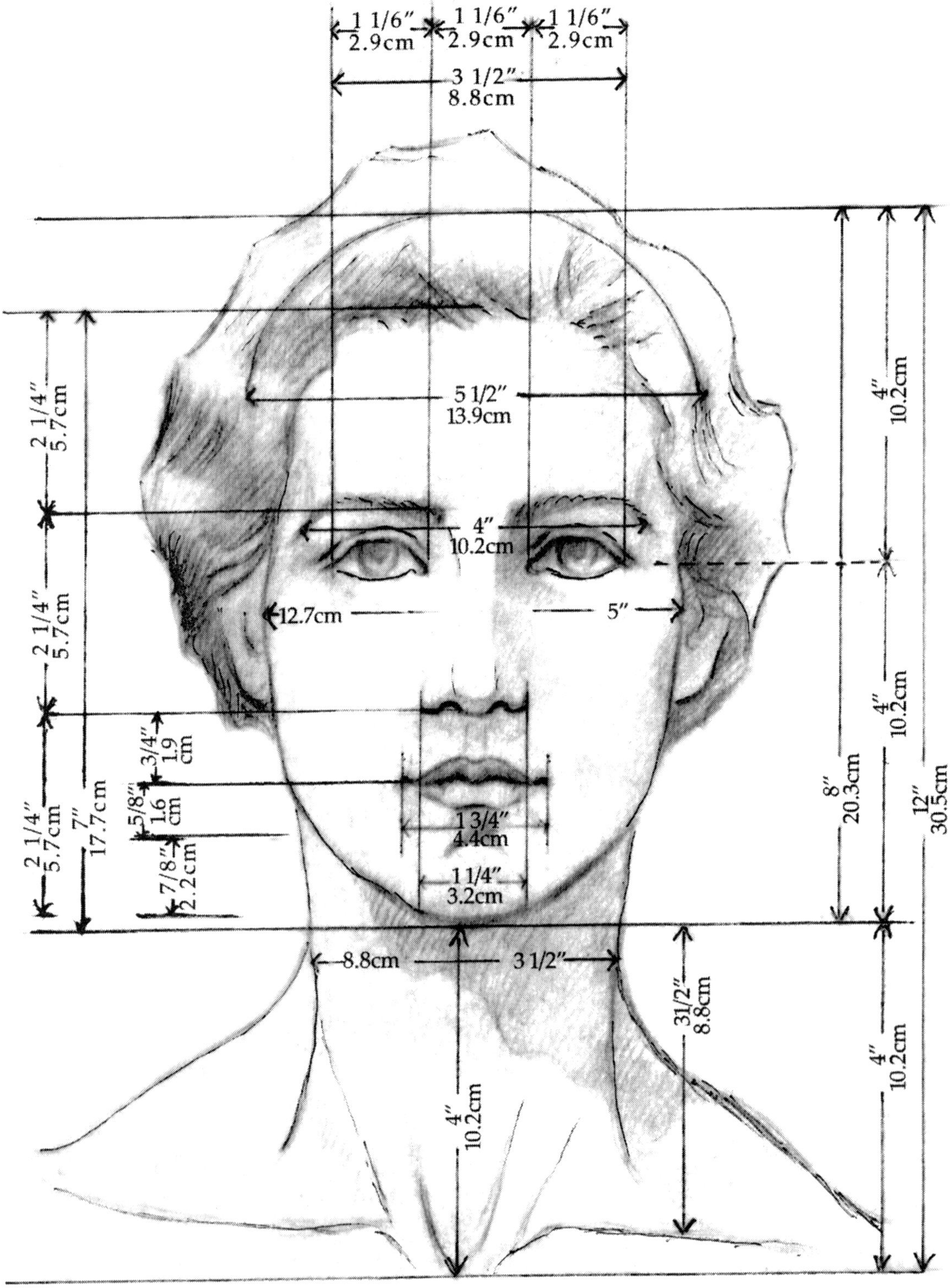

The feminine head, detailed proportions, anterior view. The head is divided in two at the level of the eyes. One half face height = distance between lateral corners of eyes. The mouth width = one half distance between the lateral corners of eyes.

Feminine Head, Length 8 inches

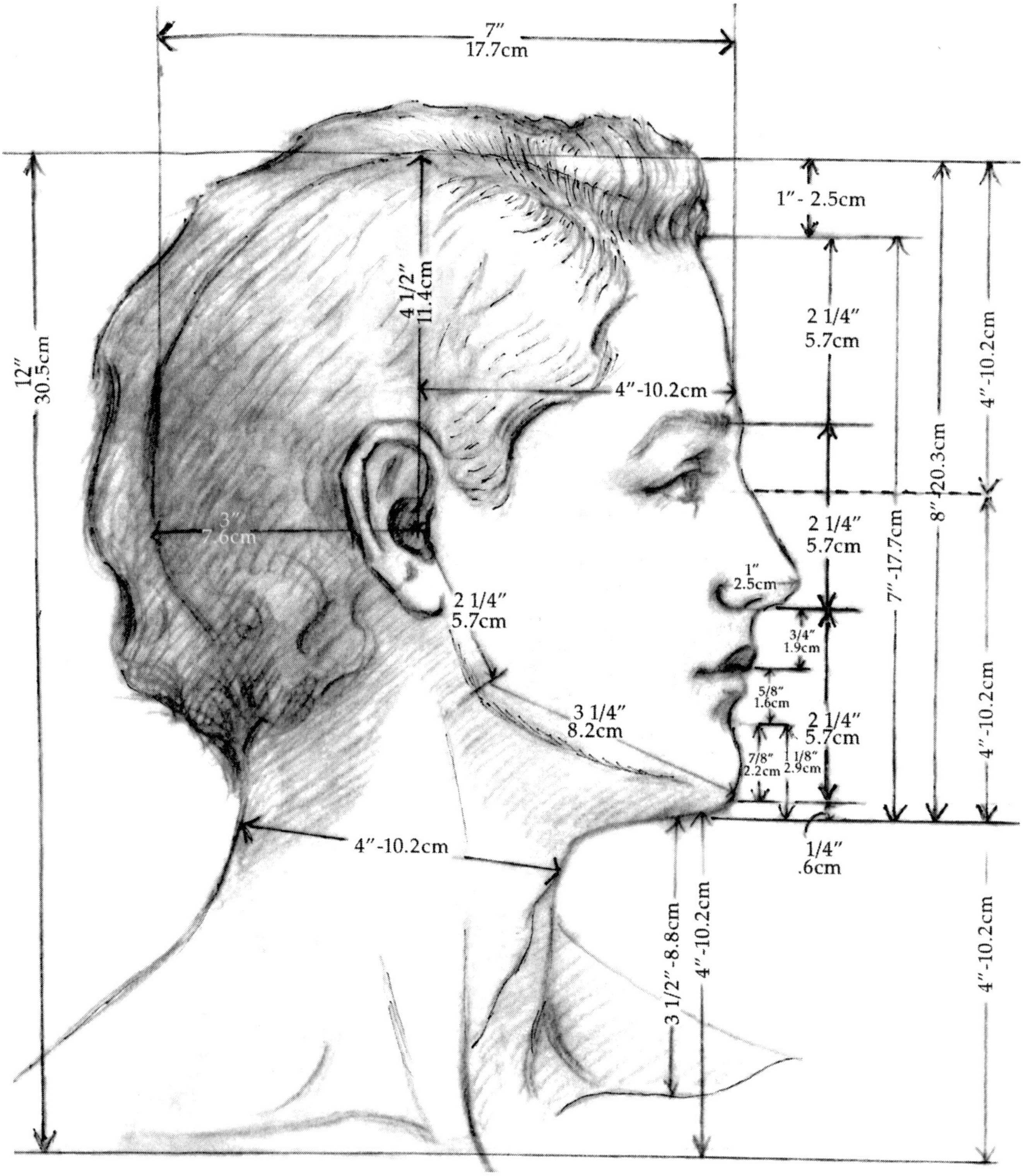

The feminine head, detailed proportions, right lateral view. Head and neck are divided into three equal proportions: Sternal notch to chin; to corner of eye; to top of head. The face also is divided into three equal proportions, commonly known as nose lengths.

Fraction of Life Size				ADULT FEMALE PROPORTIONS Inch Measurements	Fraction of Life Size		
Life size	3/4	2/3	1/2		1/3	1/4	1/8
				VERTICAL MEASUREMENTS			
inch	inch	inch	inch		inch	inch	inch
66.0	49.5	44.0	33.0	Stature, Height, Vertex to Sole	22.0	16.5	8.3
53.8	40.3	35.8	26.9	Shoulder at Acromion to Sole	17.9	13.4	6.7
38.5	28.9	25.7	19.3	Ant. Sup. Spine of Ilium to Sole	12.8	9.6	4.8
34.5	25.9	23.0	17.3	Symphysis Pubis to Sole	11.5	8.6	4.3
32.0	24.0	21.3	16.0	Crotch to Sole	10.7	8.0	4.0
19.3	14.4	12.8	9.6	Knee to Sole	6.4	4.8	2.4
12.3	9.2	8.2	6.1	Head & Neck, Vertex to St. Notch	4.1	3.1	1.5
15.3	11.4	10.2	7.6	St. Notch, Shoulder – Ant. Sup. Sp.	5.1	3.8	1.9
19.3	14.4	12.8	9.6	Sternal Notch to Crotch	6.4	4.8	2.4
19.3	14.4	12.8	9.6	Ant. Sup. Spine of Ilium to Knee	6.4	4.8	2.4
74.3	55.7	49.5	37.2	Kneeling Height	24.8	18.6	9.3
35.0	26.3	23.3	17.5	Sitting Height	11.7	8.8	4.4
39.5	29.6	26.3	19.8	Buttock, Straight Leg to Sole	13.2	9.9	4.9
23.3	17.4	15.5	11.6	Buttock to Flexed Knee	7.8	5.8	2.9
20.2	15.2	13.5	10.1	Flexed Knee to Sole	6.7	5.1	2.5
				VERTICAL HEAD MEASUREMENTS			
inch	inch	inch	inch		inch	inch	inch
8.0	6.0	5.3	4.0	Vertex to Chin	2.7	2.0	1.0
7.0	5.3	4.7	3.5	Hairline to Chin	2.3	1.8	0.9
4.0	3.0	2.7	2.0	Vertex to Lateral Corner of Eye	1.3	1.0	0.5
4.3	3.2	2.9	2.1	Vertex to Tragion of Ear	1.4	1.1	0.5
2.3	1.7	1.5	1.1	Hairline to Brow	0.8	0.6	0.3
4.5	3.4	3.0	2.3	Hairline to Infranasal	1.5	1.1	0.6
2.3	1.7	1.5	1.1	Brow to Infranasal	0.8	0.6	0.3
2.0	1.5	1.3	1.0	Sellion to Infranasal	0.7	0.5	0.3
4.3	3.2	2.9	2.2	Sellion to Chin	1.4	1.1	0.5
2.5	1.9	1.7	1.3	Infranasal to Chin	0.8	0.6	0.3
0.8	0.6	0.5	0.4	Infranasal to Lip Aperature	0.3	0.2	0.1
0.6	0.5	0.4	0.3	Lip Aperat. to Sublabial Crease	0.2	0.2	0.1
1.1	0.8	0.7	0.5	Sublabial Crease to Chin	0.4	0.3	0.1

ADULT FEMALE PROPORTIONS
Inch Measurements

Fraction of Life Size					Fraction of Life Size		
Life size	3/4	2/3	1/2		1/3	1/4	1/8
				TRANSVERSE HEAD			
inch	inch	inch	inch		inch	inch	inch
5.5	4.1	3.7	2.75	Bi-Parietal	1.8	1.4	0.7
5.0	3.8	3.3	2.5	Bi-Zygomatic	1.7	1.3	0.6
4.6	3.5	3.1	2.3	Bi-Fronto Temporal	1.5	1.2	0.6
4.0	3.0	2.7	2.0	Inter Brow Ridge	1.3	1.0	0.5
5.5	4.1	3.7	2.8	Inter Tragion of Ears	1.8	1.4	0.7
4.6	3.5	3.1	2.3	Inter Angle of Mandible	1.5	1.2	0.6
3.5	2.6	2.3	1.8	Inter Lateral Corners of Eyes	1.2	0.9	0.4
1.2	0.9	0.8	0.6	Width of Eye	0.4	0.3	0.1
1.2	0.9	0.8	0.6	Inter Inner Corner of Eyes	0.4	0.3	0.1
1.3	0.9	0.8	0.6	Breadth of Nose	0.4	0.3	0.2
1.8	1.3	1.2	0.9	Breadth of Mouth	0.6	0.4	0.2
1.3	0.9	0.8	0.6	Breadth of Chin	0.4	0.3	0.2
3.5	2.6	2.3	1.8	Breadth of Neck	1.2	0.9	0.4
				ANTERIOR-POSTERIOR HEAD			
inch	inch	inch	inch		inch	inch	inch
7.4	5.6	4.9	3.7	Brow to Occiput	2.5	1.9	0.9
4.2	3.2	2.8	2.1	Brow to Tragus	1.4	1.1	0.5
3.6	2.7	2.4	1.8	Sellion to Tragus	1.2	0.9	0.5
3.2	2.4	2.1	1.6	Tragus to Occiput	1.1	0.8	0.4
2.3	1.7	1.5	1.1	Tragus to Angle Mandible	0.8	0.6	0.3
3.3	2.4	2.2	1.6	Angle of Mandible to Chin	1.1	0.8	0.4
2.5	1.8	1.6	1.2	Length of Ear, Vertical	0.8	0.6	0.3
1.3	1.0	0.9	0.7	Width of Ear, Anterior-Posterior	0.4	0.3	0.2
4.0	3.0	2.7	2.0	Anterior to Posterior of Neck	1.3	1.0	0.5

Conversion scale of inches to centimeters:

inch x 2.54 = cm   cm x 0.39 = inch

See Appendix for other measurement conversions.

Fraction of Life Size				ADULT FEMALE PROPORTIONS Metric Measurements	Fraction of Life Size		
Life size	3/4	2/3	1/2		1/3	1/4	1/8

VERTICAL MEASUREMENTS

cm	cm	cm	cm		cm	cm	cm
167.6	125.7	111.7	83.8	Stature, Height, Vertex to Sole	55.9	41.9	21.0
135.5	101.6	90.3	67.8	Shoulder at Acromion to Sole	45.2	33.9	16.9
97.8	73.4	65.2	48.9	Ant. Sup. Spine of Ilium to Sole	32.6	24.5	12.2
87.8	65.9	58.5	43.9	Symphysis Pubis to Sole	29.3	22.0	11.0
81.3	61.0	54.2	40.7	Crotch to Sole	27.1	20.3	10.2
48.9	36.7	32.6	24.5	Knee to Sole	16.3	12.2	6.1
30.4	22.8	20.3	15.2	Head & Neck, Vertex to St. Notch	10.1	7.6	3.8
38.7	29.0	25.8	19.4	St. Notch, Shoulder - Ant. Sup. Sp.	12.9	9.7	4.8
48.9	36.7	32.6	24.5	Sternal Notch to Crotch	16.3	12.2	6.1
48.9	36.7	32.6	24.5	Ant. Sup. Spine of Ilium to Knee	16.3	12.2	6.1
125.7	94.3	83.8	62.9	Kneeling Height	41.9	31.4	15.7
89.0	66.8	59.3	44.5	Sitting Height	29.7	22.3	11.1
100.3	75.2	66.9	50.2	Buttock, Straight Leg to Sole	33.4	25.1	12.5
59.1	44.3	39.4	29.6	Buttock to Flexed Knee	19.7	14.8	7.4
51.7	38.8	34.5	25.9	Flexed Knee to Sole	17.2	12.9	6.5

VERTICAL HEAD MEASUREMENTS

cm	cm	cm	cm		cm	cm	cm
20.4	15.3	13.6	10.2	Vertex to Chin	6.8	5.1	2.6
17.8	13.4	11.9	8.9	Hairline to Chin	5.9	4.5	2.2
10.2	7.7	6.8	5.1	Vertex to Lateral Corner of Eye	3.4	2.6	1.3
11.4	8.6	7.6	5.7	Vertex to Tragion of Ear	3.8	2.9	1.4
5.7	4.3	3.8	2.9	Hairline to Brow	1.9	1.4	0.7
11.5	8.6	7.7	5.8	Hairline to Infranasal	3.8	2.9	1.4
5.7	4.3	3.8	2.9	Brow to Infranasal	1.9	1.4	0.7
5.1	3.8	3.4	2.6	Sellion to Infranasal	1.7	1.3	0.6
10.9	8.2	7.3	5.5	Sellion to Chin	3.6	2.7	1.4
6.3	4.7	4.2	3.2	Infranasal to Chin	2.1	1.6	0.8
2.0	1.5	1.3	1.0	Infranasal to Lip Aperature	0.7	0.5	0.3
1.6	1.2	1.1	0.8	Lip Aperat. to Sublabial Crease	0.5	0.4	0.2
2.8	2.1	1.9	1.4	Sublabial Crease to Chin	0.9	0.7	0.4

Fraction of Life Size				ADULT FEMALE PROPORTIONS Metric Measurements	Fraction of Life Size		
Life size	3/4	2/3	1/2		1/3	1/4	1/8
				TRANSVERSE HEAD MEASUREMENTS			
cm	cm	cm	cm		cm	cm	cm
14.0	10.5	9.3	7.0	Bi-Parietal	4.7	3.5	1.8
12.7	9.5	8.5	6.35	Bi-Zygomatic	4.2	3.2	1.6
11.8	8.9	7.9	5.9	Bi-Fronto Temporal	3.9	3.0	1.5
10.2	7.7	6.8	5.1	Inter Brow Ridge	3.4	2.6	1.3
12.7	9.5	8.5	6.35	Inter Tragion of Ears	4.2	3.2	1.6
11.8	8.9	7.9	5.9	Inter Angle of Mandible	3.9	3.0	1.5
9.0	6.8	6.0	4.5	Inter Lateral Corners of Eyes	3.0	2.3	1.1
3.0	2.3	2.0	1.5	Width of Eye	1.0	0.8	0.4
3.0	2.3	2.0	1.5	Inter Inner Corner of eyes	1.0	0.8	0.4
3.1	2.3	2.1	1.55	Breadth of Nose	1.0	0.8	0.4
4.4	3.3	2.9	2.2	Breadth of Mouth	1.5	1.1	0.6
3.2	2.4	2.1	1.6	Breadth of Chin	1.1	0.8	0.4
8.9	6.7	5.9	4.45	Breadth of Neck	3.0	2.2	1.1
				ANTERIOR-POSTERIOR HEAD			
cm	cm	cm	cm		cm	cm	cm
18.5	13.9	12.3	9.25	Brow to Occiput	6.2	4.6	2.3
10.2	7.7	6.8	5.1	Brow to Tragus	3.4	2.6	1.3
9.2	6.9	6.1	4.6	Sellion to Tragus	3.1	2.3	1.2
7.6	5.7	5.1	3.8	Tragus to Occiput	2.5	1.9	1.0
5.7	4.3	3.8	2.85	Tragus to Angle Mandible	1.9	1.4	0.7
8.3	6.2	5.5	4.15	Angle of Mandible to Chin	2.8	2.1	1.0
6.0	4.5	4.0	3.0	Length of Ear, Vertical	2.0	1.5	0.8
3.3	2.5	2.2	1.65	Width of Ear, Anterior-Posterior	1.1	0.8	0.4
10.2	7.7	6.8	5.1	Anterior to Posterior of Neck	3.4	2.6	1.3

Conversion scale of inches to centimeters:

inch x 2.54 = cm cm x 0.39 = inch

See Appendix for other measurement conversions.

Anatomy

Embryological Development of the Nose and Lips

While presenting a demonstration lecture, Sculptor Fairbanks talked about the lips, and he explained features in the developmental anatomy in which the central form grows down forming the nose and the center of the upper lip. The features of the face may be better understood by a review of the embryonic development, as illustrated. In the fourth week, when the embryo is 3.5 cm in length, there are five tiny prominent folds or processes in the developing face: the upper midline nasal process is growing downward. It approaches the paired maxillary processes and the mandibular processes.

At five weeks, the embryo is 8 mm long and more form is evident. The nasal process is central and has paired lateral nasal processes. The paired maxillary processes have grown. The paired mandibular processes have fused. A view from below demonstrates added details.

At six weeks, the embryo is 12 mm long. Additional growth is evident. During fetal growth, an extension of the septum of the nose grows down between the lateral forms or maxillary processes that are growing towards the center. The maxillary processes approach the central nasal processes.

At seven weeks, the embryo is 19 mm long. The maxillary processes have joined the central nasal process. The tongue and lips have begun to develop. The eyes have also grown. The columella of the upper lip in infants and adults indicates the fusion of the central nasal process and the paired maxillary processes. When a cleft lip (hare lip) is noted at birth, it is due to an incomplete fusion of a maxillary pro-

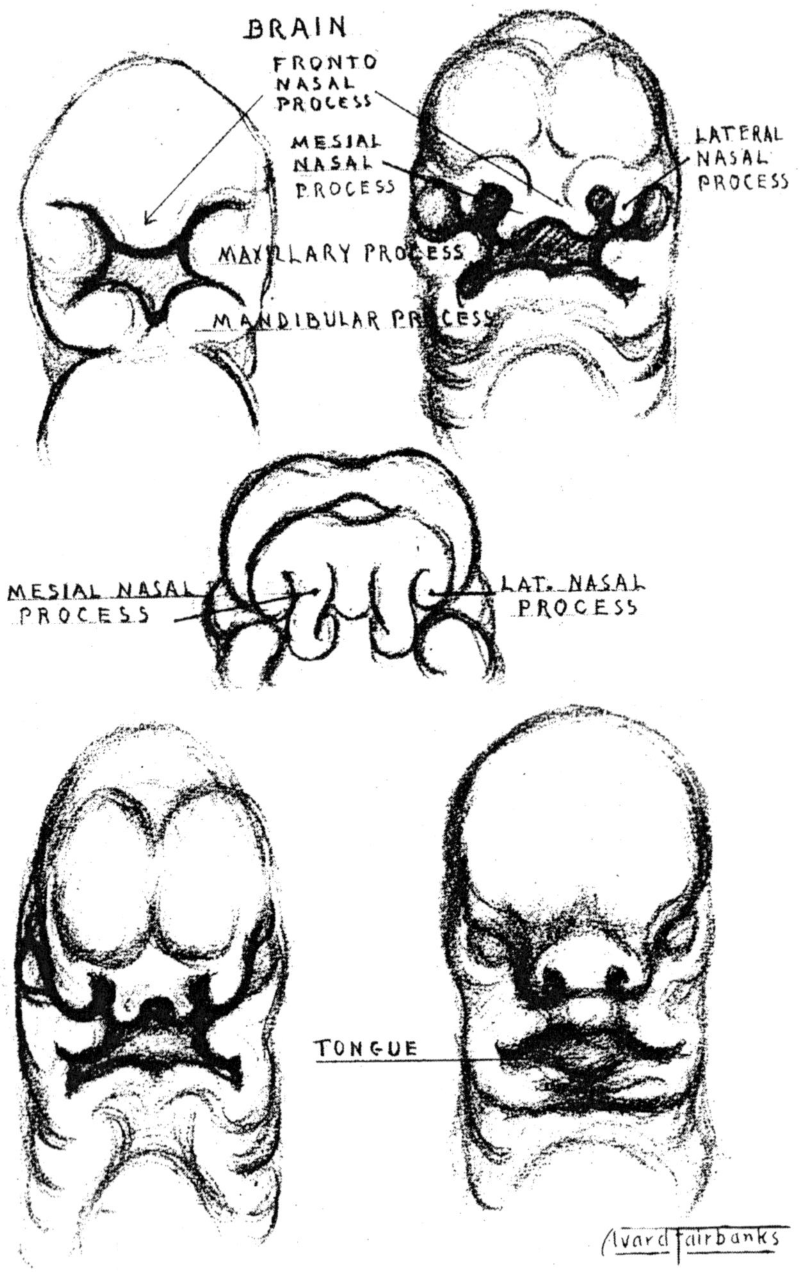

Development of the face in embryo.

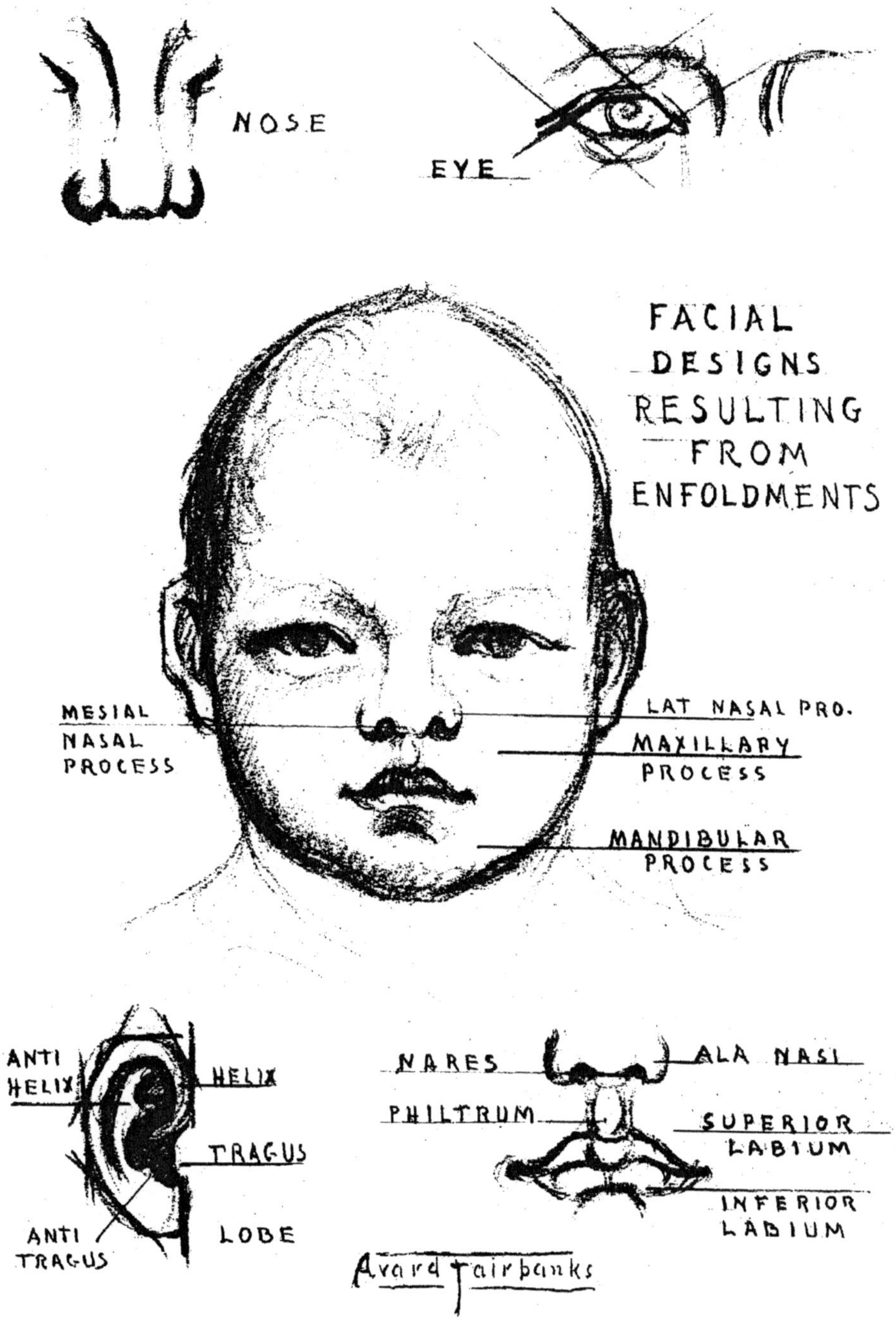

Facial designs resulting from enfoldments.

cess to the nasal process. Where the mandibular processes fuse there is a median raphae in the center of the lower lip, where a cracked lip may occasionally occur.

By three months gestation, the embryo is about 7-cm long, the elements of the embryonic face have fused and a tiny human face can be recognized. The cranium is much larger than the face. Both of them are growing rapidly. At birth the features of the human face can be appreciated. The two vertical ridges, the columella, of the upper lip below the nose represent where the maxillary processes joined the center process of the septum. There is a concave groove between these two columella on the upper lip. The two central incisor teeth are also derived from this central process of the septum. An illustration by Avard Fairbanks, of a young infant, is included that correlates the embryonic components of its face.

---

adapted from
Children's Proportions for Artists

Anthropometry Points of Reference on the Head

Physical anthropologists are also interested in the measurements of the human body. A subspecialty of anthropology is titled anthropometry, and it is designated for human measurement. Terms have been used to describe various points of reference to standardize information. When considering the skull, references are now made to the neurocranium, the portion containing

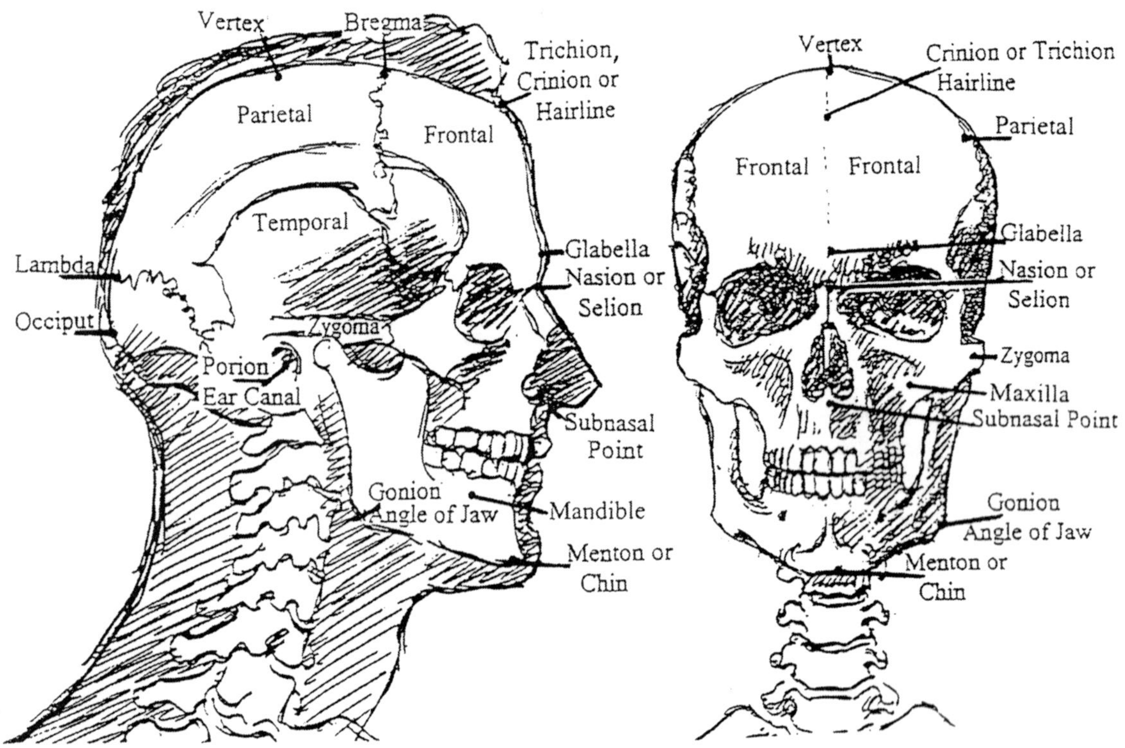

Anthropometry reference points on the head.

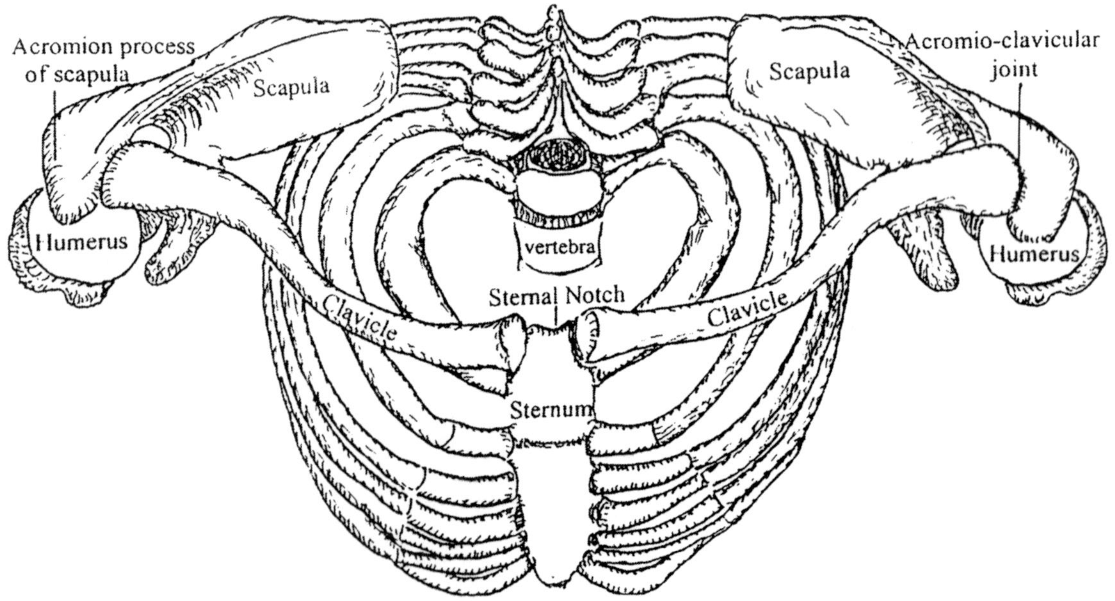

Thorax and shoulder girdle viewed from above.

the brain, and the viscerocranium, essentially the face. For simplicity, in this study, the skull will be construed to mean both the neurocranium and the viscerocranium. Precise points can often be determined by observing junctions of suture lines on some ancient skull. Sculptors deal with live human form and must try to use reference points that are covered with soft tissues. To facilitate understanding, these points will be described and illustrated in depicting a skull. It is interesting to note that Leonardo da Vinci chose many points that are now in use by anthropologists. Of prime interest to the serious artist is the human head. Beginning the list is the top of the head, the vertex.

Vertex is the uppermost portion of the skull vault in the midline, a little posterior to a vertical line to the ear.

Bregma is the junction of the midsaggital suture and the coronal sutures joining the frontal and parietal bones. It is anterior to the vertex and is often in a groove or depression. It is the soft spot or anterior fontanel, a quadrangle, of an infant skull until bone fusion occurs by growth.

Parietal Prominences are indefinite prominence of the parietal bones at the widest part of the cranium, posterior and above the ears. Biparietal measurement is between these two prominences.

Glabella is the midpoint of the frontal bones above the nasal root, essentially the midline of the brow.

Zygoma, or **zygomatic arch**, cheek bone, is at the greatest breadth of the face. It is about the same breadth as the biparietal breadth of the upper part of the skull.

Nasion or **Sellion** is the point at which the nasal bones join the frontal bones, commonly called the bridge of the nose. It is usually an indentation below the brow. The exception is in some ethnic groups with a high nasal bridge. In sculpture history, it is noted as the classic Greek nose.

Ala nasae, or wings of the nose, these semicircular structures are supported by cartilage and outline the nostrils.

The **subnasal point** is at the upper lip juncture and the nose. On a skull, it is a definite projection that supports the cartilage of the nasal septum in the midline.

Gonion is the angle of the jaw. Rather than a definite point, it is rounded, but it is a bony landmark that is easily palpable.

Menton is a designation for the bony border of the chin in the midline. Soft tissues on living subjects serve as a cushion in front and below the bone.

Porion is the ear canal. On living subjects, the tragus, the cartilaginous flap just anterior to the ear canal, is essentially the same point for anterior-posterior measurement.

Lambda of the posterior skull, so named for a Greek letter of three intersecting lines, is a slight indentation at the posterior skull, the location of three sutures that join. It is a remnant of the posterior or triangular fontanel of infancy.

Occiput is the maximum posterior point of the skull.

There are other designated points for measurements of interest to anthropologists but of less significance to artists and therefore will not be listed. Many soft tissue features are supported by bony features and the localization of these need to be recognized. Other soft tissue features of living subjects have common names. They need the attention of serious students and amateurs, and are indicated in illustrations.

Reference: Hrdlicka, Arles. *Practical Anthropometry.* Philadelphia: Wistar Institute of Biology and Physiology, 1939, pp. 122-125.

Anatomy for a Portrait

developed from lecture notes
of Avard T. Fairbanks

The Skull

The skull is composed of many bones, some of which are important to anatomists and physicians. However, the beginning sculptor need only become familiar with the most salient features. Many of these may be palpated by a finger on a person's head.

The bones of the cranium include the frontal bone, the parietal, the temporal, and the occipital bones. Prominent bones of the face are the nasal bone, the two maxillae, or cheek bones, the two zygoma, and the mandible, or jaw bone.

The size of the mandible varies with age and sex. The widest portion of the cranium is about two-thirds the distance from the frontal bones to occipital bones or front to back. Usually there are parietal prominences above and behind the ears. There are occipital prominences at the posterior of the head.

There are also frontal prominences in the forehead. A low midline ridge is usually present, on the forehead; although sometimes it is barely perceptible; it is often prominent. Other prominent features include the supraorbital ridges above the eyes and the infraorbital ridges below the eyes, outlining the upper and lower arcs of orbits or eye sockets and superciliary, or brow ridges, above the eyes.

The zygomatic arches and zygomatic prominences give form to the cheeks. The mastoid processes are behind the ears. These features may vary with age, sex, racial, and ethnic background, as well as with the individual.

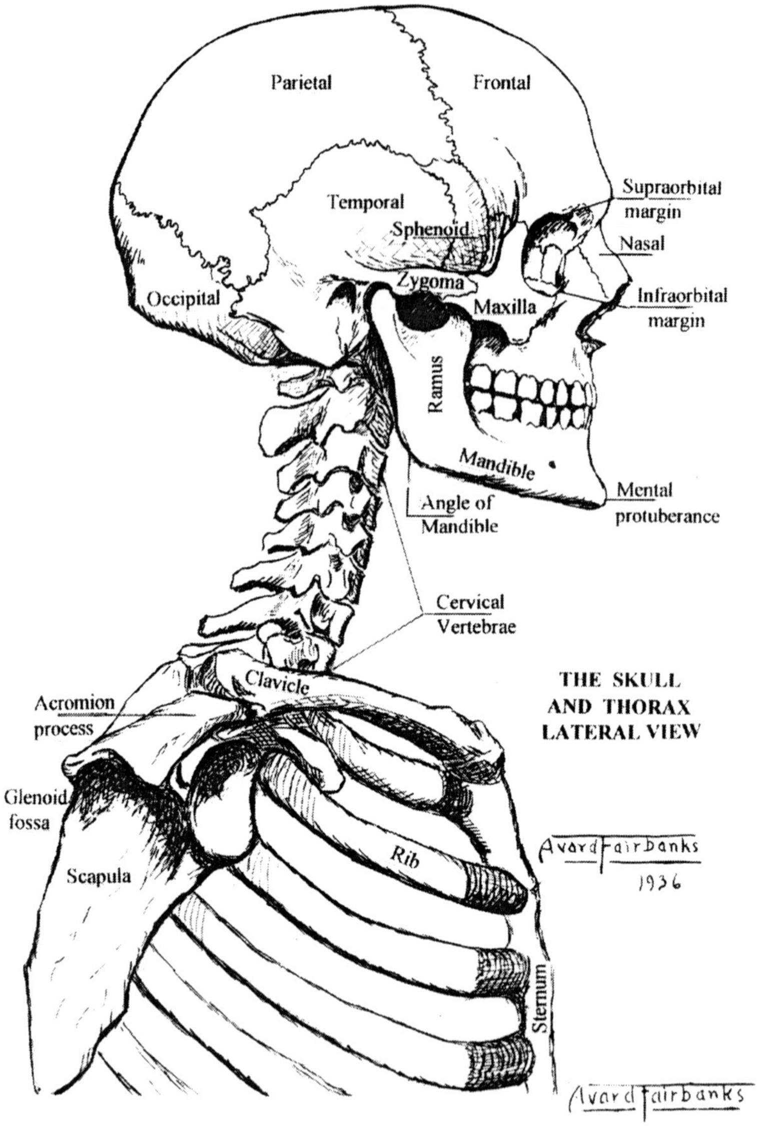

The skull and thorax, lateral view.

The female skull has a less prominent brow ridge, maxillae, or cheek bones and mandible. Children have proportionally less development of facial bones and mandibles. The ears and lower two-thirds of the nose are flexible features composed of cartilage. These features are even more variable than bone structures. They also change more with age. The ears often become larger and longer in old men. The nose may also become longer and droop in with age.

When a sculptor is modeling a portrait, the large features of the skull to be considered include the neurocranium, often called the cranium, and the viscerocranium, or facial bones. The neck, thorax and shoulders can be considered later.

There are some basic proportions that must be carefully regarded if an accurate portrayal is to be accomplished. These may vary in minor degree with age, sex, and person attributes. The neurocranium is roughly spherical, though more nearly elliptoidal, actually ovoid, or egg-shaped. On anterior projection, the contours of the neurocranium conform to the arc of a circle down to the temporal ridge. This circle is intersected by the facial bones projecting downward. On lateral projection, the contours of the skull also deviate from the arc of a circle and form more of the shape of an ellipse.

One may note that the face is generally vertical from brow to chin, varying with individuals, except for the protrusion of the nose. A line from the chin to the occiput or base of the skull is at an angle of about sixty-five degrees from the vertical. The neurocranium will appear to conform, with minor deviations, to an arc of a circle.

When viewed from above, the head superficially appears oval. The widest diameter is at about two-thirds the distance of anterior to posterior, where the parietal bones are most prominent. The contour of the cranium reveals the widest measurement is between the parietal prominences.

Some skulls are long and narrow, some medium, and others relatively short. Physical anthropologists have expressed this variation as cephalic index, a ratio of width to length. This ratio varies with individuals and with ethnic groupings from dolicocephalic at 0.65 to 0.74; mesocephalic at 0.75 to 0.79; and brachycephalic at 0.80 to 0.86. These ratios are independent of skin color.

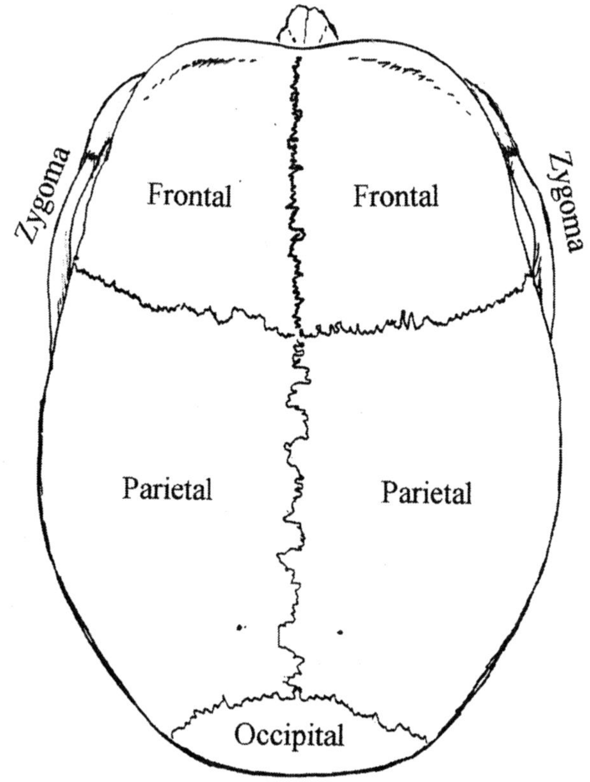

Cephalic – Superior view of the skull.

Skilled artists automatically note these features. On lateral view, the neurocranium measured from below the ear canal to the vertex is two-thirds the height of the skull. The face, on frontal view, can approximately be divided into half at the center of the orbit or eye socket. The face may be divided into thirds; chin to base of the nose, nose to brow, and brow to hairline. An additional one-sixth is hairline to vertex. The articulation or joint of the mandible, just anterior to the ear canal, is nearly one-half the distance of brow to occiput.

When one plans to model a portrait bust, the general features must first be considered. These include the neurocranium, and the facial bones. Later, the neck, thorax, and shoulders will be considered and added appropriately. There are also proportions for these which must be carefully regarded if an accurate portrayal is to be accomplished. These may vary in minor degrees with age, sex and individual characteristics.

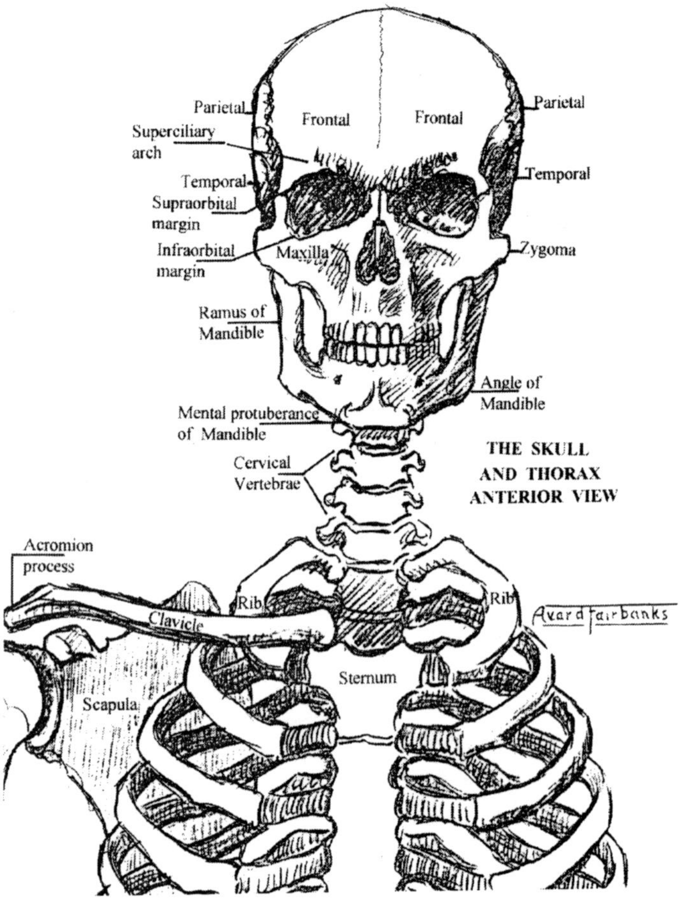

Anterior view.

The skull and thorax, anterior view and posterior view.

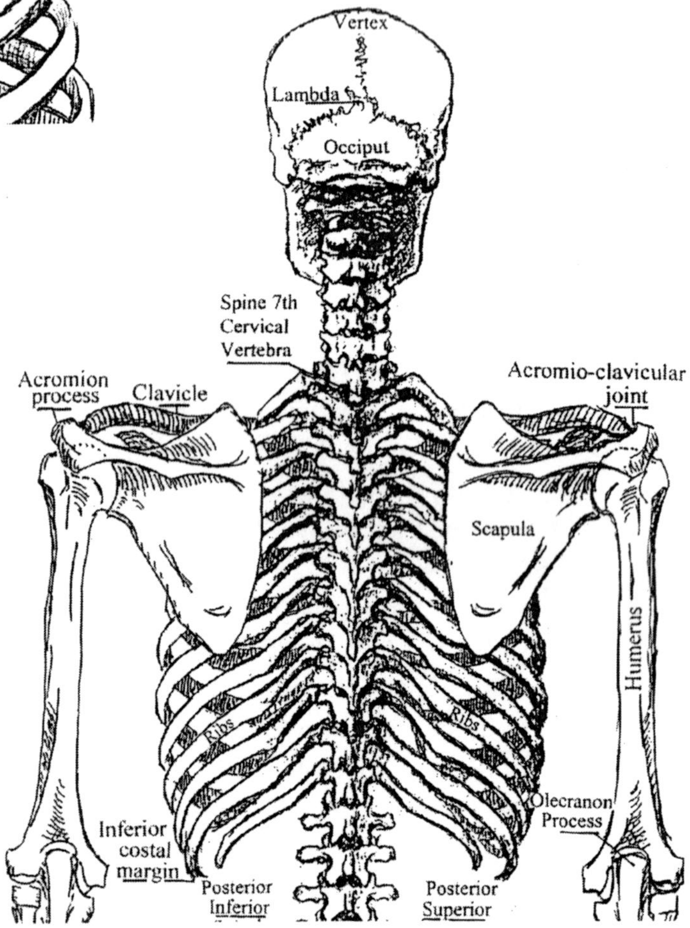

Posterior view.

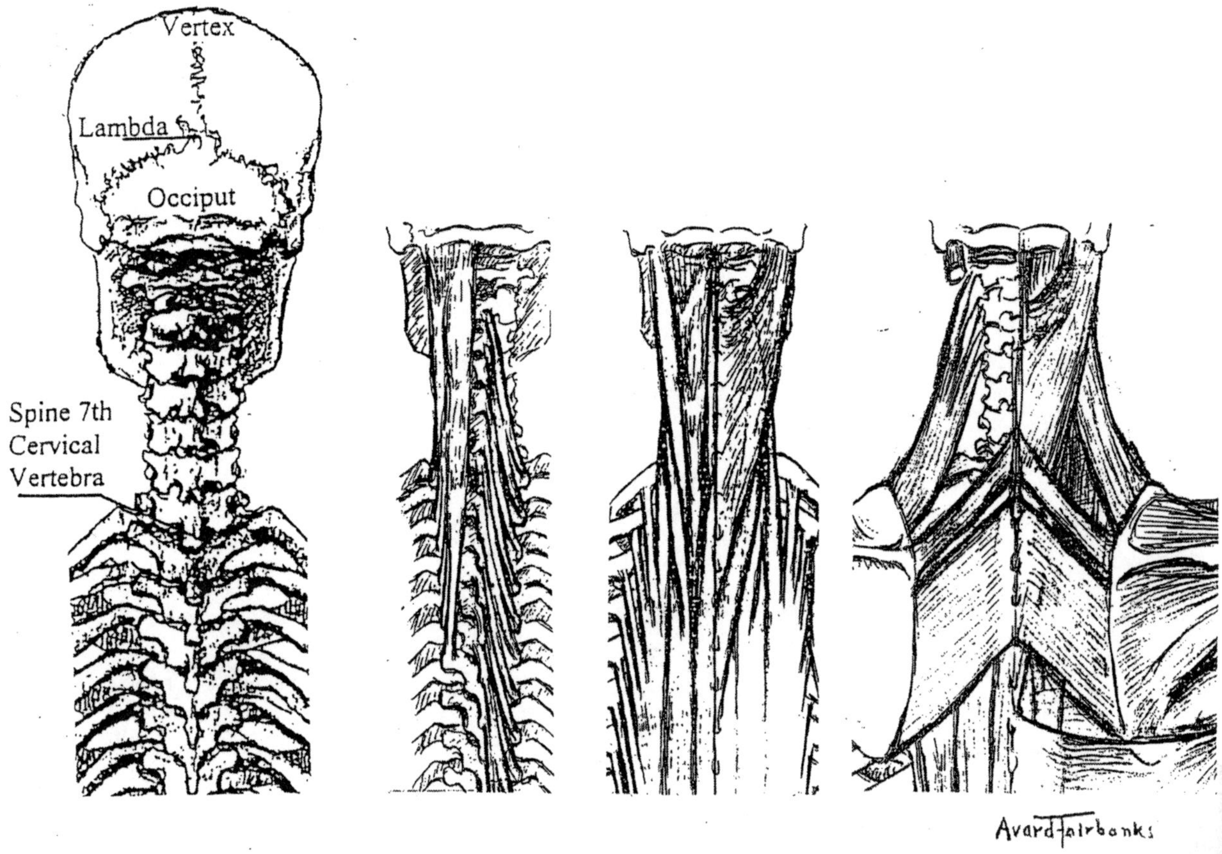

The deep muscles of the posterior neck.

The Neck

When one plans to model a portrait bust, the general features must first be considered. These include the neurocranium, and the facial bones. Later, the neck, thorax and shoulders will be considered and added appropriately. There are also proportions for these which must be carefully regarded if an accurate portrayal is to be accomplished. These may vary in minor degrees with age, sex and individual characteristics.

The significant features of the neck include seven vertebrae, the hyoid bone below and posterior to the chin, and the larynx (Adam's Apple or voice box) just below this in the anterior neck.

There are several muscle groups of the posterior neck including the rectus capitis, that holds the head erect, and the trapesius muscles. These massive trapesius muscles originate along the spinous processes and insert on the occiput, the shoulders, and scapula of each side and can affect its attachments—lifting the shoulder, stabilizing the scapula, and supporting head movements.

Anterior neck muscles include the scalene and sternocleidomastoid that stabilize and assist in head movement.

The thorax is dome shaped and its contours are modified by bones of the shoulder girdle. The scalene muscles originate on the first rib and insert at the base of the cranium. The sternocleidomastoid muscles are prominent in the anterior neck. They originate on the sternum and its attached clavicles or collar bones, from which they angles up and lateral to the mastoid processes.

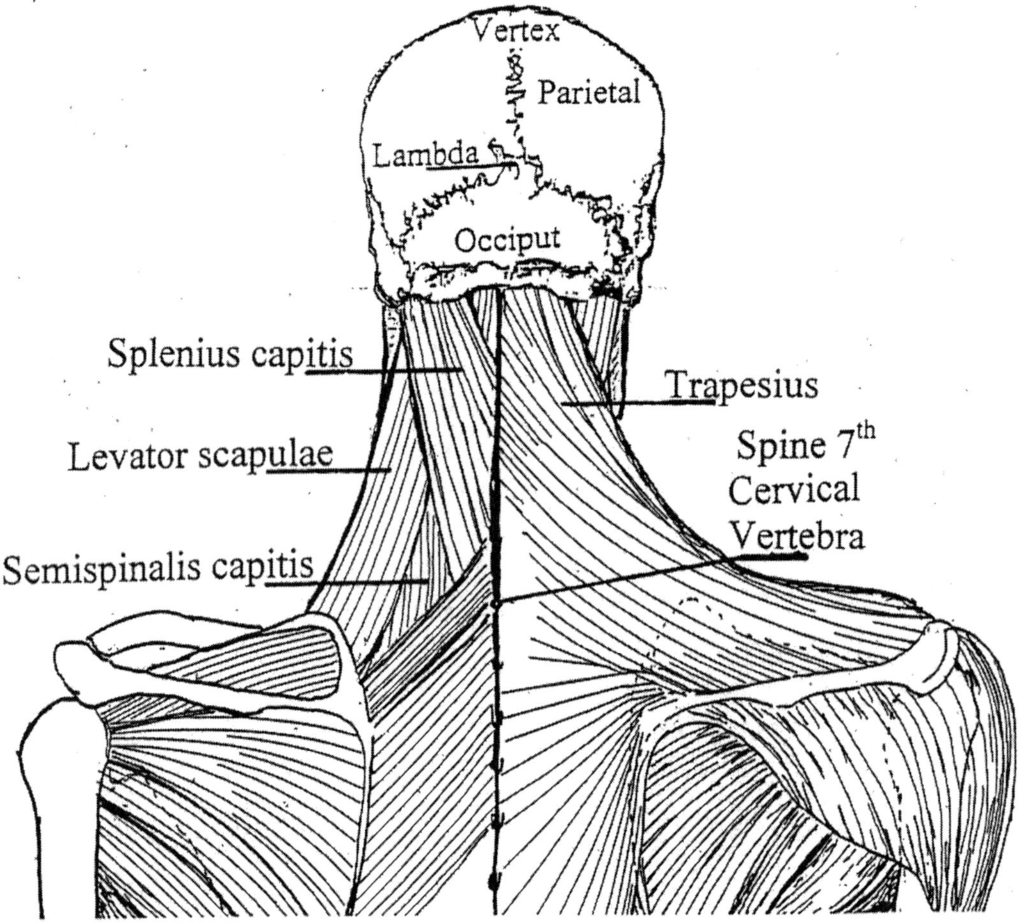

The muscles of the posterior neck.

Anatomic Details of the Neck

The neck serves as a column to support the head. This is accomplished by bones ligaments and paired muscles that are best considered in groups.

In the posterior midline is the nucal ligament, composed of fibro-elastic tissue that is about the same diameter as a pencil. It is attached by a fibrous membrane to the occiput, the spines of the seven cervical vertebrae and the first thoracic vertebra. It assists the muscles to return the head to the erect position after bending forward.

There are many deep posterior muscles whose form is not apparent on the surface. Some assist in turning and others is flexing and some for extending the neck. Prominent muscles among them are the longissimus capitis and the semispinalis capitis that arise along neck vertebrae and go vertically to insert on the occiput. They form the prominent paramedian muscular columns to the occiput.

The splenius capitis arise on the vertebrae, ascends more obliquely and inserts on the mastoid processes. There is a shallow triangular concavity below the occiput and the splenius capitis attachments to the mastoid process. Superficial to these muscles are the large paired trapezius muscles that originate along the spines of cervical and thoracic vertebrae and insert on the occiput and bones of the shoulder girdles, including the distal clavicles and the scapulae and their olecranon processes of the shoulders.

The posterior neck consists primarily of

bone and muscles. The anterior neck contains some large muscles and physiologic organs. These include the esophagus for eating, the trachea for breathing, blood vessels for circulation, the larynx (Adams apple) for vocalizing and separating swallowing from breathing, and the nerves directed laterally for muscular control of the arms.

Deep anterior neck muscles include the paired three scalene muscles that originate on the first and second ribs and insert on the upper neck vertebrae. They act to stabilize the neck like guy wires to a telephone pole. Like other deep muscles, they are not evident for neck contours.

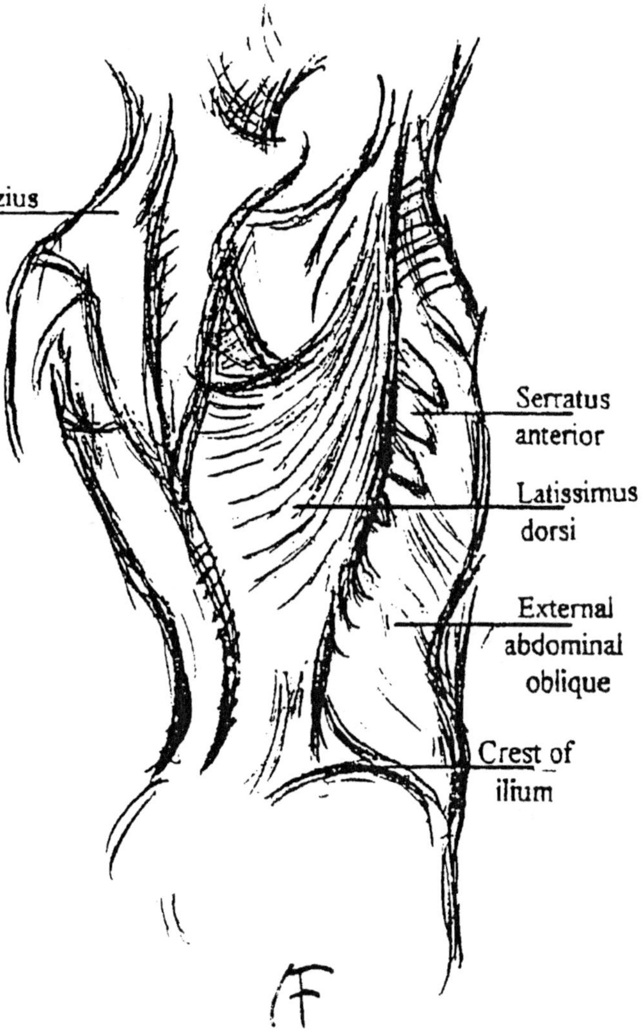

Muscles of the back, from the sketchbook.

Prominent muscles are the diagonal sternocleidomastoid muscles of which one part originates at the sternal notch on the sternum and another part originates along the clavicle or collar bone. These muscles insert on the mastoid processes of the skull and are important in neck support and motion. They divide the anterior-lateral neck into two triangles; the anterior triangle is outlined by the midline, the chin to the angle of the jaw, and the sternocleido-mastoid muscle.

The posterior triangle is bordered by the sternocleido-mastoid muscle, the clavicle and the trapesius muscle on the posterior border. In the anterior triangles, between these two diagonal sternocleido-mastoid muscles is the larynx or Adam's apple and deeper muscles that involve the larynx. These include the sternothyroid and the sternohyoid muscles.

There are other muscles that are deep and whose contraction are not evident on the surface. the myelohyoid muscle is partially cone shaped and extends from the mandible to the hyoid bone above the larynx. There are paired, superficial thin broad sheet of muscle fibers, the platysma muscles in the superficial fascia of the skin that extends from the thorax across and up the neck to the chin, and some fibers extend into the face. This is one of the muscles of expression that flares the skin of the neck in moments of anxiety and stress.

Anatomical Divisions of the Nose

Just as the lower third of the face may be divided into thirds, the nose may also be divided into four parts, however with less apparent division points. The nasal processes of the frontal bones attach to the nasal bones at the sellion.

Below the sellion the nose is divided into thirds. The upper third, or bony portion, consists of the nasal bone and the forward, upward extension of the nasal processes of the maxillae, both left and right.

The junction of the nasal bones with the middle third may easily be felt on oneself with the fingertip. The middle section is composed of three cartilages, the nasal septum in the midline, and the superior lateral cartilages on each side. They are closely attached to the nasal bones with fibrous tissue.

The lower third also consists of cartilages including the midline septum and the two inferior lateral cartilages. These originate as the central column of the nose, at the nostrils. They sweep up, form small domes, and curve laterally and out where they are fused into the fibrocartilages of the ala nasae, forming the wings of the nose.

Nose Anatomy

A better appreciation for the form of the nose involves a study of its development and anatomy. The purpose of the nose is to warm and moisturize air on the way to the lungs. The supporting anatomy of the nose consists of some bone and some cartilage. The paired frontal bones of the skull form the brow. On their lower medial aspect of these bones there are paired projections or nasal processes that curve down and posterior forming the upper part of the saddle or sellion, (Latin for saddle) of the nose. These nasal processes of the frontal bones attach to the paired nasal bones at this junction. This short suture line on the skull is termed the nasion, but it is beneath the soft tissues of the sellion, which is a less precise term, but it is more appropriate for art.

Other designations are the bridge, root, or notch of the nose. The nasal bones, on their lateral borders, join the adjacent, paired frontal processes of the maxillary bones that point up and forward. The shallowness or depth of the sellion depends on the growth of these bones during infancy and maturation prior to bone fusion.

The cartilaginous septum of the nose is a central plate that helps support the lateral cartilages like a central vertical partition. The septum helps support two lower, lateral paired structures composed of cartilage. Below the sellion are three segments of joined, paired components. The upper third is nasal bones and the adjacent maxillary attachments. There is dense fibrous tissue that joins the nasal bones to the middle third of the nose. That portion consists of the paired superior lateral cartilages that slant laterally to form about a sixty degree angle. They are triangular in form. The bases of these triangles are along the leading edge or upper border of the nose that is essentially flat on top. The apices of these triangles are down and lateral. At the flat leading border of the nose, these cartilage edges (which are separated by the septum) can easily be felt. There may be a slight flare at the nasal bone and superior lateral cartilage junction and a slight prominence in many people, resulting in the leading nose border varying from a straight to a humped line on profile.

The septum or central cartilage with the inferior lateral cartilages gives the form to the tip of the nose. The lower segment to the tip of the nose is supported by paired inferior lateral cartilages. These are attached wherever the borders are adjacent to the superior lateral cartilages and to the maxilla by dense fibrous ligaments.

The bulbous tip of the nose varies with individuals. On lateral view it conforms to two rounded obtuse angles. The nostrils in the lower third are supported by curved cartilages, somewhat elliptical, that consist of the bulbous tip and the flair of the wings or ala of the nose. These are supported by curved dense fibrous tissue that outlines and gives form to the nostrils. The vertical central support of the lower

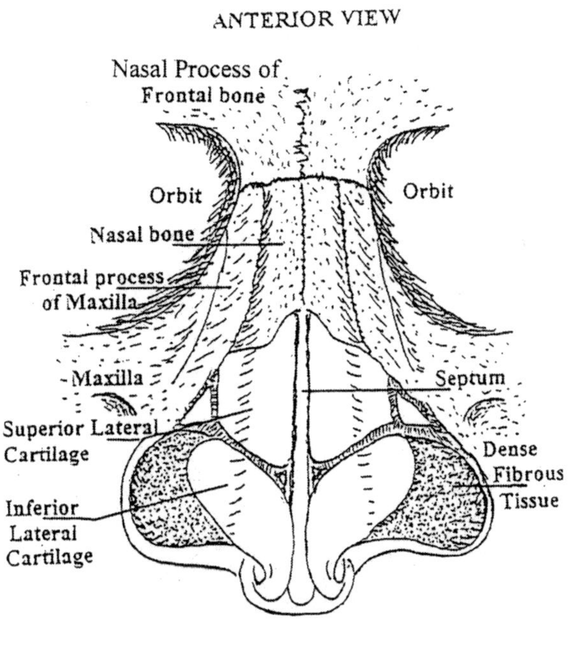

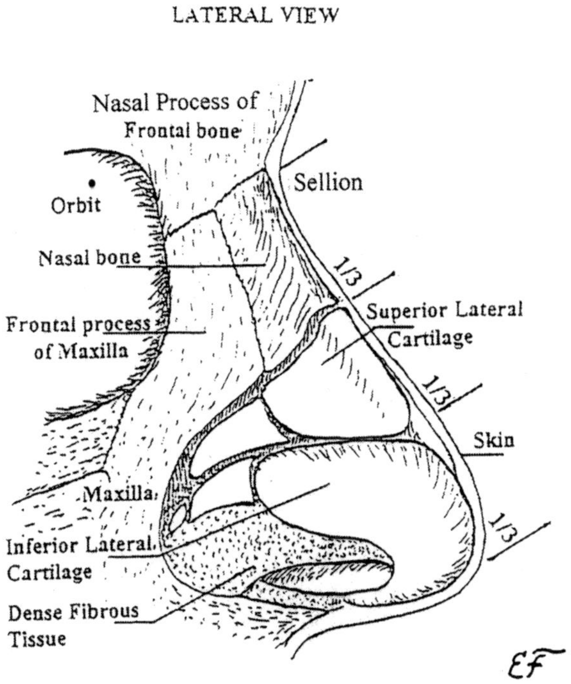

Nose anatomy.

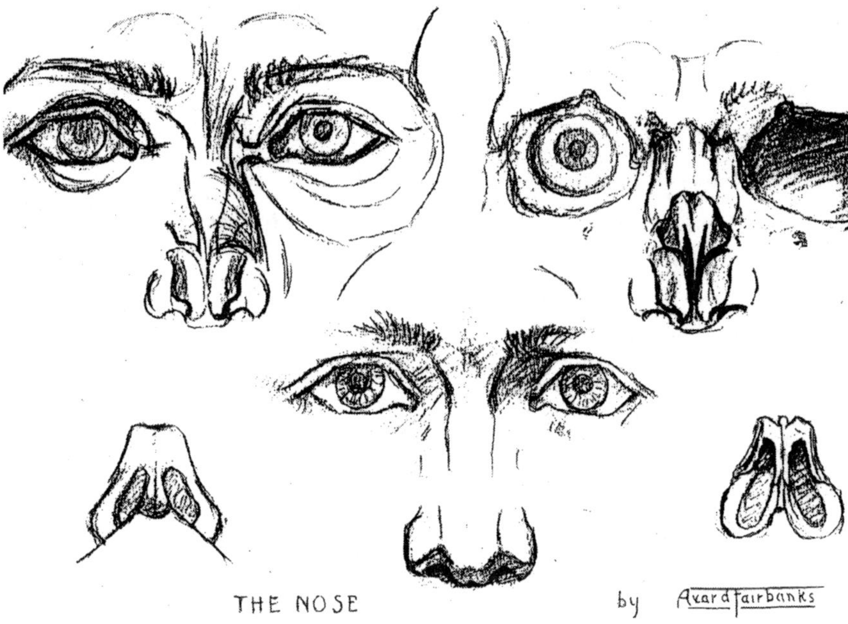

Nose anatomy by A. Fairbanks, from his sketchbook.

segment is the cartilaginous septum. At the sub nasal point, there is a bony prominence of the maxilla just above the upper lip. It is essentially a midline pedestal for the cartilaginous septum of the nose. The profile of the nose depends on the development of these three segments of the nose. They may all develop uniformly, or one segment may develop more than the others.

Generally, the nose of the adult male is more prominent than the adult female. The nasal bones of the infant are undeveloped. This gives the baby a cute little pug nose. A blow to the bridge (sellion) of the nose in infancy may cause a fracture of these nasal bones resulting in a deformation with a low broad nose. Other injuries may cause the septum to deviate to one side.

When modeling a portrait, these irregularities may be modified toward a more normal or ideal feature. The alert artists note these variations of the details, and model the portrait to the characteristics of the individual. However, if a caricature is intended, the elements of the nose may be exaggerated along with other exaggerated features, as ears, eyebrows. lips, and chin.

As a person ages, the cartilages of the nose may grow longer and become less ridged or soft, allowing the nose to sag. Just as the artists soften the wrinkles of the brow, he or she may also render a more youthful appearance by a slight upward adjustment of the nasal contours

Recognize that people rarely see a profile of themselves in a mirror and may be unaware of the aging changes of their nose. A review of an earlier photograph may be helpful. Since the nose is one of the most prominent facial features, it is important for individual's image. A careful study of the nose and its anatomy is beneficial to the sculptor.

Anatomy of the Ears

It is important to define the parts of an ear. The whole external ear is called an auricle or a pinna. The width of the pinna is about one-half the vertical height of an ear. The pinna is supported by a pliable framework of elastic cartilage that is covered with skin. There are several prominent features of the pinna. The curved outer border of a pinna is called the helix.

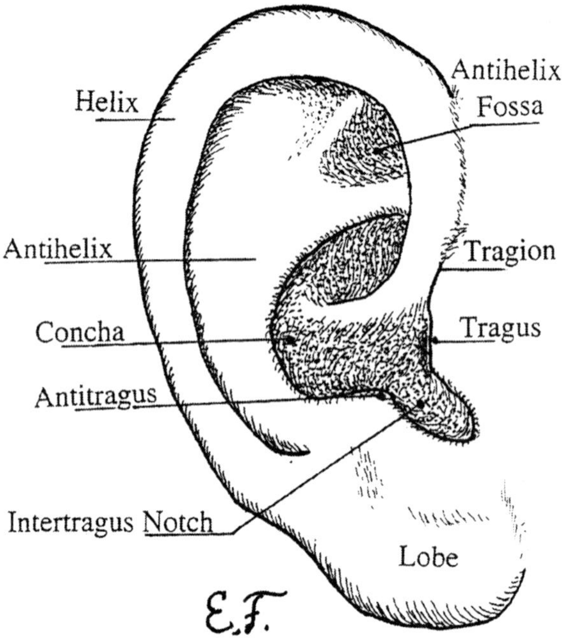

Lateral view of ear.

The curve of the helix is a geometric spiral that demonstrates dynamic symmetry. It begins at about the middle half of the ear just above the tragus or ear flap. It is first directed anteriorly, and then curls up and out away from the temporal plane. The helix curves around the ear's apex to become the upper and outer border of the ear. Curving down, it descends nearly vertically then slightly anterior and medially as it approaches the lobe. The helix' course is similar to a whorl.

The groove inside the helix is the fossa of the helix. The ridge inside the fossa of the helix is named the antihelix. It originates in the upper ear with two ridges which join the antihelix to form a "Y" between which is the antihelix fossa. The antihelix curves down inside the helix.

The cavity between the tragus and the antihelix is a concave space, a depression within the mid portion of the curve of the antihelix is called the concha, a word derived from Latin meaning a shell. Anterior to the concha and partly covering the ear canal is a blunt projection called the tragus or ear flap.

Anterior to the concha is the ear canal, or the auricular canal (named the porion by physical anthropologists). It is an important reference point on the skull at the base of the cranium, and is a relatively fixed point during head growth. The position of the porion is independent of other facial development. There is a small groove between the upper border of the tragus and the beginning of the helix. This is named the tragion and is a surface point of reference on the skin for the porion, the external auditory canal.

Posterior to and below the tragus is a small ridge, the antitragus that is joined to the antihelix. Between the tragus and the antitragus is a definite notch, the intertrageal notch. All of these structures of an ear are supported by cartilage, a firm flexible type of tissue that retains its shape. Below the tragus and antitragus is the ear lobe. It is composed of fibrous and fatty tissue, but

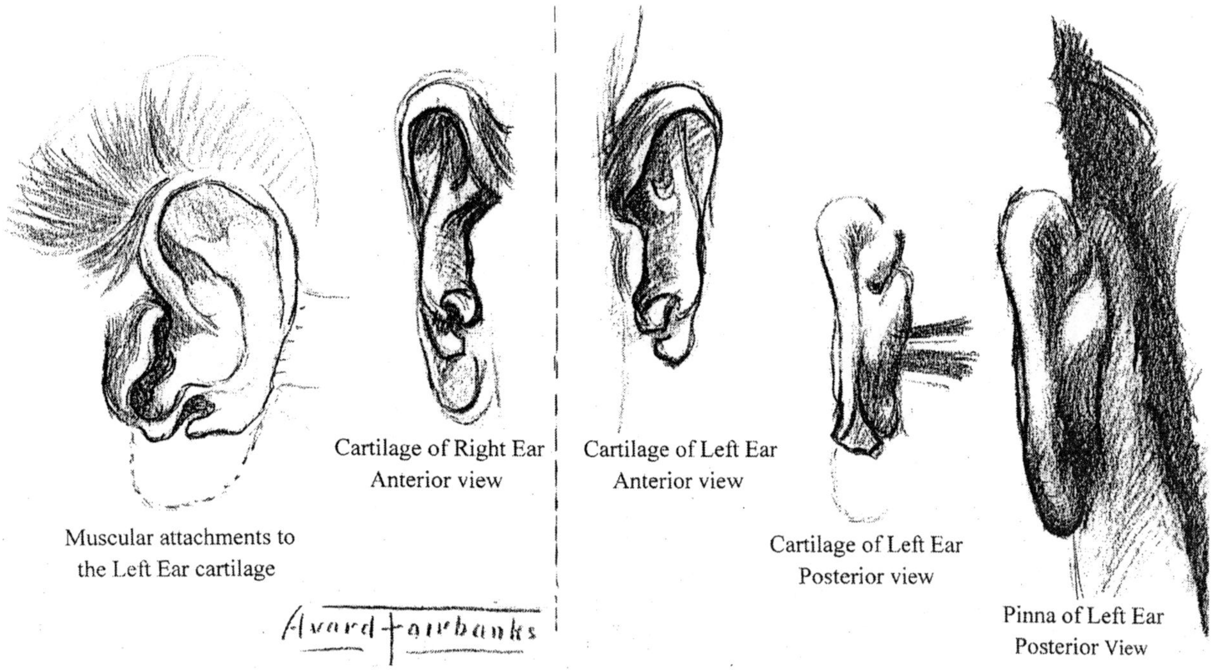

Ear structures, from the sketchbook of Avard Fairbanks.

since it contains no cartilage, it is soft and pliable.

The lobe is characterized by even greater variations in shape. In many people the lobe has a definite crease and a notch at half of its distance, separating it from the face. In others the lobe is less developed and attaches without a separation. On frontal view, the helix is prominent in the upper third, but the antihelix hides it in the middle third. The lobe is more evident in the lower third.

The ears vary with individuals and may grow with age. On some persons, they may be somewhat unequal or at slightly different elevations. Since they are not a feature of expression, artists may model them and de-emphasize any unusual characteristic.

If one is intending a caricature, the features of the forehead, hair, eyes, ears, nose, lips, and chin may be exaggerated. However, the artist with idealistic intent and the portrayal of character may minimize unusual or gross features while endeavoring to capture the expression, personality, and spirituality of the individual. This renders a more life-like appearance. This quality of incorporating animation into a portrait is the true measure of the artist's abilities.

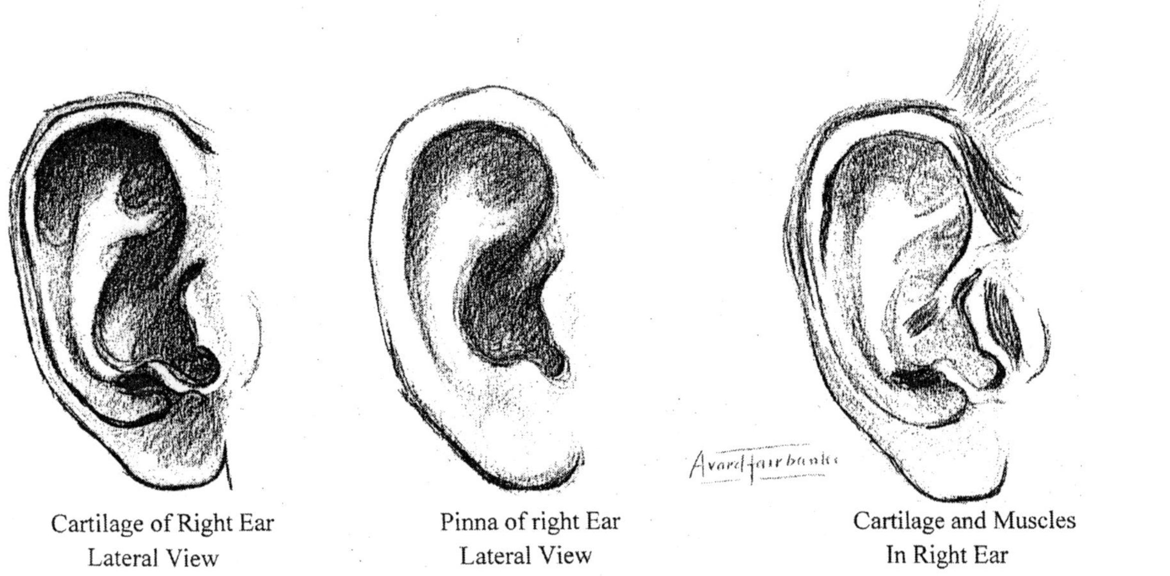

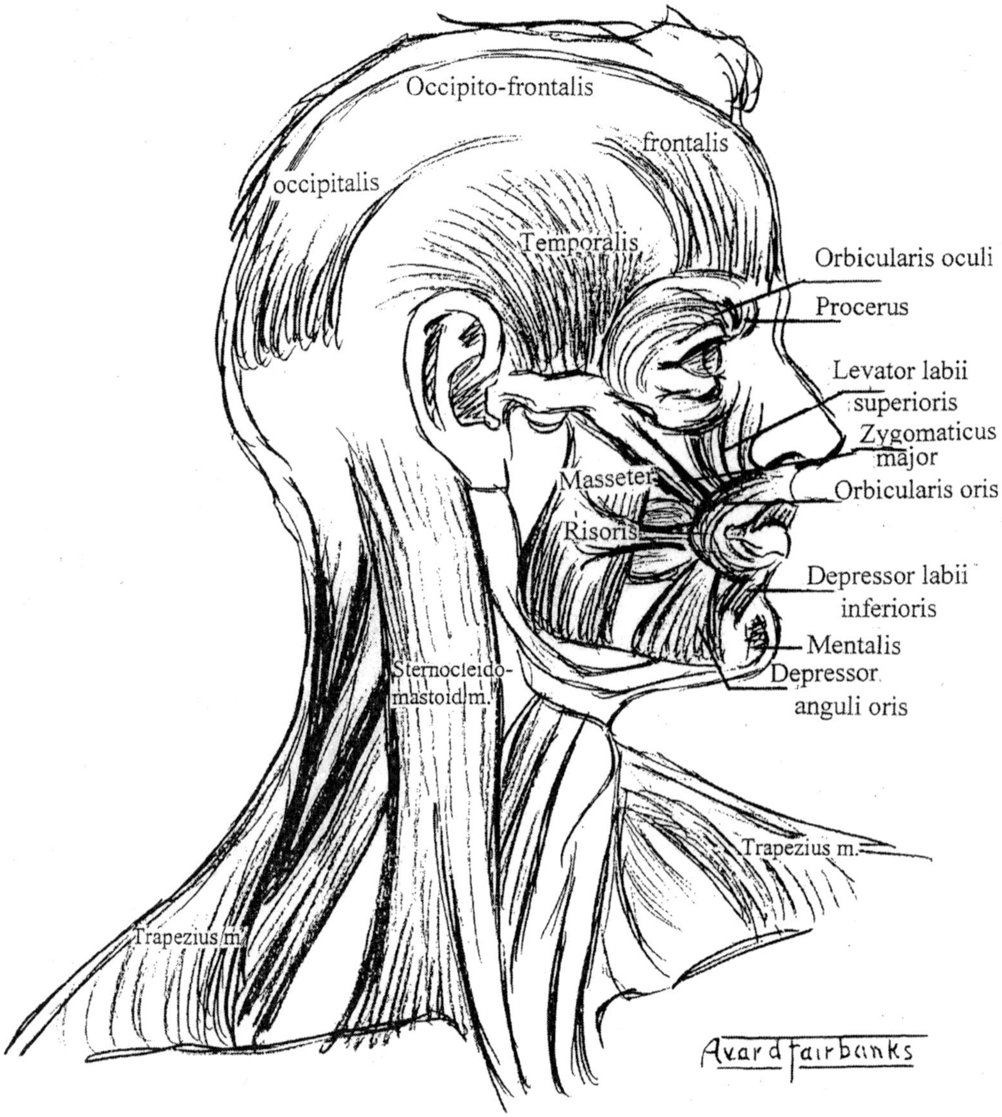

Muscles of the head, lateral view, from the sketchbook.

The Muscles of the Head

The muscles of the head can be divided into two categories: the muscles for mastication of food and the muscles of facial expression. The two mastication muscles, of importance to artists, are the temporalis and the masseter. Two other muscles exist on the inner aspect of the mandible, the medial and lateral pterygoid muscles, but they do not contribute to external form and will not be discussed. The temporalis muscles are large flat, fan like muscles on both sides of the head. They originate on the temporal fossa of the skull (from the forehead to above the ear) and insert on the coronoid process on the ramus of the mandible. These muscles serve to elevate the mandible to close the mouth and chew. The masseter originates along the lower border of the zygomatic arch (cheek bone to just in front of the ear) and inserts along the lower border of the ramus of the mandible, anterior to the angle of the mandible. This muscle also serves to elevate the mandible and can be recognized when someone is chewing or clenches teeth in anger.

The second category, the muscles of facial expression form a large group. People have a broad range of facial expressions that involves many muscles. Therefore, a good understanding of theses muscles and their actions are necessary

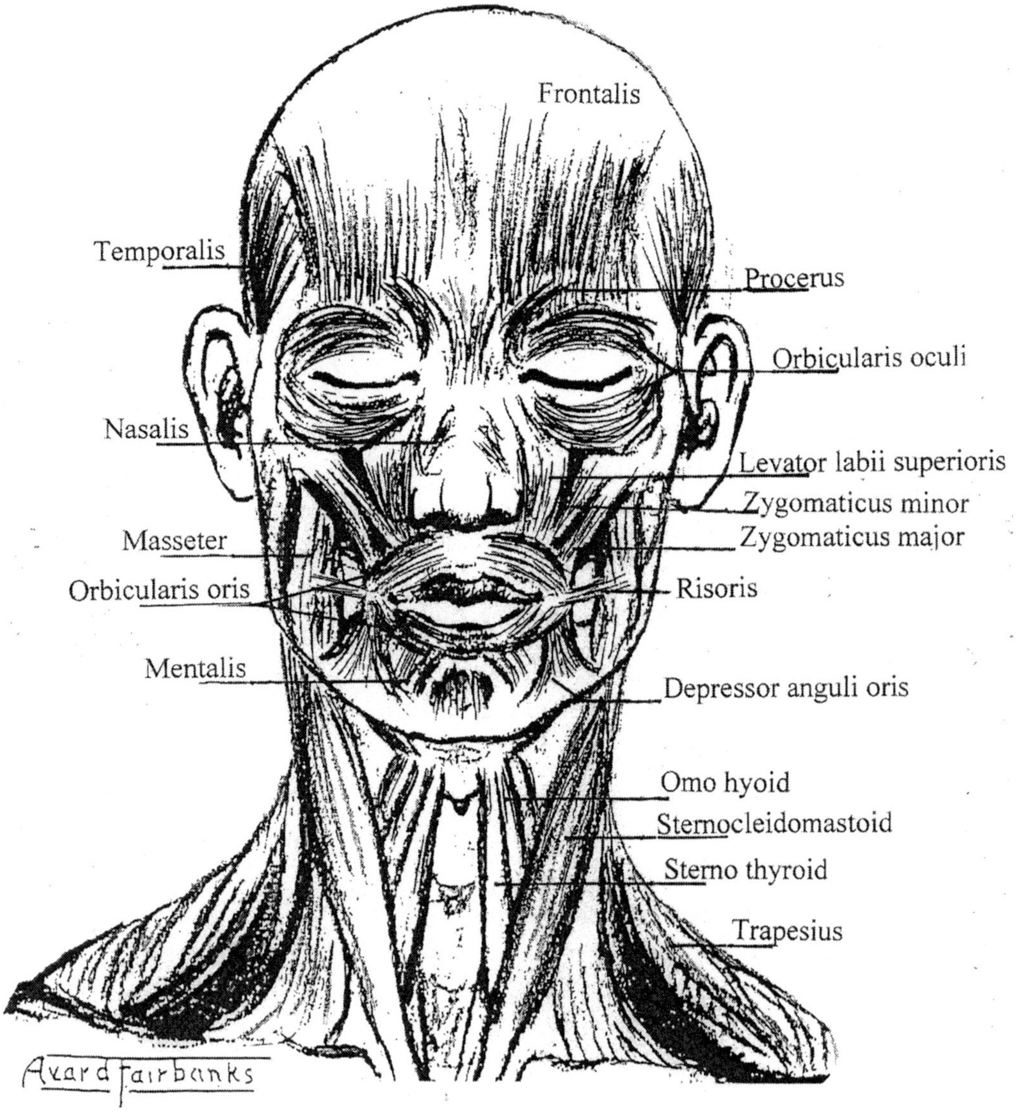

Muscles of the head, anterior view, from the sketchbook.

to accurately convey on a portrait the thoughts and feelings through expression. These are named primarily for their action rather than their attachments. The muscles of the scalp are paired and are referred as epicranius (outside of cranium) muscles. A main component is the occipito-frontalis muscle. It is composed of frontal and occipital bellies. Both join onto the galea aponeurotica, (a broad tendinous sheath that covers the cranium and can be moved about one centimeter both forward and back as well as side to side).

Beginning above the orbit, the frontal belly attaches to the skin of the eyebrows. Its contraction will produce horizontal wrinkles in the forehead up to the hairline or where the hairline once existed on a bald person. The posterior belly arises along the occipital bone and inserts on the posterior galea aponeurotica. When activated in conjunction with the anterior belly, alternate contractions of these two muscles will move the scalp alternately forward and back.

The orbicularis (circular around) oculi (eye) muscles surround the orbits and extend into both eyelids acting to close the eyelids. Another muscle originating deeper, the levator (raises) palpebrae (eyelid) serves to open the eyelids, but this pair does not contribute to external anatomic form. Deep to the orbicularis oculi are two broad muscles that run laterally from the frontal bone just above the nose. These corrugator (wrinkle) supercilli (above eyebrow) attach to the skin of the eyebrows and pull the eyebrows together to produce vertical wrinkles in the forehead between the eyebrows.

Horizontal wrinkles between the eyebrows are created by contraction of the procerus muscle. This thin muscle arises from the nasal bone an attaches to the skin of the forehead. The muscles of the nose are not well developed. The paired nasalis muscles arise from the maxillae and insert on the lower part of the ala (wings) of the nose. They draw the ala up and laterally. A small tendon crosses over the dorsum of the nose to connect these two muscles.

Encircling the mouth is the orbicularis oris (mouth) muscle to close the lips. Fibers of this muscle add to the form and substance of the lips. Many of its fibers are continuous with adjacent facial muscles. The levator (raise) anguli oris arises on the maxilla and inserts with the skin around the mouth and with fibers of the orbicularis oris. Another muscle, the levator labii (lip) superioris originates on the maxilla and inserts into the orbicularis oris. Both the levator anguli and the levator labii superioris serve to elevate the upper lip.

Other muscles inserting on the upper lip include the zygomaticus major and minor. Both arise from the zygomagtic bone; the zygomatic major arises more laterally and both insert on the orbicularis oris and the skin at the angle of the mouth. They serve to draw the lip upward and laterally as in a smile. Another strap-like muscle arises from the fascia (fibrous tissue) in the cheek and inserts in the angle of the mouth. This muscle is named the risoris, indicating the laughter or grinning muscle, because it pulls the angle of the mouth laterally. Deep to these, the muscular part of the cheek is composed of the buccinator muscle. Its name is derived from a Latin word for blowing a trumpet. It also serves to draw the cheek and side of the mouth laterally.

Other muscles attach from below and serve to pull the lower lip and corner of the mouth in a downward direction. A triangular muscle, the depressor anguli oris, arises from the lower border of the mandible and tapers moving upward as it blends with muscles at the corner of the mouth. Medial to it lays the depressor labii inferioris muscle. Its course begins at the lower border of the mandible and inserts by blending with the orbicularis oris along the lower lip.

Between these two muscles appears the mentalis (chin) muscle. It also arises from the mandible, but its course runs downward to insert on the chin. Contraction will elevate the skin over the chin.

The muscular complexity of the mouth can be more effectively recognized and appreciated by looking in a mirror while performing the enormous number of lip and facial movements that are necessary in speaking, creating gestures, and making faces.

Actions of the Facial Muscles of Expression

The muscles of facial expression can be grouped into upper and lower face areas. Both eyes and mouth are surrounded by circular muscle sheets. These muscles contracted will close the openings which are in reality slits in the skin of the face. Most of the expression muscles originate on bone, but run into or fuse with these orbicularis muscles and they alter the form of the opening. The upper group activates expression about the eyes and forehead. The lower group acts on the nose, cheeks, and chin.

Smiling and Laughing

Pleasant expressions utilize most of the same muscles of expression. Laughing, a more intense degree, activates the same muscles more completely as well as several additional strands.

The zygomatic major muscles pull at the corners of the mouth diagonally upwards, laterally, and posteriorly. They are assisted by the zygomatic minor muscles. In so doing, they bunch up the flesh of the cheek under the eye. At the same time, the risorius, or laughing muscle, pulls laterally and posteriorly on the corners of the mouth.

The levator labii superioris (upper lip lifter) and the levator anguli oris (mouth angle lifter) lift the upper lip and lateral mouth. This action deepens the cheek furrow. At the same time, the orbicularis oculi contracts to partially close the eye. This produces smile wrinkles laterally from the eye.

Laughing widens the mouth further and opens the mouth. In addition, a nasalis muscle over the nose contracts to wrinkle the nose and the dilatores muscles on the ala of the cartilages contract to flare the nostrils.

Compassion and Sincerity

Emotional expressions of sympathy and concern may be demonstrated by a slight wrinkling of the forehead by contraction of the Frontalis muscle and a slight twist of the eyebrows upward and inward by action of the corrugator muscle.

Discontent, Disagreement, Indignation, Scorn, and Hate or Rage

These expressions evoke, a different combination of muscle action. The risorius muscle draws the mouth back while the triangularis muscle draws the corners downward and backward. The orbicularis oris muscle tightens the lips. The depressor labii inferior depresses the lower lip and extends the furrow around the corner of the mouth, while the levator menti raises and wrinkles the chin and causes the lower lip to protrude. This is especially true in children.

Expression in the brows and eyes occurs when the corrugator muscles draw the eyebrows downward and together, while the orbicularis oculi contract causing the brow to overhang. Several muscles of the nose flare the nostrils and deepen the furrow.

In addition, the masseter, a muscle of mastication, may tighten as the jaw sets. When the mood is intense, the platysma, a thin sheet of superficial muscle fibers originating in the chest and shoulders, contracts to widen the neck and produce vertical, divergent strain folds.

Excitement, Astonishment, Surprise, and Suspense

The first effect of astonishment is a raising of the eyebrows and eyelids. The frontalis muscle lifts and arches the brows, producing longitudinal furrows in the forehead. The levator palpebrae superioris raises the upper eyelid so that not only the whole iris is exposed, but also the border of the sclera or white of the eyeball.

As surprise and excitement increase, the head may tilt back and the mouth may open as the mandible drops, activated by deep muscles of the neck. As the mouth opens, the Triangularis muscle and the depressor labii inferior give a downward pull on the corners of the mouth elongating the cheek furrow.

When excitement progresses to the stage of yelling, the risorius muscle may effect a widening of the mouth. The dilator muscles of the nose may flare the nostrils. Yawning uses essentially the same muscle action about the mouth. However, the orbicularis oculi contract to close or partly close the eyes and the corrugators contract to draw the brows down and together.

Supplication, Worry, and Suffering

Expressions of sincere concern have increased muscle tone of the frontalis and corrugator muscles producing more wrinkling of the brow and more upturn of the center eyebrows. The lower face contours change by action of several muscles that includes the risorius which pulls the corners of the lips laterally.

The knowledge of facial anatomy benefits the artist's effort to portray expressions of emotion from demonstrative reactions to more solemn occasions. Observation and analysis of various people in a range of situations will further enhance portrayal.

Avard T. Fairbanks

Sculptured Anatomical Displays

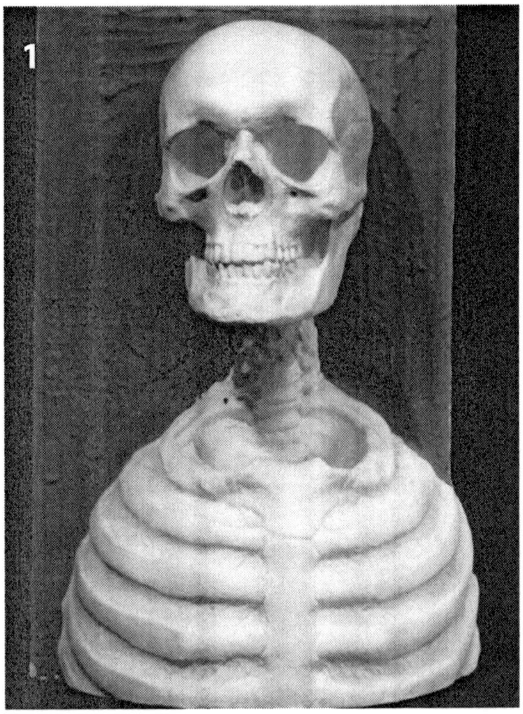

1. The anterior view of the skull, and the upper thorax down to the fifth rib is first in the series.

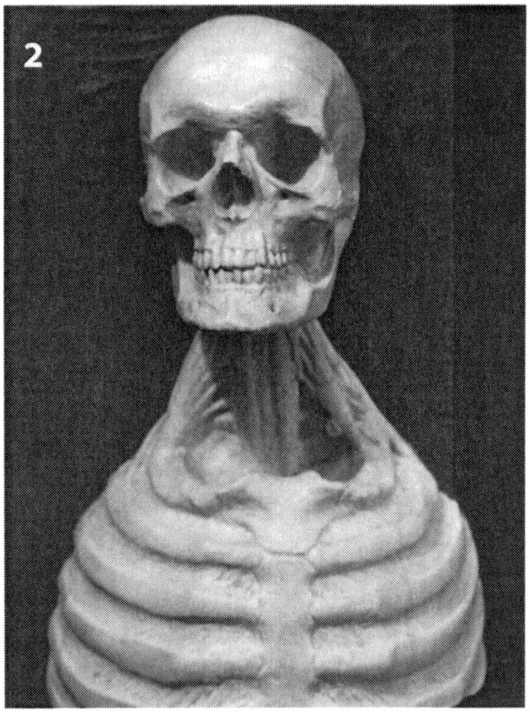

2. The anterior view of the skull and upper thorax demonstrates the first layer of supporting muscles to the head. The three scalene muscles connect the transverse processes of upper neck vertebrae to the first and second ribs. They act like guy wires to telephone poles that add stability.

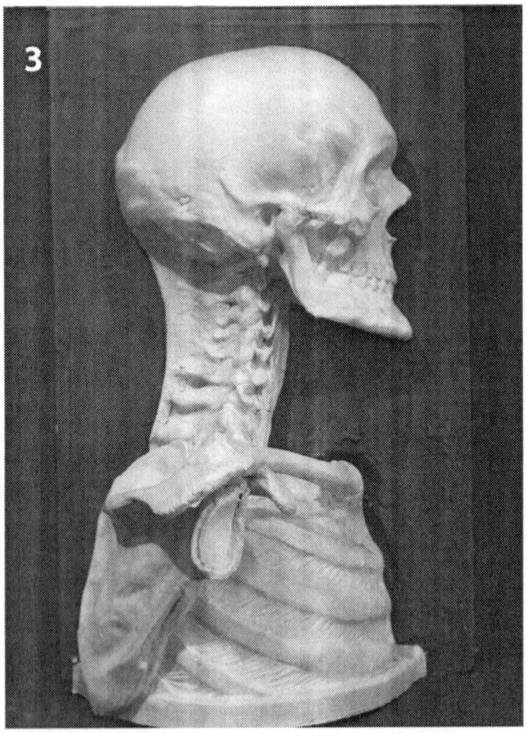

3. A lateral view of the skull, neck, and upper thorax reveals the nuchal ligament, a fibrous elastic membrane that extends from the occiput to the spinous processes of the neck vertebrae and the upper thoracic vertebrae. It facilitates the head to return to an erect position. The bones of the right shoulder girdle, consisting of the clavicle and scapula, have been added.

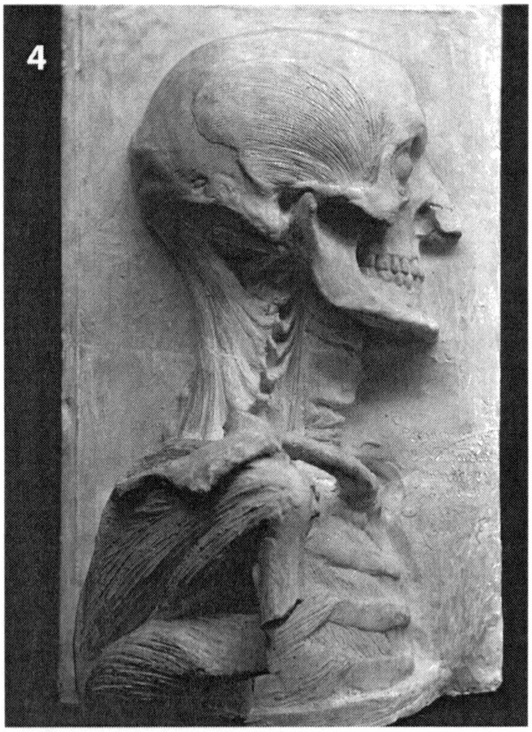

4. Additional development of muscles is demonstrated in this lateral view. The temporalis muscle on the skull which acts to close the jaw has been added and cartilage has been added to the nose. Erector spinae muscles cover the ligamentum nuchae of the neck, and muscles that activate the arm have been placed appropriately.

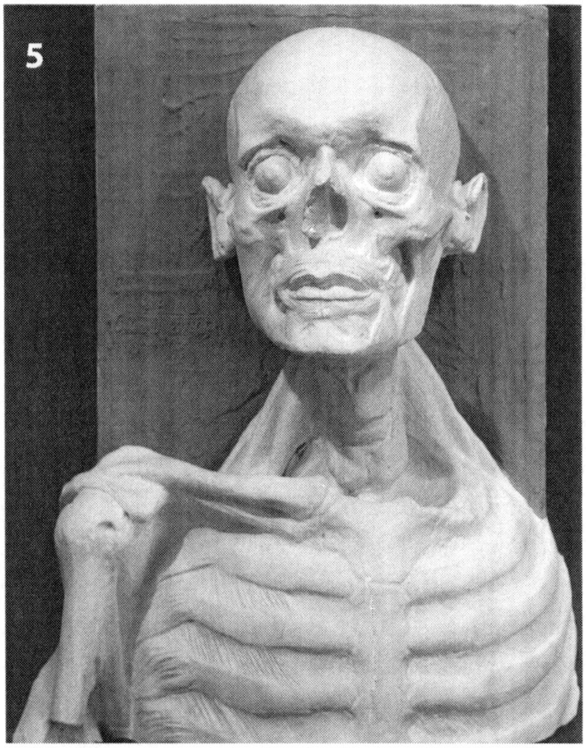

5. Additions to the frontal view include the right shoulder girdle, the ears and eyes, and mouth. The masseter and temporalis muscles which activate chewing are in place. Muscles about the mouth are muscles of expression.

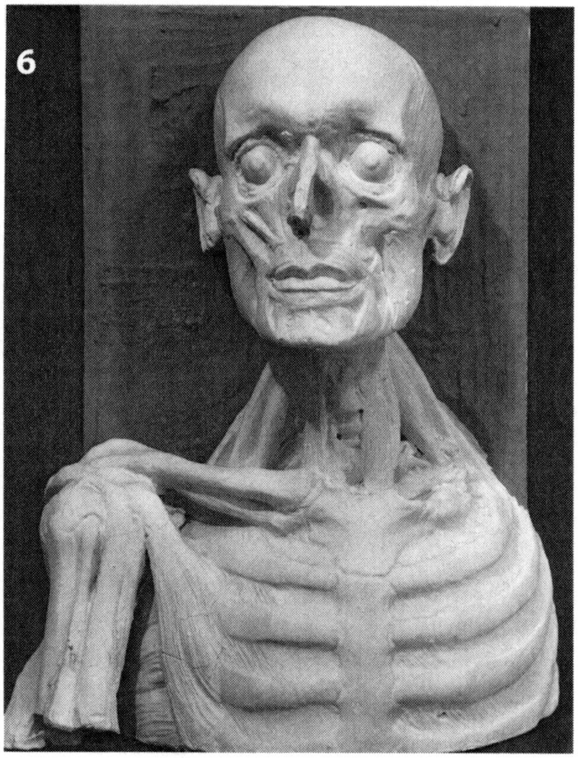

6. The nose and more facial muscles are added.

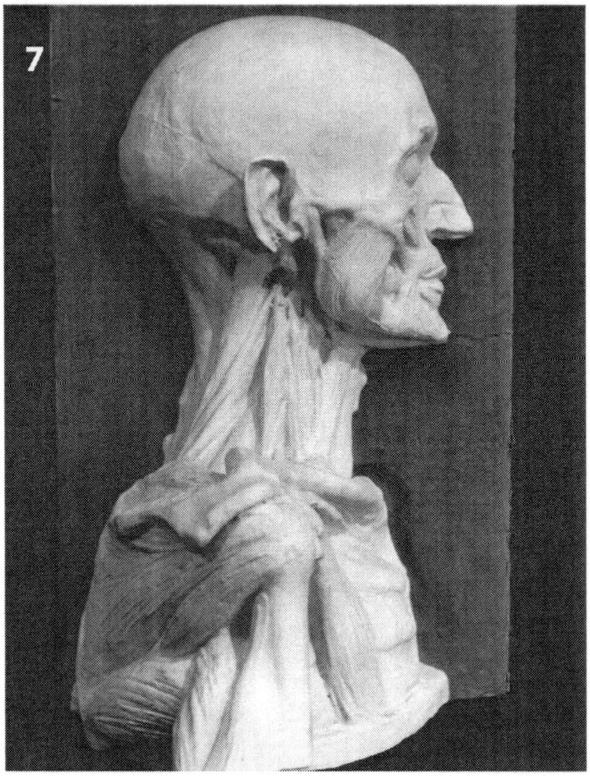

7. Further development of the lateral view demonstrates additional muscles of the neck and the shoulder girdle.

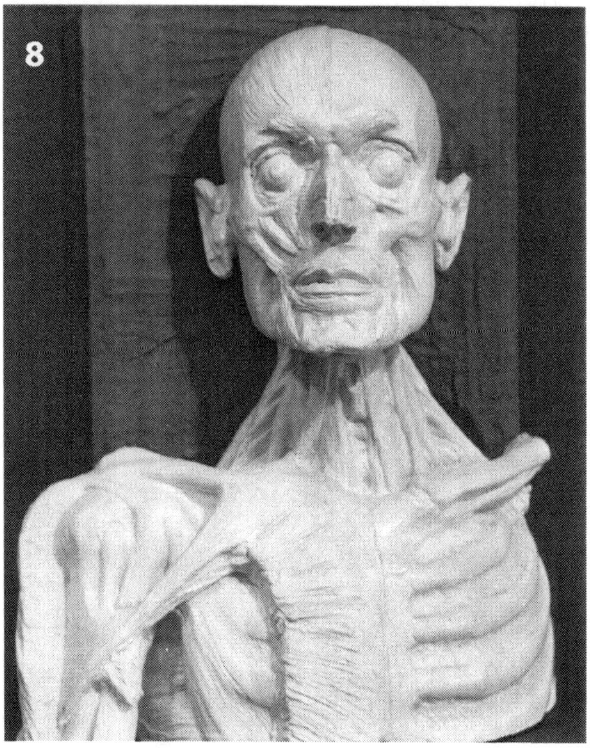

8. Cartilages of the nose have been added to the frontal view. Additional muscles of expression are in the face. The larynx and the sterno hyoid muscles are in the neck. The large pectoralis muscle is indicated over the right upper thorax.

APPENDIX

Contraposto, Dynamic Balance

Alterations of the torso form represent the big change from the ancient Egyptian art to the Greek classic art. It is sometimes called weight shifting, one point balance, dynamic balance, and with a few other modifications, *Contraposto* in Italian, or counterpoise in English. It was incorporated and fostered by the master sculptor, Michelangelo.

For a description, it is placing all of the weight on one foot (example, left). When this is done, there is a high hip where the weight is supported (left), and a low hip on the opposite side (right). This causes the vertebral column, the back bone, to bending an "S" curve, creating a low shoulder (left) with the low hip and a high shoulder, (right). The sternal notch becomes the center of balance. This is a position of rest.

Many variations of this concept can result as soon as an artist grasps how the body moves. For example when the foot without the weight is put forward, the weight is supported by the back foot and the figure is not moving. It is at rest like Michelangelo's *David.*

However, when the weight must move forward the non-weight foot becomes posterior, and the figure appears to be ready to take a step as if it is to be moving forward. Normally, when one foot is forward, the opposite shoulder goes forward. When this configuration is included with the weight shift, it is known as *Contraposto.*

It becomes clear when one understands how the weight of the body moves. This dynamic action also puts the body into alternating rhythms, which are the rhythms of movement. This was one of the most important of advancements of art from the ancient Egyptian to the classic Greek sculpture. The dynamics of motion gave a semblance of life to the inert materials of art. During the Renaissance these concepts were revitalized when the artists learned how to utilize balance in art.

When the weight is shifted to the forward foot, the dynamics change; the right shoulder moves up, and the shoulder above the rear foot (left) becomes low. The torso moves forward. The curve of the vertebral column reverses. The high shoulder (right) moves forward, as the low hip (right) receives the weight and moves back. The low shoulder (left) moves back as the high (left) hip moves forward.

In walking and running there is an alternation of positions. One side has a high shoulder forward and a low hip back, while the opposite side has a low shoulder back with a high hip forward. This is clearly demonstrated in the illustration comparing a man and a lizard walking. The dedicated amateur may choose to observe people walking and running with more close attention in order to better understand how to portray action.

---

after Avard T. Fairbanks

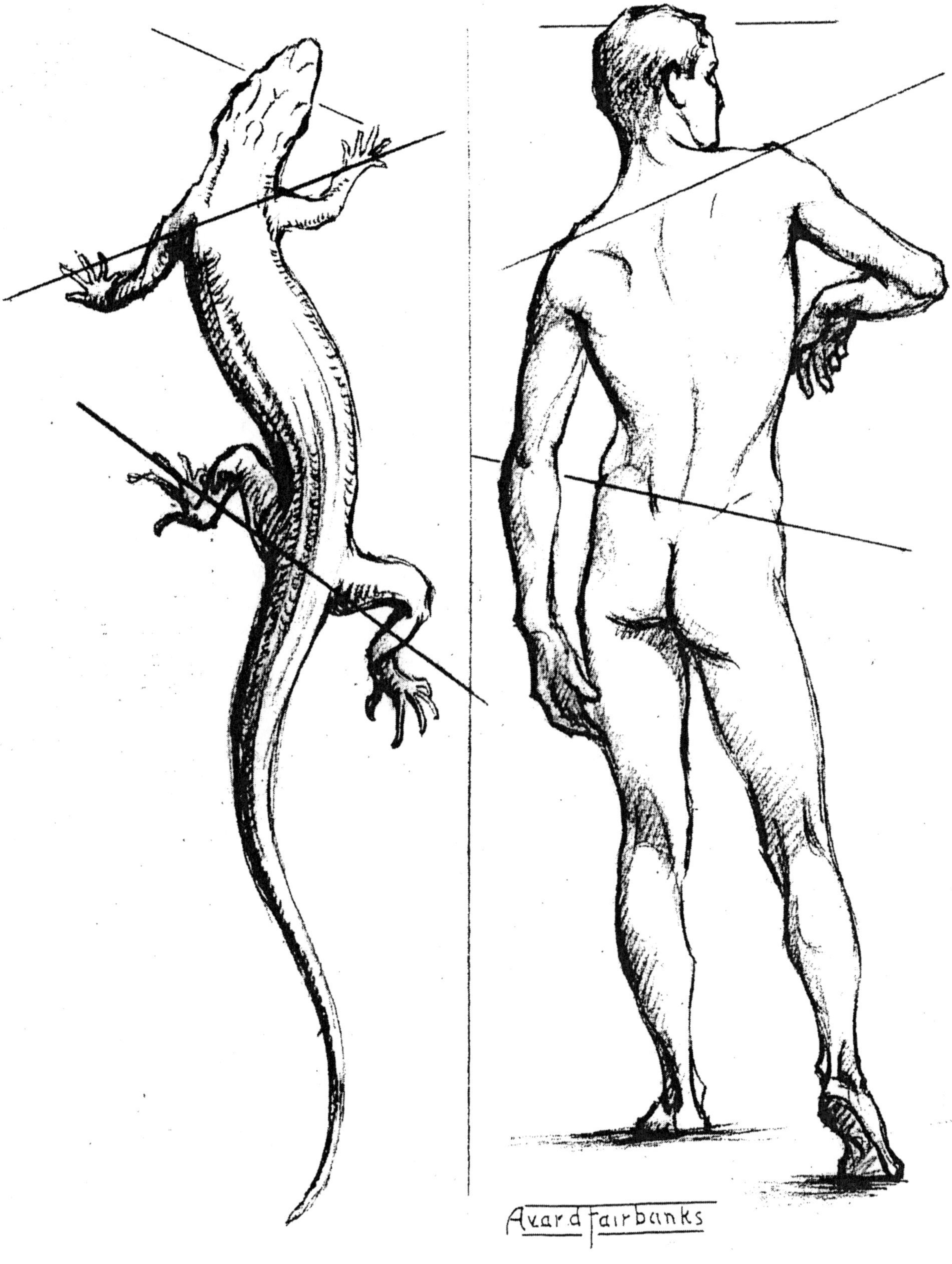

Illustration of *contraposto*.

Concepts in Creating Fine Art

In order to create a fine statue, there are various steps that the artists may consciously or automatically follow by experience, by training or by naturally endowed, organized behavior.

A. **Perception** of a thought, an incident, an historical event, an object of interest, or of beauty may attract an artist's attention sufficient to study details. Perception of a memorable experience or impression that is retained in the person's consciousness may later be re-created in a three-dimensional form.

B. **Recognition** of forms and details. These may bear a resemblance to simple geometric or pleasing configurations that enhance a composition.

C. **Analysis** of forms or details, such as arches, curved lines or planes, may be made either consciously or unconsciously by training and experience or by habit, or developed by study.

D. **Retention** in memory of significant images and the important details that enhance the central theme, image, or person.

E. **A concept** that can communicate a message, a feeling, a mood or enlightenment is beneficial. The creation of a fine composition may then follow by factors that result in an expression, whether it is in actions, in music, dance, in a graphic art or in a three-dimensional or sculptural artistic creation.

F. **Synthesis** may then result in a composition, or a restoration of a scene or an image. It may be an experience or a moment in time. The composition may join features together in a two- or three-dimensional object that will impart an experience to the observer, preferably a positive and enlightening experience.

Creative imaginative thinking may produce a design that will communicate a thought or a feeling that others can comprehend and appreciate. For a re-creation of a moment in time, art needs to have a message that can be conveyed and comprehended.

Art is a means of communication: the finer the art, the better is the communication of the message.

Artistic Design

There are important fundamental phases in creating a masterpiece:

A. **Observation** in an astute manner of the person as to age, sex, stature, and ethnic characteristics.
   1. Familiarity with form of the usual expected features of the person and the differences that make the individual special.
   2. Perception with special attention to the individual features.
   3. Recognition of the expected features, the slight variations, and the distinct variations from usual or expected features.

B. **Retention** of observed features and details of any slight or distinct individual variations from the usual features.

C. **Synthesis** of the retained information when reproducing an image.

D. **Reproduction** of a likeness in an image that recreates the expression of the personality.

E. **Restore** the animation and character of the individual, so that it also recreates a moment in time of his or her existence.

Art is a means of communication. Fine art is at a high level of communication that renders an opportunity of experience to the observer.

The artist must so organize a masterpiece in beautiful proportions, and with such orderly lines, masses and forms that an observer, in the presence of such art objects, feels a sense of reverence and has the higher level of consciousness aroused to the harmonic orders of life, truth and beauty.

Any complete design must result from the harmony of all of its parts. While the form is modeled using the material into an orderly arrangement that renders an expression, the goal of design is an endeavor towards perfection.

The Elements of Art and Design

A. The elements of art first include lines. These one-dimensional features may be straight or curved lines to express the limits and direction of form.

B. **Form** is the shape of an object, which in a two-dimensional composition may be combinations of straight and curved lines with subtle inclusion of plane geometric figures like triangles and quadrangles and many others to create an image. Plane figures include curvilinear triangles, quadrangles or others which result wherever series of lines intersect.

In a three-dimension composition, *Form* uses curved and straight lines combined with portions or sections of plane and solid geometric configurations. These aspects of *Form* should be modeled in a subsidiary but contributory manner, so that they do not attract any special attention as a form to the viewer. Yet they can be analyzed as resembling spheres (spheroids) such as the head, cylinders (cylindroids, similar to cylinders) like the fingers, tapered cones (and conoids, similar to cones); with sections like thighs and other geometric contours joined in a pleasing complex composition to create an image that is visually appreciated.

C. The modification of *Form* is achieved by:
   1. Tone variations of light to dark intermingled with various shades of gray;
   2. Color in various hues; and intensities.
   3. Texture, either real or apparent, which ranges from bold to subtle and may accentuate the Color and Tone.

Content is very important. Art is a means of communication. A message is needed to be conveyed to the viewer, especially a theme expressed in a manner that can be comprehended by the expected observer.

Arrangement in Design

Three fundamental components in design are: *Symmetry, Balance* and *Rhythm. Symmetry* is often thought to be static, but in a design it may be modified to demonstrate action. *Balance* begins static but an interrupted balance with a restoration of balance represents action and motion.

Rhythm implies a beat with repetition. We are creatures of rhythm. Our hearts beat with a regularity of about eighty impulses a minute. With vigorous activity the pulse increases and at rest it decreases. Irregular rhythms often signify heart disorders. The lungs have a rhythm of breathing, about sixteen to twenty a minute with a sigh, a deeper breath, about each minute. Walking, running, and many tasks demonstrate repetitive actions and therefore rhythms.

This repetition in rhythm may be further modified by variation of intervals and intensities. Associated with these elements may be a *gradation* in which there is an orderly diminution as in arms to forearms to hands to fingers. In contrast, a *progression* is an orderly increase of intensity, size or appearance. With these modifications there may also be an *alternation* from one side of an axis to the other side. Alternation may then be with equal elements or alternation of elements may be seen in a progression or an alternation may be included in elements of a gradation.

By combining these elements, a *harmony* can be achieved, and with action a *dynamic harmony* becomes possible. By incorporating an *emphasis* more *expression* is possible. Other important factors include *proportion* and *perspective.* Attention to *proportion* renders recognition of, normality and a pleasing quality to a composition. *Perspective* arranges an object to appear appropriate in its surroundings.

A master Gothic builder said in 1398, *Ars sine scientia nihil,* [art without knowledge, (science) is nothing].[1] In this book there is an emphasis on the science involved in art generally and for sculpture in particular. The understanding and application of knowledge of human structure combined with more significant design considerations should add to the general appreciation of fine art and generate a higher consciousness in society. Fine Art may become a positive factor and a beneficial force throughout the world.

Substances, which may be acted upon by human intelligence, may be arranged into orderly and harmonious patterns to awaken a sense of aesthetic delight in the beholder. These are the ingredients and raw materials with which the artist labors. According to the type of work and the substance by which expression is exercised, the artist may be classified as a sculptor, a painter, a decorative designer, an architect, a musician, a poet, a dancer or a dramatist.

1. Ghyka, Matila. *The Geometry of Art and Life.* New York: Dover Publications Inc., 1977, p. xi.

...pose of Design

The purpose of design is to act on forms so that they have an inherent and recognizable expression. The mind of man is capable of appreciating harmonious design through sensory impulses, and through these impulses humans are able to correlate the impressions of existence and elevate them into knowledge and understanding.

Through the power of coordinated nervous and muscular activity a person becomes capable of producing an evocative and pleasing design. The ultimate purpose of design is, by means of creative effort, to compose forms by a knowledge and understanding of fundamental principles.

Design therefore may not only produces a sensory delight in the beholder, but should lead to a conscious appreciation of the effort and the means by which the artist created the work. Any observed form which attracts attention is a challenge. It says, "know me if you can, follow me in my plan."

Any design then is the basic idea upon which forms are built or the plans by which they are developed. The real function of artistic design is to attract a person through sensuous means, to cause one to know order and to guide one's self in the harmonies of physical and mental realms.

The artistic design of three dimensional forms in plastic substance modeled with balance and rhythm, are akin to the word symbols of poetry. Some trivial designs may be nothing more in art than a jingle is in poetry. The greater values of artistic design lie in the power to bring man into accord with the harmonies of existence and to cause him to be conscious of them.

Like poetry and music, artistic design in plastic forms may deal with the most profound and significant features of life and existence.[2]

The elements of design including: *form, content, symmetry, balance, rhythm, and harmony* with the significant modifying features are discussed and illustrated with an effort for correlation of inter-related aspects in *Human Proportions for Artists* by Avard T. Fairbanks and Eugene Fairbanks.[3]

2. Fairbanks, Avard T. *Anatomical Design,* Doctorate thesis. Ann Arbor, Michigan: The University of Michigan, 1936, pp. 16, 17, 46, 47, 50.

3. Fairbanks, Avard T. and Eugene F., *Human Proportions for Artists,* A Basis for Design. Bellingham Washington: Fairbanks Art & Books, 2005. pp. 147-217.

Preservation of a Portrait After Creation by a Sculptor

When the modeling of a portrait in clay is complete to the sculptor's satisfaction, it can be and should be preserved in a semi-permanent and hopefully a permanent medium. The semi-permanent medium is usually plaster, also called Plaster of Paris, which is a form of gypsum. Permanent mediums are ceramic, bronze and stone. In order to preserve the form and the intricate details, a mold is first made.

If only one cast is intended, a waste mold that is disposable can be made of plaster applied to the clay image. It is made in two halves separated by a fence of tin strips. After the plaster is hardened, the cast halves are lifted off, cleaned, shellacked, and greased. When the cast halves are reunited and secured, a plaster slurry is poured into the void to make about a two-inch-thick image cast. When it is hardened, the waste mold is carefully chipped away from the image.

When multiple casts were desired, multiple-piece molds or flexible molds are needed. Multiple-piece molds have been used for many years, but need a very skilled caster to create the mold.

In the first half of the twentieth century, the available flexible mold material was of a tough gelatin material, also called a glue mold. Hot molten gelatin was poured into the space between a rigid, plaster master mold and the sculpture. When it cooled, the master mold was removed and the gelatin (glue) mold was split and removed from the clay image. After the gelatin (glue) mold was cleaned and greased, the mold was put back together inside the master mold and secured. A plaster slurry was poured into the cavity sufficient for a two-inch-thick image. When the plaster was sufficiently hard the master mold and gelatin molds were removed, revealing an impressive white plaster image that needed retouching.

With each casting some detail was lost and the maximum number of castings was about eight.

After about 1950 a rubber compound called Black Tuffy was developed and became popular. More copies could be made, but the mold deteriorated with time. When silicone-rubber mold material became available, the molds were more durable and many more copies could be made. A rigid master mold was still necessary. The molds could be stored for years and could also be used for images cast in wax, suitable for the lost-wax process of bronze casting.

Although sculpture can be cast in other metals, bronze is preferred for its beauty and resistance to corrosion. The lost-wax process was developed before written history. The wax was lost, not the process. It is the finest casting process. It is used for dental inlays, sculpture, and much larger castings.

A wax image is first created, much like a plaster image, but only about one-fourth-inch thickness. Multiple applications of a ceramic slurry are applied and allowed to dry, building up to an adequate thickness called an investment. This investment is then heated and the wax melts out and is "lost," but most of it may be recovered and re-used.

Molten bronze is then poured into the hot ceramic investment and allowed to gradually cool. When cool the ceramic shell is crumbled off the bronze cast, which must then be retouched and finished with a patina that highlights the features.

Marble sculpture is carved in the finest permanent material. The stone image is a duplication of a plaster image done by skilled marble carvers. Many of the carvings are done at studios in Pietrasanta, Italy, near the Carrara Mountains where the finest white marble is quarried.

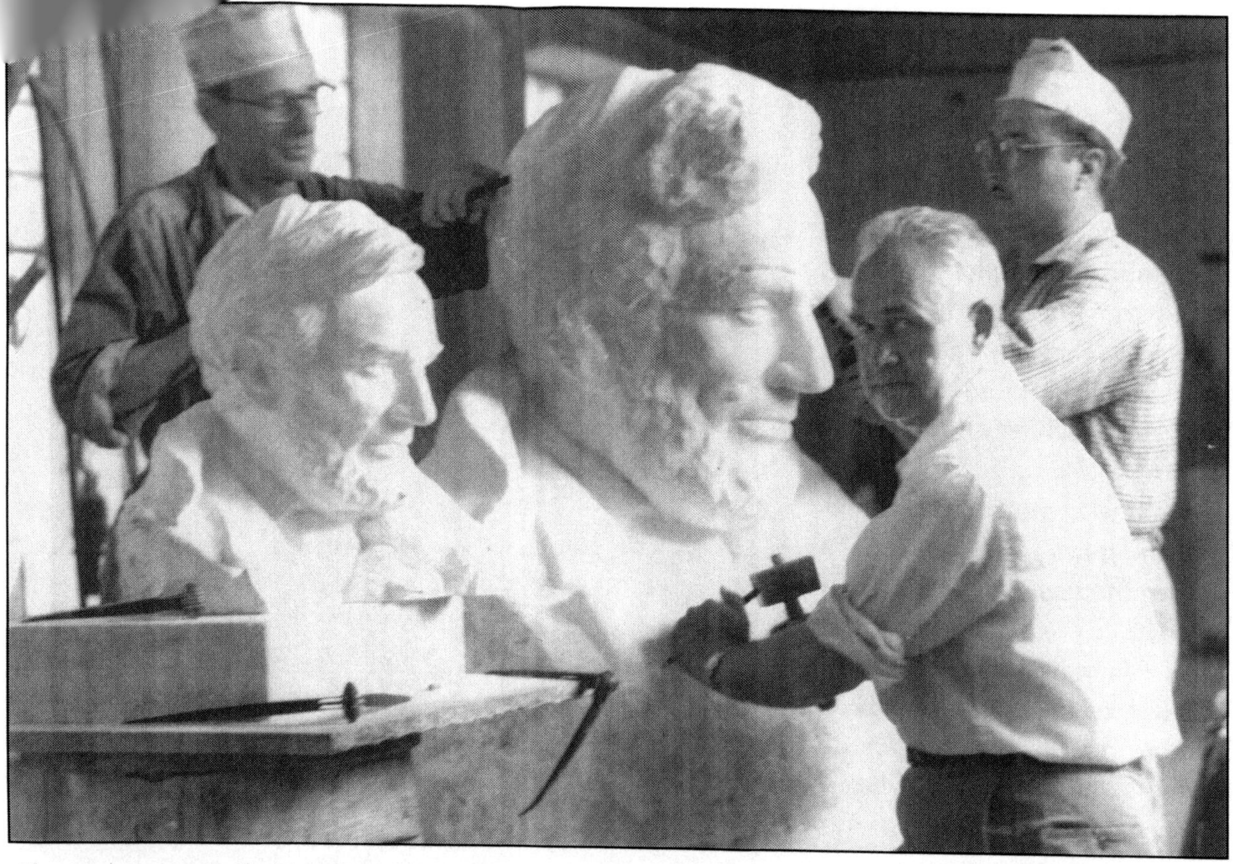

The colossal portrait, *The Enduring Lincoln,* is illustrated as it was being carved in Carrara marble at the stone carving studio in Pietrasanta, Italy. A heroic plaster image is used as a model to carve from in a three dimensional enlargement process. Avard Fairbanks is in the foreground finish carving with mallet and chisel, while technicians in the background use pneumatic chisels.

They use a pointing device that has a three point fixation, an adjustable arm and a long pointing needle that can slide through a small tube in a bracket. The needle has an adjustable stop that can be set at an appropriate distance.

Three fixation points are prepared on the plaster cast, and three points are located on the block of marble. The arm and the pointing needle are set on a prominent point of the plaster cast. The pointing device is then placed on the block and marble is chipped away with a pneumatic chisel until it is near the set of the pointer needle. This is repeated many times over the plaster cast and the marble until the image appears out of the block of marble.

The skilled marble carvers can carve down to an accuracy of about one-sixty-fifth of an inch. The sculptor then needs to finish the carving using fine pneumatic chisels adding expression to the portrait.

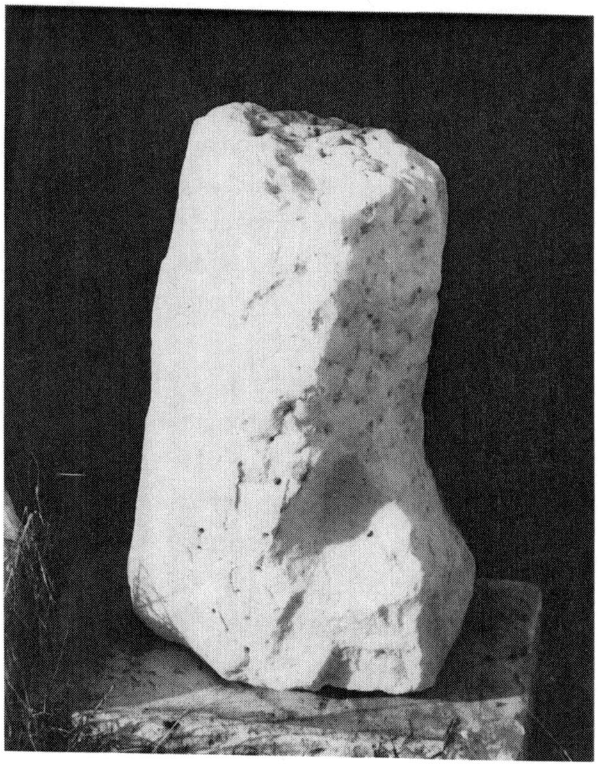

A block of marble from a quarry.

Marble Carving

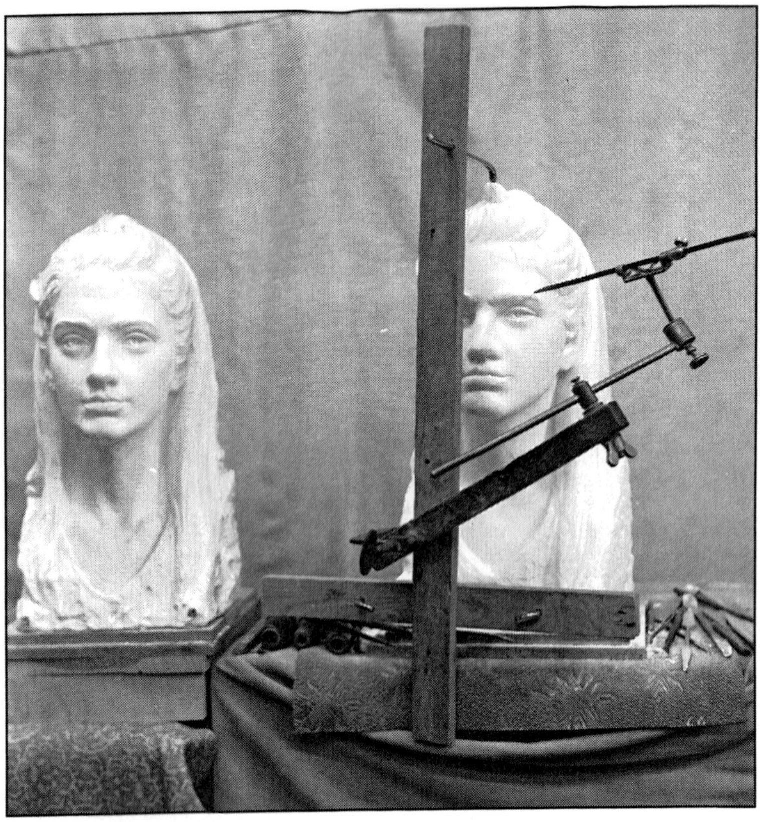

A three-point pointing device on the portrait of granddaughter Theresa Fairbanks.

Marble is a form of limestone. Its chemical name is Calcium Carbonate with a formula of $CaCO_3$. It is a metamorphic rock created by recrystallization under great heat and pressure over many millions of years. It comes in many colors due to impurities and is used extensively in architecture for public buildings.

The finest white marble comes from the quarries in the Cararra Mountains east of Pietrasanta, Italy. The city is named for sacred stone. There are other sources in the Alps of Europe. Grecian or Permian marble is noted for its hardness and durability. A beautiful rose colored marble comes from quarries in Portugal. United States sources are in Georgia, Tennessee and Vermont and in some other locations of the Appalachian Mountains.

Marble carving begins with a rude block of marble from a quarry. A point is drilled in the apex of the block with a pneumatic chisel. A point is drilled near the base of each corner of each four vertical surfaces of the block. The points are the same distance apart on each face of the block. These will be location points for the three point carving device to gage the depth of carving.

Each of the four surfaces would use the apex point and the two points at the base for an exact three-point fixation on each of all four sides. This device was developed in ancient times for carving in stone and is still used today. The ancient carvers used manual tools, but modern carvers use pneumatic hammers that use compressed air and speed the progress.

The image to be carved in stone is a plaster cast. On it a point is prepared by a small cone of plaster at the vertex with an incorporated metal cap having an indented point. This metal cap is usually a rivet with the head indented by a hammer and a center punch. The apex cap will receive the upper point of the device. Small plaster cubes about one-inch deep are attached near the corners of each side of the base. These also have metal caps with an indented point to receive points on the lower part of the pointing device. The distance between points on the base is carefully prepared to be equal to the points on the device.

The pointing device has an adjustable arm that has a bracket with two holes for a spindle to glide through. The spindle (like a long needle) has an adjustable stop so that it can slide through the holes of the bracket to a determined distance.

The three-point pointing device is first placed on the plaster image. The arm is adjusted and the

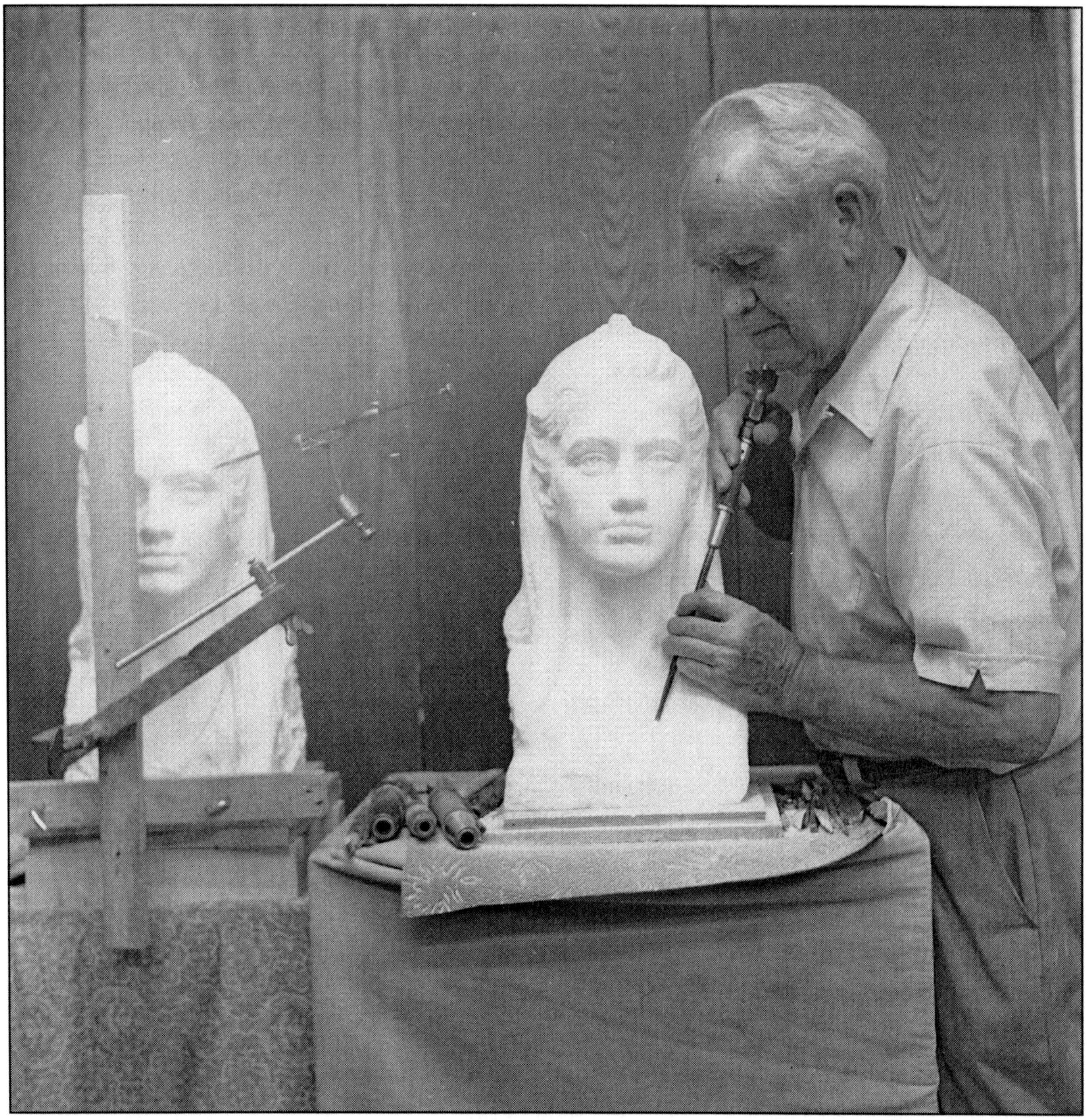

The illustration demonstrates Avard Fairbanks carving a marble portrait of his granddaughter Theresa, daughter of Jonathan. He is using a three-point pointing device and a pneumatic hammer with chisel. The plaster cast is used as the image to copy, and the three-point pointing device is shown.

spindle is advanced first to a high point on the surface of the image and the stop is adjusted. A small 'x' is marked on the image for reference. By moving the pointing device to the marble, chiseling with a pneumatic hammer chiseling device will make the chips fly.

At first, the marble block is chiseled down to about ¼ inch from the intended finished surface. The pointing device is progressively moved from point to points that are located about one-half inch apart. After the carving is roughed in, fine carving will proceed using more care and finer tools.

This fine workmanship is time consuming as the pointing device is moved back and forth from the image to the marble carving. When the carving nears completion, the beautiful result can be gratifying.

Measurements of Face and Head for Portraits

While Avard Fairbanks modeled a portrait, he made a number of measurements. However, he had a photographic memory and may not have needed to record as many measurements as would benefit a beginner.

The following measurements are suggested and recommended for students, amateur sculptors, and graphic artists to achieve a more accurate portrayal.

An aspiring artist may start by doing more detailed measuring and with more experience may rely on the major measurements. Experienced artists may automatically calculate some of them as they are modeling the portrait.

1. Bi-pairetal breadth, maximum width.
2. Bi-frontal width, forehead width at the fronto-temporal line.
3. Vertex to chin.
4. Vertex to trichion, hairline or point above forehead wrinkling on raising eyebrows.
5. Hairline to chin, trichion to chin.
6. Hairline to brow, trichion to glabella.
7. Brow to nose, glabella to subnasal point.
8. Note angle of nose to upper lip, male 90 degree or less, female 90+ to 108 degrees.
9. Subnasal point to chin.
10. Subnasal point to lip aperture, mouth; note the thick ness of the upper lip.
11. Lip aperture, mouth to sub-labial crease; note the thickness of the lower lip.
12. Breadth of mouth.
13. Breadth of brows, to the down-turn angle of the eyebrows.
14. Malar Breadth, width of cheek.
15. Eye breadth between lateral corners.
16. Width of one eye.
17. Width between the eyes, between the medial corners of the eyes.
18. Ear position, length of apex to lobe, and angle of tilt.
19. Nose length, depth of sellion or saddle, prominence of nose and breadth of ala.

Conversion scale of inches to centimeters:

inch x 2.54 = cm cm x 0.39 = inch

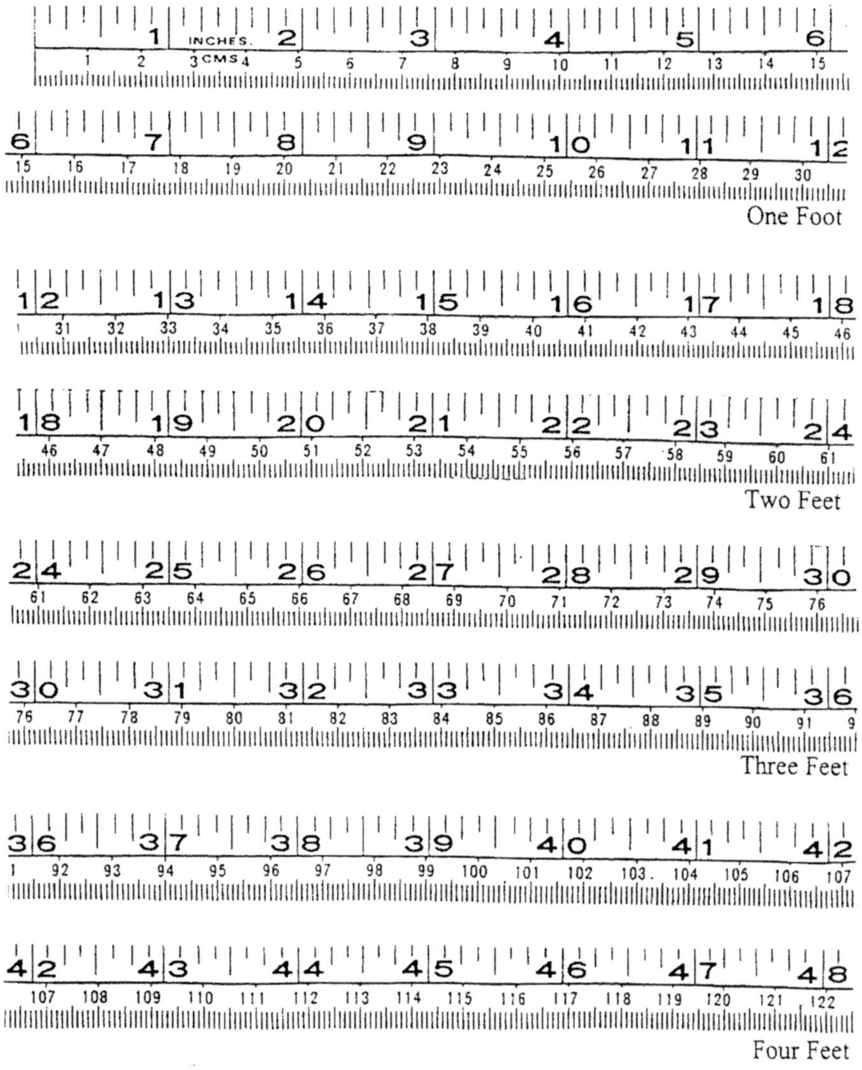

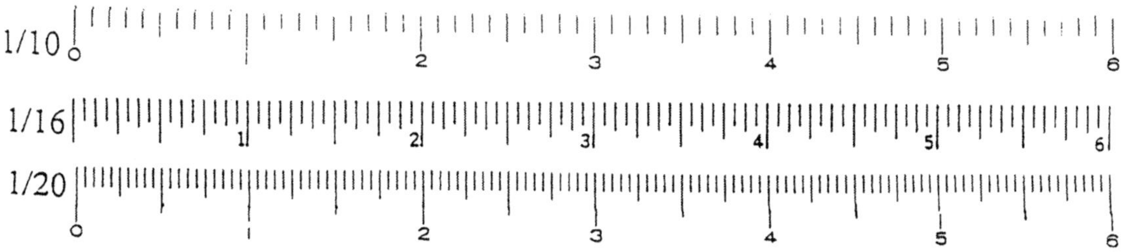

Conversions of Inch Fraction in 1/16ths to Inch Decimal

Inch fraction	1/16	1/8	3/16	1/4	5/16	3/8	7/16	1/2
Inch decimal	0.06	0.13	0.19	0.25	0.31	0.38	0.44	0.50
Inch fraction	9/16	5/8	11/16	3/4	13/16	7/8	15/16	
Inch decimal	0.56	0.63	0.69	0.75	0.81	0.88	0.94	

Sculpture Materials

During no period in history have there been such excellent and varied materials, tools and processes for creating fine sculpture as there are today. Modeling clay is available in many art and hobby supply stores. When larger quantities are needed, they can be ordered by sculpture supply houses.

The clay used by Avard Fairbanks in his productions was Roma Plastilina, a time-honored green-colored Italian formulation that contains clay, suet, and sulphur. For large statues he used water clay, which is preferred by many sculptors because of its fine texture. Many newer formulations are now available in different colors, firmness and many are sulphur free.

A leading sculpture clay producer is Chavant, chavant.com.

Tools, books and other supplies are available in other leading sculpture supply houses. They have comprehensive catalogs that are available on request.

Three of these are advertised in *Sculpture Review,* the quarterly magazine of the National Sculpture Society, sculpturereview.com.

- Sculpture House, sculpturehouse.com;
- The Compleat Sculptor, sculpt.com;
  both in New York, and
- Sculpture Depot in Loveland, Colorado. sculpturedepot.net.

Foundries and other suppliers also have advertisements in the publication, and some have catalogs of equipment and supplies.

Armatures

An armature is a supporting structure. In architecture it is the supporting framework when arches are being created. In an electric motor, it is the rotary steel framework on which coils of wire are wound to create magnets. In sculpture it is the supporting framework on which clay is applied. It must be strong enough to maintain the desired shape, but adaptable to the desired form or changes. There are several types and materials used.

Avard Fairbanks developed a simple armature of a one-by-one-by-eighteen-inch wooden upright for the head and a crossbar for the shoulders. It fit into a wooden socket on the baseboard, but was easily dismantled and could be carried with the baseboard and clay in a suitcase to the place of a lecture.

Another workshop-created armature that is commonly used is constructed of a gas pipe fitted into a floor flange that is screwed to the baseboard. Two iron rebars or heavy cables are bent into circles with projecting segments that are pushed into the upright gas pipe so that the circles are intersecting at right angles. This is satisfactory for a portrait with the head, neck and collar. A portrait bust includes shoulders and upper chest and needs additional support for the upper torso and shoulders.

Anatomically formed armatures in several sizes are available at some art supply stores. These may save some time for initial application of clay. A company in Novasota, Texas, has developed TruForm Armatures, a series of portrait and full-body skeleton-like armatures in plastic, with supporting metal and adjustable joints to assist sculptors. Visit truformarmatures.com.

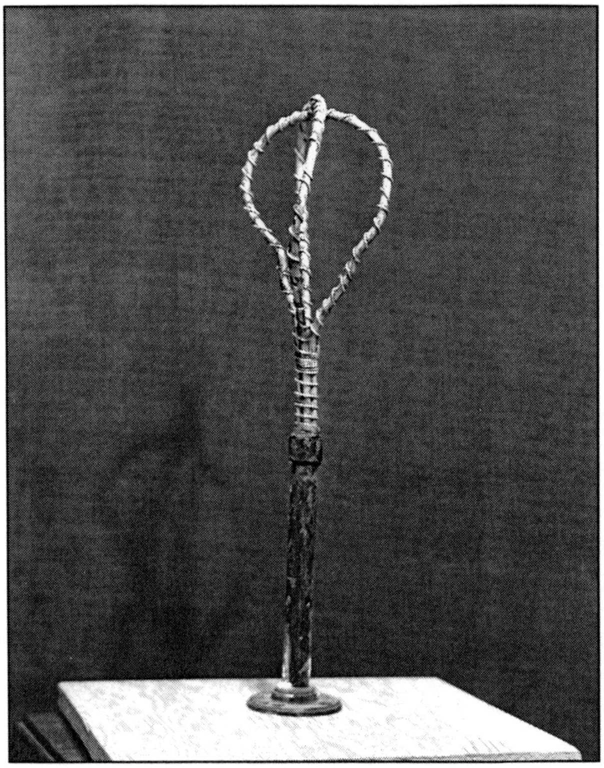

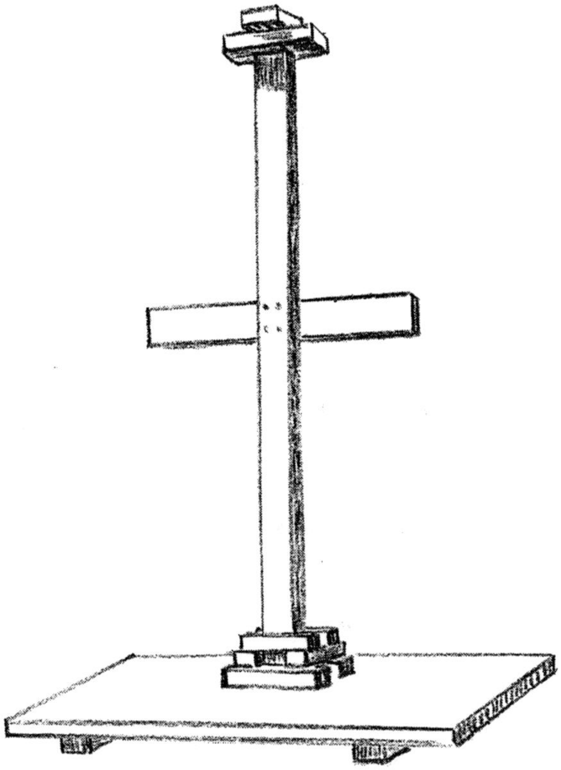

Simple workshop-created armatures are shown above, TruForm armatures shown below.

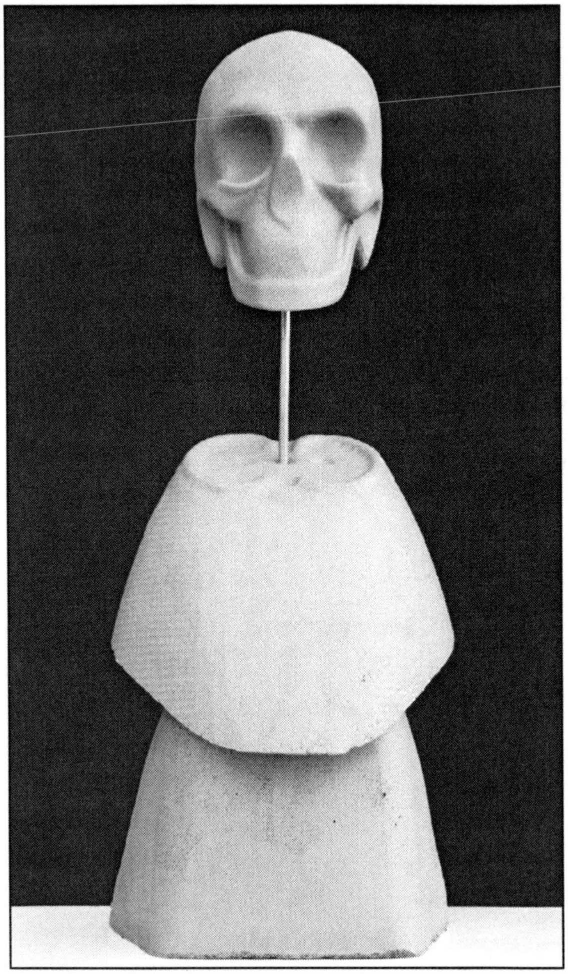

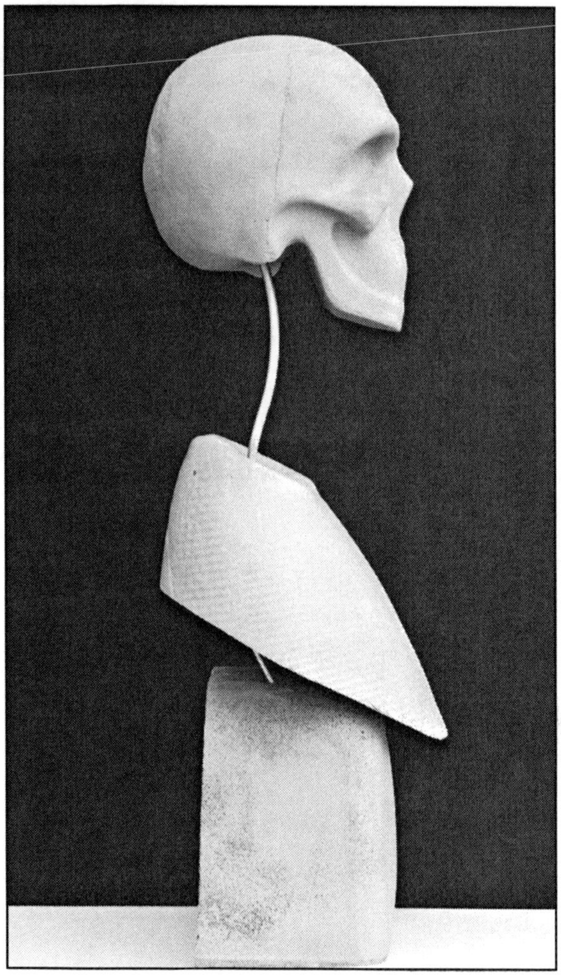

Modeling Tools

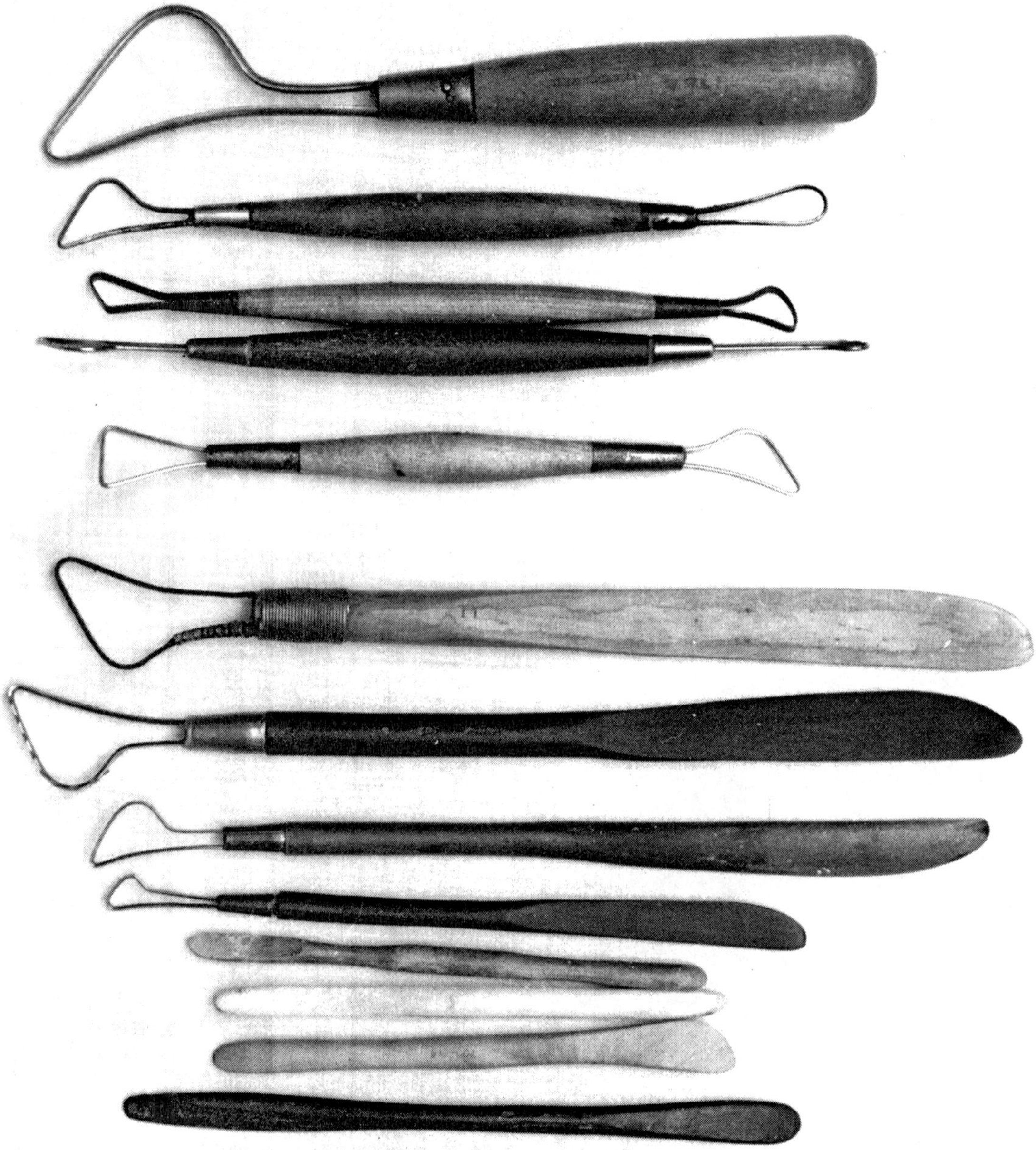

A collection of sculpture modeling tools.

GLOSSARY

Acromion process: the lateral point of the shoulder

Ala, ala nasae: the lateral border of the lower third of the nose, literally, wings of the nose.

Anterior aspect: ventral, it is the front of a standing human figure.

Anterior superior spine of ilium: a prominence of the pelvic bone anterior to the crest of the ilium. It is often used and referred to as a point for measurement.

Anthropometric, anthropometry: measuring the human figure.

Aperture: an opening, as the parting of the lips for the mouth.

Axilla: arm pit.

Axillary: reference to the arm pit.

Axillary folds: anterior, formed by the pectoralis muscle; posterior, formed by the latissimus dorsi muscle.

Axillary pivot: the center pivot for extension or raising of the arm.

Biceps muscle: a large muscle on the anterior aspect of the upper arm.

Braccio: an old Italian measure from the shoulder to the wrist.

Brachychepalic: a head configuration that is short, width to height, with a cephalic index of 80 to 86 .

Brachymorphic: short body build.

Bridge of the nose: a notch just below the brow at the upper part of the nose.

Buttock: the rump or protuberant hinder part of human.

Canthus: the corner of an eye where the lids join, the inner canthus and outer canthus.

Caudal: toward the tail in most vertebrates or towards the coccyx in humans.

Central: is toward the center axis, the vertebral column which is generally vertical and generally but not entirely central. The axis is on a plane, but is not a plane, it is a theoretical straight line, but in body development it has developed gentle curves.

Cephalic: also Superior: toward the head.

Cervical: refers to the neck.

Chryselephantine: sculpture carved in elephant ivory.

Clavicle: the collar bone; it is attached to the acromion process of the shoulder and to the sternum at the sternal notch.

Costal margin: costal refers to ribs and the costal margin is the lower border of the ribs of the thorax, starting in back near the vertebrae and forming an arc attaching to the sternum in front.

Crest of ilium: a prominent ridge of the pelvis bone on the lateral aspect of the abdomen.

Crotch: the apex of the angle where the legs join in the midline.

Cubit: ancient unit of measure from the tip of the flexed elbow to the tip of the middle finger of the straightened hand.

Deep: inside and deep to the surface.

Deltoid muscle: a large triangular muscle at the lateral aspect of the shoulder.

Distal: a part of an extremity away or farther from the body; compare to proximal.

Dolicocephlic: a type of head that is long and narrow with head width to height about index of 70 to 75.

Dolicomorphic: tall and slender body form.

Dorsal aspect: posterior, it is the back of a standing human figure.

Dorsal spines: posterior vertebral spinous processes of vertebrae.

Epicondyle: prominence at lateral aspects of a joint, especially on the humerus.

Fathom: a span of the out-stretched arms, finger tip to fingertip.

Fibonnaci series: a summation series of numbers in which a number is the sum of the previous two numbers, such as: 3, 5, 8, 13, 21, 34. . . .

Frontal plane: any theoretical plane that intersects the erect human body from side to side, parallel to the central axis and perpendicular to the mid sagittal plane.

Frontotemporal: a junction of a frontal bone of the forehead with a temporal bone on the lateral aspect of the skull.

Gluteal cleft: the crease between each buttocks.

Gluteal furrow: a prominent transverse crease below a buttock.

Gluteus maximus: prominent large muscle of the buttocks.

Gonion: an anthropometry term for the angle of the jaw bone.

Greater trochanters: the widest prominences of the femurs, thigh bones at the hips.

Helix of an ear: the lateral, outer border of an ear.

Humerus: the upper arm bone.

Ilium: a prominent bone of the pelvis.

Infra-: below, compare to supra, above.

Infranasal point: the junction of the base of the nose and the upper lip.

Labium: lip; labial, pertaining to a lip.

Larynx: the voice box or Adam's apple, an anatomical feature of the neck composed primarily of the thyroid cartilage.

Lateral: is away from the mid-sagittal plane.

Mandible: a jaw bone.

Nasion: at the bridge of the nose, see sellion.

Malleolus: a bony prominence at the ankle, either medial or lateral.

Manubrium: the upper part of the sternum.

Mastoid process: a bony prominence just behind an ear.

Medial: is toward the midsagittal plane.

Menton: chin.

Mesocephlic: medium head, a head width to height index of 75 to 80.

Mesomorphic,: medium body build.

Mid-saggital plane: a theoretical plane that intersects the human body from front to back through the central axis, perpendicular to frontal planes and creating two equal halves.

Occiput: the low posterior prominence at back of the skull.

Olecranon process: the tip of the flexed elbow.

Orbit: the bony socket of the skull for an eye.

Patella: knee cap.

Pectoralis muscles: anterior chest muscles inserting on the upper part of a humerus.

Phalanx, phalangeal: segments of digits, fingers or toes.

Popliteal crease: the popliteal fossa is a cavity behind the knee and when bent forms the popliteal crease.

Posterior aspect: dorsal, it is the back of a standing human figure.

Proximal: a part of an extremity near or closer to the body; compare to distal.

Pubis: a bone of the pelvis fused to the ilium. It is prominent at the base of the genitals.

Radius: a bone of the forearm parallel to the ulna.

Rod: an English measure of sixteen feet.

Scapula: shoulder blade.

Sellion: a junction of the nasal bones with frontal bones at the bridge of the nose.

Sternal notch: the top of the sternum, or breast bone, between clavicles or collar bones.

Sternocleidomastoid muscle: a prominent muscle of the anterior neck originating at the sternal notch and inserting on the mastoid process behind an ear

Sublabial: below the lip.

Supercilliary arch: the brow ridge that is above the orbit or eye socket.

Superficial: toward the surface; compare to deep.

Supra-: above; compare to infra-, below.

Symphysis pubis: a midline pelvic junction of both pubic bones of the pelvis, also considered a base of the genitals.

Thorax: the chest, composed of vertebrae in back, ribs, and sternum in front.

Thyroid cartilage: the prominent cartilage structure of the larynx or voice box in the anterior part of the neck.

Tibia: the shin bone of the leg.

Tragus: a cartilaginous prominence or flap anterior to the ear canal.

Tragion: a point on the tragus of an ear, just anterior to the ear canal.

Transverse plane: any theoretical plane that intersects central axis at right angles; in most vertebrates, top to bottom; in the erect human body, from front to back.

Ulna: a bone of the forearm parallel to the radius.

Umbilicus: belly button.

Ventral: in most vertebrates inferior or abdominal aspect; in humans, anterior, or the front of a standing human figure.

Vertex: the highest part of the human head.

Xiphoid process: a midline bony prominence below and attached to the sternum or breast bone.

Zygomatic arch: a lateral cheek bone in front of an ear.

Symbols:

- $=$: Equal to
- $\cong$: Approximately equal to
- $\neq$: Not equal to
- Φ : Phi, ratio 1.62...

BIBLIOGRAPHY

Backhouse, Kenneth, and Ralph T. Hutchings. *Color Atlas of Surface Anatomy, Clinical and Applied.* Baltimore: Williams and Wilkins, 1986.

Enlow, Donald H., PhD. *The Human Face.* New York, Evanston, London: Hoeber Medical Division, Harper and Rowe, 1968.

Enlow, Donald H., PhD. *Handbook of Facial Growth.* Philadelphia: W.B. Saunders Company, 1975.

Fairbanks, Avard T., PhD. *Anatomical Design,* a Doctoral Thesis. Ann Arbor, Michigan: The University of Michigan, 1936. pp. 16, 17, 46, 47, 50.

Fairbanks, Avard T. and Fairbanks, Eugene F., *Human Proportions for Artists,* Bellingham Washington: Fairbanks Art & Books, 2005. pp. 147-217.

Fairbanks, Grant R., MD. *Medical Life Drawing and Sculpture.* New York City: American Society for Aesthetic Plastic Surgery, 2001.

Fairbanks, Jonathan L. "America's Measure of Mankind, Proportions and Harmonics." *Smithsonian Studies in American Art* 2.1, 1988, pp. 73-87.

Fairbanks, Justin F. Dictated and manuscript notes and discussions with author about creating a portrait in clay. 1976.

Faraut, Philippe, and Charissa Scott Faraut *Portrait Sculpting.* Honeoye, NY: PCF Studios, Inc. 2004.

Faraut, Philippe, and Charissa Scott Faraut. *Mastering Portraiture.* Honeoye, NY: PCF Studios, Inc. 2009.

Fitzpatric, John C., Editor. *The Writings of George Washington from the Original Manuscript Sources,* 1745-1799. Publication of the U.S. Army Corps of Engineers.

Frothingham, Thomas, *G. Washington Commander in Chief.* Boston and New York: Houghton Mifflin Company, 1930, pp. 234-241.

Ghyka, Matila. *The Geometry of Art and Life.* New York: Dover Publications Inc., 1977, p. xi.

Hrdlicka, Arles. *Practical Anthropometry.* Philadelphia: Wistar Institute of Biology and Physiology, 1939, pp. 122-125.

Kinncaid, Clark. *George Washington, The Pictorial Biography.* New York: Bonanza Books, 1958.

Lockhart, R.D., G.E. Hamilton, and F.W. Fyfe. *Anatomy of the Human Body.* Philadelphia: J.B. Lippincott Company, 1972.

Oliver, George. *Practical Anthropology.* Springfield, IL: Charles C. Thomas, 1960.

Olson, Todd R., PhD. *PDR Atlas of Anatomy.* Montvale, NJ: Medical Economics Company, 1996.

Patterson, Carl G., MD, and Donald G. Powell, AB. "Facial Analysis in Patient Evaluation for Physiologic and Cosmetic Surgery." *The Laryngoscope.* March 1974, pp. 1004-1019.

Swift, Al. Narrator of the television feature presenting *Avard Fairbanks Demonstration Lecture Modeling a Portrait Bust of General George Washington.* KVOS Television, Bellingham, WA. 1962.

Williams, P.I. and Wendell Smith, C.P. *Basic Human Embryology.* Philadelphia: J.B. Lippincott Company, 1969.

Note, a special comment: The two books by Phillipe Faraut and Charissa Scott Faraut are superb references and belong in any serious portrait sculptor's personal library. The excellent photography is impressive in the initial steps of sculpture creation and in the finished heads and faces in both *Portrait Sculpting* and *Mastering Portraiture.* Expression and a broad variety of ages, ethnic types and moods are demonstrated in *Mastering Portraiture.* They have also authored and published a new book, *Advanced Sculpting,* and P. C. F. Studio will supply Anatomical Reference Casts to sculptors.

Justin Fox Fairbanks

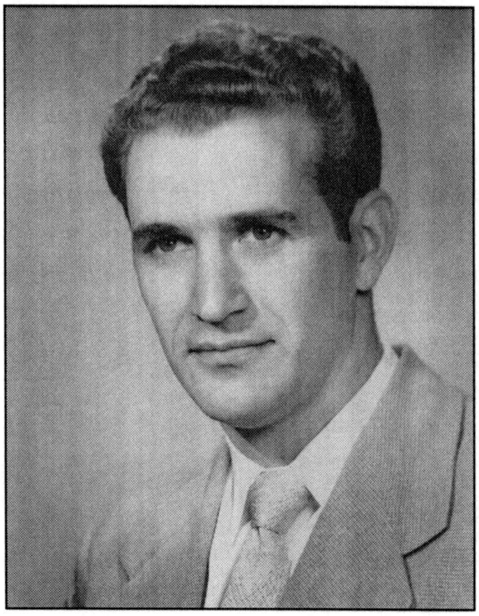

Justin Fox Fairbanks was born in Eugene, Oregon, July 12, 1926, the fourth son of Avard and Maude Fox Fairbanks. During his childhood and youth he lived with his family in Ann Arbor, Michigan. He graduated from Ann Arbor High School and entered The University of Michigan, 1944, studying Engineering. This was during World War II. He joined the Navy V12 Program there for one year then enlisted in the U.S. Navy and served for three years.

He studied at Brigham Young University for one year, and was called on a mission to France by the Church of Jesus Christ of Latter-Day Saints in 1948-1951. Following this, he studied French culture and language at the University of Paris (the Sorbonne). After these studies he traveled through Egypt, Palestine and continental Europe. Other later travels included Scandinavia and Russia

He enlisted in the U.S. Air Force Reserve (1953-1960) and was commissioned 1st Lieutenant. He studied at the University of Utah and earned a BA degree in Business Administration. In 1956 he earned a Master of Fine Arts degree and continued as an instructor in sculpture and other fine arts. He assisted his father in administrative duties as a Dean's Assistant, in teaching sculpture, and in the creation of many heroic monuments. He also developed a bronze foundry in Salt Lake City.

Teaching Experience

Between 1954 and 1967, he taught art in several private schools in Salt Lake City, Utah, while also serving as teacher and assistant to the department head, which included college course development, student counseling, and maintaining records at the University of Utah.

He taught Fine Arts at Eastern Utah College in Price, Utah, 1967-1968 as the Art Department Chairman. He was appointed in 1969 to the Faculty at Eastern Arizona College, Thatcher, and became Chairman of the Art Department.

Besides Fine Art he often was requested, because of his diverse experience, to also teach classes in French, Business and Mathematics. He continued until retirement in 1993.

Creative Sculpture

Prominent among his creative sculptures are a colossal statue in cast stone to Pope Gregory at Saint Gregory's Chapel in Phoenix AZ; a statue in Snowflake, AZ, honoring the Flake family, early pioneers, and Erastus Snow; a memorial to the First School in Kansas City, Missouri; a Ram, the mascot of Highland High School, Salt Lake City; The Golden Eagle for the College of Eastern Utah, Price, Utah; Equestrian statue of Geronimo in Las Cruces, New Mexico, Provo, Utah, and Columbus, Indiana; The Rainmaker at Foxwoods, Connecticut; Bear Cubs for Vladivostok, Russia; the Bell Tower Memorial Plaques, at the Eastern Arizona College in Thatcher, AZ; and Moses the Prophet in Orem, Utah.

Portraits have been created by him of more than ten prominent public leaders. Other significant sculpture includes six medallions and six low relief memorials. He rendered expert assistance to his father and other brothers in monuments that they have erected.

Justin retired to Mesa, Arizona, where he died in January 2007.

Justin's son Daniel Fairbanks studied art with his grandfather and later studied Plant genetics at Cornell University, earning a Doctor of Philosophy degree. Besides his accomplishments as a Plant Geneticist, he was appointed professor of Biology at Brigham Young University, and at Utah Valley State University. He is a Master Sculptor and has also created many fine masterpieces. He is continuing his father's and grandfather's tradition of fine art and dynamic sculpture.

Our brothers and sisters

Although our other brothers and two sisters did not contribute directly to this book, they were all taught in the development of statuary and were involved in the family production of sculpture. They all contributed a fair share of their time and effort toward the family's artistic projects and endeavors.

Avard F. Fairbanks (Jr.), the oldest of the eight boys, modeled a knight in armor in his early youth. He helped on several heroic monuments. He did much of the early photography and assisted in casting and retouching of many plaster casts. He studied art and created some fine paintings. His major interest was in engineering and he became an aerospace engineer.

Eugene F. Fairbanks, one of the authors, was the second son (see next page).

Elliott A. Fairbanks, the third son, studied engineering and sculpture. He created some fine sculpture and assisted his father in some of the fine monuments. He was also interested in the Boy Scouts organization and became an executive in the Portland, Oregon Council. With management experience, he was called to work in several large firms and became a Dean of Eastern Utah College, as assistant to the president. He later served in management of a prominent firm that produced office equipment.

Justin F. Fairbanks was the fourth son and is recognized as a contributing author of this book.

Virgil F. Fairbanks also studied under his father, but developed an interest in medicine. He specialized in Internal Medicine and joined the staff of the Mayo Clinic. His field of endeavor was Hematology.

Jonathan L. Fairbanks also studied art under his father and became a fine artist. His interest was in graphic art and in oil painting, both of landscape and portraits. This interest also led him into a study of American antiquities. He was on the staff at the Wintertur Museum in Delaware and then was appointed to be a curator at the Boston Museum of Fine Arts. He has authored several fine books on American antiquities with an emphasis on furniture.

David N.F. Fairbanks studied under his father, but developed an interest in Medicine. He specialized in Otolaryngology and was a professor at George Washington Medical School in Washington, DC. He has authored books on antibiotics and some special procedures. He volunteered editorial recommendations for this book. He honored his father by promoting several important monuments.

Grant R. Fairbanks also studied under his father. He created an improved and enlarged replacement for the eagle at Eagle Gate at State Street and South Temple in Salt Lake City, Utah, when the original was damaged in an accident. He had continued interest in art, but chose Medicine as a career and became a plastic surgeon. He has lectured and taught significant art principles to fellow plastic surgeons.

When Avard and Maude Fairbanks visited Greece for the dedication of his heroic statue to Lycurgus, Maude visited an orphanage and was impressed by the many beautiful children that needed homes. She offered to adopt girls. Two sisters of a fine family, impoverished by World War II, were adopted and adjusted to American life. They, in turn had experience in assisting at sculpture. Maria married and reared a fine family. Georgia was talented in voice and became a music teacher in Salt Lake City High Schools.

Eugene F. Fairbanks

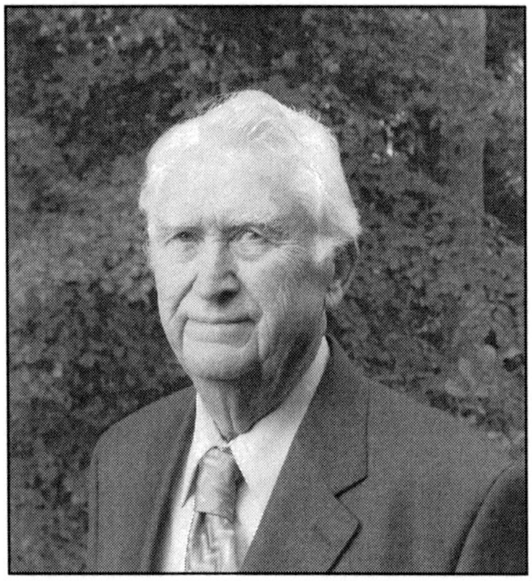

Eugene Fox Fairbanks, the second son of Maude Fox and Avard T. Fairbanks, was born 1921 in Eugene, Oregon. He was involved in the studio at an early age. When the family was in Florence Italy, he modeled his first sculpture under the direction of Dante Sodini, one of Italy's most famous sculptors at that time. When Sculptor Avard Fairbanks was appointed to the faculty of the University of Michigan in 1930, his sons often helped at the studio. They did some modeling, assisted the plaster caster, retouched casts, and were taught photography for sculpture. There was a progressive increased expectation in skill and responsibility. This continued from grade school through high school and into college. An older brother chose engineering as a vocation. Younger brothers studied engineering, art, and medicine.

Eugene chose to study Medicine. He married Florence Sundwall in 1944 in his last year of the University of Michigan Medical School, and graduated in 1945. He interned at Wayne County General Hospital near Detroit, Michigan. Subsequently, he served in the Army Medical Corps as a transport surgeon on a troop transport which sailed from the Seattle Port of Embarkation. Following military service he practiced medicine as a family physician in Pasco and Kennewick, Washington. After an Anesthesiology residency in Seattle, he moved to Bellingham, Washington, and practiced Anesthesiology and Family Practice. He was certified as a diplomat of the American Board of Anesthesiology and the American Board of Family Physicians. In time Florence and Eugene became the proud parents of five sons and five daughters. He practiced medicine in Bellingham, Washington, until retirement in 1995.

In 1995 he was asked to create a heroic bronze monument honoring fishermen of Bellingham who have been lost at sea. This was titled *A Safe Return,* and was dedicated on Memorial Day 1999 in Zuanich Point Park in Bellingham, Washington.

With Dr. Charles J. Flora he co-authored an invertebrate marine biology species identification handbook, titled *The Sound and The Sea,* published in 1966 and 1977.

Over many years he collected photographs and made many enlargements of Fairbanks sculpture for projected publications.

His first book about Avard T. Fairbanks' sculpture, *A Sculptor's Testimony In Bronze And Stone* featured sacred sculpture (1972 and 1994).

During spare moments in the practice of medicine, Eugene composed poetry to complement his father's fantasy sculpture. In 2001 he published *A Sculpture Garden of Fantasy,* featuring the fantasy sculpture of Avard T. Fairbanks.

A third book titled, *Abraham Lincoln Sculpture Created by Avard Fairbanks,* was published in 2003.

His books for working artists include *Human Proportions for Artists* in 2005 and abridged version in 2012. This book is of particular interest to students and serious amateurs as it discusses human proportions. Included are profuse illustrations and tables of about 120 representative human measurements of both male and female figures.

Children's Proportions for Artists was published in 2011. Studies are presented for figurative artists about the yearly growth and development of children of each gender from infancy to young adulthood. Illustrations are included with charts of about 130 representative measurements and proportions.

Please visit
www.fairbanksartbooks.com
to see examples of other books about Avard Fairbanks sculpture
and how to purchase them.

CPSIA information can be obtained at www.ICGtesting.com
Printed in the USA
LVOW10s0420230215

427940LV00025B/617/P

9 781482 724639